1986

Virginia Berridge
and
Griffith Edwards

OPIUM
and the
PEOPLE

Opiate Use in
Nineteenth-Century England

ALLEN LANE/ST MARTIN'S PRESS

ALLEN LANE
Penguin Books Ltd
536 King's Road
London SW10 0UH

ST MARTIN'S PRESS
175 Fifth Avenue
New York, NY 10010
USA

First published jointly in 1981
Copyright © Virginia Berridge and Griffith Edwards, 1981

ISBN 0 7139 0852 1 (Allen Lane)
ISBN 0-312-58684-1 (St Martin's Press);
Library of Congress Card Catalog Number 81-40630

Set in Monophoto Plantin
Printed in Great Britain by
Butler & Tanner Ltd
Frome and London

Contents

List of Plates

List of Text Figures

Preface

It is surprising that the vast outpouring of words on the 'drug problem' in the last ten years has produced no serious historical examination of the place of narcotics in English society. Reactions to contemporary events have been immediate and specific, strangely isolated in their assumption that drug use is peculiarly a feature of the 1960s and 1970s. This book attempts to fill at least part of that gap by examining the place of opium in nineteenth-century society, in language which it is hoped will appeal to that much sought-after being, the 'general reader', as much as to the academic historian or drug researcher. Technical language is kept to a minimum. But where it is unavoidable, as for instance with the term 'narcotic' or the battery of language used to describe drug habits and their pharmacological basis, readers will find definitions in the Introduction.

This book is, like any history, the product of its own time. It reflects the interests of the 1970s, and in particular the efflorescence of writing on social history which has taken place in the last twenty years. Social history as 'history with everything else left out' is no longer acceptable; its place has been taken by a concern for the structure of social groups, the study of social movements, popular culture, for urban history and demography. Had this history of opium in the nineteenth century been written say even ten years ago, it would undoubtedly have been classified as 'medical' rather than 'social' history. It would have concentrated on the 'public health' aspects of opium, and would have accepted at face value the testimony of the official reports and inquiries. Today there is a greater awareness of the bias of the sources which earlier writers so unhesitatingly and unquestioningly used, a willingness to use a wider range of evidence or to ask different questions of it. There is a desire to re-create not just 'official opinion' but the actual experience of people living at the time, and to consider more analytically the contribution of the social groups involved. This book, in devoting itself primarily to such matters as the 'popular culture' of opium, the place of opium in working-class life, and the contribution of the medical and pharmaceutical professions to changed perceptions of opium use, rather than to the individual experience of 'famous opium eaters' such as Thomas De Quincey and Samuel Taylor Coleridge, is very much the product of those concerns.

Any writing, historical writing in particular, is the outcome of co-operation and help, both practically and in terms of ideas and insights, from a large number of people. In a joint publication, this is particularly the case. Virginia Berridge, as a social historian, has been responsible for the historical section (part of the Introduction and Chapters 1 to 17) and Griffith Edwards, as a psychiatrist concerned with drug research and the formation of control policy, for the consideration of the nineteenth century in relation to the present position and for the section of definitions (Chapter 18 and part of the Introduction). The inter-disciplinary nature of the project was an unusual one. It is not often that a historian is so directly confronted with the contemporary implications of historical arguments, or that a psychiatrist looks back to the perceptions and structures which moulded present-day approaches to drug use. Comments and criticisms on each other's drafts have thus flowed freely. The disjunction between the conclusions of academic historical research and present-day concerns in many respects remains great; but the authors feel that they have at least attempted an exercise in collaboration which could prove productive in other areas of social policy.

The historical research on which the nineteenth-century section is based has involved the assistance of many others. Virginia Berridge would like in particular to thank the staffs of the Pharmaceutical Society and Miss Jones, the librarian; those of the Wellcome Institute for the History of Medicine, and the Royal Society of Medicine, the Society of Friends, the University of London Library, Goldsmiths' Library, the Guildhall Library and the library of the Institute of Actuaries. Her thanks are due to the staff of the Greater London Council Record Office, Pauline Sears in particular, and the Middlesex Record Office, to Dr Charles Newman, Harveian Librarian at the Royal College of Physicians, and to Patricia Allderidge, archivist of Bethlem Royal Hospital. The Librarian of Tower Hamlets Local History Library was helpful in providing access to that library's unrivalled collection of material on East London opium 'dens'. The staff of the British Museum and the Public Record Office gave considerable assistance; ar.l the pharmacists and others who provided reminiscences about the open dispensing of opium at the turn of the century have added a valuable perspective.

A debt is owed to the many historians who contributed suggestions and criticisms when earlier versions and sections of the book were presented as papers. For an historian working in a non-historical environment there is a danger of becoming isolated; and particular thanks are due to members of research seminars at the Institute of Historical Research, at Bedford College Social Research Group and at University College History of Medicine department who helped ensure that this did not take place. Members of the Pharmaceutical Society, the British Society for the History of Pharmacy, the Social History Society and the Society for the Social History of Medicine also gave valuable help. A transatlantic perspective was provided by the contributions from members of the Social Research Group of the University of California at Berkeley and the staff of the Center for Socio-Cultural Research into Drug Use at Columbia University in New York. Professor E. J. Hobsbawm and Professor F. M. L. Thompson gave helpful guidance as did Alethea Hayter, Pat Thane, Meta Zimmeck, Anna Davin and Linda Deer. Phil Kuhn, the late Stella Cripps and Pat Whitehead worked hard as research assistants on the project at various stages.

We both owe a considerable debt to our colleagues, ex-colleagues and friends in the Addiction Research Unit. Particular thanks must go to Margaret Sheehan for unfailingly patient help, to Gerry Stimson, to Nigel Rawson and Edna Oppenheimer. Earlier drafts have been patiently typed by Pat Davis, Sara Marshall, Jean Crutch, Linda Stevens and Diane Hallett. But we are especially indebted to Julia Polglaze, who has provided much more than secretarial assistance and advice, and to Jacqueline May, who patiently and expertly produced the final version.

PREFACE

The research on which the book is based was funded by generous grants from the Drug Abuse Council in Washington and the United Kingdom Social Science Research Council, and we would like to express our thanks to both these organizations.

Introduction

The most acute anxieties of the 1960s 'drug epidemic' have quietened. Drug stories appear less often, and more prosaically, in the newspapers. Yet attitudes towards the use of 'dangerous drugs', and 'narcotics' in particular, remain restrictive. The legislative control of drugs and public reactions to their use is more stringent than the restrictions on those other recreational substances, tobacco and alcohol. The Misuse of Drugs Act (1971), the latest of a long line of 'Dangerous Drugs' Acts, continues the practice of control through fines and imprisonment under the aegis of the Home Office. Since 1968, heroin and cocaine have been available to addicts only through treatment clinics, where doctors licensed by the Home Office may prescribe.[1] For other 'recreational' substances, the system of control is much less stringent. For alcohol, the equivalents are the liquor licensing laws, the duty on whisky and the sale of alcohol in pubs and supermarkets. For tobacco, they are the health warnings on cigarette packets and the no-smoking carriages in trains. The contrasts in reaction are instructive.

Regulations and legislation applicable specifically to 'dangerous drugs' were not passed until the early decades of the twentieth century. The 1916 Defence of the Realm Act regulation 40B dealing with cocaine and opium and the 1920 Dangerous Drugs Act were the first legislative measures to establish narcotics as a matter of social policy.[2] But it was in the previous century that the bases of control were laid down, and new and restrictive ways of looking at opium established.

The nature of the drugs[3]

This book is concerned with the factors involved in that process, with the advent of legislative control over opium in the nineteenth century, with the growth of a view of opium as a 'deviant' activity and with the factors which went to make it so. But first it is necessary to be armed with some basic knowledge of the pharmacological, therapeutic and addictive properties of opiates and of some other drugs. The paragraphs which follow attempt to compress a lot of the relevant science into a short space. The aim is not to produce a scientific section of pharmacology, but to deal specifically with issues which are relevant to an understanding of social reactions and perplexities. And although more is known about these scientific issues than a century ago, it must of course be borne in mind that current concepts are no more final than the nineteenth-century ideas which were their predecessors.

A simple classification

To anyone who has no specialized knowledge, the great variety of substances which act on the mind create a rather bewildering situation. Is every drug different or is there some simple way of grouping these substances? There is in fact a simple classification which can help to guide one through the seeming complexities: there are just four different basic categories of mind-acting drugs.

1. *Opiates.* Opiates (or opoids in the American phrase) are drugs of the morphine type, which have the common property of relieving pain and inducing euphoria. Opium is of importance because of the opiates it contains.
2. *Cerebral stimulants.* This group includes cocaine, a drug which came into the story during the latter part of the nineteenth century. Amphetamines are the familiar present-day representative of the stimulants. These drugs cause excitement and increased mental and physical energy. They can give rise to brief psychotic illness. Although there are no remarkable physical withdrawal symptoms, the stimulants can be highly addictive.
3. *Cerebral depressants.* Here can be grouped together a variety of substances which have the common property of inducing sedation and sleepiness: there may also be disinhibition so that

the drug appears to be causing stimulation and excitement. Alcohol provides a prime example. In the latter part of the nineteenth century, chloral, a synthetic depressant, began to enjoy a vogue and gave rise to problems of misuse.

4. *Psychomimetic substances, or hallucinogens.* Cannabis is probably best placed in this group, although it also has depressant properties. Mescaline is another member of the group, which became known in England during the nineteenth century, while LSD is the well-known modern example. Members of this group have the capacity to induce complex changes in the way the world is perceived and given meaning – experiences which are in short described as transcendental. Acute psychotic disturbances may also result.

Thus the nineteenth century was engaging with a range of drugs which nicely represented the complete spectrum of drug types – opium as the source of opiates, with morphine and heroin later added, alcohol as the pervasive depressant and chloral as the new medical substance, cocaine as the first encounter of this society with a powerful stimulant, cannabis as a psychomimetic which received quite a lot of attention and mescaline as an exotic.

Cocaine and cannabis

As we have seen, these two very different drugs made an appearance in nineteenth-century history, and they will receive some attention in this book. Their importance was, however, very minor compared with the opiates, and here it seems appropriate to dispose of questions relating to their pharmacology and their place in therapeutics very briefly.

The *coca leaf* comes from a shrub known as *Erythroxylon coca*, which grows in Peru and other parts of South America. When chewed it can be used as a stimulant, and it is still widely used in the Andes for this purpose. *Cocaine* is the alkaloid obtained from the leaves of the coca bush, and was first isolated by Niemann in 1860. It is a white powder which can be sniffed, or dissolved and injected. Medically it had its importance as a very effective surface anaesthetic.

Cannabis is the general term used to describe the various products of the plant *Cannabis sativa*. The major natural products are known by many names in different parts of the world, but consist primarily of two types of material – the resinous exudation of the flowering top and leaves, often known as *hashish*; and the material derived by chopping the leaves and stalks, collectively called *marijuana*. The activity of both is largely due to a tetrahydrocannabinol, or T.H.C. In the nineteenth century, cannabis or its extracts enjoyed some medical popularity for their analgesic and sedative effects.

Opium, opiates and their preparations

For many of the remedies which make up the doctor's armentarium the history of therapeutics is firstly that of a plant product with medical use going back for thousands of years. Then follows the isolation, chemical identification and extraction in the nineteenth century, or sometimes as late as the twentieth, of the therapeutically active ingredients of that plant. The final stage of development may then be the production and marketing of a synthetic drug identical with the natural product, or of a drug with alterations in chemical structure which result in a substance which in some way improves on nature – the synthetic may for instance be more potent than the original plant extract, or have fewer untoward effects. The pharmacological history of opium and opiates provides an example of this type of general technological sequence.

Opium is the plant product. Its effects on the human mind have probably been known for about 6,000 years, and it had its early and honoured place in Greek, Roman and Arabic medicine.

Opium is the name given to the brown tacky substance which is obtained after drying the milky exudate which oozes when the poppy capsule is incised. The original plant material yielded a crude substance containing all kinds of organic material and extraneous matter. Crude or not, it was this material which, eaten, made up into a drink or smoked, provided the drug in effective form over the millennia, and it was still only in this traditional plant form that the drug was available at the start of the nineteenth century.

The *opium poppy* – the species cultivated for opium production – is *Papaver somniferum*, a white poppy growing to a height of about one or two feet. Opium may though also be obtained from certain other varieties of this plant. The poppy is, or has been, grown chiefly in Asia Minor, China, Iran and some Balkan countries.

In the nineteenth century, many preparations based on opium, or patent remedies with opium as their active ingredient, were to be found listed in textbooks and on sale. Among the best known and most widely used were: *laudanum*, otherwise known as tincture of opium, made by mixing opium with distilled water and alcohol; *paregoric*, or camphorated tincture of opium ('paregoric' is derived from the Greek word for 'soothing' or 'consoling'); *Battley's Sedative Solution*, known officially as 'liquor opii sedativus', opium mixed with calcium hydrate, alcohol, sherry and water; *Dover's Powder*, a preparation first made and used by Dr Thomas Dover and consisting of opium, saltpetre, tartar, liquorice and ipecacuanha. Although a patent preparation, Dover's Powder was widely used in hospital practice in the nineteenth century. *Chlorodyne* was the best known of the opium-based patent medicines. It was originally made up by Dr John Collis Browne and marketed by J. T. Davenport of Great Russell Street, London. Its main constituents in the nineteenth century were chloroform and hydrochlorate of morphia, although some analysts also detected a small quantity of Indian hemp. *Godfrey's Cordial* was a 'children's opiate', made according to various recipes, but based on laudanum. Other children's soothing syrups included *Mrs Winslow's Soothing Syrup*, *Atkinson's Infants' Preservative*, and *Street's Infants Quietness*.

The active therapeutic principle in many plant medicines has the chemical structure of an *alkaloid*. *Morphine* (or morphia) was the first alkaloid to be isolated. It was named after Morpheus, the god of sleep. Many other alkaloids of opium were later identified, but those other than morphine which are of medical interest are few in number, and include *codeine*, as well as the much less popularly familiar substances thebaine, papaverine and noscapine.

The next stage in technology was in this instance not development of a synthetic, but what is called a *semi-synthetic* – a substance produced by a chemical process which, taking a natural alkaloid as starting point, modifies in some way the structure of the original substance. Taking morphine as the starting point, a potent semi-synthetic which can be produced by a remarkably simple chemical process is *heroin*. Heroin was first produced in 1874 at St Mary's

Hospital in London. It was rediscovered in Germany in the 1890s and marketed by Bayer under the trade name heroin. This probably derived from the German 'heroisch', or large and powerful in medical terminology. It was not used in medical practice in England in the nineteenth century. Weight for weight, heroin is several times as powerful in its drug action as morphine. There have subsequently been developed a host of fully synthetic opiates – drugs such as methadone and pethidine – but these play no part in the nineteenth-century story.

Actions of opiates

Opiates can produce a great variety of effects which will be modified by expectation, but of prime importance to medicine is their ability to relieve pain. Any young medical student who sees for his first time the acute relief which an injection of morphine can bring about when, say, a person with a badly broken leg is brought into an Accident Department must have a sense of being in the presence of something almost magical. Very severe pain is brought rapidly under control, and from being in a state of agony and apprehension the patient is calm and at ease. Opiates are used in daily practice throughout the world for trauma and accident, for the relief of post-operative pain, in childbirth, and for the control of the pain of advanced cancer and some other very painful conditions. The difference here between the present and the nineteenth century is that, though they are still essential drugs for relief of pain (it is almost impossible to think of medical practice without the availability of opiates), these drugs are now used almost exclusively by doctors and, by them, much more conservatively and with stricter criteria for their deployment and dosage. Today opiates are, for instance, not drugs to be prescribed or self-prescribed for toothache or for ordinary menstrual pain – aspirin and similar non-narcotic analgesics do that sort of job adequately and without the same dangers. But aspirin was not introduced until 1899, and the popularity of opiates for all manner of pain relief in the nineteenth century can be seen in one sense as related to lack of any alternative.

Closely allied to the pain-relieving effect of opiates is their ability to influence mood. This effect is again a property of great value to medicine and very much the therapeutic ally of the pain-relieving effect; even when the severe pain of a spreading cancer is not fully abolished by the drug injection, the mood effect can make the residual pain more tolerable and generally produce a lessening of emotional distress. The patient is in a way emotionally distanced from what is happening, and floats as it were on the surface of his experience. The drug has a *euphoric* effect. It is difficult to describe a complex feeling in precise words, but the tranquil pleasantness of this experience can be very positively enjoyable. This effect is not exactly equivalent to sedation, for neither do the opiates bring about the type or degree of drowsiness that barbiturates produce, nor do the barbiturates produce the same type of euphoria as the opiates. The euphoric effect of opium is what was meant by the nineteenth-century term the 'stimulant' use of the drug. As we have seen, opiates are in present terminology not classified as stimulants, and to apply this word to a class of drugs which produce drowsiness and passivity today seems rather bizarre. The word obviously had a different connotation in the last century, and may be taken as broadly meaning the pleasure-seeking use of the drug. In general the effects of the opiates, like those of any other drug, can vary enormously according to the expectation of the user and setting in which the use takes place.

Opium and the opiates are also sometimes classified, along with other drugs, as *narcotics*. Technically narcotic drugs are those which have a sedative and sleep-inducing effect. The description of opium's pain-relieving and mood-altering effects already given indicates that this 'narcotic' designation is not wholly accurate. The term 'narcotic' has also been applied in control legislation to drugs like cannabis and cocaine which do not have any true family resemblance to the opiates, and the word might indeed be seen as something of a vehicle of confusion.

So much then for a brief account of the two medically most important actions of opiates – pain relief and mood effect. The pharmacological element in the history of nineteenth-century opium use can largely be seen in terms of the history of these two attributes of the drug: the history of a pain reliever which had no rival or substitute, and of an euphoriant and tranquillizer with a usage which was in part 'medical' but which easily crossed over the borderline to what was then termed the 'stimulant' use of the drug. These two aspects, pain relief and mood alteration, are thus the essential and primary pharmacological themes for understanding the nature of the actual drug with which society was dealing. They are the fundamental attributes of the drug which proposed its use and brought reacting social processes into play, and this whether it was the story of 'infant doping', the use of opium by Romantic poets and Fenland labourers, the enormous and uncontrolled sale of opium as a popular remedy, or the medical utility of the drug.

Opium before the nineteenth century [4]

A knowledge of the utility of opium was not, of course, confined to the nineteenth century, or even particularly novel at that time. The properties of the drug, and its use as a 'stimulant' and in dealing with pain, had already been widely known for many centuries. References to the juice of the poppy occur in the Assyrian medical tablets of the seventh century B.C., and in Sumerian ideograms of about 4000 B.C. the poppy is called the 'plant of joy'. Mesopotamia saw the growth of the opium poppy, and in both Egypt and Persia doctors treated patients with opium from at least the second century B.C. In fragments of the veterinary and gynaecological papyri and in the Therapeutic Papyrus of Thebes of 1552 B.C., opium is listed among other drugs medically recommended. From Egypt, growth of the poppy plant spread to Asia Minor and from there to Greece. Descriptions by Theophrastus and Dioscorides show that the toxic effects of the drug were already well-known. Even the famous nepenthe of Helen is likely to have been an opium draught. Homer states in the *Odyssey* that when Telemachus visited Menelaus in Sparta and memories of the Trojan war and the death of Ulysses made them depressed and tearful, Helen brought them as a drink a drug dissolved in wine which had the power to bring 'forgetfulness of evil'. Although the effects of the drink have been attributed to hashish rather than to opium, Helen's draught seems to have produced the euphoria of opium rather than the excitement of the other drug.

Roman medicine was as familiar with opium. Galen was enthusiastic about the virtues of opiate 'confections' or mixtures, and Virgil mentioned it as a soporific both in the *Aeneid* and in the *Georgics*. It was so popular in Rome that, as in nineteenth-century

England, it was sold by ordinary shopkeepers and itinerant quacks.

The Arab physicians used opium extensively, writing special treatises on its preparations; Avicenna himself, who recommended it especially for diarrhoea and diseases of the eye, is said to have been an opium addict or at least to have died from an overdose of the drug. Arab traders spread the use of opium over a much wider area – to Persia, India and China. When they penetrated into the eastern part of the Roman Empire – into Egypt, North Africa and Spain – they took opium with them. During the Mohammedan conquest of the tenth and eleventh centuries, the opium trade was firmly established in Europe, and returning Crusaders, too, brought back knowledge of the Arabs' use of the drug.

By the sixteenth century at least, then, opium was well established in Western European medicine. The famous German physician Philippus Aureolus Theophrastus Bombast von Hohenheim, better known as Paracelsus (1490–1540), owed much of his success to the way in which he administered opium to his patients. He is said to have carried opium in his saddle pommel and to have called it the 'stone of immortality'. His followers were as enthusiastic: Platerus of Basle strongly recommended it in 1600, and Sylvius de la Boe, a well-known Dutch physician, declared that without opium he could not practise medicine.

In England the drug had early been used, chiefly for its narcotic properties. In the middle of the fourteenth century John Arderne used salves and elixirs containing opium to procure sleep and also apparently, externally applied, as a form of anaesthetic during operations: 'he schal slepe so that he schal fele no kuttyng...'. The drug's soporific and narcotic qualities reappear in Chaucer's *Canterbury Tales* and in Shakespeare, in particular in the famous passage from *Othello*:

> Not poppy, nor mandragore,
> Nor all the drowsy syrups of the world,
> Shall ever medicine thee to that sweet sleep
> Which thou ow'dst yesterday.

Bullein's *Bulwarke of Defence against all Sicknesse, Soarenesse and Woundes* of 1579 likewise recommended the white poppy, which 'hath all the vertues', and opium made from the black poppy, 'which is cold and is used in sleeping medicines: but it causeth

deepe deadly sleapes'. The stock-in-trade of a Lancashire apothecary of the same period had its half ounce of opium (valued at
sixpence).

Opium was to be found too in the four great standbys of the
medicine of that period: mithridatum, theriaca, philonium and dia-
scordium. The last-named, a product of the early sixteenth century, mentioned among its principal ingredients cinnamon, cassia
wood, scordium, dittany, galbanum, storax, gum arabic, opium,
sorrel, gentian, Armenian bole, Lemnian earth, pepper, ginger and
honey. Such preparations remained popular as general palliatives
and antidotes, but opium was used more specifically, too. It was
Paracelsus who first used the term laudanum to describe an efficacious opium compound, but his was probably in solid pill form.
The alcoholic tincture which is now known as laudanum was originated by the English physician Thomas Sydenham in the 1660s.
Sydenham's enthusiasm for the drug is well-known and his praise
unstinting:

> ... here I cannot but break out in praise of the great God, the
> giver of all good things, who hath granted to the human race,
> as a comfort in their afflictions, no medicine of the value of
> opium, either in regard to the number of diseases it can control,
> or its efficiency in extirpating them... Medicine would be a
> cripple without it; and whosoever understands it well, will do
> more with it alone than he could well hope to do from any single
> medicine.

With this widespread use of opium, addiction was known, but
quite rarely discussed and generally calmly accepted. Thomas
Shadwell, the Restoration dramatist and poet, was an opium
addict whose habit was a matter for jest rather than concern. Shadwell was the subject of Dryden's *MacFlecknoe*, the Prince of Dull-
ness, who 'never deviates into sense'. But neither Dryden nor Tom
Brown, who wrote a mock epitaph on Shadwell, considered him
in the modern terminology of addiction, nor did they apparently
consider his use of opium had any effect on him or his readers:

> Tom writ, his readers still slept o'er his book,
> For Tom took opium, and they opiates took.

In general, the reaction to sustained opium use at this time was
calm, and indeed the subject was rarely discussed. Dr John Jones's
Mysteries of Opium Reveal'd, published in 1700, was one of the

earliest books specifically to treat addiction, but its tone was not hysterical. In fact Jones, although listing unpleasant physical and mental symptoms from excessive doses, was also inclined to emphasize the pleasurable aspects of opium use, those which the nineteenth-century writers might have termed its 'stimulant' effects. After taking opium, '... if the person keeps himself in action, discourse or business, it seems ... like a most delicious and extraordinary refreshment of the spirits upon very good news, or any other great cause of joy ... It has been compared (not without good cause) to a permanent gentle degree of that pleasure which modesty forbids the name of ...' Medical authors, too, in the eighteenth century, such as George Young in his *Treatise on Opium* published in the 1750s and Dr Samuel Crumpe in his *Inquiry into the Nature and Properties of Opium* of 1793, stressed the main features of addiction and the possibilities of withdrawal, but with no sign of moral condemnation or alarm. Crumpe himself reported that he had taken opium frequently and had experienced its euphoric effects. Nevertheless, the majority of descriptions at this time still saw opium eating or smoking as a peculiarly Eastern custom. In Dr Russell's *History of Aleppo* for instance, or the tales of Baron de Tott, the Eastern opium eater was a regular feature of the travellers' tales of the period, an object of interest and wonder, but not of condemnation.

Opium and history

At the opening of the nineteenth century, then, doctors and others still thought of opium not as dangerous or threatening, but as central to medicine, a medicament of surpassing usefulness which undoubtedly found its way into every home. It is with the way in which these attitudes changed and the restrictions placed on opium use during the course of the nineteenth century that the rest of this book will deal. These historical roots of contemporary events have already attracted a certain amount of attention. The 'drug consciousness' of the 1960s was in particular marked by an interest in historical material which could provide 'relevance' for the contemporary debates. Often this was quite superficial. A reference to the mid-nineteenth-century opium wars, or a mention of De Quincey's *Confessions of an English Opium Eater*, did duty as historical input to the debate. This interest in the historical dimension was particularly noticeable in the United States. The discussions which took place there in the 1960s over the direction which American drug-control policy should take were marked by continual references to, and analyses of, the past. The struggle to graft disease ideas of addiction, the view of the addict as a patient rather than a criminal, on to a policy which still stressed a penal approach established in the 1920s was rooted in historical as well as scientific and medical discussion. Detailed and valuable work was done on the historical roots of American narcotic policy.[5] The historical background was used as a vantage point from which to criticize current American policy. In the work of the anti-psychiatrist Thomas Szasz, perhaps the best-known exponent of such views, historical material was used to criticize both penal and medical approaches to drug control. Szasz's *Ceremonial Chemistry* (1975) argued that heroin and marijuana are different from alcohol and tobacco not for chemical but for ceremonial reasons and put forward a view of medicine as social control, not an agent of progress.[6]

To any historian, the deficiencies of many such polemical approaches are obvious. The lack of a certain socio-cultural or class perspective in Szasz is notable. Easily accessible historical examples from a variety of cultures and social structures have often been a substitute for a more rigorously researched analysis of drug use in a particular society. In another sense, too, the history of narcotics has been misused in the contemporary debates. There has been a tendency to read the preconceptions and values of the present too directly into the past. A recent study of the historical origins of social policy makes very much this point. Matters have been looked at 'through the wrong end of the telescope; taking insufficient account of the difficulty of understanding past events in the very different context of their time'.[7] Those concerned with present policy have been too intimately involved with the assessment and selection of material from the past. Facts and opinions to a large extent divorced from their historical context have been used to provide 'relevance'. Narcotic history has been used in a mechanistic way to justify particular departures in policy or specific ways of looking at drugs. The statistics of the past have been quoted in comparison with those of the present with little realization of the pitfalls of historical data, the very different cultural and social situations of drug use in historically distant societies.

Writers on opium and other narcotics, seeing a problem of contemporary drug use, have discussed opium in the past within the same problem framework. But what most needs analysis is not the dimensions of a problem – the statistical and epidemiological approach has spilled over in historical discussions from its dominance of contemporary scientific writing on drug use – but the definition of it. It is the establishment of attitudes and perceptions, of shifts in focus and ways of looking at drug use which should concern us. The description just given of opium use before the nineteenth century is an indication of rather different reactions to opium and its regular use. The nineteenth-century story makes this differing reaction more explicit. How did a drug like opium, on open sale in Britain in the early nineteenth century, its use widespread for what would now be termed 'non-medical' as well as 'medical' reasons, come to be seen as a problem? In the 1850s, opium could be bought in any grocer's or druggist's shop; by the end of the century, opium products and derivatives and opium-based patent medicines were only to be found in pharmacists' shops. Regular opium users, 'opium eaters', were acceptable in their communities and rarely the subject of medical attention at the beginning of the century; at its end they were classified as 'sick', diseased or deviant in some way and fit subjects for professional treatment. It is these broader questions of shifts of focus which need explanation, the establishment of a whole new way of looking at drug use which requires analysis.

An obvious explanation would lie in the inherently dangerous properties of the drugs themselves, the obviously profligate way in which they were used when freely available. This, indeed, is the type of drug-centred explanation which has often been adopted. The restriction of opium use has been seen as little more than a public health matter. The public health issues which concerned nineteenth-century society are considered in Chapters 7 and 8 of this book, and indeed some accounts of opium use and restriction have dealt with them alone. The testimony of official reports and inquiries has been taken at face value rather than analysed as a product of the values and perceptions of the society of the time. For drug use must also be considered in relation to its social context; individual and drug-centred explanations of use and control need replacement by a consideration of the whole socio-cultural setting in which such use was established. Most obviously, narcotics have been a scapegoat for wider tensions within society. There were undoubtedly problems associated with its open sale. The adulteration of the drug and the high level of overdosing and mortality from opium were the most obvious. Even these issues, however, were closely allied with the social situation of opium users. The large number of deaths from opium poisoning were the outcome of established popular traditions of self-medication and the lack of continuing accessible medical care. The popular acceptability and utility of opium as an everyday remedy in such a situation badly needs reconstruction; it has in the past signally failed to emerge from the concentration on child 'doping' and poisoning.[8]

The perception of issues like these as part of an opium 'problem' owed more to structural change. The 'problem' of opium was, at various stages in the nineteenth century, seen very much as one of lower-class use, as Chapter 9 makes plain. Opium use by the working class was much more likely to be considered problematic than use of the drug in any other class. The belief in working-class 'stimulant' use of opium helped justify the first restriction on the drug in the 1868 Pharmacy Act. Consumption of chlorodyne – as a patent medicine, a preparation with much popular utility – brought further control in the 1890s. Fear of the spread of opium smoking among lower-class Chinese in dock areas encouraged more restrictive attitudes. The question of who used the drug was central; and the control of lower-class deviance was undoubtedly important. The problem of opium use was in this sense the outcome of the class basis of Victorian society. It was in part a question of social control. Despite recent criticism of the unthinking overall application of this concept, control of lower-class usage of opium was at certain stages in the nineteenth century a clear aim in the formulation of legislation.[9]

The changed perception of opium and its use also demonstrated the establishment of the ideological and practical dominance of opium use by the medical and pharmaceutical professions, the former in particular. The medical profession was in the process of legitimizing its own status and authority; opium was translated into a problem in the process. In a practical sense, this was achieved by professional controls over availability and use, as discussed in Chapters 10 and 11. The restrictions of the 1868 Act – the 'professionalization' of the sale of patent medicines, the curbs on prescriptions – were part of the establishment of a professional élite. Controls symbolized the substitution of a new view of opium use for the popular culture which had hitherto existed. It was notable, too, how the profession, in helping to forge a problem out of opium use, concentrated attention where it was least needed in objective terms. Once the 'stimulant' scare was over, working-class use was largely ignored. Instead, as Chapter 12 indicates, doctors concentrated on the question of hypodermic morphine, where a small number of injecting addicts were magnified by the medical perspective on the drug into the dimensions of a pressing problem.

The medical dimension to the 'problem' of opium use was more than a case of professional strategy. There is a danger, in stressing the theme of professionalization in connection with narcotics, that doctors come to be seen as some autonomous body, working out their designs on opium in an isolated way. This is one of the deficiencies of the approaches which simply stress social control. For in reality the medical profession merely reflected and mediated the structure of the society of which it was the product. Social relations lay under the apparent objectivity of medical concepts and attitudes. This was at its clearest in the new ideological interpretation of narcotic use which began to be established in the last quarter of the century. What Michel Foucault has called 'the strict, militant, dogmatic medicalization of society...' found its expression in the nineteenth century in the establishment of theories of disease affecting a whole spectrum of conditions.[10] Homosexuality, insanity, even poverty and crime were re-classified in a biologically determined way. Concepts of addiction, discussed in Chapter 13, of 'inebriety' or 'morphinism' in the nineteenth-century terminology, were part of this process. These emphasized a distinction barely applied before between what was seen as 'legitimate' medical use and 'illegitimate' non-medical use. They established an apparently objective system of ideas which in reality had its foundation in social relations. For the 'disease model' of addiction arose through the establishment of the status of the medical profession in society. It was formulated by a section of the middle class, and the model of addiction thus presented was peculiarly attuned to the characteristics of addicts of the same status. Lower-class addicts were notably neglected in disease theory. The respectable addicts to whom the theories were most often applied accepted their provenance; and, at that level, the need for medical intervention was rarely questioned. The 'problem' of opium use found a major part of its origin in the establishment of this form of ideological hegemony. Putting forward individual rather than social explanations, it nevertheless proposed the scientific objectivity of disease views as a means of progress towards greater understanding. The moral prejudices of the profession were given the status of value-free norms.

This was never a monolithic process. Many doctors, particularly those in general practice (as opposed to the expanding numbers of addiction specialists), doubted the necessity for treatment and intervention even if they accepted the conceptual framework of disease. And at the lower levels of society, opium use and self-medication was still quite calmly accepted even at the end of the century. Theories of disease were in any case rarely applied to the working-class addict; the response here epitomized in the agitation over chlorodyne in the 1890s simply emphasized that the availability of the drug should be limited. The distinctive ideological shift had nevertheless already taken place. Drug use was a developing social problem by the end of the century. Opium was already contolled; certain of its users were classified as 'deviant' or 'sick'.[11] The rest of this book will examine how and why this was the case.

PART ONE

The Import and Cultivation of Opium
at the Beginning of the Century

I

The Import Trade

Opium use in English society in the nineteenth century was completely unrestricted until 1868, when the first Pharmacy Act became law. The first chapters of this book will attempt to describe how such a situation of free availability and sale operated at all levels of society over this seventy-year period, not simply in the medical profession, who might, from a contemporary point of view, be thought the most likely legitimate users of the drug, but also among the generality of consumers, whether of the middle, lower or upper class. Opium was sold and used freely and largely unselfconsciously throughout this time, and it was imported, too, through normal channels of commerce as one more item of trade, to be dealt with as objectively as any other variety of goods to be shipped and passed through the hands of a broker. The other, very minor, source was British-grown opium, dealt with in Chapter 2. Here too the concern was with profit and quality, not with controls or the dangers of the drug.

It might have been expected that the opium bought and sold in this way in England would come from the Far East. After all, Britain was involved in the Indian opium trade with China, to the extent of fighting two 'opium wars' with that country in 1839–42 and 1856–8. But these Far Eastern connections had little effect on English opium use until the last quarter of the century, well after the opium wars were over. The opium sold and used in England for most of the century came not from India or China, but from Turkey. In the eighteenth century, the anonymous *Short History of Druggs and Other Commodities* had stated that imported opium came 'chiefly . . . from Turkey, where they prepare it much better than what comes from India, which is much softer and

3

fouler than the Turkey...'.[1] This was still the case in the nine-teenth century. For over forty years, between 1827 and 1869, between 80 and 90 per cent of opium imported into the country was Turkish. Even at the end of the century, Turkish opium still had over 70 per cent of the market (Table 1, p. 273).

Indian opium could occasionally be found on the English market. In 1829, Dr Webster exhibited a 'specimen of pure opium' before the Westminster Medical Society, sent to him from Calcutta. Webster expressed the forthright hope that 'if it could be obtained from one colony, we should have it thence rather ... than that we should go to the rascally Turks'.[2] Small quantities of Indian opium were occasionally imported, and the disruption of normal channels of trade during the two 'opium wars' also brought more of the drug onto the London market. Indian opium also had an increasing share of the market from the late 1880s.[3] But Persian opium gained the most notable increase. It formed over 10 per cent of the total in the 1890s. Previously the Persian drug had been sent to Constantinople, where it was made up into an imitation of the Turkish variety. The new Persian variety (shipped from ports in the Persian Gulf) attracted much interest in pharmaceutical circles.[4] But the major proportion of imported opium at the end of the century still came from Asiatic or European Turkey.

Turkish opium was of either the Smyrna or the Constantinople variety, although in practice there appears to have been little difference between the two. Some opium simply found its way to Constantinople direct instead of going through the market at Smyrna, which was the central market for all the opium grown in Asia Minor. The actual opium-growing areas in the nineteenth century were chiefly in Kara Chissar and around Magnesia.[5] Peasants, rather than large landowners, were the main cultivators. The labour-intensiveness of poppy cultivation and of opium collection – a major drawback when experiments were made with British opium – made it uneconomic for large-scale production. Every peasant who could tried to grow his own opium for sale on whatever land he owned or could rent. The whole family was pressed into service, in particular at the time of the opium harvest.

Sowing of the opium poppy took place three times in one season. One acre was sown in mid-November, a second in December and the last in February or March. The plants were grown partly from white, partly from blue, seeds, and in the temperate Turkish con-

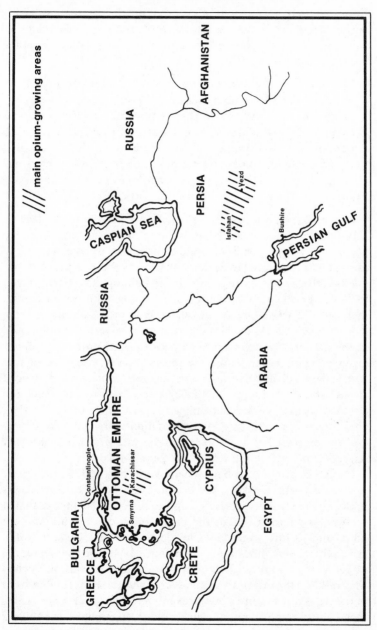

Sources of opium imported into Britain.

ditions could reach a height of six or eight feet. Peasants working in the poppy fields were quite invisible as they made their incisions. The concentration together of so many opium poppies could have unusual effects:

> The exhalations emitted by these plantations especially in the morning and after sunset, are described by the Turks as very dangerous, and they avoid them by retiring towards evening to their huts, which they do not leave until after the rising of the sun ... As soon as the moisture of the atmosphere ... begins towards evening to be condensed, a strong narcotic smell is developed. This, in those unaccustomed to it, gives rise, in about a quarter of an hour, to headaches and nausea.[6]

Harvesting by the traditional incision methods took place in July in the higher areas, in May lower down the slopes. Every part of the poppy plant was used. The plants were given to the cattle, the seed pressed to produce oil used by the peasants in cooking as well as for lighting, and the remaining cake partly given to cattle, partly used by the poorer families who mixed it with their bread. Part of the seed was also sold to merchants at Smyrna, who shipped it to Marseilles where it was converted into oil used in the manufacture of soap. The peasant cultivators were under heavy obligation even before the opium was ready, for speculators and dealers had already purchased the crop. Money was advanced at high rates of interest (18 to 25 per cent was moderate) and although peasants were not obliged to give their opium to their creditors if they could find buyers at a higher price, nor were merchants compelled to take opium at the rate first fixed after the harvest if no one would take it off their hands.

Packed in grey calico bags which were then sealed and placed in oblong wicker baskets, the opium came down to Smyrna by mule, although the vagaries of opium speculation meant that it sometimes passed through the hands of three or four different merchants before it reached the port. The first baskets would arrive there sometimes around the end of May or the beginning of June. They were sold without examination. It was only when they reached the buyer's warehouse that they were opened in front of the seller himself and a public examiner. The latter was a skilled man. The judging of opium, where colour, appearance, weight and scent all had to be taken into account, was a matter of many years' experience. Seated on the ground wearing an apron and armed with a strong knife, he would examine the opium piece by piece as an assistant emptied each basket in turn; each one took him about ten minutes. Practice enabled him to tell by weight if the opium was pure. Any suspect piece was cut open and immediately thrown aside if adulterated. The strength and quality of the opium was measured on a 'carat' scale, twenty-four carats being pure opium. By custom, everything over twenty was counted as pure and anything under was thrown out. This examination usually took place several weeks after the first batches of opium had arrived from the growing areas, partly because the opium, if too fresh, tended to become over-heated. It lost weight over the weeks as it dried out (damp opium always did poorly on the market) and adulteration was not so easily detected when the drug was fresh. Shipments from Smyrna began in August, and the opium was packed in hermetically sealed zinc-lined wooden cases, each one large enough to take the contents of a single basket.

In Persia, the whole process was much the same, although on a smaller scale. Here Yezd, Isfahan and some of the Khorassan districts were the main opium-growing areas. Isfahan was the centre of the opium trade – a great market place through which Persian opium passed on its way to Hong-Kong or London. Much of the Persian drug went on to the Chinese market, but already in the 1880s about a quarter of Isfahan opium was exported by London firms.

The varieties of opium were immediately distinguishable by appearance, although, as the example of Persian opium shows, it was not unknown for opium from an inferior area to be disguised in the form of one from a more highly prized district. Smyrna opium came in irregular flattened masses of around two pounds in weight. It was blackish brown, waxy and enveloped in leaves. Constantinople opium was generally found in small lens-shaped cakes, covered with poppy leaves. It was redder, softer and weaker in quality than the Smyrna type. Egyptian opium was marketed in round, flattened cakes, also enveloped in leaves. It was redder and harder than both the Turkish varieties. Persian opium came in the form of agricultural sticks, each covered in smooth glossy paper and tied with cotton. Indian opium (or at least that coming from Patna and Benares) was made into balls the size of a double fist and weighing about 3½ lb. each. Again covered with a hard skin made of poppy petals, it was packed in two-storey mango-wood chests, each storey with twenty compartments for twenty balls.[7]

At the beginning of the nineteenth century, the old trading routes by which opium had long been imported into England, along with other drugs and spices, from Turkey and the Middle East, still maintained a tenuous existence.[8] By mid-century, however, so far as opium was concerned, the last relics of the old trading company routes had disappeared and a new pattern of importing had been established. In the 1820s and 1830s, some opium was still imported by way of the Netherlands, Gibraltar, Malta, Germany, France and, most important, Italy. These were relics of the old trading routes through Europe, centred on Venice and Leghorn. It was along these that the merchant companies had imported drugs and spices (currants in particular in the case of Turkey) in return for the goods exported there. By the 1850s, however, the bulk of the drug imported came direct from Turkey itself. The 'Italian connection' had died away and other European staging posts were of minute significance[9] (see Table 1, p. 273). The S.S. *Crimean* for instance, which went aground off Smyrna in 1865, was carrying quite considerable quantities of opium direct.[10]

Later in the century, alternative routes did begin to open up. Increasing quantities of the drug were arriving by way of France in the last quarter of the century. Marseilles was becoming an important staging post in the opium trade, a historic link with its later importance as a drug 'laboratory'. By the 1890s between 4 and 10 per cent of imports each year came that way; the Netherlands, too, was an important trading centre.

In the early years of the century, opium was imported through a variety of British ports. Liverpool, for instance, imported 120 lb. in 1792, Dover 261 lb. in 1801.[11] But the bulk of dealing in the drug was increasingly centralized in the capital. In London, a small group of importers initially controlled the supply of opium. These were the Turkey merchants, offshoots of the earlier Turkey, or Levant, Company, the mercantilist organization originally given its charter by Elizabeth I. This had controlled all trade to and from Turkey until the eighteenth century; its demise in 1825 left the import of opium open to free trade.[12] The drug wholesaling houses were by the mid nineteenth century importing many other drugs direct, but opium at this period still remained the province of the Turkey merchants. Drug brokers, active in the Mincing and Mark Lane areas of the city since the seventeenth century, were used by these merchants to conduct detailed sale negotiations.[13]

Many drugs were sold on the open market and auctions of opium did take place at Garraway's Coffee House by the Royal Exchange, the centre for London drug sales.[14] But opium seems to have been dealt with more often by private arrangement than by public auction. Most often some form of arrangement was agreed between the large London wholesale houses – Allen and Hanburys, the Apothecaries' Company and others – and the opium brokers.[15] A representative of the wholesaler would go down to the docks to examine the opium in bond, and any suspect cases would be immediately rejected. Drug broking was an expanding occupation in early nineteenth-century London. There were only three brokers specializing in drugs and spices in the 1830s, but around thirty by the 1850s.[16]

The Apothecaries' Company, which had a superior status as a body with rights both to examine in medicine and to visit apothecaries' shops (although the trading department of the Company was a separate entity), expected to be approached by the brokers themselves. Every Saturday a list was put up in the outer room of the Company's counting house giving notice of drugs needed the following week. Brokers and merchants who wished to sell to the Company sent in samples by one o'clock the following Tuesday. The Buying Committee, a group of 'medical gentlemen', assisted by specialist chemists from the Company itself, then examined and tested the samples and selected the best of them.[17] Opium was just a commodity like so much tea.

The records for calculating the cash and profit of the opium import business – what money there was to be made – are no longer in existence. But profits were clearly sufficient for unscrupulous dealers to try to obtain a share. In the mid 1840s, one importer tried to sell completely worthless opium, but his effort did not meet with much success. It was offered on the market, but met with no customers – 'he made it so completely worthless,' a buyer recalled, 'that its detection was not difficult.'[18]

There was as much speculation in opium in London as there was in Smyrna. Prices could vary considerably, depending, too, on the quality of the opium purchased. Opium paid an import duty in the first half of the century. This stood at four shillings a pound between 1828 and 1836, and was reduced to one shilling a pound in 1836. It stayed at this level until, as part of the introduction of a free-trade policy, duty on the drug was completely abolished in 1860. Few reliable figures are available prior to the 1850s. Nevertheless, the gradual reduction of the opium duty did lead, at least initially, to a considerable cheapening in the wholesale price of opium. In 1819, when duty stood as high as nine shillings a pound, Turkey opium could be had at around £1 a pound – the addition of duty brought this up to around thirty shillings a pound. In February 1819, it reached a price of twenty-seven shillings and sixpence in bond, thirty-six shillings when duty had been paid. Opium's basic price had altered little by the 1850s, but the reduction of duty to one shilling meant that it could be bought wholesale for around twenty shillings a pound. This was the price Thomas Herring gave for 'common good opium'. Opium from less favoured areas could be had at a cheaper price. Egyptian opium, known to be of poor quality and generally deficient in morphine, sold in 1858 for only six shillings and eightpence a pound without duty. Times of scarcity and bad harvest could lead to a steep increase in prices, and this may have been behind the sudden rise which took place in the late 1860s when Persian opium first came directly on to the London market. Turkish opium rose to over twenty-five shillings in 1868 and higher in the succeeding year. Even Egyptian opium was around seventeen shillings and the newly arrived Persian drug sold at about £1 a pound[19] Considered in these quantities, opium was an expensive drug. Twenty shillings was an agricultural labourer's weekly wage. But it was no more expensive than other drugs on the market, and, of course, was sold and made up in ounces rather than pounds.

The question of the quantity of opium imported and consumed inside England became a matter of public discussion in the first half of the century. Import statistics are, indeed, an index of what was happening to consumption levels in the country. This point is discussed in Chapter 3. But the mechanics of opium importation, the fact that opium was just another commodity on the market, were in themselves an indication of the normality of the trade in the first six decades of the century.

2

The Cultivation of Opium in Britain
1790–1820

The bulk of the opium used in England at this time was thus imported. But there were also small-scale attempts at domestic cultivation of the drug in the early years of the nineteenth century. Opium was a very minor, if surprising, part of the move towards agricultural 'improvement' in Britain at the end of the eighteenth and beginning of the nineteenth centuries. Although much of the fundamental transformation of landownership and farming was already established by the middle of that century, the later eighteenth and early part of the nineteenth century was a time of increasing output and productivity, when changes in crops and crop-rotation, new methods of stock-breeding and an increase in the size of farms consolidated the move to commercial farming techniques.[1] Opium's inclusion with turnips and rhubarb in the agricultural discussions of the period was one sidelight on the content of agricultural innovation. It was an indication, too, of the drug's acceptability; the 'home-grown' product bore witness to the place of opium in society at the time.

'I make no doubt it may be brought to the greatest perfection in this country, and rendered at one half the price at which we have it from the East, and without the least adulteration...' John Ball, who wrote this letter in 1796 to the Society of Arts, was referring to his cultivation of opium. In a letter two years previously, he had written:

I think amazing quantities are consumed every year; and am of opinion, that there is twenty times more opium used now in England only, than there was fifteen or twenty years since, as great quantities are used in outward applications, and it is continually advancing in price...[2]

Ball was a small farmer from Williton in Somerset, and was among the first seriously to consider the commercial possibilities of cultivating opium.

The beginnings of experimentation had a lengthier history, for the white opium poppy was indigenous in certain areas of the country, most notably in the Fen ditches in parts of Norfolk and Cambridgeshire. Poppy-head tea and fomentations made from poppy capsules had long been widely used in domestic remedies, in particular in that area. One of the first to produce opium rather than poppy capsules was Dr Alston, Professor of Botany and Materia Medica at Edinburgh in the middle of the eighteenth century. Alston had begun his experiments in the 1730s, although he did not write them up until 1742. He used primarily the white poppy, taking little account of debates on which variety was the best to use. He thought that there was little difference, it was simply that the white had the biggest head and so gave the most opium.[3]

Other eighteenth-century experimenters followed Alston's example and used methods of collection adapted from Far Eastern experience. Mr J. Kerr, Surgeon to the Civil Hospital in Bengal, estimated in 1776 that one acre harvested in this way in Britain could yield sixty pounds of opium.[4] Woodville, in his *Medical Botany* (1793), held out very favourable hopes of the possibilities of domestic opium cultivation. He himself had 'appropriated a part of the garden at the Small-pox Hospital'. It was, he thought, 'highly probable that the White Poppy might be cultivated for the purpose of obtaining opium to great advantage in Britain'.[5]

Such hopes were the forerunner to the main period of experimentation and discussion. This lasted for roughly thirty years, from the late 1790s until the mid-1820s, although individual attempts at cultivation continued later in the century. The Society of Arts, which had taken an interest in the introduction of new medicinal plants, was the agency which encouraged extensive experimentation. Its interest in the general area of drug cultivation dated back to 1763, when it had appointed a committee to encourage the introduction of rhubarb cultivation, offering a gold medal as inducement. At the end of the century it began to take an interest in opium as well, primarily after the approach by John Ball, to whom the Society eventually awarded fifty guineas for his home-grown opium. Fifty guineas or a gold medal were also offered in general for those producing considerable quantities (at least twenty pounds) of the drug. Another experimenter, Thomas Jones, used five acres of ground near Enfield after an initial experiment in 1794. He managed, despite numerous setbacks when seeds were strangled by weeds, and cold and dry weather in May was nearly fatal to the growing plants, to produce twenty-one pounds of opium. In 1800 he was the next recipient of the financial prize.[6]

Other learned societies began to take an interest. The Caledonian Horticultural Society aimed primarily to encourage the production of lettuce opium, which it hoped might lack the 'distressing consequences' which sometimes resulted from the medical use of opium. In 1810 it offered two prizes. One was for the best method of preparing 'soporific medicine' from the juice of the common garden lettuce, the other for the best method of preparing opium in Britain and the most advantageous manner of cultivating poppies for that purpose. One of the first to claim the opium prize was Dr Howison, ex-Inspector of Opium in Bengal, who, in 1813, described how he had found the double red garden poppy the best plant for use in Scotland. He had experimented with the white poppy in a plot about ten miles from London and had found that he could collect milk better both in quality and in quantity from it there. But the size of the plant was a disadvantage for cultivation in Scotland, where strong winds were likely to break it down. Dr Howison received the Society's prize medal.[7] But no further successes were reported until 1820, when John Young, who had described his collection of lettuce opium to the Caledonian Society, also received the Society of Arts' gold medal. Young, an Edinburgh surgeon, aimed to demonstrate that opium could be successfully cultivated in a cold wet climate. This he amply did, for his experiments in cultivating poppies not just for opium but for oil as well had given a profit of £50–£80 an acre. A yield per acre of fifty-six pounds of opium, several hundred pounds of oil and oil cakes, and a quantity of early potatoes prudently planted in addition produced the handsome sum of £110 7s. 6d. profit.[8]

Perhaps the most successful opium cultivators were Dr John Cowley and Mr Staines of Winslow in Buckinghamshire, who, in 1823, received thirty guineas from the Society for '143 pounds of opium, of excellent quality, collected by them from about eleven Acres of Land, planted with the Papaver Somniferum'.[9]

Opium cultivation did not end with their efforts. Isolated experiments continued in various parts of the country. But the main period of competition to produce the most and best of the domestic variety was over. Opium cultivation, with reports coming in from places as far apart as Edinburgh and Somerset, appears not to have concentrated in any particular area of the country, although cultivation was obviously more successful in southern England. There was no generally agreed method of cultivation and each experimenter tried to improve on that used by his predecessor. Mr Arnot in 1742 was the first to describe cultivation:

What I have found most successful is to trench a spot of new rich ground, where Poppies had not grown the preceding year; for if they are continued several years on the same Ground they degenerate. A chusing the ripest and whitest Seed of the great single-flowered Turkey Poppy, I sow it in the month of March very thin and superficially in Drills at two Foot Distance each, to allow Place for Weeding, etc. As soon as the young Plants spring up, I take most of them away, leaving only the strongest most thriving Plants at about a Foot distant from each other.

The opium was collected by roughly the same method as it generally was in the Far East – incisions were made into the poppy capsule and the milky juice allowed to run out. This was then scraped from the poppy head into a tin or other container and evaporated to obtain the pure opium. Dr Alston had 'collected the pure Milk with a little Silver Spoon and my Finger into a China Tea-cup'.

This was an age of cheap and exploitable labour. The harvesting of opium was still costly in man-hours and ways of circumventing this cost were much discussed. Ball, Jones and Jeston explained the possibilities of child labour. As Ball pointed out, with children making the incisions and taking off the opium, 'the expence [sic] will be found exceedingly trifling'. Jones and Jeston both carried the possibilities of child labour to greater lengths, establishing a clear pay structure with financial inducements. Jones, employing seven or eight boys between eight and twelve years old with a man as superintendent, based his pay scale on age and behaviour. 'To the youngest, I gave threepence a day, and, if tractable and well disposed, an additional penny for every additional year.' Jeston favoured a productivity deal, with a rate of eightpence a day and a penny for every extra bottle of opium collected.

Cheap labour was the main requirement. Cowley and Staines employed two women for nine days in 1819, paying them a shilling a day. They commented that 'a general cultivation of opium would certainly be beneficial by calling into action a description of persons not calculated for common agricultural labour, and that between hay-time and harvest'. A later experiment used unemployed lace-makers from the Winslow neighbourhood. They had also employed six 'peaceable and industrious' Irish migrant labourers (also paid a shilling a day for eleven hours' work) and noted that if cultivation was expanded beyond their present fifteen acres of land then: 'We must do it by the Irish, great numbers of whom are every year seeking employment during the Opium Season.'[10] One commentator even suggested that opium cultivation might be a means of rejuvenating Irish economic life – 'the cultivation of poppies ... might be very profitably undertaken in IRELAND, where labourers ... are abundant...'.[11] Opium could even provide the solution to the Irish problem.

The growers of opium experienced little difficulty in finding profitable outlets for their produce. Druggists were very ready to buy a variety of the drug which was pure and unadulterated. John Young, in his 1820 schedule of cash and profits, estimated the selling price of his opium variously at between 17s. 6d. and thirty-six shillings a pound, roughly equivalent to variations in the current price of best Turkey opium.[12]

Home-grown opium found ready acceptance in medical circles. Thomas Jones's opium was used by a hospital physician in cases of acute rheumatism, disease of the bowels and a case of hysteria. An apothecary at the Middlesex Hospital used the home-grown product on Elizabeth Spraughton with a 'diseased state of the stomach', giving her a grain of opium every four to six hours. Dr Latham of Bedford Row tried a one-grain soap and opium pill made with John Ball's opium and found it relieved his tickling cough.[13] Experiments were made with regular consumers of the drug, who were asked to try British opium to see if it produced the same effect. British opium was found more efficacious than the Turkey variety.[14]

There was glowing testimony to the efficacy and purity of

English opium. Some observers even thought that local cultivation could supply domestic medical needs. But British opium did not live up to such expectations. The cultivation of the opium poppy never became widespread. The existence of a domestic variety of the drug was quite widely known in the first half of the century; and the various experiments obviously made some public impact.[15] It was unlikely that production continued on any great scale. But some growers did continue the experimentation of the early years of the century. Sir Roger Martin of Burnham Westgate in Norfolk collected English opium there in the 1840s. As late as the 1870s a Mr Dymond of Birmingham and Mr Sutton of Norwich were describing experiments in its cultivation to fellow pharmacists.[16] Clearly many such small-scale attempts could have been made, particularly in Norfolk, where the white opium poppy grew wild. At a time when attempts were being made to produce opium on a commercial scale in Western Europe, most notably in France and Germany, where trials were made in the 1820s and again later in the century, it was very likely that further attempts were made in England too.[17]

The only successful commercial production was not of opium, but of poppy heads. This was well-established in the neighbourhood of Mitcham as early as the 1830s. The London drug market obtained the bulk of its supplies from the Mitcham growers. The poppy heads yielded an extract known as 'English opium' which contained 5 per cent morphia, a lower proportion than in either the imported or home-grown variety. An average bag of three thousand poppy capsules sold for about £4 10s. in the 1830s.[18] There were attempts to use the obviously congenial Mitcham climate for the production of cannabis, too.

But British opium and British cannabis never became large-scale commercial propositions to rival the pre-eminence of the imported drug in the early decades of the century. The 'precariousness of our climate', problems with 'marauding hares', the attractions of more easily grown and harvested crops were all reasons for failure. The short-lived domestic experiment in cultivation was an interesting, if very minor, facet of the general move towards agricultural innovation and change in this period, the establishment of a capitalist agricultural structure to parallel that of industry. The calm discussion of its medical and agricultural possibilities, the use of child labour, the balance sheets of profits and losses which were drawn up, were in another sense interesting. For the experiments, like the import of the drug, emphasized society's acceptance of opium use in any form at this time.

PART TWO

Opium Use in the First Half of the Nineteenth Century

3

Open Sale and Popular Use

Opium, once imported, passed through a mechanism of whole-saling and retailing which finally brought it within reach of the ordinary consumer of the drug. Until 1868, there were no bars on this process at all (and even after 1868 restrictions were still quite minimal). The chapters in this Part will analyse how such a system of free availability and sale operated in the early decades of the century and how opium was used not just medically but for non-medical reasons as well at all levels of society.

Opium was an everyday part of the drug trade. Once sale negotiations had taken place, it became the property of a whole-sale drug house. There had been such wholesalers in London since the seventeenth century, and firms like William Allen & Company, of Plough Court (ancestor of Allen and Hanbury), had been in existence since the early eighteenth century. It was in the early part of the following century, however, that the process speeded up. Not only wholesale drug houses but manufacturing druggists, too, were established in profusion. Meggeson and Company in 1796 and May and Baker in Battersea in 1834 were among the earlier examples. Often there was no initial distinction in function. The early businesses dealt with many aspects of what later became specialized fields of the pharmaceutical industry. Thomas Mor-son and Sons Limited, for instance, the first commercial manufac-turer of morphine in Britain, began as an apothecaries' business in Fleet Market in 1821. Wholesaling, manufacturing and retailing were at that stage all part of the same operation; not until 1900 did Morsons actually give up their retail business.[1]

The wholesale druggists did not just sell but also manufactured their own opium preparations, a process which naturally provided much scope for adulteration, at a time when there was no legislative control.[2] The Apothecaries' Company, perhaps the most prestigious of the wholesaling houses, was manufacturing twenty-six opium preparations in 1868, including two morphine preparations, the hydrochlorate and the acetate, as well as its popular 'Cholera number two' mixture. In 1871, it had twenty-five on its books, including the oddly titled Fire Brigade mixture (Mist pro. Fire Brigade) which contained opium.[3] William Allen, in Plough Court, had sixteen opium preparations on his list in 1810, twenty in 1811. One wholesale druggist was selling poppy capsules at 1s. 10d. for a hundred, opiate plaster, Hemmings' extract of opium and syrup of white poppies, Battley's Sedative Solution, morphine acetate and hydrochlorate, Turkey opium, as well as Black Drop and the special Godfrey bottles (three dozen for 10s.).[4] Top sellers in the opium line are difficult to pin-point. Allen's kept most stock of opiate confection, extract of opium, the gum (or raw) drug, various varieties of laudanum, and syrup of white poppies. Later in the century, morphine hydrochlorate, paregoric, raw and powdered opium, laudanum, and gall and opium ointment were the Apothecaries' Company's most popular products.

In the eighteenth century, the central wholesalers had dealt direct with provincial apothecaries. In the latter years of the century, however, and increasingly in the nineteenth, a number of provincial wholesale houses established themselves, often developing as specialist businesses from grocers who found drugs their most profitable line.[5] Some chemists still dealt directly with the central wholesalers,[6] but it became customary for local chemists to buy opium from local wholesalers rather than direct from London. In 1890, W. Kemp and Son at Horncastle, one of these local businesses, still offered nine opium preparations. There were special quotations for twenty-eight-pound and fifty-six-pound lots of Turkey opium. More specialist opium preparations continued to be obtained from London. George Meggeson was the manufacturer there who led the market in the production of lozenges, and many opium and morphine based ones were on his price list (Figure 1).[7]

The opium stocks of such wholesalers, in the years before the 1868 Pharmacy Act limited the sale of the drug to professional pharmacists, were available to any dealer who chose to purchase. There was no limitation at all. Qualified pharmacists and apothe-

OPEN SALE AND POPULAR USE

GEORGE MEGGESON,

Druggist, and Manufacturer of

MEDICATED LOZENGES, REFINED LIQUORICE, PATE DE JUJUBES, &c., &c.,

No. 61, CANNON STREET. LONDON.

---o---

MEDICATED AND PROPRIETARY LOZENGES FAITHFULLY PREPARED.

---o---

Refined Liquorice, super	1	6
Pure Extract of Liquorice Lozenges	3	3
Liquorice Drops	1	3
Pontefract Cakes, genuine	1	7
,, refined Liquorice	1	7
Solazzi Juice		
Barracco Juice		
Corigliana Juice		
Pate de Jujube, Pink and Amber	1	4
,, ,, Pink and Rose	1	4
,, ,, Liquorice	1	4
,, ,, Sedative	1	9
,, ,, Crystallized	1	8
,, ,, Black Currant	2	0
,, ,, Strawberry	2	0
,, ,, Raspberry	2	0
,, ,, Crystallized	2	0
,, ,, Vanilla	2	0
French Jujube, Pine and Pink	1	9
,, ,, Rose	1	9
,, ,, Liquorice	1	9
,, ,, Crystallized	1	10
Pate de Guimauve	2	6
Pastills de Guimauve	2	6
Pate de Lichen	2	6
Peppermint Lozenges, extra strong		
Super, extra trans. Peppermint do	2	4
Super Transparent and Opaque	2	2
A Peppermint Lozenges	2	1
B ,, ,,	1	11
C ,, ,,	1	9
D ,, ,,	1	6
E ,, ,,	1	4
F ,, ,,	1	3
G ,, ,,	1	1
H ,, ,, genuine	1	0
Fluted Peppermint Lozenges		
Peppermint Pipe and Rock		
Same prices as above		
Peppermint Pearls or Seeds	2	2
Regent or Variegated Pipe	1	4
,, ,, ,,	10	2
Peppermint Drops 1 9 to	3	0
Absorbent Lozenges	2	6
Aniseed ,,	1	10
,, ,,	1	6
,, Pipe	1	7
Antacid Lozenges	1	5
Aromatic ditto	2	2
Bath Lozenges	2	6
,, Pipe	1	6
Balsamic Lozenges	1	7
Black Currant ditto, very superior	2	8
,, ,, Paste	2	6
Bismuth Lozenges	3	0
Brilliants, superfine	2	1
,, A	2	4
,, B	2	0
,, C	1	8
Calomel Lozenges, 1 grain	1	6
,, ,, 2 grains	3	3
,, ,, 3 ,,	3	6
Each Lozenge marked.	3	9
Cachou de Rose	4	0
Camphor Lozenges	2	0
Calomel and Jalap Lozenges	3	6
Cardamon Lozenges	3	6

Chocolate Lozenges	2	3
Caraway and Ginger Candy	1	6
Camomile Lozenges	2	3
Catchu	2	3
Cayenne and Acidulated ditto	2	1
Cinnamon ditto, extra strong	3	0
,, ,, White	2	6
,, ,, Pink	2	0
Chalk Lozenges	2	0
Clove ditto	2	6
Colt's-foot ditto	1	8
Conf. Opium Lozenges	1	7
,, Aromatic ditto	3	0
Comp. Chalk and Opium Lozenges	3	0
Dandelion Lozenges	2	6
Long Life or Digestive Candy	2	6
Long Life Lozenges, stamped	3	0
Voice	3	0
Cough	2	10
Worm	3	0
Steel-Tonic	2	6
Ingestive	2	3
Pine Apple ,,	2	6
Orange Marmalade ditto	2	6
Cherry Lozenges	2	6
Delectable Lozenges, superior	2	4
Digestive Tablets	2	2
Cachou Lozenges	3	0
Bouquet Lozenges	2	6
Pectoral Jujubes	2	3
Edinburgh Lozenges, P. E.	3	0
Fruit Cough Lozenges	3	6
Fruit and Ipecacuanha ditto	2	8
,, Opium ditto	2	8
Ginger Lozenges, extra strong	2	10
,, ,, super.	2	0
,, ,, A	1	8
,, ,, crystallized	1	4
Gelatine ditto (Nelson's)	1	6
Ginger Seeds or Pearls	1	7
,, ,, A	2	0
,, Pipe, super.	2	0
,, ,, A	2	10
Glauce-te-r Pipe	2	0
Gum Arabic Lozenges	2	9
Heartburn ditto	2	0
Hop ditto	3	0
Horehound ditto	2	0
,, Candy	0	11
,, ,, oz. and 1 oz. Hearts	1	1
Iceland Moss Lozenges	3	0
Ipecacuanha ditto, ½ grain each	2	2
,, ,, ,, & 1 grain each	2	2
,, ,, with Camphor	2	0
Kino ditto	2	0
Lactucarium ditto	2	10
Lavender ditto, very superior	2	0
,, Pipe	2	0
,, ,,	1	10
Lettuce Lozenges	2	8
Lemon ditto	2	2
Magnesia Lozenges	2	2
,, and Peppermint ditto	2	2
Marshmallow ditto	2	2
Morphia Lozenges, 1-24 grain	4	0
,, with Ipecacuanha ditto	4	6
Each Lozenge marked.		
Musk Lozenge, superior	2	6
Nitre Lozenges	2	2
Nutmeg ,,	2	2

Gum Lozenges		2	4
Orange		2	2
,, genuine		2	1
Patinea		1	10
Poppy		2	8
Quinine		4	6
Raspberry Lozenges		2	6
Rhubarb and Ginger Candy		2	6
,, ,, Lozenges		2	6
,, Ginger and Soda ditto		2	6
,, ,, and Cardamon		2	6
Rose Otto ditto		2	1
,, Acidulated ditto, White		2	4
,, saffra ditto		2	0
,, dry Soda and Bicarb Lozenges		2	0
,, Soda and Peppermint ditto		2	0
,, Soda & Ginger ditto		2	0
Snuff ditto		4	4
,, ,,		2	2
,, Ipecacuanha ditto		2	2
,, Aromatic ditto		2	2
,, Cubeb ,,		2	2
,, Lozenges		2	2
Cameral ditto		2	6
Snuff ditto		4	0
,, ditto, super.		2	3
,, ditto, A		2	1
Aniseed ditto		2	1
Acid Cayenne Drops		0	11
,, in ¼ lb. and 2 oz. canisters	5	9 & 3	3
,, Lemon Drops		0	10
,, ,, in ¼ lb. canisters	10	0	
,, ,, in ¼ lb. and 2 oz.	5	9 & 3	3
,, Orange Drops		0	11
,, Rock ditto		0	11
,, Rose ditto		0	11
,, ,, in ¼ lb. & 2 oz. canisters	5	9 & 3	3
,, Raspberry and Cayenne ditto		0	11
,, Strawberry ditto		0	11
,, Pine Apple ditto		1	2
Cayenne Drops		1	6
Horehound ditto		1	0
Barley Sugar ditto		1	3
Nonpareils and Pearls		2	2
Brown Candy		0	11
Pink ditto		1	4
White ditto		1	2
Candied Lemon Peel			
,, Orange ditto			
,, Citron ditto			
,, Iceland Root		3	6
,, Angelica Root		1	9
Drained Lemon Peel			
,, Orange ,,			
,, Citron ,,			
Black Currant Jam			
,, ,, Jelly			
Raspberry Jam			
Strawberry Jam			
Powdered Sugar			
Barley Sugar (Lemon)		0	11
,, ,, (Ginger)		0	11
Capillaire		1	3
Pastilles, Aromatic Fumigating			
Raspberry Vinegar ... gall.	10	6	
Nelson's Gelatine, Opaque and Trans.			Nelson's
,, 2 oz., ¼ lb. and ½ lb. packets			Prices.

Fig. 1.   George Meggeson's price list containing morphia lozenges alongside blackcurrant jam and barley sugar.

caries, grocers and general dealers all sent in their orders. The carriers' carts would bring out fifty-six-pound lots of raw opium or gallons of laudanum for delivery; or opium arrived regularly by parcel post. Opiates were freely available to all who could buy.

The opium preparations on sale and stocked by chemists' shops were numerous. There were opium pills (or soap and opium, and lead and opium pills), opiate lozenges, compound powder of opium, opiate confection, opiate plaster, opium enema, opium liniment, vinegar of opium and wine of opium. There was the famous tincture of opium (opium dissolved in alcohol), known as laudanum, which had widespread popular sale, and the camphorated tincture, or paregoric. The dried capsules of the poppy were used, as were poppy fomentation, syrup of white poppies and extract of poppy. There were nationally famous and long-established preparations like Dover's Powder, that mixture of ipecacuanha and powdered opium originally prescribed for gout by Dr Thomas Dover, the medical man and student of Thomas Sydenham, turned privateer (and discoverer, in 1708, of Alexander Selkirk, the model for Robinson Crusoe).[8] An expanding variety of commercial preparations began to come on the market at mid-century. They were typified by the chlorodynes – Collis Browne's, Towle's and Freeman's. The children's opiates like Godfrey's Cordial and Dalby's Carminative were long-established. They were everywhere to be bought. There were local preparations, too, like Kendal Black Drop, popularly supposed to be four times the strength of laudanum – and well known outside its own locality because Coleridge used it. Poppy-head tea in the Fens, 'sleepy beer' in the Crickhowell area, Nepenthe, Owbridge's Lung Tonic, Battley's sedative solution – popular remedies, patent medicines and the opium preparations of the textbooks were all available.

Laudanum and the other preparations were to be found not just in high-street pharmacies but on show in back-street shops crowded with food, clothing, materials and other drugs. The profession of pharmacist barely existed before the 1840s and those who sold drugs were a motley group, with all varieties of qualifications from customary usage, or apprenticeship, through to examination. Some idea of those who might call themselves druggists is given in a letter from Edward Foster, a chemist in Preston and secretary of the United Society of Chemists and Druggists, a semiprofessional body agitating for reform of the open sale of drugs. He told George Grey, Home Secretary, in 1865, that those selling drugs in Preston included a basket maker, shoe maker, smallware dealer, factory operative, tailor, rubbing stone maker and baker, and a rent collector, who, as he pointedly noted, was 'connected with a burying club'.[9]

Not all drug sellers were of this type. There were, for instance, those pharmacists who had taken the, as yet, voluntary examinations set by the Pharmaceutical Society. There were also apothecaries under the jurisdiction of the Society of Apothecaries, which although it had theoretically extended its authority throughout the country by the 1815 Apothecaries Act, exerted only lax inspection even in its traditional metropolitan area of control. And there were those who had learnt the trade through apprenticeship. These various groups appear sometimes to have surrounded the sale of opium with certain precautions even prior to 1868. Some, for instance, sold laudanum in a special poison bottle, or inquired for what purpose the purchaser wanted it. Others refused to serve persons u   to them with drugs, or limited the purchaser to a certain amount. A friend of Professor Alfred Taylor of Guy's Hospital had been refused a drachm of laudanum for toothache in this way by a City chemist.[10]

In the small corner shops, it was usually different. There, 'They put down their penny and get opium. Many of the people engaged in selling drugs and chemicals would sell opium with complete freedom, and their number was estimated in the 1850s to be between 16,000 and 26,000, although even this number probably did not include small 'general' stores dealing in all manner of goods as well as opiates. 'You have a great medley of and variety of classes, some who will not sell at all, others who will sell under caution, and others who will sell anything on application.' Many of the small shops were kept by people little removed in status from the population of the surrounding area they served. In factory areas, the wives of factory workers often kept a small shop to supplement the family income.[11] Such shops were plentiful; the vendors were often ill-educated. The prescription book of a Scarborough business (Figure 2), compiled just after the 1868 Act, details not only 'red oils for cattle' and methods of dressing rabbit skins, but an infants' preparation remedy and one for 'coff drops', based on 'Loddanum, parreygorick' and other drugs.[12] These small

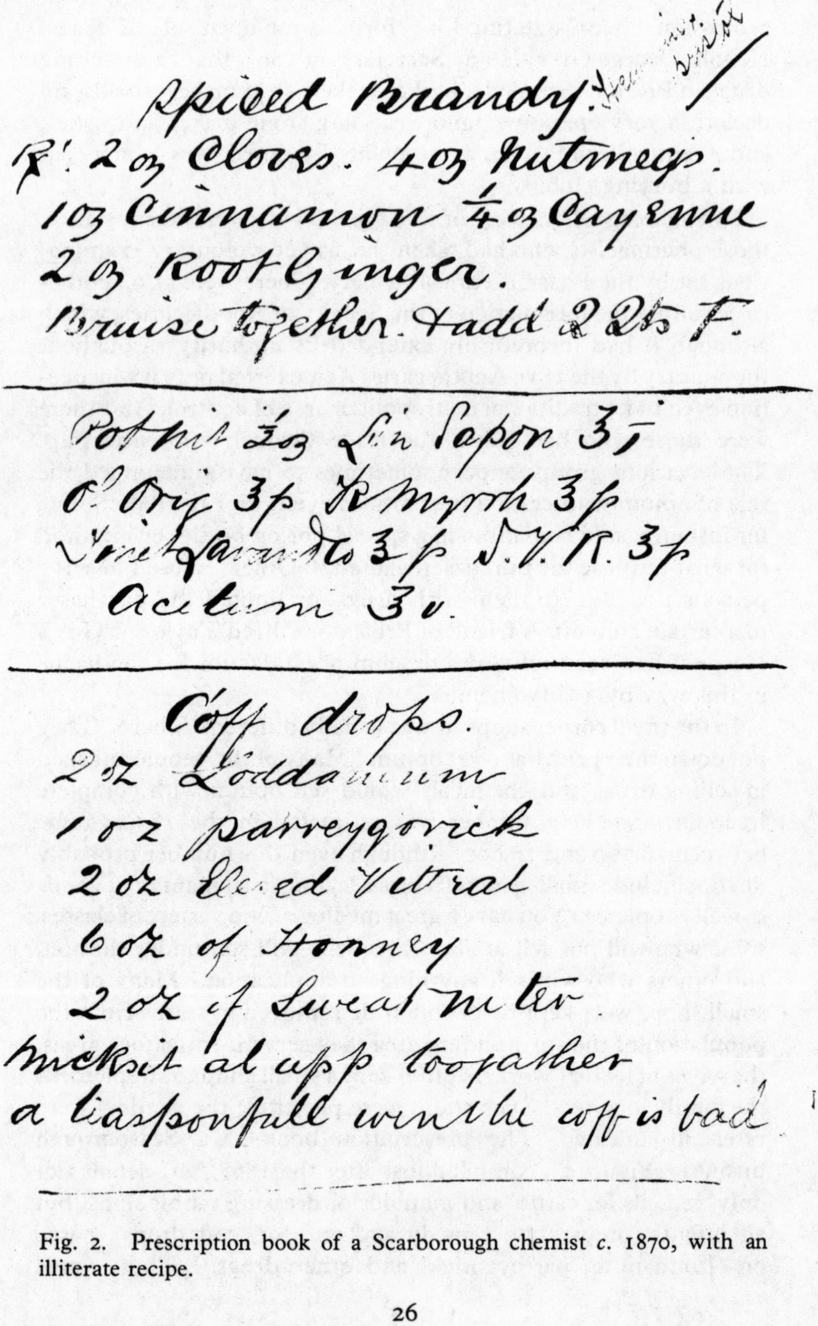

Spiced Brandy.

℞. 2 oz Cloves. 4 oz Nutmegs.
1 oz Cinnamon ¼ oz Cayenne
2 oz Root Ginger.
Bruise together. & add 2 Qts F.

Pot nit ½ oz Lin Sapon 3ᵢ
O. Orig 3p ℞ Myrrh 3p
Vinet far onto 3p S.V.R. 3p
Acetum 3v.

Coff drops.

2 oz Loddanum
1 oz parreygorick
2 oz Eliced Vitral
6 oz of Honney
2 oz of Sweat niter
mick it al upp toogather
a teaspoonfull wen the coff is bad

Fig. 2. Prescription book of a Scarborough chemist *c.* 1870, with an illiterate recipe.

businesses were everywhere to be seen, an everyday part of both urban and rural life. In a back street in Chorlton in 1849 surrounded by mills, there was a 'shop in the "general line", in the window of which, amongst eggs, candles, sugar, bread, soap, butter, starch, herrings, and cheese, I observed a placard marked "Children's Draughts, a penny each"'.[13]

It is easy enough to point to the mistakes and tragedies which undoubtedly occurred as a result of the system. The public health campaign of mid-century made great play of the sometimes horrifying carelessness of open sale. Professor Taylor himself had nearly lost a friend through the ignorance of a village shopkeeper near Windsor, who had sent an ounce of laudanum instead of the syrup of rhubarb ordered. There was indeed no guarantee that the shopkeeper would have any knowledge of poisons at all, even though some obviously learnt by experience. In 1858, when Mr Story took over a shop at Guisborough, with its existing stock of groceries, draperies and drugs, 'he was not thoroughly acquainted with' the latter commodities 'and objected to take the whole of them, but the person leaving pressed him to do so'. When, in April, Fanny Wilkinson, a servant at Guisborough, sent for powdered rhubarb, that Mr Story confused the jar marked 'Pulv. opii Turc. Opt' with Turkish rhubarb was hardly surprising. Fanny Wilkinson died after taking a teaspoonful of powdered opium; Mr Story had to stand trial for manslaughter.[14] Many such small shopkeepers, the 'chemists and grocers' who were still usually to be found in any city or town, picked up their dispensing knowledge where they could. It was for them that books like William Bateman's *Magnacopia* (1839) were produced. Its opium-based recipes for astringent balls, gout remedies and corn plasters mingled with others for ink, cleaning grates and making preserves. It was intended as a 'chemico-pharmaceutical library of useful and profitable information for the practitioner, chemist and druggist, surgeon-dentist etc.'.[15]

Even the small shops held a varied stock of opiates, or concocted their own preparations based on opium.[16] Vendors sometimes had their own speciality, particularly in the 'Children's Draught' line. Local varieties of 'quietness' for soothing small babies were quite commonly to be found. The raw drug was often prepared for sale in the shop. It was purchased in square one-pound blocks which always came wrapped in red paper, labelled 'opium (Turc)'.

An ex-apprentice remembered that 'we ... peeled off the skin, softened it by pounding with a little honey in a mortar and then making quarter ounce, or half ounce and one ounce "loaves", wrapping them in Rouse's red waxed paper'. Opium was put on sale in one-drachm or two-drachm packets. The 'gum' was dug from the cake of opium with a palette knife, weighed, rolled in French chalk and wrapped in greaseproof paper. In the better druggists an apprentice was often put in charge of weighing out the penny and two-penny portions of opium sold over the counter. These shops would also make up their own laudanum and other preparations. In the hands of an inexperienced druggist, this could be a source of error. Cutting opium fresh from a damp lump which should have been left until dry, together with careless weighing, could result in a preparation stronger than intended.[17]

Nor were such shops the only places where opiates could be obtained. Street markets had their opium preparations. According to Samuel Flood, a surgeon in Leeds in the 1840s, Saturday night purchases of pills and drops were a regular custom as much as the buying of meat and vegetables – 'in the public market place ... are to be seen ... one stall for vegetables, another for meat, and a third for *pills*! ...'[18] London costermongers were still selling the preparations in the 1900s, even if the paregoric they sold no longer contained opium. Opium was to be found on sale in pubs, too. Medical herbalists were common, and untrained midwives in working-class areas often had their own recipes as well. It was quite usual for an untrained doctor to act as medical adviser to the families in his area, prescribing mixtures containing laudanum for conditions such as diarrhoea and dysentery.

What needs greater emphasis than the mistakes which emerged as evidence in the public health campaign is the complete normality of open sales of opium to both seller and purchaser. An area of opiate use existed where doctors were never consulted and which, except at times of particular anxiety, was largely unremarked. Working people rarely encountered a trained doctor on any regular basis. A visit to a hospital out-patient department, a dispensary order or a subscription to a provident dispensary was, for most, the limit of professional medical care. Mostly such care was self-administered, and many of the preparations used were opium-based. The 'official' medical uses of opium were paralleled by a quite distinct popular culture of opiate use. The 'medical'

use of opium was, by the end of the century, almost the only legitimate one. But earlier in the century popular use was as extensive,
if not more so. Many subsequent medical developments were
adaptations of, or prefigured by, established trends in self-medication; popular and medical forms of knowledge mingled. It is with
this popular culture of opium use, the sale and use of opium among
working-class consumers of the drug, that the rest of this chapter
will deal.

The opium preparations sold in chemists and back-street shops
were only commercial developments of practices common before
industrialization. Poppy-head tea had long been a well-known
rural remedy, for soothing fractious babies and for adults, too. Its
use continued in the nineteenth century. Bob Loveday, Hardy's
character in *The Trumpet-Major*, fell into a stupor through using
poppy heads in the time-honoured way. '... I picked some of the
poppy-heads in the border, which I once heard was a good thing
for sending folks to sleep when they are in pain...'[19] Poppy heads
made into fomentations (often with camomile flowers) were still
in regular use at the end of the century.

For over-the-counter sales, however, laudanum was universally
recognized to be most popular for poor customers, although
powdered opium was used, in making suppositories, for example,
and in certain areas taking raw opium, rolled into pill-like masses,
appears to have been quite common. Everyone had laudanum at
home. Twenty or twenty-five drops could be had for a penny. Laudanum was also sometimes sold at threepence an ounce. The
extent of such sales was barely realized in mid-Victorian England.
Professor Taylor told the Select Committee on the Sale of Poisons
in 1857 that 'in many large manufacturing towns ... labouring
men come to the extent of two hundred or three hundred a day
for opium'.[20] Some idea of the extent of demand became clear
when Edward Hodgson, a pharmacist in Stockton-on-Tees, noted
details of the number of customers he served with opiates over
a summer month in 1857. Two hundred and ninety-two customers
had bought opium from him over the month. As Hodgson was
one of the six qualified chemists in the area, this presupposes that
at least sixty people were buying opiates each day from this type
of source alone, in a town with a population of twelve or thirteen
thousand.[21]

The sale which went on in general dealers made the evidence

of accredited pharmacists bound to be an underestimate. The day-book of William Armitage, a 'chemist and grocer' in Thorne, a village near Doncaster, gives some indication of the way in which sales were undramatically made. Between June and December 1850, he made twenty-nine over-the-counter sales of opiates, not including the opium-based doctors' prescriptions he dispensed in the same period. Thorne, where Armitage had his business, was hardly representative of the extent of urban purchasing. Yet the pennyworths of laudanum he sold, the two-pennyworth of pare-goric to Mrs Coulam on 6 October, the mixed order of laudanum, acid drops and turpentine noted on 10 July, the fivepence left owing for opium by Stephen Webster, all give some flavour of the acceptability of opium as an everyday purchase.[22]

The corner shop, and not the doctor's surgery, was the centre of popular opium use. The balance of the drug seller/purchaser relationship often inclined to the latter. Customers often dictated the type of remedy they wanted. Families had their own private recipes which the shopkeeper or chemist would make up. It was laudanum and ipecacuanha for coughs in one Hoxton family, lau-danum and chloroform (known as 'Gasman's mixture' from the person who had first suggested it) in another area. Twopenceworth of antimony wine with twopenceworth of laudanum for whooping cough was a remedy passed on in a Woolwich family.[23] Sometimes the vendor interposed some degree of expertise in this process. One in Manchester recalled in 1849 that such 'home-made' opium recipes often contained dangerous quantities of laudanum. He tried to convince the possessors of the remedies of the danger in-volved, and was sometimes allowed to change the proportions. There is little doubt that such remedies derived from the poppy recipes of pre-industrial living (many had been handed down in the same family for generations). The conditions of urban society brought the vendor of the drug into the situation when families could no longer produce their own remedies.

Opium was sometimes sold ready packaged in pill boxes, but the liquid preparations were measured into any container the cus-tomer provided. Shopkeepers kept their laudanum in large con-tainers. It was measured into 'bottles of all kinds ... dirty and clean'. This was in fact a strong argument against having a special type of poison bottle – 'They would take it ... to have some syrup of poppies, or any little innocent thing put in; it would be bought with the word "poison" upon it, and taken home, and it would become a very common bottle. . . .' This practice meant too that the final strength of a preparation could sometimes be rather different from its original recipe. A half-emptied bottle of cordial would be bought, so that more laudanum could be put into it. Few opium preparations, patent medicines apart (Godfrey's Cordial had its own distinctive steeple-shaped bottles), were pre-packaged, the 'jug and bottle' method of sale was almost universal.[24]

Going to the grocer's for opium was often a child's errand. In a large family, a harassed mother would send the eldest child, often kept at home to nurse younger brothers and sisters, out shopping. With such a system, there was often an instinctive bond between vendor and purchaser. The small corner shops, even the pharmacist's and druggist's businesses in areas where most sales were in pennyworths, did not see themselves as a group separate from their customers. There was a relationship of mutual dependence, which often resulted in a barrier of evasiveness presented to an outsider. Several told the *Morning Chronicle* reporter investigating Manchester conditions in 1849 that they knew nothing of the drug, while 'several of them had their windows covered with announcements of different forms of the medicine which they were cool enough to declare they did not deal in'. Many accepted that some, at least, of their customers would be dependent on opium. If a large quantity was asked for, it was the custom to ask if the purchaser was in the habit of taking the drug and was accustomed to it.

Working people were relying upon opiates purchased in this way to deal with a whole range of minor complaints. They were a remedy for the 'fatigue and depression' unavoidable in working-class life at the time. They acted as a cure-all for complaints, some trivial, some serious, for which other attention was not available. Medical herbalists and botanists, untrained midwives and self-trained doctors were used by the poor. For the most part, ailments were dealt with on the basis of community knowledge; and there was often positive opposition to the encroachment of trained doctors. It was in this situation where opium came into its own. It was, for instance, widely used for sleeplessness.[25] Many working-class consumers appear to have followed this advice. An inquest at Jarrow in 1891 revealed that the deceased had been

31

accustomed to take laudanum for sleeplessness. The inquest on Amos Withers of Hull in 1881 noted that for four years he had been in the habit of taking 1/12 drachm of opium to alleviate pains in the head and stomach and to help him sleep.[26] A pharmacist remembered that, as late as the 1900s, '. . . we sold laudanum, and before we closed on Saturday nights we had a few old ladies wrapped in shawls, bringing their old bottles for 3 d and 4 d of "lodlum" which helped them with their coughs and sleeping'.[27]

Middle-aged prostitutes, according to a factory area druggist, took it when they felt low or to relieve pains in their limbs. There was a large sale of gout and rheumatic pills each containing a grain of opium, colchicum extract and liquorice powder. These were an indication of the drug's popularity in the treatment of rheumatism. It was also a great standby for coughs and colds.[28] Families could follow the advice given in domestic medical texts. Many chemists had their own opiate cough recipes. An octogenarian chemist remembered in the 1950s how 'customers often asked for four-pennyworth each of oil of aniseed, oil of peppermint, laudanum and paregoric to be mixed with sugar syrup for a cough mixture'. The numbers of opiate-based cough remedies, 'chest tonics' and rheumatic and diarrhoea pills in chemists' recipe books give an indication of the range of popular usage.[29]

It was always in the treatment of minor ailments, whose symptoms might or might not mask more serious complaints, that opiates were most useful. Dr Rayner at Stockport prescribed opiates in the form of eye drops as well as for sleep. The *Doctor*, a medical magazine offering advice to non-professionals, told one correspondent, 'A.Z.', to bathe a sore eye three or four times daily with a warm decoction of poppy heads. Elizabeth Adams, who died of an overdose of laudanum in Sussex in the summer of 1838, had taken it to cure toothache 'unintentionally in too large quantity'.[30]

Medical reliance on the drug to combat cholera or dysentery was paralleled by its popular currency as a remedy for diarrhoea. It was as popular for earache as for toothache – 'mix equal parts of purified ox-gall and liquid laudanum together, and let fall into drops every night into the affected ears'. For stomach cramp, 'flatulencies, or wind', headaches, and nervous diseases in general, it was at least a palliative. In medical practice it was recommended for the treatment of insanity. There was advice in domestic texts for its use in hysteria. 'Women's ailments' and the menopause were popularly treated with opium, just as the drug was used in professional medicine to subdue such symptoms.

External use of the drug was common in popular usage. Buchan's *Domestic Medicine*, which ran into numerous editions in the first half of the century, recommended an anodyne plaster containing powdered opium and camphor for use in acute pains, especially of a nervous kind, and clysters or suppositories containing opium. A 'liniment for the piles' was based on two ounces of emollient ointment and half an ounce of laudanum, mixed well together with the yolk of an egg. Buchan recommended anodyne balsam to be used in violent strains and rheumatic complaints. It should be rubbed 'with a warm hand' on the affected part, or a linen rag moistened with the mixture and applied.[31] For ulcers, bruises, sprains and chilblains (one text recommended a poultice of bread and poppy liquor renewed every six hours) it was in regular use. These were the type of small 'non-medical' ailments occurring in every home where opium came into its own.

The uses of opium in self-medication paralleled and prefigured those of professional medical practice. Self-medication with opium, if anything, encompassed more than the professional spectrum of use. A particular example was the connection of opium use with drinking. Certainly the conjunction of opium and alcohol in popular usage was more extensive than its orthodox use. Opium was generally accepted as a medical remedy for the treatment of delirium tremens. But it was popularly used to counteract the effect of too much drink. In many industrial working-class areas, children's cordials containing opium were on sale in the pubs. The *Morning Chronicle* reporter found this to be the case in Ashton, and probably, he thought, in Manchester as well. It was customary to sell laudanum there also. In Liverpool in the 1850s much was sold by publicans during the cholera season, and in the fruit season in the summer, 'It is the custom for the publicans to keep a supply of laudanum to add to the brandy....' The criminal usage of the drug which such proximity could lead to was recognized.[32]

This appears to have been a widespread popular means of controlling and counteracting excessive drinking. The number of cases where overdoses of opium were accidentally taken in these circumstances is some indication of this. A Manchester blacksmith took six drachms of laudanum while drunk; a Liverpool widow of 'intemperate habits' was 'accustomed to take a few drops of laudanum after indulging in drink'.[33] These were only exceptional instances – in that they took too much and so their cases received publicity – of what seems to have been a common enough practice. Medical men were known to use this type of remedy on themselves after excessive drinking. How far such usage extended both above and within the working-class is impossible to estimate. This informal means of sobering up had its local variations – the adding of opiates directly to beer in the Fens, for instance. This practice was the origin of the 'stimulant' working-class use of opium which much concerned outside observers in the 1830s and 1840s and which is discussed in Chapter 9.

How much opium was in fact being consumed, not just among the working class, but indeed at all levels of society in a situation of open availability? This is difficult to assess, for the available data on mortality and consumption have severe drawbacks.[34] Many contemporary discussions used the statistics to support the argument that the use of opium was rising out of control. The belief in 'stimulant' opium use among the industrial working class (to be discussed in Chapter 9) owed much to the picture presented through the figures.[35] The detailed mortality data will be considered in Chapter 7 as part of the public health case. Certainly deaths from opium were high (140 died from narcotic poisoning in 1868), and the level of accidental overdosing was notable, even though deaths by other violent means - suffocation, drowning – were always far more numerous. But there is less evidence of a steep overall increase in either mortality or consumption in the first half of the century. The rate in 1840 of 5 per million population for narcotic poisoning deaths had risen to 6.1 per million in 1863, not a startling increase, since the early figure was most likely an underestimate. Absolute import figures, too, were increasing. But home consumption figures per thousand population show a less steep progression than a simple comparison of import totals. Table 2 (p. 274) shows that in the 1827–60 period home consumption varied between 1.3 and 3.6 lb. per thousand population. Figure 3 shows that in the same period the five-year average home consumption varied between 2 and 3.3 lb. per thousand population. Home consumption was rising, although not as swiftly or as astronomically as contemporaries believed.[36]

34

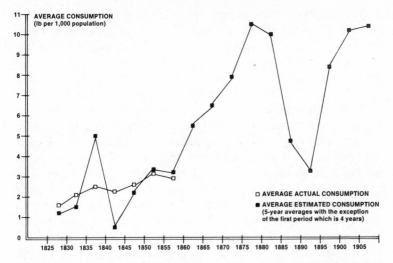

Fig. 3 Five-year averages of actual and estimated home consumption of opium per 1,000 population.

Certainly given the level of self-medication which prevailed, dependence or addiction among working people was likely to be common. No precise quantification can be given. A survey was conducted by Professor Robert Christison of Edinburgh and G. R. Mart, a Soho Square surgeon, in the early 1830s, but this was unique. The sample was small and unrepresentative, since only those whose dependence was obvious and well known were included. A total of twenty opium eaters were recorded. Of that number, seven of the thirteen females would be classified as working-class, two of the seven males.[37] Knowledge of the extent of dependence is otherwise piecemeal. It can be estimated through the mortality rate. But of course not all overdose cases would have been working-class consumers, nor would all have been dependent on the drug.[38]

Patterns of use necessarily emerge haphazardly. Martha Pierce of Hughenden, a sixty-year-old lace-maker, a widow with eight children, while in prison in 1854, told the chaplain that she had 'been used, for 4 years, last past, to take 5 pennyworth of laudanum per week. Can take 2 teaspoonfuls per day. States that great numbers of women in her neighbourhood, and some men, take large quantities.'[39] It was only in exceptional circumstances like this that dependence was ever revealed. An inquest on Ann Kirkbride, for instance, a child of twenty-two months, who died in Liverpool in 1854 'of the effects of taking opium', revealed that her mother 'had been accustomed to chew opium, which she had been in the habit of buying by pennyworths at a time'.[40]

Generally, dependence on opium went largely unrecognized, either by the consumers themselves or by those who sold opium to them. Doctors could be quite unaware of the drugs the patients they saw briefly were using in self-medication. The only occasion on which the situation was made clear to both user and the medical profession was when supplies were for some reason cut off. During the cotton famine in Lancashire in the 1860s, the purchase of even pennyworths of opium was difficult. Robert Harvey, later Inspector General of Civil Hospitals in Bengal, was at the time of the famine assistant to the house surgeon at Stockport Infirmary. 'Many applications were made at the infirmary for supplies of opium, the applicants being then too poor to buy it ... I was much struck,' he later recalled, 'by the fact that the use of the drug was much more common than I had any idea of, and that habitual consumers of ten and fifteen grains a day seemed none the worse for it; and would never have been suspected of using it.' In Salford, customers who regularly took a teaspoonful of laudanum would come and beg for a dose in bad times when they had no money.[41]

Doctors who worked closely with the poor elsewhere also had their eyes opened about the extent of use and dependence. Dr Anstie, editor of the *Practitioner*, commented on the prevalence of opium taking among the poor of London. He had had this point brought home to him. 'It has frequently happened to me to find out, from the chance of a patient being brought under my notice in the wards of a hospital that such patient was a regular consumer, perhaps, of a drachm of laudanum, from that to two or three drachms per diem, the same doses have been used for years without any variation.' His comments on the habit were a realistic appraisal of why there was a large sale of opium to the working class. The consumers were 'persons who would never think of narcotising themselves, anymore than they would be getting drunk; but who simply desire a relief from the pains of fatigue endured by an ill-fed, ill-housed body, and a harassed mind'.[42]

The official sources are, except in special instances like this, mostly silent on the question of popular opium use. It is easy enough, using the testimony of coroners' inquests, of accidental overdosing and casual 'non-professional' sales reported in the medical journals, to write of it solely in terms of dangers and problems. The particular bias of the sources to an extent determines the conclusion. Alternative information is barely available. Pharmacists' day-books and workhouse medical records can give some indication, but the records of small corner shops where most purchases went on have not survived, if they ever existed. Yet even from the official sources and the testimony of those who remember some part of the system emerges a picture where opiate use in the early decades of the century was quite normal, where it was not in general a 'problem'. There were reasons for concern, as later chapters will indicate. Opium did not arise as a problem simply from the minds and outlook of the medical profession. But the framework within which opium was subsequently placed should not serve to erase the positive role it played in working-class life at this period. Robert Gibson in Manchester, manufacturing vermin killer, medicated lozenges (including morphine) and 'wholesome sweetcakes'; opium lozenges given like sweets as a treat to a shopkeeper's child; a pub keeper sucking morphine lozenges for a sore throat – these are incidents which, slight in themselves, recall the time when opium was freely available and culturally sanctioned. Opium itself was the 'opiate of the people'. Lack of access to orthodox medical care, the as yet unconsolidated nature of the medical profession and, in some areas, a positive hostility to professional medical treatment ensured the position it held in the popular culture of the time.

4

Opium in the Fens

Despite the difficulties of reconstructing patterns of opium use, a detailed picture can be put together of what was happening at this time in one particular area. Opium consumption in the Fenland was arguably untypical in that it was high, and extensive enough to attract particular attention at the time. The spotlight thrown upon it by the mid-century public health inquiries, and its importance as evidence during the later anti-opium agitation, is invaluable. It is possible to reconstruct the incidence of popular opium use, however imperfectly, in a rural setting.

The low-lying marshy Fens covered parts of Lincolnshire, Cambridgeshire, Huntingdonshire and Norfolk. Remote and isolated by reason of their geography, there had been attempts to drain them and to improve the agricultural land on an individual basis since the sixteenth century. Work in northern Fenland had been carried out in the following century with the aid of Dutch engineers. Yet Arthur Young in his late-eighteenth-century *Annals of Agriculture* commented that much of the Fenland was still subject to frequent inundation. It was only at the turn of the century, with the drive to agricultural improvement and enclosure which paralleled industrial developments, that further drainage work was undertaken on a major scale. For much of the first half of the century, the Fens remained an unhealthy, marshy area, where medical assistance was limited, especially for the poor, and where large numbers of the working population of the countryside were prone to the ague, 'painful rheumatisms' and neuralgia.[1]

The fact that these conditions had led to a noticeably high consumption of opium was commented on at the time. 'There was not a labourer's house ... without its penny stick or pill of opium,

38

and not a child that did not have it in some form.' According to
an analysis made in 1862, more opium was sold in Cambridgeshire,
Lincolnshire and Manchester than in other parts of the country.[2]
As elsewhere, poppy-head tea had been used as a remedy long before other narcotics were commercially available. Charles Lucas,
a Fenland physician, recalled the widespread use of the remedy.
'A patch of white poppies was usually found in most of the Fen
gardens. Poppy-head tea was in frequent use, and was taken as
a remedy for ague. . . . To the children during the teething period
the poppy-head tea was often given.'[3] Poppies had been grown
in the area for the London drug market, where they were used to
produce syrup of white poppies; and there had even been attempts
made in Norfolk to produce opium on a commercial scale.

Although the use of opium, in one form or another, was certainly
not new in the Fenland area, in the nineteenth century commercial
opium and opium preparations were more widely used. Shifts in the
structure of agrarian society may also have made the use of opiates
more widespread (the practice of enclosure degraded the status
of the agricultural labourer). A greater awareness of, and concern
about, the practice grew up through the numerous social surveys
and statistical exercises which characterized these years. The impression is of a long-established habit suddenly brought to light
by growing interest in, and increased access to, the Fenland area.

The high general death rate in agricultural Lincolnshire – 22
per 1,000 living in Spalding in the 1840s, as high as industrial
areas like Huddersfield and Keighley – was enough to single it
out. It was notable too that the death rate from opium poisoning
(primarily based on laudanum deaths) was 17.2 per million living
average over the 1863–7 period in the Midlands area, which included Fenland Lincolnshire. This figure had risen to 23.8 per
million in 1868, the year when the restrictions of the Pharmacy
Act were introduced. This was far higher than the national opium
death rate, averaging 6 per million in the same five years.[4] It was
this type of evidence which stimulated investigations by Dr Henry
Julian Hunter in the 1860s. Reporting to Sir John Simon, as Medical Officer to the Privy Council, in 1863, on the excessive mortality
of infants in some rural districts, he wrote:

A man in South Linconshire complained that his wife had spent
a hundred pounds in opium since he married. A man may be

39

seen occasionally asleep in a field leaning on his hoe. He starts when approached, and works vigorously for a while. A man who is setting about a hard job takes his pill as a preliminary, and many never take their beer without dropping a piece of opium into it. To meet the popular taste, but to the extreme inconvenience of strangers, narcotic agents are put into the beer by the brewers or sellers.[5]

Others who had practical experience of the area told the same story. The basis of adult opiate use in the area appears to have been what a pharmacist who practised there in the early 1900s termed 'The three scourges of the Fens ... ague, poverty and rheumatism'.

The area where opium eating was common can be delineated fairly clearly. It appears to have stretched from Boston in the north (although there is some indication that there was a lesser incidence of the habit as far north as Louth), into the Isle of Ely, where it concentrated, and on round King's Lynn and towards Castle Acre in the east. St Ives and the Fenland area of Huntingdonshire was its south-west boundary; Burwell, Soham and Methwold on the south-east, the area round Whittlesey in the west. Opium was, of course, used well beyond these limits; but dependence on the drug was not so exceptional as in the Fens.

A pharmacist who arrived in Louth from Edinburgh to take up a new post in 1913 still remembers her feelings of surprise at the much greater quantities of opium sold there. Twenty years earlier, Dr Rayleigh Vicars had been equally perplexed by the unaccountable symptoms of a patient of his in Boston. One of her friends soon set him right. 'Lor', Sir, she has had a shillings worth of laudanum since yesterday morning.'[6] Holbeach, too, had an opium-eating reputation. 'It has always been understood that Holbeach is a great laudanum district, and, as might be expected, the drug is sold in immense quantities....' Dr Harper, working at the Holbeach Dispensary, was surprised at the longevity of the opium eaters who came. Fifteen who attended had an average age of seventy-six years, although all were taking over a quarter of an ounce of the drug each week. Even as late as 1909, a pharmacist apprenticed in the town remembers several addicts who were supplied, and the large quantities of opium sold.[7]

The habit centred on the Isle of Ely. Ely itself, 'the opium-

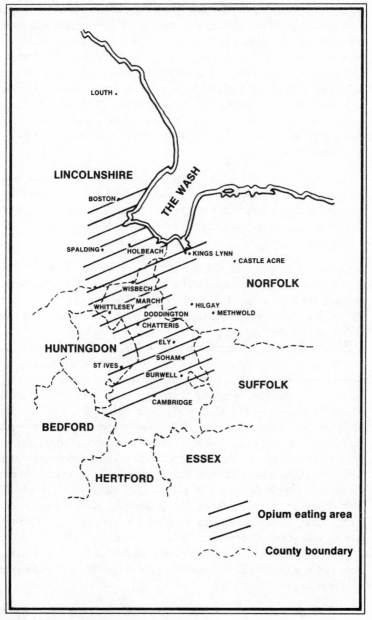

Opium eating in the Fens.

eating city of Ely', as a *Morning Chronicle* reporter called it, was a well-known centre of opium distribution.[8] The surrounding market towns and villages were also well known for their opium consumption. In March, Doddington, Chatteris and Whittlesey, opium taking was widespread. Wisbech, too, was said to be the town consuming the highest proportion of spirits in proportion to population and also the highest proportion of opium. A letter, in 1894, from Thomas Stiles, a ninety-six-year-old druggist, who had practised in the town from 1813, gave evidence of the quantities consumed:

> ... daily I supplied a vast number with either opium or laudanum... The amount of opium consumed in the commencement of the present century in this form was enormous, and it is surprising the quantity of laudanum which was taken with impunity, after being habituated to its use...[9]

A visitor to the town in August 1871 soon became aware of the complete freedom with which the drug was sold. The Saturday evening crowds in the chemists' shops 'come for opium ... they go in, lay down their money, and receive the opium pills in exchange without saying a word'.[10]

Croyland had its 'opium slaves', according to Mrs Burrows, who was brought up there in the 1850s. A shillingsworth made up twenty good-sized pills; these would be taken at one dose.[11] Burwell Fen had an opium-eating 'Fen tiger' as late as 1910, a local character known as old Daddy Badcock. Spalding, too, was an opium-eating town – Thomas Stiles had begun to practise there on his own account in 1826 and 'disposed of large quantities of opium and laudanum'. An apprentice there some ninety years later was still selling raw opium to elderly people 'to alleviate fever'. Dr John Whiting, physician to the West Norfolk and Lynn Hospital, stressed the prevalence of the habit in King's Lynn, too. In his view, drunkenness and debauchery were rife in the town, and so was the use of drugs, opium above all.

Opium was even to be bought in Cambridge itself on market day, as Charles Kingsley, himself a parson in the county, related in *Alton Locke*:

> 'Yow goo into druggist's shop o' market day, into Cambridge, and you'll see the little boxes, doozens and doozens,

a'ready on the counter; and never a ven-man's wife goo by, but what calls in for her pennord o' elevation to last her out the week. Oh! ho! ho! Well, it keeps women-folk quiet, it do; and it's mortal good agin ago pains.'

'But what is it?'

'Opium, bor' alive, opium!'[12]

As soon as the marshlands were left behind, the habit died away. The custom was established in these higher lands to only a 'limited extent' and evidence of its incidence in adjoining areas, as for instance in Leicestershire, is only fragmentary.

High opium consumption may have been to some extent characteristic of all agricultural populations in such low-lying, marshy areas. Historically there were other pockets of ague (a malarial disease) round the Thames Estuary and in Romney Marsh.[13] There was little evidence of exceptional opium taking in the former area; but the practice did occasionally emerge in the Kent marshlands. Dr Thomas Joyce of Rolvenden noted some strange developments there after the 1868 Pharmacy Act had restricted the sale of opium by unqualified vendors: 'In my own village and immediate neighbourhood this practice exists to a considerable extent, the opium being retailed by the grocer and other small shopkeepers. I am credibly informed about 3 oz a week are so distributed. Since January last, four cases of opium sickness and purging have come under my own immediate notice . . . and I have heard of others.'[14] It can reasonably be assumed that the Fens remained the opium-taking area *par excellence*; the practice in other marshlands was only a pale reflection.

The largest consumers were the country people, the labourers who came in from the outlying marshy fens into the towns to buy it on market day, 'not the villagers, or people of the little towns in which the shop was, but rather the inhabitants of small hamlets or isolated farms in the Fens'. In Wisbech it was the country people who came to do their marketing on a Saturday evening who crowded out the chemists' shops. It was the 'Fen tigers', the small dark people of the remoter districts, who were most noted for their opium consumption. In such isolated areas, laudanum was shared indiscriminately with the farm animals. Many buying the drug stated that they wanted it for their pigs, not for themselves – 'they fat better when they're kept from crying'. The use of opium in cattle medicines was not unique to the Fens, although its use was said to be on the increase in the 1850s. Six drachms of laudanum for a sheep and two or three ounces for a horse were not unusual. One child who died from opium poisoning in Cambridgeshire in 1838 had accidently drunk laudanum intended for a calf. Opiates were mostly used throughout East Anglia, and probably elsewhere as well, to dope vicious or unmanageable horses before they went for sale.[15]

It was the doping of young babies that had first attracted attention to the high consumption of opium in the Fens. The introduction of new methods of exploiting the land had resulted in particular in declining standards of child care. The drainage of areas under water and their cultivation led, in the nineteenth century, to the use of itinerant 'public gangs' composed of both women and children, and employed by a gang master. The under-populated nature of the drained areas meant that the gangs, supplying the lack of a settled labour force, ranged over wide areas. Although the public gangs were by no means the norm in the Fenland, it is true that, where they existed, women were away from home for long periods and the care of young babies suffered.[16]

The extremely high infant mortality rates in the Fenland towns, 206 per 1,000 living in Wisbech, higher than in Sheffield in the 1860s, were sufficient to indicate the special circumstances there. The old custom of dosing children with poppy-head tea was to some extent replaced by the sale of the commercially produced opiate, or at least 'Godfrey's' which the chemist made himself. But the dosing of babies was not overly peculiar to the Fens (child dosing with opium is discussed in Chapter 9). It went on in areas far beyond the marshlands – in Yarmouth, Walsingham, Downham, Goole. It is possible, too, that opiates were used, inadvertently or not, to dispose of unwanted children – 'Twins and illegitimate children almost always die.' This may have been the case outside the Fens as well.

The habit was also noticeable among working-class women, their use of the drug perhaps originating from 'tasting' the opiates which they gave their children, as well as from the tradition of self-medication, 'the wretchedness of their homes', and the demands on some women of the gang system. A woman came into a druggist's shop in Ely while the *Morning Chronicle* reporter was there, asked for a pennyworth of laudanum and drank it off with the 'utmost unconcern' before his startled eyes.[17] Other elderly females took up to thirty grains a day and an old woman at Wisbech was accustomed to a daily dose of ninety-six grains.[18]

The origins of such a situation lay not in unwise medical prescription, since few of the most obvious consumers would have seen a doctor at all regularly – Dr Harper's surprise at the opium eaters who came to the Holbeach Dispensary is proof of that. The druggist's shop, not the doctor's surgery, was at its centre. It symbolized the dominance of the consumer of the drug, not its prescriber, as already noted in Chapter 3. It had its basis in the peculiar circumstances of the area, but also in the tradition of popular self-medication. Use for simple euphoric effect was a possibility in the Fens. The writer Thomas Hood, on a visit to Norfolk, 'was much surprised to find that opium or opic, as it was vulgarly called, was in quite common use in the form of pills among the lower class, in the vicinity of the Fens ... the Fen people in the dreary, foggy, cloggy, boggy wastes of Cambridge and Lincolnshire had flown to the drug for the sake of the magnificent *scenery*...'[19] Dr Rayleigh Vicars also recognized this as the case. He found a patient 'apparently unconscious of everything excepting the strange visions floating through the sensorian and giving rise to the erratic movements and gestures'. He commented, after this abrupt introduction to the popularity of opium among his patients, that '... their colourless lives are temporarily brightened by the passing dreamland vision afforded them by the baneful poppy'.[20]

It is possible to make some estimate of the amount of opium sold and taken individually in the Fens. It came into the area on farmers' carts and was sold, as elsewhere in the country prior to 1868, through a multiplicity of outlets, of which chemists' shops were only the most obvious. Opium was sold 'by almost every little country shopkeeper and general dealer', on market stalls, and hawked from village to village by itinerant vendors. The British Medical Association estimated in 1867 that Norfolk and Lincolnshire consumed half the opium imported into the country.[21] This, estimated on the basis of 1859, the last year for which home consumption figures are available, would be at least 30,000 lb. and possibly more. Shop counters in the Fenland towns were loaded every Saturday night with three or four thousand laudanum vials. One firm sold two hundred pounds of opium a year in the March/Wisbech area. In Spalding, the druggists' sales in the 1860s averaged approximately 127 grains per head of the local population there. A druggist in Ely sold three hundredweight a year, and two others eighty or ninety pounds each.[22]

This was only the relatively 'respectable' and obvious tip of opium sales. The turnover in grocers' and general shops went unrecorded. Poppy-head tea was brewed at home. The main opiates sold commercially were, as elsewhere, laudanum and crude opium itself. The latter, sold either in pill form, or carved in square lumps about an inch in length, seems to have been most popular, although laudanum was said to be favoured by women consumers. 'Pills or penny sticks' were what Dr Hunter saw on sale, and others describe farmers' wives and labourers buying their penny packets of opium. Actual consumption and expenditure are difficult to estimate. Thirty grains was a pennyworth, the average daily dose of those who had taken the drug over a long period. Dr Elliott found that an average dose was half an ounce a week of solid opium or four ounces to half a pint of laudanum in the morning and the same in the evening. Many took more. A St Ives druggist remarked that people had come into his shop and drunk off two scruples of opium.

> I have been really frightened to see them take it in such quantities, I thought it would have killed them. When they came into the shop I have seen them look very bad, and have asked them if they were used to taking it in such large doses, and they have said 'Oh yes!' But I certainly thought by the ravenous way in which they took it out of the box, that they wanted to poison themselves.'[23]

Actual expenditure is even more difficult to estimate. It was said later on, in the 1870s, that families were spending eight-pence to one shilling a day on it. A Croyland addict, buying enough to make forty pills, was spending two shillings a day, a very sizable proportion of an agricultural labourer's wage. In Holbeach, laudanum was fourpence an ounce; so weekly consumption of eight ounces was less expensive. Laudanum had been sixpence an ounce early in the nineteenth century; by mid century it was threepence in Ely and fourpence in St Ives.

Opiate use in the Fens was culturally accepted and sanctioned in a way which might not seem strange in South-East Asia, but which is striking in such an English setting. The majority of the

labouring part of the Fenland population and those shopkeepers
selling opium clearly accepted its use on a regular basis as something quite normal, not only in the early decades of the century,
but, to a lesser extent, well into the 1870s and 1880s. The case
of the Fens emphasizes the general attitude of poor users to
the drug. There was a general absence of concern. In Boston, Dr
Rayleigh Vicars had to struggle against the community support
offered his opium-eating patient in order to impose a medical imprint on the situation. 'The neighbours,' he reported, '. . . indulge
in the same lethal habit, and encourage the fatal termination by
goodnaturedly lending their own private store of laudanum.' In
Croyland, as elsewhere, buying opium was an errand for a child
to go on, just like any other small purchase. One had the 'daily
duty . . . to go every morning for a shillings worth of opium, or,
as it was nicknamed, "stuff" . . .' The unconcern of Fenland society
is perhaps best demonstrated by the encounter in the Wisbech
chemist's shop in 1871. The writer:

> Went into a chemist's shop, laid a penny on the counter. The
> chemist said – 'The best?' I nodded. He gave me a pill-box
> and took up the penny, and so the purchase was completed
> without my having uttered a syllable. You offer money, and get
> opium as a matter of course. This may show how familiar the
> custom is.[24]

The existence of a domestic population which could apparently
control and moderate its consumption became a matter of interest
later in the nineteenth century. The public health concern of mid-
century abated; but the case of the Fens continued to be important
to those involved in the debate on the Indo-Chinese opium trade
and the allied issue of the effects of regular opium use. The interpretation of opium eating in the Fens at mid-century was marked
by a relative absence of the sort of concern which was evoked by
opium use in an industrial setting. The possibility of the 'stimulant' use of opium by the industrial working class was one of the
reasons behind the drive to control sales of opium at mid century.
Lower-class use in urban areas was important as an argument in
seeking greater professional control over the sale of drugs. This
is dealt with in Chapter 9. Yet opiate eating in the Fens was used
by professional interests in exactly the opposite way. For opium
was removed from the more restrictive Part One of the poisons

schedule of the 1868 Pharmacy Act (the controlling legislation) precisely because of protests from Fenland pharmacists, who feared their trade would be affected by too much control.[25] This was indicative of the way in which views of opiate use were coloured by social and class setting. 'Stimulant' opium use in the cities was part of the threat posed by the industrial working class. The opium-eating labourer in the Fens was a different matter, even if, as Hood surmised, he had taken the drug in part for its stimulant effect. Middle-class and 'respectable' opium use was of course rarely a matter of concern, even in the case of stimulant use by the Romantic writers.

Regular and widespread opium use was clearly in decline by the last quarter of the century, although consumption in the Fenland area remained notably higher (in particular in the eyes of pharmacists who practised there) as late as the 1900s.[26] It had been, in its time, a notable example of the operation of a system of open availability of opium. It had demonstrated how a population could succeed in controlling by informal social mechanisms its consumption of the drug, with only minimal medical and legislative intervention. The reminiscences and accounts of the practice given by doctors have the air of being given by outsiders standing on the periphery of a quite different cultural tradition of drug use. The Fens were a specific instance of the popular culture of opiate use in the first half of the century – opium used in a rural setting in a manner which varied only in degree from the pattern of consumption in the rest of society.

5

Opiate Use in Literary
and Middle-Class Society

Popular use always attracted most attention. But at all levels of society, opium and laudanum were commonly and unselfconsciously bought and used. Few who took the drug regularly would have bothered to analyse the reasons behind their consumption. As the discussion of popular self-medication has shown, the drug could originally have been taken for what can be called a 'medical' need – sleeplessness, headache, depression – but as it was often and quite normally self-prescribed, the use continued perhaps after the strict 'medical' condition had gone. In reality the medical uses of opium shaded imperceptibly into 'non-medical' or what can be termed 'social' ones. The type of terminology now taken for granted in discussing opiate use and abuse was not at all applicable to the situation when opium was openly available.

What would now be called 'recreational' use of opium (and what in the nineteenth century was termed the 'luxurious' or 'stimulant' use of the drug) was, however, rarely spoken of. Although, as reminiscences of the Fens indicate, even working-class use could have its 'stimulant' and recreational effects, at first opium was not usually taken with such effects in mind, even if it did in practice produce them. Self-medication was the most common reason for opiate use. It is therefore surprising that historically the most attention has always concentrated on examples of recreational use. The use of opium in the early part of the nineteenth century by the circle of Romantic writers and poets, and by their friends and associates, has attracted the bulk of interest, even though, as Chapters 3 and 4 have shown, popular usage was far more extensive at that time. In the Romantic circle, the opium addiction of Thomas De Quincey and Samuel Taylor Coleridge has been particularly emphasized. Some discussions have drawn very direct and unsubtle parallels between the life of these opium eaters in nineteenth-century England and the current drug 'scene'. De Quincey has been equated with a 'high-school drop-out', and his pattern of opiate use has even been related to the current American programme of methadone maintenance.[1] A paraphrase of De Quincey's life was quite a regular component of medical journals at the height of the drug 'epidemic' of the 1960s. Calculation of his dosage of opium in current terms and analysis of his psychology, or of his experiences under the influence of opium, somehow did duty as historical input to the debate on drug use. Analysis of his untypical individual case was easier than an examination of the place of opium in nineteenth-century society as a whole.

Much more valuable work has been done from a literary point of view; and the Romantics' use of opium has been widely studied in so far as it contributed to their literary output. De Quincey and Coleridge have attracted most attention in this respect, too. Abrams, in a short study, *The Milk of Paradise* (1934), long ago stated the view that opium had affected patterns of imagery in the addicted writers, leading to 'abnormal light perception' and 'extraordinary mutations of space'. Elizabeth Schneider, however, in *Coleridge, Opium and Kubla Khan* (1953), discussed in some depth the poet's composition of the poem long considered the epitome of an opium reverie. Casting doubt on whether Coleridge really wrote the poem when he said he did, in the summer of 1797, she traced its origins from a 'complex literary tradition' involving pseudo-oriental writing, the Gothic fashion and even Milton. 'There is reason to believe,' she concluded, 'that its special character was not determined or materially influenced by opium.'[2] Alethea Hayter's recent work, however, allows opium a more active role in literary creation. Her view, and Schneider's, that the 'stimulant' effects of opium were new, and largely confined to the Romantic circle, is open to criticism. A study of opiate use in eighteenth-century society indicates that such effects were widely known, but unrevealed because of 'cultural prejudices' and literary convention. The Romantic recognition of the value of the imagination brought to the fore not new, but unspoken effects.[3] But her main assessment, that opium did indeed have an effect on literary creation, stands as the most acceptable current analysis. In her view the opium dreams of De Quincey, Crabbe or Wilkie

Collins 'crystallized the particles of past experience – sensory impressions, emotions, things read – into a symbolic pattern, an "involute", which became part of the life of the imagination and could be worked into literature'.[4] The difficulty, however, remains, in proving that it was indeed opium that aided the literary result. As De Quincey himself noted, 'If a man whose talk is of oxen should become an opium eater, the probability is that ... he will dream about oxen.'[5]

The poets' use of opium was also not without its wider social significance. The life histories of opium eaters like Coleridge and De Quincey are in no sense a substitute for an analysis of opium's place in nineteenth-century society; but they do indicate what were contemporary attitudes and practice. De Quincey's flight from school, his wanderings through Wales, his journey to London to raise money, his months of near starvation there in the winter of 1802–3 and his friendship with the fifteen-year-old prostitute, the famous 'Ann of Oxford Street', are well-known, and particular to his own experience. But the ease with which he could buy the drug and the self-medication thereby involved were typical of any opium user in the first half of the century. De Quincey's first purchase was in 1804, from a druggist near the Pantheon in Oxford Street: 'when I asked for the tincture of opium, he gave it to me as any other man might do; and furthermore, out of my shilling, returned to me what seemed to be a real copper halfpence ...'[6] De Quincey's dose may at times have been enormous – 320 grains a day in 1816, 480 grains in 1817–18 and in 1843. But the self-treatment of minor complaints involved in his story was entirely commonplace. De Quincey first took it, on the recommendation of an undergraduate friend, as a remedy for gastric pain and also to ward off the incipient tuberculosis to which he was thought to be succumbing. Indeed, at the height of the debate on Britain's involvement in the Indo-Chinese opium trade at the end of the century, Surgeon-Major Eatwell even made an analysis of De Quincey's medical history from which he concluded that he had been suffering from 'gastrodynia' and a chronic gastric ulcer – 'whatever might have been the degree of abuse of opium, this drug had in reality been the means of preserving and prolonging life'.[7]

The origin of each other's opium habit was always subject to intensive debate between De Quincey and Coleridge. Each was anxious to accuse the other of taking opium for the pleasurable sensations which resulted. After Coleridge's death in 1834, Gillman, in a life of the poet, published a letter in which De Quincey was said to have taken opium solely to obtain pleasurable effects. Coleridge, on the other hand, maintained that he himself had taken it only as an anodyne – 'nor had I at any time taken the flattering poison as a stimulus, or for any craving after pleasurable sensations. . .'.[8] De Quincey, who had become friendly with Coleridge while on a visit to Somerset in 1807, was deeply wounded. In response, his *Reminiscences of the Lake Poets* were not charitable in their treatment of Coleridge. In *Coleridge and Opium Eating*, De Quincey reiterated his view that Coleridge had begun opiate use solely as a source of luxurious sensations. 'He speaks of opium excess ... the excess of twenty-five years – as a thing to be laid aside easily and for ever within seven days; and yet, on the other hand, he describes it pathetically, sometimes with a frantic pathos, as the scourge, the curse, the one almighty blight which has desolated his life.'[9]

In reality, the origin of both writers' opium habits was a particular illustration of the intertwining of 'social' and 'medical' usage so much a feature of opiate use at the time. De Quincey may have begun taking the drug in self-medication – but he also took it for pleasurable sensations and as a relief from anxiety. At times of particular stress – for instance after the death of little Kate Wordsworth in 1812, of whom he was particularly fond – his opium consumption was enormous. Coleridge, too, was less than honest about his habit. His contention that he was 'seduced' into the use of narcotics during a period of painful illness at Keswick in 1801 has been widely accepted. In a letter to Poole in May of that year, he described 'the disgust, the loathing, that followed these fits, and no doubt in part, too, the use of the brandy and laudanum which they rendered necessary'.[10] But Coleridge had been known to take laudanum before this date. It had been given to him in Christ's Hospital sick ward; and in 1796 he had taken large quantities of laudanum for toothache while at the cottage near Stowey. *Kubla Khan* was written in the following year while Coleridge was taking opium ostensibly for dysentery, but possibly, too, to combat the anxiety caused by financial problems.[11]

Such controversies are clearly important in any evaluation of the poets' lives and writings. But they ignore the point that self-medication could easily shade into recreational use. Similarly, Coleridge's accusation, made in 1830 and repeated by Gillman, that De Quincey's *Confessions* had 'seduced' others into 'this withering vice through wantonness' ignored the established place of the drug in society.[12] The accusation that more of the pleasures than the pains of opium eating appeared in the *Confessions* was to some extent remedied by De Quincey himself in his 1856 revised version. Examples of opium eaters who attributed their experimentation to reading the book are undoubtedly to be found. The writer James Thomson and the poet Francis Thompson both acknowledged such a debt. Certainly the author of the anonymous book *Advice to Opium Eaters* (1823) maintained that it had been hastily brought out to warn others from copying De Quincey.[13] De Quincey's own defence against this charge stressed the links between 'stimulant' and 'narcotic' use, medical and non-medical. 'A man has read a description of the powers lodged in opium,' he wrote in 1845, 'or ... he has found those powers heraldically emblazoned in some magnificent dream due to that agency ... but if he never *had* seen the gorgeous description of the gorgeous dress, he would (fifty to one) have tried opium on the recommendation of a friend for toothache, which is as general as the air, or for earache, or (as Coleridge) for rheumatism. ...'[14] The 'medical' use of the drug could, he recognized, easily develop into something more, even without specific advocacy.

The acceptability of non-medical opiate use comes out most clearly in the public response at the time. When the *Confessions* were first published in the *London Magazine* in 1821 (and republished in book form in the following year), the literary reaction was one of excitement. The opium eating of the anonymous author and his stimulant use of the drug was a matter for moral condemnation from some quarters. But in general the reaction was interested and calm rather than hysterical. The *Confessions* were the first detailed description of English opium eating, although there were earlier, less widely circulated, medical analyses. The majority of descriptions available up to that time had presented the habit, along with opium smoking, as a peculiarly Eastern custom.[15] De Quincey's eulogy of the drug proved the reality could be different, and that English opium eating was possible. Reaction was indeed a 'mixture of intelligent appreciation and sanctimonious condemnation'.[16] The *Confessions* undoubtedly caused a furore, but the overriding impression is of calm interest even where the reaction was condemnatory. *John Bull* mounted a libellous attack on the author in 1824; Sir James Mackintosh praised the piece. The poet James Montgomery, writing in the *Sheffield Iris*, and the *North American Review* both cast doubt on its genuineness.[17]

Opium eating was a prime concern, but the literary value of the work and the identity of the anonymous author were as important. The *British Review* was not 'disposed to acquiesce in the justness of this panegyric on opium'.[18] The *Medical Intelligencer*, however, was full of admiration for the 'beautiful narrative' and concluded that opium itself should be more widely used.[19] The *Confessions* aroused interest, not fear or a desire for control. They even became a subject for humour. De Quincey appeared as the 'English opium eater' in his friend John Wilson's 'Noctes Ambrosianae', semi-humourous literary dialogues published in *Blackwood's Magazine*. General Hamley, a regular contributor to *Blackwood's*, wrote 'A recent confession of an opium eater', a humorous 'take-off' of De Quincey's work, when it was republished in a collected edition in 1856.[20] Opium eating as a subject for humour, however heavy-handed, indicated a relaxed reaction.

On the other hand, Coleridge's attempts to reduce or break off his habit also indicated increased medical intervention in the condition and the beginnings of changed reactions. Between 1808 and 1814 he consulted many physicians and tried to restrict his quantity without success. After a period under the care of Dr Brabant, he removed finally to Highgate in 1816 to be permanently under the medical supervision of Dr Gillman. Here too, however, he continued to obtain lesser amounts of opium secretly. Dunn, the Highgate chemist, supplied him with three quarters of a pint of laudanum at a time, enough for five days' supply.[21] Coleridge's habit was never as notorious as De Quincey's in his own life-time, and was not well-known even to his close friends. Campbell states that his indulgence in opium may have been suspected by the Wordsworths in 1802. But it was only on his return from his stay in Malta in 1806 that his friends were acquainted with the secret. Joseph Cottle, while on a visit to Coleridge in Bristol in 1813, noted the strangeness of his look. When both men called on Hannah More, Coleridge's hand shook so much that he spilled wine from the glass he was raising to his lips. Cottle was told by a friend that this 'arises from the immoderate quantity of opium he takes'.[22]

The social context of opiate use is thus implicit in the life-histories of the two men – the use of the drug in self-medication, its availability and the lack of concern evoked. But their own impact on the place of opium in society was also important. Their opium eating affected, as well as illustrated, the response to opium.

Cottle's own revelation of his friend's opium eating in his *Reminiscences of Samuel Taylor Coleridge and Robert Southey* was one indication of how later reactions to such usage were no longer as tolerant as they had once been. Cottle waited until after Coleridge's death before publishing. By the late 1830s there was more concern about the practice than there had been in the early 1820s. Taking as justification a letter of the poet's to Mr Wade in which he had expressly ordered that a 'full and unqualified narrative of my wretchedness' be given after his death, Cottle heightened, as well as expressed, the changed response. 'When it is considered also, how many men of high mental endowments have shrouded their lustre, by a passion for this stimulus, and thereby, prematurely, become fallen spirits,' he declaimed, 'would it not be a criminal concession to unauthorised feelings, to allow so impressive an exhibition of this subtle species of intemperance to escape from public notice? . . . In the exhibition here made, the inexperienced, in future, may learn a memorable lesson, and be taught to shrink from opium, as they would from a scorpion. . . .'[23]

The 'lesson' of opium eating came increasingly to be read into the experience of the two men. Indeed in some respects the social significance of Coleridge and De Quincey was in the last, rather than the first, decades of the century. Although the *Confessions* and evidence of Coleridge's opium use were never absent from discussions on opiate use in the first half of the century, it was during the period of anti-opium debate that their experiences were most directly related to changed reactions to opiate use. De Quincey and Coleridge were an established part of the domestic evidence with which the protagonists in the debate could buttress their arguments for and against the drug's consumption. Reissues of De Quincey abounded. There were at least thirteen editions and reissues of the *Confessions* between 1880 and 1910, more than in the first half of the century. The poets' consumption of opium, their dosage, their periods of moderate addiction and their longevity were all cited as evidence.[24] Coleridge, De Quincey and Wilkie Collins were 'melancholy and well-known instances' of opium eating to the Society for the Suppression of the Opium Trade (even if in this case the object was to stress the harmfulness of smoking rather than eating the drug). In evidence to the Royal Commission on Opium in the 1890s, by contrast, their longevity and the consequent possibilities of long-continuing consumption were the point at issue.[25]

De Quincey and Coleridge were, after all, only exceptional and well-publicized instances of the commonplace use of opium in respectable circles in the first half of the century. Excessive concentration on their spectacular histories of addiction, and, at times, enormous dosages, has tended to disguise the overlapping of addiction, social and medical usage throughout middle-class society at the time. Among the writers, medical men and friends of the two men, use and addiction intermingled. In the circle which gathered round Dr Thomas Beddoes of Bristol, a disciple of Dr John Brown, were Coleridge and De Quincey, Charles Lloyd and Tom Wedgwood, the photographer, whose reliance on opium was notable in the last years of his life. It was through a recommendation of opium in Beddoes' edition of Brown's *Elements of Medicine* that Coleridge was supposed to have first taken the drug. Two of Tom Wedgwood's brothers married two sisters, whose third sister was married to James Mackintosh. Mackintosh, the philosophical writer and lawyer, was, like Beddoes, also a student and admirer of Brown. He was generally reported to be an opium addict, and while out in India, as Recorder of Bombay, he was in the habit of often taking laudanum. Mackintosh was a friend of Robert Hall, the Baptist preacher. Hall, too, was an opium addict and took as much as 120 grains a day. The stirring quality of his sermons was said to result from his use of the drug.[26]

Such a chain of inter-linking addiction is remarkable only in that it was documented; patterns of literary consumption were always the most accessible. Byron, for instance, took laudanum occasionally. When his wife, thinking him insane, had his belongings searched, she found not only a copy of *Justine*, but a phial of Black Drop. In 1821, six years later, he recorded that he was using alcohol, not opium, to raise his spirits – 'I don't like laudanum now as I used to do.'[27] Shelley was also heavily reliant on laudanum at times of excessive physical and mental stress. He recorded, after a violent disagreement with Southey in 1812, that 'I have been obliged by an accession of nervous attack to take a quantity of laudanum which I did very unwillingly and reluctantly. . . .' On his parting from his wife, Harriet, at a time when he was suffering much bodily pain in addition, 'he would actually go about with a laudanum bottle in his hand, supping thence as need might be'.[28]

Keats was taking laudanum in 1819 and 1820 and at one stage intended to commit suicide with the drug before his death in Italy.[29] Sir Walter Scott wrote *The Bride of Lammermoor* in 1819 in the course of a painful illness for which he was being given up to two hundred drops of laudanum and six grains of opium a day.[30] Branwell Brontë was overtly dependent on the drug (his consumption of it originally began in imitation of De Quincey). For sixpence he could buy a measure of laudanum at Bessy Hardacre's drug store opposite The Bull in Haworth; and he sometimes wheedled opium pills out of her when he had no money.[31] Dickens took opium occasionally at the end of his life, in particular to mitigate the stresses and physical ailments induced by his reading tour in America in 1867–8. The drug's effects provided a notable theme in his unfinished novel, *The Mystery of Edwin Drood* (1870). James Thomson's poem 'The City of Dreadful Night', inspired by his use of opium; the secret addiction of Francis Thompson who, taking six ounces of opium a day, had descended into destitution before Wilfrid and Alice Meynell rescued him to write for *Merry England*; James Mangan's compensation for poverty and ill-health by laudanum and alcohol – all were part of the interlocking patterns of use and addiction.

Many other writers were undoubtedly dependent on the drug. Wilkie Collins took laudanum originally to deaden the pain of a rheumatic complaint and went on taking it for the rest of his life. Towards the end of his life Collins was in almost constant pain, carrying his supply of laudanum in a silver flask with him wherever he went. He had written in 1865:

> Who was the man who invented laudanum? I thank him from the bottom of my heart . . . I have had six delicious hours of oblivion; I have woken up with my mind composed; I have written a perfect little letter . . . – and all through the modest little bottle of drops which I see on my bedroom chimneypiece

at this moment. Drops, you are darling! If I love nothing else, I love you![32]

It was in Collins's writing that the influence of opium was most clearly expressed. *The Moonstone* itself (1868) was written under the influence of opium as Collins, aware of his mother's impending death, struggled to meet a deadline while plagued with acute pain in his eyes. Like his part-autobiographical character, Ezra Jennings, the opium addict of the novel, he found that the 'progress of the disease has gradually forced me from the use of opium to the abuse of it'.[33]

Elizabeth Barrett Browning, whom Pickering has called 'a well-balanced addict', took opium and morphia regularly. Robert Browning was shocked to find that 'sleep only came to her in a red hood of poppies'. As she wrote to Miss Mitford, in 1840, 'I took two draughts of opium last night – but even the second failing to bring sleep. It *is* a blessed thing! – that sleep! – one of my worse sufferings being the want of it. Opium – opium – night after night – ! and some nights, during east winds, even opium won't do. ....' Muriate of morphia she called her 'elixir', but she was quite able to give up the drug altogether when she was pregnant and worried about its effect on the unborn child. Her use of the drugs was simply a fact of her life and not an important one for her literary output; Julia Ward Howe's jealous contention that Mrs Browning relied on 'pinions other than her own' for the imagery and depth of her writing remains in doubt.[34] Jane Carlyle, too, although probably not addicted, was taking much morphia in the 1840s. She was using the drug quite regularly from 1846 to 1853 to help her depression and sleeplessness. A dose given for her cough in 1846 induced, according to Caroline Fox, 'not beautiful dreams and visions, but a miserable feeling of turning to marble herself and lying on the marble, her hair, her arms, and her whole person petrifying and adhering to the marble slab on which she lay'.[35]

Regular middle-class use and addiction was not simply a literary matter, although evidence for it in those circles is most plentifully documented. Throughout 'respectable' society addicts were to be found, with most note being taken of the habits of the famous. Clive of India died in a fit after taking a double dose of the opium to which he was accustomed. William Wilberforce was first prescribed opium for ulcerative colitis in 1788; Lord Carrington commented of him half a century later that 'it is extraordinary that his health was restored by that which to all appearances would be ruined by it, namely the constant use of opium in large quantities'.[36] In 1818, thirty years after his first prescription, he was still taking the same dose, a four-grain pill three times a day. Gladstone's sister Helen, a convert to Rome, was an invalid and a laudanum addict whom Gladstone himself found in Baden Baden in 1845 'Very ill from laudanum', having taken a dose of three hundred drops.[37] John Thomson, whose *Street Life in London* was one of the earliest documentary photographic series, was also an opium addict. He, unlike most other users, had developed the habit after a lengthy visit to the Far East.[38] George Harley, Professor of Practical Physiology at University College Hospital and later a writer on the uses and abuses of opium, also became dependent on morphia (which he took orally) after suffering intense eye pain. 'I ... crawled back into bed, put out my hands, laid hold of the bottle containing the draught of morphia, and drained it to the bottom.' Harley later cured himself of his addiction by an agonizing period of abrupt withdrawal. After eight sleepless nights, ten hours of oblivion left him cured.[39]

Others, although not strictly dependent on the drug, took it for 'stimulant' purposes. Horace Walpole remembered Lady Stafford saying to her sister, 'Well, child, I have come without my wit today' when she had not taken her opium 'which she was forced to do if she had any appointment, to be in particular spirits'. Jane, Duchess of Gordon, likewise took opium regularly and was lively and gay.[40]

Florence Nightingale took opium on her return from the Crimea, partly to counteract the effect of the ending of her work there, partly, too, for a medical reason. In July 1866, when suffering severe back pain, she wrote that 'Nothing did me any good, but a curious little new fangled operation of putting opium under the skin which relieves one for twenty-four hours – but does not improve the vivacity or serenity of one's intellect.'[41] Southey's mother took opium in large quantities during her last illness. Southey himself took the drug for sleeplessness, as did many others. In a letter to Sir Humphry Davy, another of the circle round Beddoes at Bristol, he complained of 'nervous feelings of pain and agitation. Tonight I try if opiates will send me to sleep, and when I sleep, preserve me from broken yet connected dreams ...'.[42]

George IV was given opiates, too, for their narcotic effect. The Duke of Wellington commented in 1826 on the King's excessive use of spirits: 'he drinks spirits morning, noon and night; and he is obliged to take laudanum to calm the irritation which the use of spirits occasions ...'. Jane Austen's mother had opium similarly to help her sleep. Lady Sarah Robinson, whose only daughter had recently died, was in 1826 calmed from 'an overwhelming rage' by the administration of 'a quantity of laudanum'.[43]

Dante Gabriel Rossetti's wife, who suffered from tuberculosis and a spinal deformity, was addicted to laudanum and died of an overdose. Yet Rossetti nevertheless strongly urged Janey Morris, in the course of a romance obsessively over-concerned with ill-health, to take chlorodyne for neuralgia.[44] Oliver, the son of Ford Madox Brown, Rossetti's associate, advised Frederic Shields, the artist and, like Rossetti, addicted to chloral, to take 'A dose of *chloral* Monday, *sour milk* Tuesday, *Laudanum* Wednesday, on Thursday a little *spirits*, while on Friday you might modestly content yourself with fifteen to twenty-five drops of *chlorodyne*. In this way you would not grow hardened to any one of them, and each would retain its full power and proper efficiency.'[45]

There were other less famous but nonetheless 'respectable' opium eaters. In Morwenstow in Cornwall, the opium taking of the Rev. Robert Hawker was exaggerated by the stress of his wife's death in 1862. Hawker had a neighbour, Oliver Rouse, whose favourite tipple was gin and paregoric.[46] Mostly the opium use of these less known circles went unremarked. In general, a gallery of such individual opium users and eaters is certainly no reliable guide to the incidence of usage at that time. It is, however, a valuable indication of how the situation of open availability operated before the 1868 Pharmacy Act and to a great extent beyond it. It is perhaps surprising to find that famous personalities of the period were dependent on, or regular users of, a drug the use of which is now shunned or regarded most usually as symptomatic of a diseased or disturbed personality. Many managed their dependence without the physical and mental deterioration, the social incapacity, or the early death which is the stereotype of contemporary narcotic addiction. Addiction, in fact, was not the point at issue for those users of the drug and their contemporaries. The experiences, and their publication, of Coleridge and De Quincey may with hindsight be seen as landmarks in the process of changing perspectives on opiate use, as helping gradually to engender a harsher, more restrictive response. But for their contemporaries, opium was a simple part of life, neither exclusively medical nor entirely social.

6

Opium in Medical Practice

The 'orthodox' medical use of opium was of relatively minor importance at this time. Doctors and pharmacists, until mid-century at least, lacked the organizational structures and professional standing even to begin to define opium use as solely a medical matter. It is easy, reading the expanding numbers of medical journals produced in this period (the *Lancet*, beginning in 1823, being among the first and most notable), to forget that they catered for a body of men very different from the later unified profession which exerted social, intellectual and political influence. 'Properly educated practitioners' were mostly lacking before mid-century. The extraordinary diversity of medical practice in the early nineteenth century, the social 'marginality' of local medical practitioners, with medical practice often still very much a trading occupation of indeterminate status, made it impossible at this stage for doctors to establish any form of unitary control over a coherent body of knowledge and practice.[1]

Opium's uses within medicine were nevertheless legion. The opium preparations on sale and stocked by chemists' shops were numerous enough; but a glance at the opium section of any textbook of materia medica of the period is enough to show that an even greater variety of preparations was available for the practitioner to use if he chose. Standardization was almost completely absent. One of the public health issues used in debates over legislative restriction of opium was the drug's widespread adulteration (to be discussed in Chapter 8). Even the opium preparations of the textbooks themselves could differ in their formulae. There was no agreement, before the 1858 Medical Act established the British Pharmacopoeia, on what were standard preparations. There were separate Pharmacopoeias in London, Edinburgh and Dublin; and all had different laudanum formulae. Nevertheless the fourteen opium preparations (as well as some preparations of poppy capsules and of morphine) listed in that first national British Pharmacopoeia were witness to the drug's popularity. They were all still there in the 1880s (with, of course, a vastly expanded morphine list); and Squire's semi-official *Companion* to the Pharmacopoeia had twenty-one opium preparations in medical use.[2] When John Murray commented of opium, in his *System of Materia Medica and Pharmacy* in 1832, that 'As a palliative and anodyne, it is indeed the most valuable article of the materia medica, and its place could scarcely be supplied by any other', he was no more than echoing the almost unanimous opinion of his medical contemporaries.[3]

Opium was by no means a newcomer to medical practice in the nineteenth century. It had been in limited medical use almost since it was first imported. Dr Turner, the apothecary in Bishop-gate Street, London, was selling a compound called Laudanu in 1601. It was said to be 'good for alleviating pain', and 'will temporarily put a man in a sweate trans'.[4] It was from beginnings such as this that opium had, by the eighteenth century, become an accepted part of medical practice. The prevailing monistic system of pathology used 'heroic' methods such as blistering, bleeding and purging. Opium was also used in tension pathology, which involved the use of remedies to increase (stimulate) the tone, or lessen it by relieving tensions. The burgeoning of English texts which dealt specifically with the use of the drug – George Young's *Treatise on Opium* for example, Alston's 'Dissertation on opium' or Dr Samuel Crumpe's *Inquiry into the Nature and Properties of Opium* (1793) – was testimony to its increased importance in English medicine.[5]

There was greater documentation of medical use of opium in the nineteenth century, simply because many of the standard medical journals were established at this time. Debates over methods of treatment raged more fiercely too, as part of the process of establishment and differentiation of a separate medical profession, and opium came to the fore. The old heroic therapies involved in humoral pathology, whereby an imbalance in body fluids was removed by physical means, gave place to a greater emphasis on drug treatment and a more localized notion of pathology. There were attempts to identify previously unclassified diseases, to evolve a more scientific mode of treatment. The use of opiates spanned both the old system and the new – and indeed the break between them was never so sharp.

Despite opium's importance to medical practice of all varieties, there was still a great deal of disagreement, even in the nineteenth century, over the actual effect of the drug and how it really worked. The debate on whether it was stimulant or sedative had been very much part of eighteenth-century medicine; and there were still echoes of the controversy in the nineteenth. Opium had been assigned by those physicians declaring allegiance to the Galenic School to the 'cold' group of drugs because of its soporific and sense-deadening effects. But rival physicians saw it as a 'hot' drug, as a stimulant rather than sedative in its action. Perhaps the most noted of all the exponents of the stimulant view was Dr John Brown of Edinburgh, who in his *Elements of Medicine* laid down what became known as the Brunonian system of medicine and whose influence on Beddoes and the Bristol circle has been described in the preceding chapter. Brown, like them, saw both opium and alcohol as stimulants, increasing the tone of the nervous and vascular systems.[6]

Opium has always been classified in the twentieth century both legally and in popular parlance as a soporific, narcotic drug. Its imaginative literary effects are regarded as something peculiar to a small circle of creative writers. 'Stimulant' usage of this type has been seen as abnormal and definitely non-medical. Yet, as discussion of the Brunonian system and tension pathology indicates, medical practice once took a very different position. Although terms were never closely defined, the drug's claims to what was called a 'stimulant' effect were urged by medical writers well into the nineteenth century. An element of euphoria was recognized as being among the effects of opium. Samuel Crumpe strongly disagreed with the compromise position that the drug had both stimulant and sedative properties. If this was the case, he pointed out, one principle would neutralize the other and the drug would turn out inert. In his view, a stimulant would be productive 'of most considerable anodyne effects, which conjunctly possesses the greatest degree of stimulant power, the most ready diffusibility, and which is, at the same time, the most suddenly exhausted. The whole of these properties are accordingly discoverable in opium, to a considerable degree'.[7]

In the following century, the drug's stimulant effects, although still a matter of lively interest, were to a much greater degree isolated from medical practice. Many writers in the newly established medical journals, in the textbooks of materia medica, reserved the drug's stimulant properties for exceptional, non-medical circumstances, seeing its narcotic effects as the true medical ones. Professor Robert Christison of Edinburgh, the greatest authority on poisons in the 1820s and 1830s, maintained that continuous excitement could be sustained by taking repeated doses. But this, as he pointed out, was rarely done in medical practice. The effect of a full 'medicinal' dose of three grains of solid opium, or a drachm of tincture, was to produce a general transient excitement and fullness of pulse, with torpor and sleep a short time after. A book by Michael Ward on the opiate friction, or the external application of the drug, also stressed its sedative properties.[8] Most medical men appear to have agreed that the drug's narcotic properties were indeed paramount, even if there was a short period of primary stimulation. Some even disputed that the stimulant effect existed. F. E. Anstie in his *Stimulants and Narcotics* (1864) thought opium produced 'nothing resembling mental excitement'.[9] By the end of the century 'stimulant' use of opium had been excluded from orthodox medicine.

The question was also bound up with that of how the drug really worked on the body, whether by the medium of the blood, or by 'nervous communication'. F. Robinson, a Hammersmith surgeon, gave as his opinion in 1846 that opium would be capable of producing quicker and more deadly effects on 'a person of thin spare habit and highly nervous temperament than on a large robust individual of lymphatic sanguineous temperament'.[10] There were echoes of the earlier medical emphasis on a humoral pathology, and perhaps the most sensible conclusion was that the effect very much depended on the person and the setting. The use of opium to aid public speaking was a particular example of conflicting tendencies and the differing effects the drug could have. It was also a notable example of the 'social' use of this drug which prevailed at the time. Opium was a 'pick-me-up' and a 'calmer of nerves'. Wilberforce was known to take opium before his speeches in the Commons, and Gladstone, too, took laudanum in a cup of coffee with the same aim. The practice was not unknown in medical circles, and could have some unforeseen effects. A doctor elected

President of the Hunterian Society in Edinburgh, through anxiety, took a larger dose of opium than usual before a crucial speech, and promptly fell fast asleep. When another member of the society also took a dose, it induced exactly the opposite effect. He was laughed out of the room, calling and crying out incoherently. The last of the trio, 'a crack man of the "Medical" and one of its possible presidents', went to make a speech on the evening prior to the election. He appeared to others present to be in a state of profound reflection. Time passed; the other speakers finished, and the meeting was declared over. The aspirant to office awakened from his opium stupor to find his chance of the presidency gone.[11] Such were the wayward and conflicting effects of opium. It could be 'stimulant' or 'sedative' depending on dosage and tolerance, and also on the consumer himself and his own expectations. Its mode of action remained a matter for investigation. But medical discussions increasingly emphasized its sedative, not its stimulant effects.

This uncertainty over its action did not prevent the widespread use of the drug for every variety of complaint. It was indeed a palliative. There were few specific cures for conditions in the first half of the century and many diseases were still to be medically defined. Opium, if not the cure-all which its most strenuous advocates saw it as, at least provided a relief from pain and a period of intermission which might aid recovery. It would almost be easier to list those areas where it was never employed than to attempt to deal with every therapeutic possibility. Jonathan Pereira noted in his textbook of materia medica in 1839 that it was used, in general, 'to mitigate pain, to allay spasm, to promote sleep, to reduce nervous restlessness, to produce perspiration, and to check profuse mucous discharge from the bronchial tubes and gastro-intestinal canal'.[12] Its popular uses give some idea of the range of minor complaints in which it was invaluable. It performed basically the same function in major illnesses, too. In gout, sciatica and neuralgia it was 'a most efficient palliative'; and the pain of cancer, or gangrene, and the effects of ulceration were also dealt with by opium. Its use to 'allay spasm' was extensive. Cases of hydrophobia were commonly narcotized with opium, even if the results were never that successful. As in cases of tetanus, it brought often a temporary amelioration which served to confirm the belief in its powers. It was often recommended for cases of intestinal obstruction; and its utility for ague and malarial conditions has already been demonstrated by the case of the Fens.[13]

It was a recognized standby for bronchial affections. There were no specific cures for tuberculosis, pneumonia or bronchitis and opium helped to alleviate symptoms, subduing coughing, expectoration and pain even if it could not touch the root cause. Discharges of all sorts, too, were dealt with by the drug. Its use in haemorrhage was well-known – 'of all the wonderful influences ... exerted by opium, that by which it sustains the powers of life when sinking from haemorrhage, and arrests the flow of blood, is the most extraordinary,' commented a medical journal in 1846.[14] In diarrhoea, it was the major remedy, sometimes combined with camphor, sometimes with nitric acid or calomel. Its use in dysentery was common, although it was argued that the constipation it produced could mask other, more serious symptoms. And, of course, for cholera its use remained virtually unchallenged. Despite the existence of a rudimentary knowledge of saline intravenous injections, owing much to the work of O'Shaughnessy, the young doctor who also brought cannabis into English medical practice, there appears to have been as much reliance upon opium in the last major cholera epidemic in England, in 1866, as there had been in those of 1831–2 and 1849–53.[15]

In some areas opium was rediscovered. Diabetes was a case in point. Earlier medical texts had noted the drug's utility in the condition; but the method then slipped from notice. Dr Anstie, in fact, was strongly against its use. But in 1869, cases published by Dr F. W. Pavy of Guy's Hospital demonstrated that opium and its alkaloids, morphine and codeine, had the ability to check the elimination of sugar in the urine. The codeine and opium treatment he advocated was not uncritically accepted but it soon became standard. It was still in use in King's College Hospital in the 1890s. William Osler, author of the standard medical text of the period, commented that 'opium alone stands the test of experience as a remedy capable of limiting the progress of the disease'.[16]

Opium also had a long history in the treatment of 'female complaints'. Its efficacy as a palliative came into its own in the treatment of dysmenorrhoea or menstrual pain, and in childbirth perhaps most notably. It was a useful anodyne for puerperal fever. It was occasionally given during labour, in particular to compose a patient during a lengthy delivery; and it was also used to dull 'after-pains', although this practice caused some controversy.[17] It was used for the 'nervous disorders' which were thought to be specifically sex-linked. Indeed, it was the medical administration, and consequent self-administration, of hypodermic morphine to 'hysterical women' later in the nineteenth century which was said to have originated the problem of hypodermic morphine abuse. The female bias of morphine use is, however, as doubtful as the idea of female fragility and ill-health which informed most discussions. It may well be, too, that, despite many assertions to the contrary, female consumers of the drug were no more numerous than males. Certainly the male death rate from opium overdoses was higher.[18]

One of the major medical areas where opium was used – in the treatment of insanity – provided a striking illustration of the changing focus of medical attention and the altered perception of the drug itself. Opium, at the beginning of the century, was seen as a welcome alternative to existing treatments. But by the end of the century, its use was increasingly viewed both as a cause of mental illness and as a form of insanity in itself. The 'disease' of opium addiction as then formulated owed much to the disease view of insanity, a condition with which opium had long been associated as a means of treatment.

But in the early 1800s, treatment with opium and other drugs appeared to be a means of progress away from earlier methods of restraint. Straitjackets and mechanical means of restraint were replaced by more subtle therapeutic means of control, opium among them. John Ferriar at Manchester, one of the earliest opponents of the 'old regime', advocated it as a valuable replacement for 'beatings and terror'.[19] Dr John Connolly, physician to the asylum at Hanwell – and one of the leading figures in the new attitude towards the insane – stressed that different preparations could vary in their effects, and also according to individual idiosyncrasy.

> With some patients laudanum acts with certainty, and like a charm; others derive comfort for long periods from the acetate of morphia; to some the liquor opii sedativus is alone tolerable. Whatever sedative is employed, the dose should be large. Less than a grain of the acetate of morphia is productive of no good

effect whatever; and laudanum requires to be given in doses of a drachm, or at least of forty or fifty drops. I am speaking of acute cases, for in those of longer continuance, use often makes much larger doses necessary ...[20]

There were those who were suspicious of the large claims made for it. W. Smith, at one time resident surgeon at the Lincoln Lunatic Asylum, in 1849 criticized an article by Forbes Winslow in the *Psychological Journal* advocating the sedative treatment. To Smith, the use of narcotics was 'merely an old enemy under a new guise', and the drugs, while useful in certain defined areas, were not general specifics.[21] Opium, other authorities agreed, could aggravate as well as subdue the symptoms of mania and many were cautious about its use. Haslam, for instance, in his *Observations on Madness and Melancholy* saw opium as a drug that could excite the patient even further, instead of producing the necessary sedative effect.

Practical experience of the 'stimulant' properties of the drug on an already over-stimulated mind brought stricter limits on the advocacy of its use. The uses to which opium could be put in insanity were more clearly established and circumscribed in the 1860s and 1870s. Opium was also a casualty of increased specialization in treatment. The elaboration of disease concepts, the delineation of particular forms and varieties of mental illness, encouraged diversification in methods of dealing with them. Significantly it was Henry Maudsley, whose name was synonymous with new departures in mental illness, who was much associated with the limitation of opium's use. In a series of articles on the subject beginning in the late 1860s, he noted the generally unsatisfactory definition of insanity and the consequent vagueness in the drug treatment. No one quite knew how, why and where opium was having its effect. In a piece in the *Practitioner* in 1869, he recommended that the drug be used only in the early stages of the illness. The sleeplessness, depression and 'strange feelings of alarm' which, according to him, often preceded 'regular insanity' could be relieved by opium. It was especially valuable in melancholia, or depression, but not in mania.[22]

In the succeeding years, Maudsley's advice appears to have won increasing support, in particular from medical men receptive to the new departures. Dr Thomas Clouston, Superintendent of the

Cumberland Asylum at Carlisle, won a gold medal from the Medical Society of London in 1870 for his demonstration that cannabis indica and bromide of potassium, used in conjunction, were more effective than opium in the treatment of 'maniacal excitement'. (Connolly had earlier also pushed the claims of cannabis.) Half a drachm of the bromide and of cannabis tincture was given continuously to his patients over eight months. Clouston found the mixture particularly effective in menopausal women – 'I think here we have a palliative of great value and importance.'[23]

The work of Dr Anstie, too, encouraged a dislike of 'strong narcotics', and the appearance of new drugs, in particular the bromides and chloral, hastened the move away from opium. Chloral was being prescribed increasingly in general practice from the 1860s for sleeplessness in cases where an opiate draught or a 'composing mixture' would once have been given. The first chloral addicts, Dante Gabriel Rossetti among them, were becoming known. Its use was advocated in insanity, too. Anstie supported the drug's use in the newly founded *Journal of Mental Science*. Bucknill and Tuke's standard work, *Psychological Medicine*, was said in 1874 to be in need of revision so far as the position of opium was concerned. Chloral and bromide of potassium, it was thought, 'enable us ... to dispense with opium and its preparations, or to reserve them for those cases of melancholia in which they are so eminently useful'.[24]

Opiates, however, continued to be used in the treatment of the mentally ill at the end of the century, even if advocacy was less eager or all-embracing than half a century before. Allbutt had reported on his introduction of electric treatment in the West Riding Lunatic Asylum reports in 1872. Digitalis, calabar bean and hyoscyamus also had their devotees. But opium was not completely abandoned, and its use in everyday circumstances in asylums and hospitals could have been more extensive than the academic texts indicate. John Cumming Mackenzie, assistant Medical Officer at the Northumberland County Asylum, still considered, as late as 1891, that opium was the major hypnotic in the treatment of the insane – 'experience but widens the field of its application while other hypnotics pass away'.[25]

In another area of insanity, delirium tremens, the continuing link between opium and alcohol was again demonstrated. Opium and alcohol had often been counterposed in eighteenth-century medicine, even if Dr John Brown had classified both as stimulants. As already mentioned in Chapter 3, the drug was popularly used as a means of sobering up. The connection between the two re-emerges at many stages in nineteenth-century society – in the working-class opium-eating 'scare', for instance, or in the concept of 'inebriety' and the formulation of disease theories of addiction (see Chapters 9 and 13). In the treatment of D.T.s the connection entered medical practice. Jonathan Pereira himself had known an alcoholic doctor who for many years took a large dose of laudanum if he was called out to see a patient while drunk. On one occasion, however, 'being more than ordinarily inebriated', he swallowed too much and died of apoplexy.[26] Such treatment was rather irregular in those circumstances, but was certainly standard medical practice in the first half of the century. Opium was the 'sheet-anchor' of the condition. It was in use in hospital practice in 1850; Thomas Jones, an intemperate 'gentleman's coachman' admitted to King's College Hospital and reported as seeing devils running about, was sustained on a diet of porter, beef tea and brandy, with laudanum every three hours.[27]

Its use in D.T.s was, though, the subject of increasing criticism from about this time. Isolated voices were raised against its efficacy and new treatments were suggested. Tartar emetic was found useful, and a supporting diet 'of an unstimulating nature' recommended. An onslaught by Professor Laycock, Lecturer on Medical Psychology at Edinburgh University, in 1858, marked the beginning of serious debate. Laycock questioned the total medical reliance on the use of narcotics. He himself had treated twenty-eight cases without opium or stimulants and all had recovered rapidly. Recommending that the patient be kept warm and on a suitable diet, he urged the abandonment of opium – 'while many have recovered without opium, and some in spite of it, none can be said to have died for the want of it'. George Johnson, Professor of Medicine at King's College, in a series of lectures on delirium tremens, supported Laycock's views. Large doses of opium were, in his opinion, to be avoided, although the drug could be given in small quantities and often worked best when combined, surprisingly enough, with alcohol.[28] It was a remedy with as many possibilities for evil as for good. Anstie, always opposed to the free use of opiates, supported this line of reasoning. 'The idea that patients in delirium tremens require to be narcotized into a state of repose, may now be said to be abandoned by those best qualified to speak on the subject,' he wrote in 1866.[29] The drug nevertheless remained in limited use in particular varieties of the conditions. Few were prepared to recommend its use in large quantities indiscriminately. Dr Latham, however, told the Cambridge Medical Society in 1882 that patients in moderate health could be given opium without risk – $\frac{1}{2}$ or $\frac{1}{4}$ grain injections of morphia were best until the delirious person fell asleep. But for those in broken health, opium should only be given with great caution.[30]

Opium indeed continued as one of the most valuable drugs in medical practice well into the 1860s and 1870s. It was not simply recommended in the official texts, but actually used in everyday practice. How much opium was in fact prescribed and dispensed must remain in doubt. Between the mid 1840s and 1860s, for instance, around 14–20 per cent of prescriptions dispensed by one Islington pharmacist were based on opium (234 out of 1,677 prescriptions in 1845). George Daniel, a chemist in the Holloway Road, dispensed a similar proportion; 16 per cent of his prescriptions in 1866 and 18 per cent in 1876 used opium.[31] Hospital case notes, too, for King's College Hospital, for instance, and the General Lying-In Hospital in London, show that opium was indeed regularly used for the conditions for which the textbooks recommended it. Most dispensing of prescriptions still took place in the doctor's surgery, and practice records have rarely survived. The amount of opiates generally dispensed must remain conjectural. Yet there can be little doubt of the established medical popularity of the drug in the first half of the century, nor of the way in which the range of complaints commonly self-treated with opium found their parallels in established medical practice.

PART THREE

The Beginnings of Restriction *c.* 1830–60:
The Public Health Case

'A Peculiar Sopor':
Opium Poisoning and the Longevity Debate

Reconstruction of patterns of opium use must always be tentative, yet it is clear from the preceding chapters that the availability of the drug in the first half of the century was rarely seen as a 'problem'. From the 1830s, however, the beginnings of a change were discernible, at least in official and professional attitudes. A climate of opinion began to emerge in which opium use was no longer regarded as an everyday part of life for all sections of society. Instead, the drug's easy availability and the effects of this began to cause concern. Among the first indications was the attention paid to opium by those involved in the mid-century public health movement, and it is with the place of opium in the general spectrum of public health at that time that the following two chapters will deal. Later chapters will show how, as the century wore on, more restrictive attitudes and practices appeared, with the classification of opium users as deviant from the norms of established society and opium itself as a problem drug.

This is a central issue. How could a drug which was openly available, was quite calmly accepted in many areas and was of proven utility come to be seen in such a different way? Was opium set within a problem framework because of the dangers of its use? Was the drug itself, with its inherently dangerous properties, the motive factor – or were other interests and strategies at work? The mechanics of establishing a problem where none had previously been thought to exist are clearly illustrated in the case of opium. It is tempting simply to see the development of a problem of opium use and resultant controls as an illustration of reform at its most benign. Indeed it is possible to present the public health and increased general concern about opium in a way which emphasizes health dangers and the response of the medical and pharmaceutical professions. But this is, at best, a one-dimensional outlook. What went to define a 'problem' were fundamental changes in social structure. The class tensions of an industrializing society had their impact as the scare about working-class opium use described in Chapter 9 makes clear. The emergence of a clearly defined medical profession was to be one of the key issues, too, in changed perceptions of opium use (this is dealt with in Chapters 10-13). As medical organization consolidated (and medical discoveries and remedies proliferated), doctors became more closely involved in the use of opium. Their own position altered. From being one among many prescribers of the drug, with nothing approaching unitary control, they began to re-define opium use as solely a medical matter, within a problem framework. Opium eating, under this medical imprint, became a disease, a habit warranting medical intervention. Doctors became the custodians of a problem which they had helped define. But it is important to see the role of the profession in this sense not simply as one of conspiratorial plotting, out to grab control of the drug for self-interested ends. The position was more complex than this. The attitudes of the profession (so far as it can ever be classified under such a unitary term) arose themselves out of the structural changes which were producing such middle-class groups; doctors, in their perception of opium use, as of other conditions, were reflecting and expressing the outlook of that section of middle-class society of which they formed an increasingly important part. This point will be discussed further in Chapter 13 dealing with medical disease theories of opium use.

Opium overdoses

This is not to deny that unrestricted opium did present problems. The dangers from a public health point of view were significant and the reformers involved in the sanitary movement did much to publicize opium as a 'dangerous drug', in particular because of the high rate of accidental opium overdoses. But these fatalities were themselves a function of a society where alternative and regular health care was mostly lacking. Indeed, given the social and cultural context of opium use already described, the level of mortality related to frequency of use was probably not high. However, the campaign for reform did not see it in this light, and open availability and the level of poisonings became a minor, if significant, part of the mid-century public health movement. Case histories in the medical journals, the evidence of the famous inquiries into social conditions in the 1840s and 1850s and those into the sale of poisons and pharmaceutical organization in the 1850s and 1860s established opium as a public health problem.

The theme of professional control was implicit in the public health campaign; for self-regulation among pharmacists, and doctors in particular, was important in bringing about increased involvement in social issues of this type. Public health was never an autonomous entity; and the move to end or reduce opium poisoning was also part of the professional movement of the 1850s and 1860s, which will be described more fully in Chapter 10. The concern about opium deaths was in another sense a form of professional self-definition and a validation of a doctor's expert status. Opium was a concern, albeit a quite minor one, for the leading public health campaigners. Edwin Chadwick mentioned the drug's use to the inquiry into drunkenness in 1834 and again in his own famous *Report on the Sanitary Condition of the Labouring Population* (1842).[1] Dr Southwood Smith, Chadwick's collaborator, considered the abuse resulting from open availability in his report on the industrial districts for the Commission inquiring into large towns in the early 1840s.[2] But mostly it was the medical contingent who brought opium to the fore. The marginal position of doctors at this period was often expressed in active support for social issues. The profession had not yet established its status to the extent that it could subside into conservatism. The public health movement was a cause which attracted many medical men; and the case of opium offered special medical scope. It was particularly through the reports made to Sir John Simon as Medical Officer to the Privy Council in the 1860s that the issue of opium overdosing was highlighted. The reports of Dr Edward Greenhow and Dr Henry Julian Hunter on infant mortality were among the first consistent medical investigations of adult as well as infant mortality from opiates.[3] The reports of Dr Alfred Taylor, Professor of Medical Jurisprudence at Guy's, on the dispensing of poisons, and his evidence to parliamentary select committees on the sale of poisons in 1857 and 1865 further demonstrated the force of professional involvement.[4]

Notable in the opium campaign was an embryo alliance between the professional sections agitating for reform and the as yet small sector of administration in government. The type of co-operation which was to characterize narcotic policy when it was established in the 1920s and which continues to operate today was already at mid century in the process of formation. For professional arguments on opium poisoning were supported by a clear emphasis on statistics, and the Registrar General's office, established in 1837, as one of the first central government agencies, provided the 'scientific' basis on which the medical and public health case was based. There were earlier localized collections of figures on opium deaths. The returns made to coroners of deaths from opium poisoning in 1838 and 1839 were the most obvious example. But the main thrust of the public health campaign came with the national Registrar General's reports. Opium statistics were used as public health propaganda. The support which they gave to the medical case (Dr Hunter, for instance, used local infant mortality rates in his report of 1864) was a first step towards an eventual alliance between medicine and the state.[5]

The agitation against opium began a drug-centred approach which, with modification, has continued to the present day. Concentration on simple statistical results without an awareness of social context or economic reality produced a situation which justified the restriction of open sale of the drug. Opium, as elsewhere, was the scapegoat for broader defects in the society of the time. With these reservations in mind, there is nevertheless no doubt that in absolute terms the number of opium overdoses revealed in the statistics was high. The earlier statistical discussions of opium mortality were generally inadequate. Professor Taylor, for instance, reported that of twenty-seven cases of poisoning admitted to Guy's over three years, five were due to opium. Other investigations were as piecemeal.[6] But the Registrar General's series on violent deaths which began in the 1860s presented a fuller picture, despite the undoubted drawbacks of early data of this type[7] (Table 3, p. 275).

Significant absolute figures were revealed for opiate deaths. There were eighty deaths in 1863 and ninety-five in 1864 from laudanum and syrup of poppies alone. There were also deaths from opium, morphia and Godfrey's Cordial. In 1863, 126 deaths out of a total of 403 poisoning fatalities were ascribed to opium. Its nearest competitors that year were prussic acid, cyanide of potassium and salts of lead; these accounted for only thirty-four deaths apiece. Around one third of all poisoning deaths in the decade were the result of the use of opiates. In relative terms such statistics were less alarming. The actual opium death rate was high but, as has already been mentioned in Chapter 3, had remained apparently static over a twenty-year period. Open availability had led neither to a dramatic rise in home consumption of opium, as import data show, nor to a rapid upturn in mortality rates.

For the public health case, however, the absolute figures were the point. The high level of accidental opium fatalities was, from this point of view, a particular illustration of the dangers of ready availability. In 1863, 106 out of 126 opium deaths were accidental, 110 out of 138 in 1867.[8] Cases where a public figure was involved attracted particular publicity. The Earl of Westmorland, given a phial of laudanum by mistake by his servant in 1834, was saved only by prompt action with the stomach pump.[9] The Bishop of Armagh was less fortunate, and his death in 1822, again from an overdose of laudanum given in mistake for other medicine, caused concern. The death of Augustus Stafford, M.P., in 1857, was also alleged, despite troubles with gallstones and a weak heart, to have been due to his injudicious use of laudanum.[10]

But mostly accidental overdoses were a simple fact of everyday life. Opium poisoning was a commonplace matter, not always worth medical attention. Like a stomach upset or a cold, it could be dealt with at home. Most 'home doctors' included instructions for dealing with a poisoning case. Buchan's *Domestic Medicine* (1803) gave full instructions for blistering plasters on the arms and legs, stimulating medicines, the use of 'strong vomits' and the drinking of warm water with oil to bring up the poison.[11] Many were familiar with what Professor Christison called the 'peculiar sopor' caused by an opium overdose. The person had an expression of 'deep and perfect repose'. He could always be roused, even though with difficulty, but as soon as the exciting cause was removed, this lethargy returned and death often followed.

The case of Fanny Wilkinson in the shop at Guisborough mentioned in Chapter 3 could be multiplied many times over. There were also habitual users who misjudged the limits of their acquired tolerance. One such was Mary Ann Beale of Bow, an opium eater for twenty years, who died in 1869 after purchasing four scruples of opium from a local chemist.[12] There were cases where occasional users took a little too much, or where those who had drunk too heavily overdosed with laudanum in an attempt to sober up.[13] Availability, the variation in strength of preparations and the tradition of popular use of the drug combined to make such incidents common. In a society where a 'sup of laudanum' did duty as a means of support, self-medication and substitute for medical care, their everyday occurrence was not surprising.

Opium was also a well-known means of suicide. The drug was said by Professor Christison to be favoured by the timid would-be suicide because of the gentleness of its operation[14] (Table 3, p. 275). Other methods were more popular – 1, 234 people cut their own throats and 2,570 hanged themselves, compared to a mere 115 opiate suicides, between 1863 and 1867. Opiates, however, were the most popular *poisons* for self-destruction throughout the century, and the rate may well have been in reality higher. Opium was not decisively displaced from top of the list of preferred suicide poisons until the 1890s, when carbolic acid replaced it in popularity. Prussic and oxalic acid, vermin killer, hydrochloric acid and strychnine were its main rivals in the 1860s. Arsenic was already being controlled by the Arsenic Act of 1851 and was less of a contender.

The drug was used by the famous for this purpose. Rossetti's wife, Elizabeth Siddal, accustomed to take up to one hundred laudanum drops at a time for the pain of tuberculosis and a spinal deformity, killed herself with an overdose. Rossetti himself later attempted suicide with a bottle of laudanum. Saved by inhalations of ammonia and strong coffee, he suffered for some time with partial paralysis as a result.[15] His action found its parallels repeatedly throughout society.[16] Young girls were presented in case histories as particularly prone to opiate suicide attempts. The owner of a lodging house in Edinburgh found one of her servants in the kitchen 'in a complete state of insensibility, with her eyes open...'. She had taken laudanum after a disappointment in love. Such occurrences were disposed of in a matter-of-fact way. When a nursery maid at a house in Covent Garden took half an ounce of laudanum in 1826 'in a fit of jealousy', she was pronounced fit to resume her duties after prompt action with the stomach pump.[17]

The histories were to a certain extent misleading, for the official statistics showed that the typical opium suicide was more likely to be male than female. The male suicide rate from opium always far exceededthe female; the disparity between the two in fact grew greater as the century progressed. The female suicide rate from opium was usually about half the male rate – 0.7 per million living female contrasted to 1.4 per million male in 1865, for instance.[18]

Even suicides could have their lighter side. Samuel Hillier, paymaster general in the Ninth Lancers, revealed in his farewell note of 1860 the problems that committing suicide with opium could bring. Wrote Hillier, 'I really believe I am poison-proof. About ten days ago I took half an ounce of laudanum, enough to poison a horse. It had no effect on me. After that I took eight grains of opium, again no effect, except a slight drowsiness. Then four grains of morphia; no effect. I then took five grains of liquor opii sedativus, with the same result.' Hillier, convinced that he was poison-proof, finally shot himself.[19] Yet the question was taken seriously enough by those urging greater restrictions on availability. John Hamill, police magistrate at Worship Street, urged such moves before the Select Committee on the Sale of Poisons in 1857, not because of accidental overdosing, but because of the drug's ready availability to would-be suicides.[20] He, like others, believed that legislation would affect the level of opiate suicides and suicide attempts, a belief which the post-1868 mortality rates prove to have been to a large extent unfounded.

The criminal use of opiates was never a public health issue to the same degree and was dealt with separately. How far opium was ever widely used either as a poisoning agent or to drug unwilling victims is uncertain. Perhaps the best known instance of its use to aid robbery came from Mark Moore, an 'investigator of intemperance' who, in 1834, reported how East End prostitutes would add laudanum to sailors' beer. Rendered insensible, they were easy prey – 'They are then robbed of every penny they possess, and very often of their new clothes . . .'. How far such stories were attempts at self-justification by sailors who had made fools of themselves is arguable. Certainly similar tales of 'drugging' circulating in London in the First World War were found, on investigation, to be groundless.[21] Professor Christison described several cases where thieves had planned 'To deaden the sense of taste by strong spirits, and then to ply the person with porter or ale drugged with laudanum, or the black drop, which possesses less odour.'[22]

At Greystoke in Cumberland in 1827, the drug was used in a rather bizarre community murder. Mary Kirkbride, a woman of weak intellect who came of a family notorious for its illegitimate children and which had 'Brought the Township to a great deal of Trouble', was deliberately poisoned by some local women, among them the wife of the overseer of the poor. 'They gave her a whole Noggin of Laudanum ... in a Large Table Spoon with Loaf Sugar to Deceive her.' Mary died after lingering for a fortnight; many in the town knew of what had happened, but few were willing to talk about it.[23] How far such practices were ever more than exceptional is difficult to assess. Opiates were known to be used in euthanasia for adults in the Fens, and for children elsewhere, too.

Whether or not the criminal use of opium was widespread must remain in doubt; but the practice was obviously given credence at the time. Laudanum was mentioned in the Offences Against the Person Act of 1861 in order to counter its supposed abuse. The 1851 Act for the Better Prevention of Offences, in increasing penalties for those who used 'stupefying things' to commit crime, had specifically mentioned chloroform and laudanum. The 1861 Act, too, established a range of penalties, including transportation and imprisonment, for those administering, or attempting to administer, 'Any chloroform, laudanum, or other stupefying or overpowering Drug...'.[24] What effect the Act had on the criminal use of opiates is impossible to estimate, since opium used simply to stun and stupefy did not enter the Registrar General's calculations. But the absence of any comment on the practice suggests that it was no longer of such importance, if, indeed, it ever had been. There were always isolated cases of murder by opium.[25] Murder with morphia remained reasonably popular as a fictional device; but the criminal use of the drug to stupefy, to aid the commission of crime, had died away.[26]

The public health discussions on opium poisoning marked the beginnings of sustained medical intervention in the question of opium. In the narrower sense opium poisoning also became a medical question. Although opium overdoses were often dealt with in a 'self-help' way, the professional was becoming more closely involved in the treatment of the condition. Opium poisoning became a medical matter. This was hardly surprising, given the number of overdoses: doctors thought of a 'narcotic poison' before all else if they were called to an unconscious patient. It was also a function of development within the profession. There was the advent of toxicology as a new medical specialism, in particular by way of the Edinburgh Medical School, many of whose graduates had studied in Paris under Orfila and Magendie, the pioneers in this subject. Professor Robert Christison's *Treatise on Poisons* (1829), with its origin in his work in Edinburgh, was the forerunner of many inquiries into the action of drugs.

Like the public health campaign, the debates on opium poisoning and its management by the profession marked the evolution of opium as a problem drug. The medical analysis of opium poisoning and its treatment was in many ways the model for later elaboration of disease theories of opium addiction. The intense debates on treatment had obvious parallels with the discussions of addiction and its treatment at the end of the century. Direct physical means were used at first in conjunction with agents to remove the poison. Emetics were employed; and the stomach pump was coming into use in English practice in the 1820s. In 1823, a Mr Jukes reported that with it he had managed to evacuate laudanum from the stomachs of 'several dogs, three persons, and himself ...'.[27] What was also later termed 'bullying' the patient was enthusiastically undertaken. Dr John Crampton of Dublin, in 1824, treated a female patient who had swallowed two ounces of laudanum by giving her emetics, shaving her head, exposing her to cold air, as well as dousing her with cold water. The whole process culminated in prolonged exercise in 'some open vehicle'.[28] One can sympathize with Sir Clifford Allbutt's later opinion that such methods were 'as useless as barbarous'.

Electrical and galvanic stimulation was another variation. Galvani's original experiments with shocks from an electric machine had taken place in 1786. It was in the 1840s that the method achieved popularity as a treatment for opium poisoning. The belief that muscle movements were due to electricity led to reliance on electrical methods as a suitable form of stimulation. In the mid 1840s, electrical stimulation from galvanic or electro-magnetic batteries was in regular use in cases at Middlesex and University College Hospitals. Dr Iliff of Kennington was certain that electro-galvanic elements applied to the various points on the body of a woman who had tried to kill herself with laudanum while depressed were responsible for her recovery. A few months later she tried again, and the same methods were used.[29] Parallels with the later electrical treatment of mental illness were clear. The electric shock treatment of opium poisoning was doubtful in its effects and fell out of favour by the end of the century.

Cruder physical methods of all kinds were being replaced by drug treatment. Drugs appeared to offer a 'scientific' means of treating opium overdoses. The attempts to find a drug cure in the last quarter of the century, and the debate between advocates of rival cures, or even of variants of particular cures, were an illustration of the process of medical self-definition and the establishment of a medical area of specialization. The controversy over atropine as an antidote was one example.[30] Caffeine, green tea and nitroglycerine had their advocates; and, at the turn of the century, Dr W. O. Moor's *The Permanganate Treatment of Opium and Morphine Poisoning* evoked interest in the use of potassium permanganate.[31]

Opium and longevity

The profession was involved in defining the problem; and was, at the same time, charged with both defining and treating the symptoms. The parallels with the later elaboration of disease theory were clear, and indeed in many textbooks a section on 'acute poisoning from opium' often preceded one on 'chronic poisoning', a term in use to represent addiction. The medical debates on opium poisoning foreshadowed later medical control of opium eating. Opium eating itself was not a matter of sustained medical interest at this time. As Chapter 13, on the growth of a disease view of addiction, will indicate, medical attention was limited in the early part of the century. But the first substantial medical intervention in opium eating, as distinct from opium poisoning, can also be traced in this period – a result of interest in the question of opium eating and longevity. Discussion centred not on the condition itself, but on its effects on life and health. The longevity debate, like the discussions about opium poisoning, was the forerunner of the disease theory of later-nineteenth-century medical thought. The question of opium eating and life insurance was the starting point, and an insurance case involving the Earl of Mar provided the opening.[32] The Earl, who had taken out several insurances on his life, died in 1828 of jaundice and dropsy. Investigations revealed that he was an opium eater of thirty years' standing, taking a tablespoonful each night before going to bed. He had at one stage informed his housekeeper that he was taking forty-nine grains of solid opium and an ounce of laudanum a day. The insurance policies led to a court case, where the insurance company argued that opium eating was a habit affecting health and longevity which should have been revealed; it therefore refused to pay out on the policy.

It was medical inquiries and medical evidence given in the course of two trials in the Scottish courts, in 1830 and 1832, which opened up the question. Professor Christison was again a prime mover in the matter. Christison, along with several other Edinburgh physicians consulted at the trial, agreed that opium eating must shorten life. There was nothing about the question in medical records and texts; his own investigations led him to conclusions different from his original ones. His survey of opium eaters, published in the *Edinburgh Medical and Surgical Journal* in 1832, was the first to consider opium eating a domestic phenomenon. Its value as an indication of the incidence of opium eating at the time is, as already mentioned, limited. But it was a clear indication of a growing medical interest in opium eating and its effects.

Christison's conclusion was that 'a certain number of opium eaters may attain a good old age' – one supported by the present judgement that opiates themselves produce no directly damaging or life-shortening effect on the body and that addiction itself is not a physically damaging condition. Opium eaters, to him, often appeared cheerful and active, and it was difficult to tell when they were under the influence of the drug.[33] Other contributors disputed the point. G. R. Mart's case histories led to the conclusion that opium eating did shorten life.[34] Some of the contributors to the debate argued from Far Eastern experience. Surgeon-General Little, for instance, who attacked Christison's conclusions in the *Monthly Journal of Medical Science* in 1850, dealt exclusively with his experience of opium eating and opium smoking in Singapore.[35] Such contributions were indicative of the relationship between Far Eastern and British use of opium to be firmly established through the anti-opium movement at the end of the century.

Perhaps the most generally adopted conclusion about the longevity question was given by Jonathan Pereira:

> . . . some doubt has recently begun to be entertained as to the alleged injurious effect of opium eating on the health, and its tendency to shorten life; and it must be confessed that in several known cases which have occurred in this country, no ill-effects have been observable . . . we should be . . . careful not to assume that because opium in large doses, when taken by the mouth, is a powerful poison, and when smoked to excess is injurious to health, that, therefore, the moderate employment of it is necessarily detrimental . . .[36]

His remarks were an adequate summing-up of the medical position on opium at this time. Opium as a 'powerful poison' was indeed already an issue by mid-century, a problem established by the public health campaign as warranting professional control. Opium eating itself was as yet of more peripheral importance, even though the discussion on longevity foreshadowed the full-scale medical intervention into the condition at the end of the century.

8

The Adulteration of Opium

One of the reasons why opiates featured so frequently in the poisoning statistics when they were first published officially in the 1860s was the extensive adulteration of the drug. Various additions made at different stages on its journey from Turkish poppy plantation to retail pharmacists and other shops made its strength variable and its effects uncertain. The different types of opium on the market were variable anyway. Egyptian opium was known to be less strong in morphine than Turkish; this made the production of exact chemical compounds difficult enough. When adulteration made this variability even more marked, it is not surprising that the rate of accidental poisoning was as high as it was. As Dr Normandy remarked in his *Commercial Hand-Book of Chemical Analysis*, '... this most valuable drug, certainly one of the most important and most frequently used in medicine, is also one of the most extensively adulterated'.[1]

The adulteration of opium was part of a general deterioration in both food and drugs which resulted from the transition to an urban society. From the end of the eighteenth century, the quality of many foods was declining. During the next hundred years, adulteration became a widespread and remunerative commercial fraud.[2] This was not simply a question of a straightforward desire for profit, but the outcome of breakdown and change in old methods of food production and, in the case of opium, of popular drug use. Just as working-class families could no longer produce their own food, so, too, the rural remedies comprising herbs and plants which could be freely picked were no longer available when the country was several miles away. The example of the Fens had demonstrated the replacement of poppy-head tea brewed at home by commercially produced laudanum, Godfrey's or paregoric bought from the local druggist or grocer.

Adulteration was fostered, too, by the breakdown of traditional methods of control. The old guilds, overseeing quality and sale, lost influence under the impact of changed conditions. The fact that medicine and pharmacy were in a state of flux in the early years of the nineteenth century has already been mentioned. The change from the tradesman status of surgeon-barber, apothecary or druggist had not yet been embodied in the professional medical and pharmaceutical organizations of the 1840s and 1850s. The medico-pharmaceutical area was at this period a complex mixture, and there is little doubt that, in general, sanctions against adulteration were lacking or impossible to enforce.[3]

The stage at which British analytical method rested in the first decades of the century also made the detection of additions difficult. The great advances in analysis and in the isolation of new alkaloids took place outside England. The influence of French scholars such as Orfila and Magendie has already been mentioned; but knowledge of this Parisian school was limited in the early decades of the century. English translations of Magendie's *Formulary for the Preparation and Employment of New Remedies* were appearing at the end of the 1820s. Toxicology as an academic subject was beginning to find its place in the medical syllabus.[4] Books like those by Christison and Pereira brought a more scientific awareness of poisons; but by themselves they could do little to check adulteration.

Given the tortuous route by which raw opium travelled from its original peasant producer, often from one merchant to another in the country of origin, it is not surprising that much adulteration had already taken place before the opium was even shipped to London. The peasants, under heavy obligation to opium merchants, augmented their crop by adding foreign matter. Further adulteration followed. Such a variety of agents were mixed in with the raw opium that analysts were hard-pressed to identify them all. The anonymous author of *Deadly Adulteration and Slow Poisoning Unmasked* (1830) noted, 'Good opium in a concrete state should be of a blackish colour, of a strong fetid smell, a hard viscous texture, heavy; and when rubbed between the finger and thumb, it is perfectly free from roughness or grittiness.' But such quality was rarely encountered. 'The drug is liable to great adulteration, being frequently vitiated with cow dung, or a powder composed of the dry leaves and stalks of the poppy, the gum of the mimosa, meal or other substances.'[5] Poppy capsules and wheat flour appear to have been the most common adulterating agents, but there were often others.[6] In one ten-ounce sample of Smyrna opium, Pereira found ten drachms of stones and gravel. Crude opium varied so much that no definite reliance could be placed on its effectiveness in given medical doses.[7] The development of 'scientific' medicine clearly needed to be able to rely on exact doses of the drug.

There were further additions to opium after its arrival in this country at both the wholesale and the retail stage. Wholesale druggists were accustomed to send raw drugs out to independent drug grinders for powdering, ready for making various compounds. Adulteration here arose from two causes: the demands of the wholesale companies, who allowed for an unreasonably small percentage of loss in the grinding process; and the desire of the grinders, too, to maximize their own profits. Arthur Hassall, a leading campaigner on adulteration, told the 1855 Select Committee how this came about:

A person having a drug which he wishes ground, forwards a given weight of it to the drug-grinder. The drug is generally returned to him of the same weight, or nearly so, and sometimes it is even ordered to be returned weighing so much more. Now, in the process of grinding, part of the moisture which all vegetable substances contain escapes ... that loss is made up by adulteration ...

The druggist knew that such a loss would occur and those with few scruples in the matter acquiesced in the process. The retail chemist also had a part to play in the process. There were certain tricks of the retail trade. Morphia, for instance, an expensive item, often had powdered opium with it. It was not unknown, too, for druggists to adulterate powdered opium with the dried and pulverized residue left from the process of preparing tincture of opium.

The drug was also used, to a lesser extent, as an adulterating agent itself. It was one of several substances added to increase the intoxicating properties of beer. Evidence of the practice is scant, and may have owed much to middle-class misunderstanding of the selling of opiates in pubs and beer houses, or the habit of taking opium to counteract the effects of too much drinking. It is possible, too, that adulteration with opium was declining before the movement to reform such practices got under way in the forties and fifties. As early as the reign of George III, penalties had been laid down for the addition of opium by beer brewers or beer sellers who mixed in 'any molasses, honey, liquorice, vitriol, quassia, cocculus Indicus, grains of paradise, Guinea-pepper, or opium' or any of the extracts of these substances. They were liable to forfeiture of both beer and additives and a fine of £200.[8] The Act was not enforced and adulteration continued; cocculus indicus was the main substance used, but according to Accum's pioneering study of adulteration in 1820, his *Treatise on Adulterations of Food and Culinary Poisons*, 'opium, tobacco, nux vomica and extract of poppies' were also known to have been added.[9]

It is likely that opium had been employed in a small way as an adulterating agent in the first decades of the century; but that such use was magnified by continuous repetition of the story without investigation. As late as the 1890s, allegations about the addition of belladonna, opium, henbane and picric acid were still being made in supposedly objective surveys of the drink trade, even though the last prosecution for the addition of cocculus indicus had taken place thirty years previously.[10] Opium was used popularly as an antidote to over-indulgence in alcohol, and possibly a popular preference in some areas for beer with opium added was distorted by the interpretation put on it by the public health campaign. Opiate use was a continuing undercurrent in Victorian society's reaction to alcohol. In this case it was a useful argument for the temperance side in the campaign against the brewers. But drink interests, too, were not adverse to using the dangers of increased opiate consumption as an anti-temperance bogey. Opium was a useful polemical weapon for both sides.

Opium was part of the concerns of those working to remove all harmful additions to food, drink and drugs. In itself a part of the wider public health movement, the crusade against adulteration was the same mixture of humanitarianism and professional self-interest as the moves to restrict the open sale of poisons. There was concern for the needs of working people. As Dr Thomson noted, the working class were particularly at risk from adulterated drugs – 'the labouring classes, being less capable of paying a higher price', were 'more exposed to the administration of bad drugs'.[11] But those who wished to replace such adulterated drugs by a higher-quality product largely ignored the fact that low wages effectively precluded working-class purchase of more expensive items. Without other means of effective medical treatment, drugs from the corner shop, adulterated as they were, were the only ones available for many families. Nor was it coincidence that the move-ment against adulteration coincided with, and was largely inspired by, professional organization in both medical and pharmaceutical circles. As with moves to restrict the open sale of poisons, the anti-drug-adulteration campaign owed much to professional strategies. Improvement of the quality of drugs prescribed and dispensed was a necessary corollary of the change from tradesman status to that of a qualified and monopolistic group with restricted entry.

The first landmarks in the campaign, in particular Accum's *Treatise on Adulterations of Food and Culinary Poisons* (1820), *Deadly Adulteration and Slow Poisoning Unmasked* (1830) and the inquiry of 1819 into the price and quality of beer, concentrated on the additions made to food and drink. But medical and pharma-ceutical organization brought with it a widening of the campaign to include drugs as well. Agitation among pharmacists against such adulteration began as soon as the Pharmaceutical Society itself was established in 1841. Jacob Bell, writing in the first issue of its *Journal* in 1841, chose adulteration as his subject and recognized at least in part that the campaign would lead to a more expensive product.[12] Jonathan Pereira's early work on adulteration was also addressed particularly to pharmacists.

Increased medical organization also lent weight to the cam-paign. The Edinburgh Royal College of Physicians appointed a committee to inquire into drug adulteration which reported in 1838. Detailed work by Professor Christison revealed the extent of adulteration of opium. The laudanum he purchased from seven-teen different shops, fourteen in Edinburgh and three in a major Scottish country town, gave wildly varying morphia percentages.[13] Dr Thomson's report to the 1839 Poor Law Amendment Act Select Committee confirmed Christison's findings and empha-sized the role of the drug-grinder in the process of adulteration.

Thomson's evidence was given wide publicity in the *Lancet* and it was this journal, under the editorship of Thomas Wakley, which was as always in the forefront of medical and public health radicalism, and which became the driving force behind the whole adulteration campaign. Its famous 'Analytical Sanitary Commission', an inquiry published in the journal in 1853–4, revealed the details of adulteration, not only of food and drink but also of drugs, and especially of opium.[14] Nineteen out of twenty-three samples of gum opium purchased in the interests of the investigation were found to be impure, poppy capsules and wheat flour being the most common additives. The investigations and reports of a Commons Select Committee chaired by Mr Scholefield, M.P. for Birmingham, in the following years, and the publications of Dr Hassall, gave increased publicity to the adulteration of opium.[15]

Opium adulteration was left untouched in the first general attempts to control adulteration. The 1860 Act merely covered the adulteration of food and drink. In any case, the Act was largely inoperative and not until the passing of the 1872 Adulteration of Food, Drink and Drugs Act did the sale of adulterated drugs become punishable. The 1875 Sale of Foods and Drugs Act, the foundation of all present legislation, specifically provided against the addition of injurious materials to drugs in Section 4. Section 6 of the Act, stating that no food or drug was to be sold which was not of the nature, substance and quality of the article demanded, was the basis for many adulteration prosecutions. The adulteration of beer, too, was specifically dealt with by the 1885 Customs and Inland Revenue Act, although most prosecutions came under the Sale of Food and Drugs Act; Section 8 made the adding of any matter except finings an offence.[16]

Quality improved, and by the end of the century the adulteration of opium was uncommon. Of seventy samples of laudanum examined in England and Wales between 1906 and 1908, only two were adulterated. In Birmingham, 12 per cent of the samples of paregoric bought between 1892 and 1913 were adulterated; but in the fourteen years between 1915 and 1929, all sixteen samples bought were genuine. The adulteration of imported raw opium was still a matter of complaint, but inside the country both standards and quality were improved.[17] The anti-adulteration campaign was thus, so far as opium was concerned, the epitome of a successful public health reform movement. Legislation, together with improved standards of health, had succeeded in largely banishing the addition of harmful agents to the drug. It also had its implications in the context of the growth of concern about the use of opiates around the middle of the century. Poisoning statistics and the evidence of adulterated opium's uncertain and sometimes dangerous action were the first factors which emphasized a need to impose controls and gave a role to the professional groups.

PART FOUR

Class Tensions

9

Opium and the Workers:
'Infant Doping' and 'Luxurious Use'

It was not simply the public health dangers of adulteration and overdosing which brought a new way of looking at opium. For the question of who was using the drug - and how - was also important. Middle-class dependence has always been much more acceptable than the establishment of the habit within the working class and this class reaction to opium was characteristic throughout the nineteenth century. But it was particularly the case in the course of the public health movement at mid-century. The publication of De Quincey's *Confessions* was, it has already been noted, only a matter for interested comment; and one searches the journals of the time in vain for much by way of concern about the widespread use of the drug in 'respectable society'. Yet popular opium use was another matter. The dangers of urban opiate use ran as a theme throughout the discussions of opium poisoning and restriction of sale. This was seen to be more threatening than the widespread reliance on opium in the rural Fens. Misunderstanding of the popular culture of opiate use had its roots in the class tensions of the period, and found expression in two ways - in the issue of infant dosing with opium, and in the belief in the working-class 'stimulant' use of the drug.

Opium and children

The dosing of working-class infants with soothing syrups based on opium has always attracted much attention as a public health issue.[1] The practice was an undoubted reality, but implicit in the campaign against it was class interest and a desire to re-mould popular culture into a more acceptable form. Opium was the immediate concern, but the campaign against it criticized basic patterns of working-class child-rearing too. The rationale, however imperfect, behind practices like child doping was ignored. Opium, as elsewhere, was a useful scapegoat. Criticism of its use diverted attention from the social situation to the individual failings of working-class mothers.

Numerous soothing syrups were on the market. The best known names were Godfrey's Cordial, Dalby's Carminative, Daffy's Elixir, Atkinson's Infants' Preservative, Mrs Winslow's Soothing Syrup and Street's Infant Quietness. Other preparations in use for this purpose were, like syrup of white poppies, also made up commercially. Some, especially in rural areas, were still brewed at home.

Godfrey's was, though, the most famous of all the 'infant's preservatives'. With origins dating back to the eighteenth century, it had originally been sold as a 'general cordial' by Thomas Godfrey of Hunsdon in Hertfordshire and after his death remained on the market 'prepar'd according to a receipt written by his own hand . . .'.[2] Like Dalby's, which also dated back to the eighteenth century, it was sold in distinctive steeple-shaped bottles. In an 1837 medical catalogue, F. Jacobson and Son were rather quaintly advertising 'Godfrey's round' and 'Godfrey's flat'.[3] Small chemists and corner stores selling patent medicines were in the habit of making up their own 'Godfrey' and one of its dangerous features was therefore that it could vary widely in its composition. For instance, in Hull in the 1850s, Godfrey's bought from one chemist had half a grain of opium per fluid ounce; from another the proportion was four grains to an ounce.[4] A pharmacist remembered the days when he used to make up Godfrey's by the gallon: 'I . . . can see with memory's eye the fluted green syrup bottle with its recessed label in red and gold in which it was kept. I can smell still the oil of sassafras which, with alcohol and laudanum, I stirred into the black treacle. One of the recognized perquisites of the apprentice was to lick clean the sticky film adhering to the wooden spoon at the end of the operation.'[5]

There were local preferences – Atkinson's Infants' Preservative, the product of an old-established Manchester firm, was more popular than Godfrey's in the 1840s in Midland towns like Dudley and Sedgley. Claiming a sale of 70,000 bottles a year, it declared itself free of 'pernicious stupefactives, whose basis is laudanum or other opiates', but was in fact a mixture of chalk and laudanum.[6] 'Children's Draught', 'Infants' Quietness', 'Soothing Syrup', 'Nurses' Drops', 'Mothers' Quietness' – the names were legion, but opium the one invariable ingredient of these many different preparations. Slowe's Infants' Preservative was popular in the Manchester area. In Kentish Town a notice on Thomson's in Queen's Crescent still urges passers-by to 'Try Thomsons Soothing Syrup for Baby'. The actual dosage of opium which was given to a child was highly variable and could be very large. The usual dose of Godfrey's was said to be from half a teaspoonful to two teaspoonfuls. Where weighing was erratic and the preparation evaporated to such an extent that it was much stronger than expected, two or three teaspoonfuls would be *stronger of poison than anybody knew*. Babies could soon develop tolerance of the drug, and mothers were then tempted to use stronger preparations, including laudanum itself.[7]

The same series of parliamentary inquiries which brought to light the issues of opium poisoning, the drug's use as a suicide agent and its adulteration brought the child 'doping' issue forward also. Dr Baker of Derby, in evidence to the Factory Commission in 1834, early made the connection with a mother's absence at work which was to be a continuing theme in all discussions. He commented, 'many mothers employed in mills are in the habit of giving opiates, such as Godfrey's cordial, Daffy's elixir, or laudanum, to their infants, that they may sleep during the mother's absence; and I have traced permanent squinting to this cause ...'.[8] Nottingham, too, was particularly noted for the practice. Women lace-makers were accustomed to use Godfrey's or laudanum to quiet their children while they worked at the frame. Lyon Playfair's survey of large towns in Lancashire collected further evidence from Rochdale, Manchester, Wigan, Bury and other centres. The Provincial Medical and Surgical Association (forerunner of the British Medical Association), the newly-established Pharmaceutical Society, the short-lived General Board of Health, all became involved in the question.

The children and opium issue came to a head in the 1860s in line with the wider campaign to control the open sale of the drug. The medical input, as in the other 'public health' issues, was striking, and Sir John Simon's reports were again particularly telling.

Nearly all the reports to the Privy Council made in this decade had some mention of the infant doping question. The statistical emphasis already noted in the public health campaign in general was used with telling effect here. Simon's anxiety about high rates of infant mortality – over twenty-four in every hundred thousand live births in towns like Wolverhampton, Ashton-under-Lyne, Preston and Whittlesey, twenty-six per 100,000 in Manchester and Wisbech – concentrated on the unrestricted sale of children's opiates.[9] His anxiety was supported by the contemporaneous publication of Registrar-General's reports. These showed that the major proportion of opium poisoning deaths occurred among young children, in particular among infants less than one year old. Between 1863 and 1867, 235 such infants had died, and fifty-six children aged between one and four; 340 children and adults over five had died. An average 20.5 such poisoning deaths per million population occurred in that period among the under-fives; there was a comparative rate of 7.8 per million among the over-thirty-five age group.[10]

The matter was brought up in Commons debate. The medical press was full of it; and infants poisoned by opiates provided a never-ending stream of patients for doctors anxious to try out the latest treatment methods.[11] The full weight of the voluntary side of the public health movement was brought to bear. The Manchester and Salford Sanitary Association gave public lectures in the 1850s and 1860s on 'The Injurious Influence of Certain Narcotics upon Human Life, both Infant and Adult'. On a national level, the Ladies Sanitary Association acted as a propagandist body. Penny tracts such as 'The Massacre of Innocents' and 'How to Manage a Baby' (along with 'Why Do Not Women Swim?' and 'The Evils of Perambulators') would, it was hoped, improve working-class child-rearing methods.[12] In the *Englishwoman's Journal*, the Association expressed its anxiety about doping: 'Few but those who have been much among the poor, know how fearfully mismanaged their little ones are – how the infant shares his mother's dram and all her food, from red herring to cucumber – how he takes medicine sufficient homeopathically to treat the whole community – and how finally, an incautiously large dose of laudanum wraps him in the sleep that knows no waking.'[13] The National Association for the Promotion of Social Science and the statistical societies took up the question. Professor Taylor added his testimony on the question of children's narcotics. Both in his evidence to the Select Committee on the Sale of Poisons in 1857 and in his textbook on poisons, he used evidence of infant mortality from opium to support his general demand for restriction.[14]

There were certain assumptions, however, which underlay this campaign. Although it is still common to find Victorian statements about child doping reproduced in discussions of disease and mortality without further analysis, the campaign against the practice was full of the class assumptions which did much to mould attitudes to the use of opium in general.[15] The campaigners assumed that the mother's absence at work was the root cause and that dosing was the habit of unqualified nurses, in whose care the infants were left. Dr Alfred Wiltshire, a medical inspector for the Privy Council in the late 1860s, was sure that maternal care was all that was needed to stop the use of cordials. 'I think if the child were kept at home it would not get opiates, but the mother would attend to it.' Nurses, rather than mothers, were criticized. These repositories of 'ignorance, tradition and prejudice' were at fault.[16] The child-minder who took in large numbers of babies and kept them quiet with liberal doses of soothing syrup was a widely disseminated stereotype.[17]

Yet professional child-minders in fact cared for a minute proportion of children in the factory areas. Most women with young babies did not go out to work, or did not work in the way presented in the parliamentary inquiries. Most women operatives were in the sixteen to twenty-one age group and tended to leave work after marriage. Domestic employment was more common and might have meant that a mother took her child along with her. Over one third of all working women in Preston in the 1850s for instance were in non-factory occupations, while others worked irregularly or part-time.[18] Child-minders were on occasion undoubtedly neglectful. But the reformers were working within a range of evidence and options which supported their own predilections. For a mother to stay at home and not work often led to lower, not higher, standards of child care; the absence of an extra wage led to a lower standard of nutrition. There was no correlation between the mother's presence and healthy infants. In Sheffield, for instance, only one per cent of mothers worked, but 21 per cent of babies were unhygienically bottle-fed.[19]

Both the culture of poverty and the economic realities of working-class life were ignored. For opium was at least a palliative for the gastro-intestinal complaints which, in conditions of poor housing and sanitation, in fact caused most infant deaths. Its ability to quieten infants made fretful by these and other digestive complaints aggravated by feeding habits based on 'scraps' should not be underestimated. Despite the undoubted dangers involved in overdosing, opium did have some role to play in a very imperfect system of infant management.

What was ignored, too, was the positive belief in the beneficial properties of opium for a baby shared by those who used it. There is no doubt that some factory hands were resolutely opposed to the dosing of their children. But there was a continuing popular belief in its powers as a restorative, reflected in the use of terms like 'cordial' and 'preservative'. This was related to a reliance on the beneficial properties of sleep and the sort of passivity which made a child easier for a harassed mother to handle. Godfrey's and laudanum were given to children on the day they were born, and were even prepared in readiness for the event. Such preparations were believed to be 'strengthening', and there was every incentive for the mother of a sickly baby to use them. Mary Colton, a twenty-year-old lace-runner in Nottingham, spoke of how women in her community had advised her to care for her illegitimate child:

> She could not afford to pay for the nursing of the child, and so gave it Godfrey's to keep it quiet, that she might not be interrupted at the lace place; she gradually increased the quantity by a drop or two at a time until it reached a teaspoonful; when the infant was four months old it was so 'wankle' and thin that folks persuaded her to give it laudanum to bring it on, as it did other children.

Other examples of a popular belief in the 'stimulant' powers of opium are not hard to find. Mr Herford, the Manchester coroner, reported in the 1840s that he had seen many cases where the parents had given large doses of narcotics, 'but neither I nor the jury believed that the person who gave the drugs thought that they would kill or do harm'.[20] It is indeed difficult to see how else many working-class families lacking day care facilities, proper baby foods and access to medical facilities could otherwise have coped.

The campaign against child doping was, then, culturally and economically insensitive to this extent. It was also silent about the extent of the practice outside the working class. Working-class self-medication was wrong; yet opium was used for children both by the medical profession and in the nurseries of the well-to-do. In official medical circles, the use, and in particular the self-administration, of opiates was frowned upon. Marshall Hall had produced a paper on 'The effects of the habit of giving opiates on the infantine constitution' in the *Edinburgh Medical and Surgical Journal* of 1816.[21] John Clarke gave similar warnings in his *Commentaries on Some of the Most Important Diseases of Children* (1815) in which he stated that children's cordials had been 'ignorantly and indiscriminately given.... Nothing is more uncertain than the effects of opium on young subjects; and it ought never to be employed even by medical men, except with the greatest caution....'[22] Most medical writers, however, did not advocate a complete ban on the use of the drug for children (and there remained some prepared resolutely to advance its claims). Dr Charles West in his *Report on the Progress of Midwifery and the Diseases of Women and Children* (1844–5) stated that preparations like laudanum, camphorated tincture or Dover's Powder should be used in the treatment of children's diseases in preference to preparations like syrup of poppies, which were variable in strength.[23]

This medical tolerance of the professional use of opium for young children extended into general practice. Prescription books show that opium-based remedies for children and infants were dispensed. A chemist in Islington dispensed in 1864 a mixture containing Battley's Sedative Solution (an opium preparation) for Mrs Ballard's infant. The baby was suffering from a rash and was probably fretful; two teaspoonfuls were to be given twice a day. The mention of such preparations for infants, or for young 'master' this and that, sprinkled throughout the records indicates that the profession was not averse to prescribing opiates for young children.[24] It was primarily self-medication, or 'non-medical' use, which was objected to.

Nor did the narcotizing of middle-class infants arouse as much anxiety. For many middle-class children, confined more severely in this period to a life based on the nursery and separate from that of their parents, were likely to be cared for by a nursemaid accustomed to using opium as a quietener. This was recognized at the time. The standard text on children, Thomas Bull's *Maternal Management of Children in Health and Disease*, warned that 'Godfrey's Cordial and other preparations of opium are too often kept in the nursery, and secretly given by unprincipled nurses to quiet a restless and sick child'. Bull advised that teething or restlessness at night should be dealt with, not by a drug, but by taking the child frequently out of its cot and carrying it about in an airy room.[25] Nurses who already worked long hours, whether 'indiscreet and lazy' or not, must surely have preferred sedation to getting out of bed once more to quieten a crying baby in a chilly nursery.[26] Even in the 1880s, infants' preservatives were still on sale at tenpence a bottle in the respectable Army and Navy and Civil Service Stores.

The passing of the 1868 Pharmacy Act, as Chapter 10 will show, had a notable effect on overall infant mortality. But the campaign against child 'doping' by working-class mothers continued with a shift of focus after this date. It became part of the campaign to control unqualified baby-minding. As such, it was part of the move to 'professionalize' all forms of child care, midwifery most obviously. The use of opium by unqualified women again served to detract attention from the wider context of living conditions and environment. A report was published by the Harveian Society on infanticide in 1867, and one by the Obstetrical Society in 1869 dealt with infant mortality. Both raised the question of unqualified child 'doping'. In an address to the National Association for the Promotion of Social Science in 1867, J. Brendon Curgenven, honorary secretary of the Harveian Society, stressed this point. Unqualified nurses were at fault and also the 'pernicious use of opium', which was 'carried on to a great extent in the Midland manufacturing counties, and the poor, wizened, dull, illnourished infants are really pitiable to behold', comments which were illustrative more of the role of malnutrition and poverty than of opium.[27] Nevertheless, as secretary of the Infant Life Protection Society, founded in 1870, Curgenven agitated for the registration of child-minders, compulsory registration of births and deaths, and an end to infant dosing.[28]

There were undoubtedly scandals involving opium and children in these years. The Waters and Ellis baby-farming case in 1870, where illegitimate children were being taken off their mothers' hands for a fee and later disposed of, was shown to have involved the use of laudanum to keep the babies quiet.[29] The Infant Life Protection Act of 1872, put on the statute book in part as a reaction to this case, limited its provisions to those who looked after two or more children under one year old; it thus effectively excluded the working-class child-minder, who could go on using opium as she pleased. The compulsory registration of births and deaths did, however, make it more likely that an opium death would be detected.

Working-class 'stimulant' use of opium

The campaign against child drugging had misjudged the issue. It showed a distinct bias in ignoring the use of opiates to dose children outside the working class. Adult working-class use of opium was treated in much the same way. For the widespread popular use of opiates already described and in particular the use of opium as an adjunct to alcohol, as an informal means of sobering up, was presented, partly through the public health inquiries of the 1830s to 1850s, as a distinct threat and a justification for control.

It was De Quincey himself, whose own 'stimulant' consumption of opium had met an interested, yet unperturbed, reception who was among the first to present working-class opium use as a problem. In the *Confessions*, he wrote:

> ... some years ago, on passing through Manchester, I was informed by several cotton-manufacturers, that their work-people were rapidly getting into the practice of opium eating; so much so, that on a Saturday afternoon the counters of the druggists were strewed with pills of one, two, or three grains, in preparation for the known demand of the evening. The immediate occasion of this practice was the lowness of wages, which, at that time would not allow them to indulge in ale or spirits ...[30]

A letter written by Coleridge in 1808 (not in fact published until 1837) confirmed this: '. . . the practice of taking opium is dreadfully spread – throughout Lancashire and Yorkshire it is the common dram of the lower order of people – in the small town of Thorpe the druggist informed that he commonly sold on market days two or three pounds of opium, and a gallon of Laudanum – all among the labouring classes.'[31]

The belief was that working people were turning to opium for 'non-medical' or 'stimulant' purposes, that their use was not for medical reasons at all, but that they used the drug as a cheaper alternative to drink. This view of popular opium use was commonly to be found at the time. In Mrs Gaskell's novel of Manchester factory life, *Mary Barton* (1848), the character of John Barton falls victim to the seductive properties of the drug.[32] Jonathan Pereira added a new section in 1853 to the third edition of his classic textbook of materia medica specifically to warn of the dangers of the drug's lower-class use.[33] The Westminster Medical Society was told in 1840 that 'the consumption of opium was increasing among the working-classes to a frightful extent'. Nor was its action among them a sedative one, for it 'affected all that was good and virtuous in woman, it acted as an aphrodisiac, and subverted all morality'.[34] Some observers of working-class life thought the extent of the practice 'somewhat exaggerated'. Nevertheless evidence was forthcoming from Glasgow, Salford and other parts of the factory districts. A druggist with a business in a Salford mill area related how, on market days, his customers 'come in from Lymm and Warrington, and buy the pure drug for themselves, and "Godfrey" or "quietness" for the children. Habitual drunkards often give up spirits and take to laudanum, as being cheaper and more intensely stimulating'.[35]

The mid-century 'public health' inquiries added to the definition of the problem. The consideration of child doping among the working class naturally led to concern about adult use too. The Factory Commissioners specifically made inquiries in the 1830s about the 'stimulant' use of opium and were met with unanimous testimony from doctors working in the factory areas that such practices did not exist.[36] Yet the dangers of lower-class use remained a continuing theme, discussed in particular during the inquiries into the open sale of poisons. Messrs Abraham and Edwards of the Liverpool Chemists' Association told the Select Committee inquiring into the sale of poisons in 1857 that laudanum was often 'very much abused' in their area. It was sold to be administered as a stimulant to adults and taken as 'a dram'. Professor Alfred Taylor concurred in condemning the 'bad use' made of opium in the manufacturing towns.[37]

Some outside observers were tolerant of the possibility; in *Blackwood's Magazine* in 1830, for instance, the habit was seen to have advantages: '. . . who can say, when eighteen hours toil out of the four and twenty have bowed down both body and soul to the dust, a few drops of laudanum may not be, in the best term, a blessing?'[38] Yet, in general, the possibility of working-class 'stimulant' use was a problem, part of the different framework within which opiate use was coming to be perceived at this time. As with children and opium, the emphasis was all on lower-class use; similar practices in the rest of society went unremarked or were viewed more tolerantly. The contrast in response to the use of opium by public speakers and the use of opium by factory operatives was, for instance, instructive. 'Medicus', writing in the *Lancet* in 1815 (which consistently publicized the dangers of lower-class use), put it thus: 'For those unfortunate creatures who daily resort of this baneful drug as a cheap species of intoxication, I have but little sympathy or commiseration. Their weakness entails a severe punishment even in this world.' However there were others, 'especially among the middle-classes of society, who resort to the use of opium, under the pressure of severe mental distress . . .'.[39]

The connection of popular opium use and drink was also a convenient argument in the much wider debate over temperance in Victorian society. The temperance movement had its origin at the time that concern over lower-class opium use began to manifest itself. The British and Foreign Temperance Society was launched in 1831 as the spearhead of the anti-spirits movements, and the more extreme teetotal movement was gaining artisan and radical support, at least in the North of England, from the early 1830s.[40] There was a belief that prohibitory or interventionist moves over the consumption of drink would inevitably lead to a corresponding increase in opium consumption. Some of the earliest investigations of opiate use did make this connection with drinking habits. Christison, for instance, in his analysis in 1831 of ten opium eaters, thought that the lower classes often combined opium eating with 'the practice of excessive drinking'. He himself found it difficult to distinguish between the two: 'I fully anticipate that this habit will be found not less destructive than the vice of drinking spirits.'[41] The idea of opium as an alternative rather than an accompaniment to drink was a later refinement. It was not until the end of the decade that the specific point mentioned by De Quincey was again raised. Jellinger Symons, one of the assistant commissioners inquiring into the state of the handloom weavers, reported that 'When the drunkards in Glasgow become too poor to satiate their appetite for spirits, they now resort in great measure to laudanum, which, in an adulterated state, is consumed in considerable quantities.'[42] This point was generally accepted, even sometimes among temperance supporters. It was a quite common argument in medical discussions of the issue, too, to point out that an opium-eating working class was indeed preferable to a spirit-drinking one, since opium eaters were not violent and spirit drinkers were. Sir Benjamin Brodie, the Queen's Physician, made this point before the Royal Medical and Chirurgical Society in 1840, and it was much discussed in the course of the more extensive anti-opium debate at the end of the century.[43]

In general this idea of opium as an alternative to drink and consequently one of the possible repercussions of temperance was accepted. Only Julius Jeffreys, who was later a surgeon in India, investigated further. Unable to find any opium eater who was also teetotal, he traced the idea back to a journal run by the drink interest, whose editor asserted that the connection was indeed possible since a decrease in the consumption of spirits had been accompanied by a rise in that of opium.[44] The argument was a fallacy, for in fact both per capita spirit and beer consumption were rising until the 1870s and declining thereafter, a pattern of consumption similar to that of opium. The pattern of concern about popular opium use however remained a subsidiary theme in the fortunes of the temperance movement. The Licensing Acts of 1872 and 1874, and the debate on Sir Wilfred Lawson's Permissive Bill in the same decade, brought the matter forward again. Opium and drink remained thus far connected in the temperance cause.

This continuing belief in the stimulant consumption of opium was an indication of how 'official' representation of popular habits could remould them into something quite different. As Chapter 3 has already shown, opium was indeed widely on sale in the factory districts, but it was consumed in rural areas, too, and at all levels of society. Working people were generally using the drug in self-medication. The connection with drink was present, but it was the sobering and not the 'stimulant' effect of the drug which most consumers expected. The distinction between 'medical' and 'non-medical' use was impossible to draw, and it was easy enough for observers to substitute moral judgement (the 'bad use' of opium) for cultural sensibility. The use of the drug in the working class, whether for children or by adults, was nevertheless considered at this time as a part of the 'opium problem'.

PART FIVE

The Professionals and Opium
c. 1860–1900:
Professionalization and Availability

10

The 1868 Pharmacy Act

In another sense, too, structural changes within society helped formulate this problem framework. Earlier chapters have already touched on how the emergence of separate 'professions' of doctors and pharmacists in the middle of the century marked a significant stage in the establishment of altered perceptions of opium. Professional medical control was to be one of the most important motives behind the new way of looking at the drug. In the second half of the nineteenth century the growing self-confidence and organization of the medical and pharmaceutical professions made a significant contribution to the altered perceptions of opium use. This came about in two ways. There was an increased concern about the availability of the drug, and that this should be in the hands of professional men. It began with the agitation leading to the 1868 Pharmacy Act and continued at the end of the century with the struggle to bring chlorodyne under pharmaceutical supervision. But there was also concern at the way the drug was used and about the medical control of its users, exemplified in the establishment of the particular problem of hypodermic morphine use and the outlining of disease theories of addiction, which are discussed in Chapters 12 and 13. In the 1850s and 1860s, however, the professional bodies concentrated on the availability of opium, not its use; the result was the 1868 Act.

Pharmaceutical organization in the 1850s and 1860s

In the 1850s and 1860s, there were moves to establish the medical and pharmaceutical professions as separate, self-regulating bodies.

These had as their corollary the restriction of the open sales of poisons, opium among them, and their reservation to one or other of the emergent medical professions. Separate professional organizations were emerging in many areas at this time; the consolidation of professional accountants, surveyors and actuaries, for instance, was underpinned by the expansion of the middle class in industrial society. A massive growth in their incomes increased the market for specialist services.[1] This process began in 1841 with the establishment of the Pharmaceutical Society, which began to organize a seperate profession out of already existing chemists and druggists, and those members of the Society of Apothecaries whose main concern was dispensing. The newly organized pharmaceutical chemists were granted a charter of incorporation in 1843. They were at first a minority body, with a membership of only 2,500 in the 1850s out of around twenty-five thousand drug sellers. The long-term aim, however, was to organize a close-knit body, membership of which would be essential in order to practise and use the title of chemist. The society laid most stress on educational qualifications as the key-stone of professional status; there was a strong desire to retrict trade in the interests of its members.[2]

Its initial objective was to limit the title of chemists to those who had passed its own examinations as well as gradually to raise the status and quality of chemists already in practice and eventually to achieve a monopoly of practice for its own members. These objectives were the main focus of activities in the 1850s and 1860s. They were partially fulfilled by the 1852 Pharmacy Act, which confirmed and extended powers already conferred by the Society's charter of incorporation. It set up a register of pharmacists and limited the use of the title to persons already members of the Society, in business before the Act, or who had passed the Society's major examination. But the exclusive powers of trade which it had sought to obtain were rejected. They were incompatible with free-trade principles and no restriction was imposed on the carrying-on of a druggist's business. The Society had not yet fully established the principle of a professional monopoly. Nor had it yet established itself as the controlling body of the profession. In the late 1850s it opposed two Poison Bills introduced by the government, in 1857 and 1859. The Society wanted restriction of sale of poisons, but only on its own terms. The Bills, instead of giving the Pharmaceutical Society control of admission, proposed a system of licensing and examination under the control of a Board in which its members would be in a minority.

Rival professional organizations were also on the scene. The newly established General Medical Council, brought into being, along with the single list of medical practitioners, by the 1858 Medical Act, was equally anxious to secure the professional standing of the general practitioner, a newly developed section. In its early days the General Medical Council aimed to close professional ranks against unqualified outsiders and to fashion a profession far from the lowly tradesman and craftsman status of the apothecary and surgeon. It also aimed to include a wide range of functions under its own aegis. There was a sustained medical attempt to include pharmacy within the ambit of the medical profession, and a claim to legislate for pharmacy as well as for medicine.[3] Surgeon-apothecaries had made a living by charging for drugs rather than for treatment, since the latter was not allowed by law, and many general practitioners continued, after 1858, to keep 'open shop' in order to dispense medicines. Before 1913, 90 per cent of all dispensing of doctors' prescriptions was still done by doctors themselves.[4] In the 1850s and 1860s, therefore, medical claims to control pharmacy were not outrageous.

In 1863, a committee of the General Medical Council proposed a new medical act in which pharmacy would come under medical control. But another 'professional' body was also on the scene, and this complicated the issue. The United Society of Chemists and Druggists was founded in 1860–61 to represent non-members of the Pharmaceutical Society who were disgruntled about that body's apparent failure to organize the trade and to defend its interests. There was rivalry between it and the Pharmaceutical Society about who was to control the profession. This led to the introduction of competing Bills by the two organizations in 1864. The Pharmaceutical Society's 'Number One' Bill sought to assert its own control over entry. The United Society's 'Number Two' draft tried to secure the position of those who were not members of the Pharmaceutical Society. This Bill included provision for the restriction of the sale of poisons to qualified men, however defined.[5]

The Select Committee to which both Bills were referred recommended that, in the light of such fundamental disagreement over control of entry, neither draft should be proceeded with.[6]

Compromise between the two organizations finally gave the Pharmaceutical Society control (although the General Medical Council was still hoping to establish its own overall responsibility). The 1868 Pharmacy Act established a system of registration involving both major and minor examinations under its direction; the United Society dissolved soon after. The educational monopoly had effectively been established.

The 1868 Act also went some way to achieving the profession's other strategic objective. This was the restriction of the availability of drugs and poisons. The same series of inquiries and draft Bills which had brought pharmaceutical self-regulation also forwarded the parallel professional aim of control of the sale of drugs. The 1868 Act continued a process foreshadowed by the 1851 Arsenic Act, which had already restricted sales of the drug. It controlled fifteen selected poisons in a two-part schedule. Those in the first part, cyanide of potassium and ergot, for instance, could be sold only if the purchaser was known to the seller or to an intermediary known to both. A detailed entry was to be made in the poisons register. The container itself had to be clearly labelled 'poison', with the name of the article and the name and address of the seller. Only these labelling restrictions applied to poisons in Part Two of the schedule.[7]

Opium and pharmaceutical organization

Those professing specialist status felt that their standing would be jeopardized if any unqualified person could sell drugs, or if any member of the general public could decide on his own medication and buy it openly. Opium as a widely used drug naturally came into the story at this point. Professional feeling, as expressed in the movement for control, complemented and paralleled the public health movement, where the presence of a large medical contingent has already been noted. For the 1860s, when the whole question of open sale had come to a head, was also the decade when the question of opium overdoses was drawing increased attention from these quarters. Sir John Simon, Medical Officer of the Privy Council, the main driving force in the public health movement since the demise of the General Board of Health, produced in his annual reports a condemnation of opium. In this he was aided

by the reports from Drs Greenhow and Hunter already mentioned
and by the advocacy of Professor Alfred Taylor. Taylor had
argued for strict control over the retail sale of poisons, and especially opium, before a House of Lords committee in 1857; and in
1863, as part of Simon's annual report, he produced a detailed
report on dispensing and sale. He put forward the professional
point of view. Only qualified persons should sell poisons and their
sale by 'chandlers, grocers, oilmen, drapers, or small shopkeepers'
should be prohibited. Taylor did, however, allow that some might
be licensed to sell medicines used by poor consumers.[8]

It was the combination of entwined professional and public
health moves, of the class tensions which had emphasized lower-
class use of the drug, which brought opium's inclusion in the 1868
Act. What was categorized as 'opium and all preparations of opium
or of poppies' was eventually placed in Part Two of the poisons
schedule. The proviso which included 'strychnine and all poisonous vegetable alkaloids and their salts' in Part One appeared
to cover morphine. It was not always interpreted in that way, and
preparations of morphine were added to Part Two in 1869. But
the decision over where opium was to go was not a straightforward one. The story of how and where this drug was included
in the Act, just because of its importance in all areas of society
at this time, showed up the weaknesses of the professional argument.

Two factors combined to limit the amount of restriction placed
on opium. The self-interest of the professional pharmacists was
in part responsible. While medical men, in particular those involved in the public health movement, were uniformly anxious
for stricter regulation of its sale, an objective consistent with their
general professional objective of creating a monopoly of prescribing, the pharmacists thought differently. They were anxious to
remove the sale of poisons from unqualified dealers, but did not
want to restrict the sale of opium to the extent that their own trade
in it would be affected. Humanitarianism clashed with professional self-interest. There was also the practical realization that
opium, in the absence of orthodox medical care, did have a large
part to play in the lives of the poor. Stringent restrictions on its
sale would only create an illicit market. The general shopkeeper
would be as important as before and professional control would
be undermined.

These considerations affected the changing place of opium in the deliberations on restriction and the draft Bills of the 1850s and 1860s. Strict control of the drug was proposed in the 1857 Sale of Poisons Bill. Opium, along with twenty-two other drugs, was to be kept under lock and key, to be sold only to persons of full age in the presence of a witness known to both retailer and purchaser, or on production of an official certificate (signed by a clergyman, doctor or G.P.) stating that the poison might be safely supplied. Its sale was to be recorded by the chemist. Medical opinion favoured this type of restriction, and Professor Taylor argued strongly for it in front of the House of Lords Committee on the Bill.[9] Even he had to modify his views when faced with the realities of opiate consumption. Recognizing the problem of small sales to working people, he conceded that the sale of penny-worths of laudanum should be allowed to continue, but only to adults, and on condition that the drug was drunk in the chemist's shop.

He had to admit that severe restriction was not practicable and that the drug was a special case. He, like the pharmacists, realized that 'a smuggled sale might go on' if its open sale was suddenly curtailed. Other professional workers agreed, in particular the pharmacists, who had most to lose in professional terms from such an eventuality. Jacob Bell, president of the Pharmaceutical Society, thought that the 1857 Bill might help control opium sales, 'but it would be almost impossible to carry it into effect in many country districts, where pennyworths of laudanum and opium are very often sold . . .' John Abraham and John Baker Edwards of the Liverpool Chemists' Association agreed. They were opposed to the scheduling of opium because they, like Taylor, believed that restriction would only produce a growth in illicit sales and the law would be impossible to enforce. Sales of the drug would remain with the back-street shopkeepers; opium would be sold, 'as it is sold now, by a low class of dealer throughout the villages in the country in defiance of the law'.[10]

Later drafts of the poison bill in the 1850s took this point. The version of 1859, for instance, proposed to exempt small quantities of opium and those dispensed on prescription from its re-quirements. Spencer Walpole who, as Home Secretary, was charged with introducing the Bill, explained the dual reason for this. 'If you put a difficulty in the way of giving it in small quantities to persons who desire it, you may interfere inconveniently with these requirements as well as with the trade of the chemist.'[11] Despite medical hostility to this limited concept of control – the Royal College of Physicians petitioned parliament urging that even small quantities of opium should be under the control of qualified people – it was generally accepted from this time onward that opium could not be rigidly controlled. The United Society's draft Bill of 1864, for instance, provided only that 'opium, its extract, and laudanum' should be properly labelled.[12]

Competing professional positions were shown at their clearest, however, in the struggle over the place of opium in the 1868 Pharmacy Act. Doctors and the public health men argued for further restrictions, while the pharmacists fought to limit control of the drug to a manageable level. The first draft of the Bill did provide for the regulation of opiate sales in Section 17, but only with labelling restrictions. By the time the measure was introduced in the Lords by Earl Granville on 19 May 1868, all mention of the drug had been dropped. No explanation of this was given at the time, but Elias Bremridge, the Pharmaceutical Society's Secretary, later told the Pharmacy Bill Committee of the General Medical Council that it had been dropped because of protests from within the profession – 'the promoters of the Bill received such strong representations from chemists residing principally in Cambridgeshire, Lincolnshire, and Norfolk, against interfering with their business – opium, as they stated, being one of their chief articles of trade – that the promoters felt compelled to strike opium out of Schedule A ...'.[13]

The passage of the Bill was therefore marked on the one hand by attempts to include the drug and even more severely to restrict its availability, on the other by pharmaceutical efforts to make regulation conform to their own professional interests. The medical profession used its political and parliamentary influence to this end. The Parliamentary Bills Committee of the British Medical Association meeting on 3 July came out strongly against the weak regulation of sale proposed by Section 17 and the 'very imperfect schedule of poisons'. The General Medical Council was more explicit. After a meeting of its Pharmacy Bill Committee with representatives of the Pharmaceutical Society on 11 July it voiced strong medical feeling that self-medication with opiates must end – 'the Committee were of the opinion that the statement that regulations as to the sale of opium would interfere with the trade profits of druggists in certain parts of England, constituted the strongest ground for inserting opium in the list of poisons'.[14]

Robert Lowe, later both Chancellor of the Exchequer and Home Secretary under Gladstone, took up the medical point of view in the Commons. He pointed out what he saw as the prime motive for the drug's non-appearance in the schedule: 'Perhaps because more profit is got out of the sale of this poison it is not proposed to deal with it.'[15] On 15 July, his amendment in committee added 'opium and all preparations of Poppies' to the Bill. This was later amended to 'opium and all preparations of opium or of poppies' by the Lords. Section 17 of the Bill in its final form provided for a two-part Schedule; poisons in the Second Part, including opium, were subject only to labelling restrictions. But Section 16 of the Act specifically excluded patent medicines, many opium-based, from its remit.

The Act was testimony to the force of professional strategies and to the conflict between medical and pharmaceutical interests. The controls it established on opium were marked by the contemporary belief in voluntary self-regulation and an absence of state intervention. The Privy Council Office had overall responsibility for the legislation and as such was the ancestor of the Home Office in present narcotics legislation; but real power and control resided with the Pharmaceutical Society. Despite its limited nature, however, the Act did have an immediate and notable effect. So far as mortality can be measured from the inadequate Registrar General's statistics, deaths from opium did indeed decline.[16] The opium death rate fell from 6.4 per million population in 1868 to 4.5 per million in 1869. After a decade, however, the rate once again climbed to over 5 per million and remained at that level, sometimes higher, until the early 1900s (Table 3, p. 275). By the end of the century, the general opium death rate was at roughly the level it had been before 1868. The number of children dying from opium overdoses was, however, permanently reduced. Among the under-five group, the death rate declined dramatically from 20.5 per million population between 1863 and 1867, to 12.7 per million in 1871. It remained at that level until the 1880s, when a further decline to between 6 and 7 per million took place. The decline in laudanum fatalities was particularly marked. But this was paralleled by an increase in the adult death rate from opium.

The death rate among those aged thirty-five and over showed an absolute increase on pre-1868 levels by the end of the century (Table 4, p. 276). The Act's effect on accidental and suicidal opiate deaths was also unremarkable. Although the accidental opiate death rate declined from its pre-restriction level of around 4 per million population, it remained until the 1890s at between 3 and 4 per million, not a notable decrease. Accidental poisonings remained the major cause of opiate fatalities, at least in the published figures. They still provided over 70 per cent of the general opium rate in the late 1870s. The Act was also ineffective in discouraging opiate suicides. The suicide rate from opium showed little variation until the 1890s. It remained at between 1 and 2 per million population until the late 1880s. Other methods of suicide were always more widely used, as the pre-1868 figures show. But opium remained responsible for a large proportion of poison suicides, and was not decisively displaced (by carbolic acid) from the top of the list until the 1890s.

The Act was not completely ineffective; and it is perhaps surprising that it is possible to trace direct results in terms of the decline in general and child death rates. For the Act often operated in practice rather more laxly than even its framers had intended. Despite the reservation of opium to professional control, general sales did continue to a limited extent. The Pharmaceutical Society itself even advocated an interpretation of the Act which made this possible. 'Preparations of opium' were distinguished from 'preparations containing opium'; only the former, defined as containing 1 per cent of opium or more, were included in the meaning of the Act.[17] Paregoric was, for instance, thus excluded; laudanum, Battley's Solution and other preparations included. This compromise in 1869 prevented some of the more obvious abuses of the Act – shopkeepers had sold lumps of opium in boxes labelled 'opiate mass' and claimed that, as patent medicines, they were not subject to control.[18] It satisfied trade interests and avoided the undermining of professional status which could have resulted from continuing open sales. Such sales did undoubtedly still proceed in some areas. Voluntary 'policing' by the Pharmaceutical Society's inspection was insufficient to fulfil the Act's purposes. The inspectors were given no powers of entry or rights to inspect business records or registers. At Ince in Lancashire, Emma Ashcroft, a patent-medicine vendor and drysalter, was prosecuted for selling laudanum in 1889 only after a child of nineteen months had died. She had been in business for twenty years.[19]

As with much legislation, the way the 1868 Act operated in practice was rather different from original legislative intentions. In many respects it made little difference. Certainly customers who could afford medical attention and obtained their opium on prescription suffered little hindrance. Proportions of opium-based prescriptions dispensed by pharmacists declined slightly, but were increasing again by the 1870s.[20] Direct over-the-counter sales to poorer customers were different only in that a pharmacist and not a general dealer was in charge, even though, as Dr Joyce's account of Rolvenden demonstrate (cited on p. 43), such consumers could suffer. Many of the features of the pre-1868 popular culture of opium remained undisturbed. Yet the long-term implications of the Act were significant. It established, at first albeit partially, that opium was a professional matter and that it must indeed be subject to some form of control. However laxly observed the regulations about the sale of opium were, however many exemptions proved acceptable in practice, a shift in attitude implicit in the public health/professional campaign had taken place and had received official legislative sanction.

11

The Patent Medicine Question

The 1868 Act was testimony to the influence which professional consolidation could have on the availability of narcotics. In one important respect, however, it was incomplete. Although the inclusion of patent medicines within poisons legislation had been one aim of both medical and pharmaceutical professions since the 1850s, such products were excluded from the Pharmacy Act.[1] The Parliamentary Bills Committee of the British Medical Association had lobbied for restrictions on patent medicines to be added, but Section 16 of the Act specifically excluded any 'making or dealing' in patent remedies. The question of patent medicines, in particular those based on opium, became a central concern of the continuing professional campaign regarding availability.

The first medicine Stamp Acts under which the government collected its licensing revenue had been passed in the eighteenth century. Duties on medicines were in fact first imposed in 1783; but the law as established throughout the nineteenth and early twentieth centuries and which required a licence to sell, or imposed a duty on the medicine sold, dated from three acts of 1802, 1804 and 1812. Few patent medicines which paid duty under the Acts actually deserved the name. Only in the seventeenth and eighteenth centuries had owners of medical formulae actually gone to the length of patenting them. After 1800, medicinal compounds were only rarely patented. Those which paid the government stamp were proprietary, rather than patented medicines. Revenue was nevertheless considerable. Around £200,000 annually was reckoned to be derived from medicine stamps in the early 1890s.[2]

Many contained opium in some form and some had a lengthy ancestry. Dover's Powder not only became a staple of popular consumption but was used also in medical practice. Daffy's Elixir, invented by the rector of Redmile in Leicestershire, was even older. It first came to public notice between 1660 and 1680.[3] As Chapter 9 has shown, the children's opiates, Godfrey's Cordial in particular, were mostly long-established.[4] There was no clear dividing line in the first half of the century between strictly 'medical' remedies and those used in self-medication, so patent medicines were often used in medical practice, or medical men made their own semi-patent remedies. Dover's Powder was widely used

Fig. 4. A chemist's recipe book of the 1800s, with chlorodyne, Godfrey's Cordial and laudanum (tinct opii) recipes listed together.

in hospital practice. Pharmacists made their own versions of Godfrey's and Atkinson's. Some patent preparations, Battley's Sedative Solution for instance, were incorporated within the Pharmacopoeia; its official name was liquor opii sedativus. Others were made by pharmacists aspiring to professional status. Peter Squire of Oxford Street produced Squire's Elixir (containing opium, camphor, cochineal, fennel-seeds, spirits of aniseed and tincture of snake-root) and later his own chlorodyne in competition with Collis Browne's.[5] The dividing line between 'medical' and 'non-medical' remedies was even less clear when medical men themselves were often involved in commercial activity.

The exclusion of patent medicines from control in 1868 was increasingly resented as establishing an area where doctors and pharmacists had little influence. The early public health legislation in the area of food and drugs continued this tendency. The 1875 Sale of Food and Drugs Act, for instance, specifically excluded proprietary or patent medicines from Section 27 of the Act, which made it an offence to sell an article falsely labelled.[6] Yet patent medicines appear to have been enjoying a vogue at the end of the century. To some extent this was a natural result of the provisions of the 1868 Act, which had made ordinary opium preparations that much more difficult to obtain. There was also a practical reason. In 1875, an Act had reduced the medicine licence duty and the number of vendors increased. Over twelve thousand licences were taken out in 1874; twenty thousand in 1895.[7]

There began in the 1880s a new professional campaign against open sale, this time concentrating on the issue of patent medicines. Press publicity was given to cases of chlorodyne addiction as early as 1880; the views of the developing anti-opium movement were also displayed in this direction.[8] Discussions took place between the Home Office, the Privy Council Office and interested bodies like the Pharmaceutical Society and the Institute of Chemistry in 1881 and 1882. It was hoped at this stage to establish that patent remedies did in fact come within the Act and that further legislation was therefore unnecessary. But a test case involving a solution of chloral sold without a poison label, and brought before a Hammersmith magistrate at this period, left the situation unclear. The professional bodies, both medical and pharmaceutical, were unanimous in demanding further restrictions on the sale of patent medicines, and they had the press and the government on their side.[9] A Patent Medicine Bill was introduced in 1884 which would have brought opiate-based patent medicines under the control of the 1868 Act, for any patent medicines containing a scheduled poison were to be sold only by a registered pharmacist. Pressure from the Society of Chemists and Druggists had ensured an added degree of freedom for the pharmaceutical profession. A pharmacist who sold a patent medicine unlawfully was not to be held responsible if he was unaware that it contained a scheduled poison.[10]

The chlorodyne issue

The 1884 Bill was unsuccessful, and patent medicines remained unrestricted.[11] In the next decade, the bulk of medical and pharmaceutical hostility was directed at one particular patent preparation. This was chlorodyne, most commonly associated with the name of Dr John Collis Browne. Collis Browne, a physician, had first used the preparation in 1848, while serving with the army in India. In 1854, while on leave in England, Collis Browne was asked to go to the village of Trimdon in County Durham to fight an outbreak of cholera. His 'chlorodyne' (the name he gave the preparation the following year) produced encouraging results. But it was not until Collis Browne left the army in 1856 and went into partnership with J. T. Davenport, a chemist practising in Great Russell Street, to whom he assigned the sole right to manufacture and market the compound, that Collis Browne's became widely known on the domestic market (Figure 5).[12]

Collis Browne's early presented an impressive list of conditions which chlorodyne was claimed to cure. 'Practical Instructions' were issued for the treatment of cholera and diarrhoea by the preparation; it was also recommended for 'coughs, colds, influenza, diarrhoea, stomach chills, colic, flatulence, bronchitis, croup, whooping-cough, neuralgia and rheumatism'.[13] Its commercial success was demonstrated by numerous attempts to find its exact formula; and to market rival chlorodynes. Chloroform and morphia were the main ingredients; the name chlorodyne was in fact made from the words 'chloroform' and 'anodyne'.[14] Rivals were soon on sale, since Collis Browne had not patented his preparation. Mr A. P. Towle communicated the formula of another chlorodyne to the *Chemist and Druggist* in 1859 and Towle's chlorodyne was commercially marketed. The advent of Freeman's chlorodyne (Figure 6) in the early 1860s was the occasion of an unsuccessful law suit brought by Collis Browne; and the ubiquitous Squire, too, was busy publicizing his own version.[15]

Collis Browne's was certainly suffering the penalties of success. The exact dimensions of its popularity are difficult to analyse. Its sales were large and advertising expenditure was high. In 1871, for instance, sales amounted to over £28,000 and advertising to over £4,000. But large sums expended on advertisements were a normal feature of the nineteenth-century patent medicine

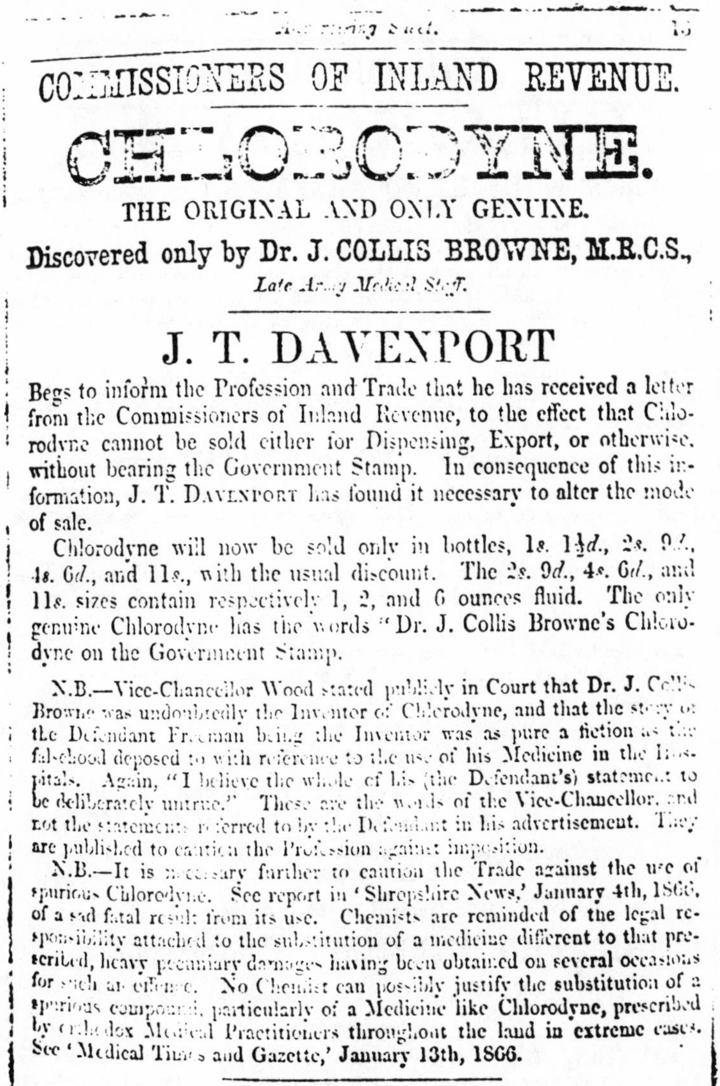

COMMISSIONERS OF INLAND REVENUE.

CHLORODYNE.

THE ORIGINAL AND ONLY GENUINE.

Discovered only by Dr. J. COLLIS BROWNE, M.R.C.S.,

Late Army Medical Staff.

J. T. DAVENPORT

Begs to inform the Profession and Trade that he has received a letter from the Commissioners of Inland Revenue, to the effect that Chlorodyne cannot be sold either for Dispensing, Export, or otherwise, without bearing the Government Stamp. In consequence of this information, J. T. DAVENPORT has found it necessary to alter the mode of sale.

Chlorodyne will now be sold only in bottles, 1s. 1½d., 2s. 9d., 4s. 6d., and 11s., with the usual discount. The 2s. 9d., 4s. 6d., and 11s. sizes contain respectively 1, 2, and 6 ounces fluid. The only genuine Chlorodyne has the words "Dr. J. Collis Browne's Chlorodyne" on the Government Stamp.

N.B.—Vice-Chancellor Wood stated publicly in Court that Dr. J. Collis Browne was undoubtedly the Inventor of Chlorodyne, and that the story of the Defendant Freeman being the Inventor was as pure a fiction as the falsehood deposed to with reference to the use of his Medicine in the Hospitals. Again, "I believe the whole of his (the Defendant's) statement to be deliberately untrue." These are the words of the Vice-Chancellor, and not the statements referred to by the Defendant in his advertisement. They are published to caution the Profession against imposition.

N.B.—It is necessary further to caution the Trade against the use of spurious Chlorodyne. See report in 'Shropshire News,' January 4th, 1866, of a sad fatal result from its use. Chemists are reminded of the legal responsibility attached to the substitution of a medicine different to that prescribed, heavy pecuniary damages having been obtained on several occasions for such an offence. No Chemist can possibly justify the substitution of a spurious compound, particularly of a Medicine like Chlorodyne, prescribed by orthodox Medical Practitioners throughout the land in extreme cases. See 'Medical Times and Gazette,' January 13th, 1866.

SOLE MANUFACTURER,

J. T. DAVENPORT, Pharmaceutist,
33, GREAT RUSSELL STREET, BLOOMSBURY.

Fig. 5. Dr Collis Browne's chlorodyne. The advertisement cautions the trade against the sale of 'spurious' chlorodynes.

THE ORIGINAL
CHLORODYNE,
Invented by RICHARD FREEMAN, Pharmaceutist,

Is allowed to be one of the greatest discoveries of the present century, and is largely employed by the most eminent Medical Men, in hospital and private practice, in all parts of the globe, and is justly considered to be a remedy of intrinsic value and of varied adaptability, possessing most valuable properties, and producing curative effects quite unequalled in the whole *materia medica*.

It is the only remedy of any use in Epidemic Cholera.—*Vide* EARL RUSSELL's *Letters to the Royal College of Physicians of London and to the Inventor*.

It holds the position as the BEST and CHEAPEST preparation.

It has been used in careful comparison with Dr. Collis Browne's Chlorodyne, and preferred to his. *Vide Affidavits of Eminent Physicians and Surgeons*.

It has effects peculiar to itself, and which are essentially different to those produced by the various deceptive and dangerous Compounds bearing the name of Chlorodyne.

See the Reports in 'Manchester Guardian,' December 30th, 1865, and 'Shropshire News,' January 4th, 1866, of the fatal result from the use of an imitation.

Sold by all Wholesale Druggists.

For Retail—½ oz., 1/1½; 1½ oz., 2/9 each.

For Dispensing—2 oz., 2/9; 4 oz., 4/6; 8 oz., 9/; 10 oz., 11/; and 20 oz., 20/

THE USUAL TRADE ALLOWANCE OFF THE ABOVE PRICES.

Manufactured by the Inventor,

RICHARD FREEMAN, Pharmaceutist,
70, KENNINGTON PARK ROAD, LONDON, S.

CAUTION.—The large sale, great success, and superior quality of FREEMAN'S ORIGINAL CHLORODYNE is the cause of the malicious libels so constantly published from interested motives by another maker of Chlorodyne. The Profession and the Trade are particularly urged not to be deceived by such false statements, but exercise their own judgment in the matter, and to buy no substitute for "The Original Chlorodyne."

Fig. 6. Freeman's chlorodyne. This advertisement attacks Collis Browne's product.

business – Holloway at the same period was spending £40,000–£50,000 a year in advertising his pills and taking a similar sum in profit.[16] Collis Browne's clearly had a long way to go before it joined the giants in the patent medicine world. Sales were, however, increasing – they brought in over £31,000 in 1891 (a modest 10–11 per cent increase in twenty years). Many of the earlier patent medicines – the soothing syrups in particular – had been developed in the north. Collis Browne's, as a relatively late arrival on the scene, gained the bulk of its sales from London and the southern part of England. More than half its sales came from this part of the country.[17]

There is no reason to suppose that all chlorodyne users were working-class, but the continuing cultural traditions of self-medication ensured that such patent medicines had considerable popular usage. In some instances, consumption was aided by the generosity of those further up the social scale. The Rev. W. R. Dawes, a country parson in Buckinghamshire, who treated with medicine 'his numerous gratuitous patients', wrote to Davenport in 1858 asking for fresh supplies: 'The trying weather lately having caused a large demand for this medicine, my stock is suddenly exhausted and I shall be particularly obliged by your sending me a *pint and half* of the Chlorodyne safely packed in a box by the *Oxford coach* ...'[18] Sarah Williams, the wife of an engine-room artificer at Portsmouth, who after her death in 1889 was reported to have been buying at least three bottles of chlorodyne a week from her local branch of Timothy Whites, was one instance of a poor consumer who took too much.[19]

Chlorodyne use and addiction was the central core of the medical campaign against patent medicines at this time. Unlike morphine, however, the use of the preparation was not consistently seen from a 'disease' point of view. It was largely outside the medical sphere of control. Chlorodyne use was seen more as a matter of availability and limitation of sale, and less as one of disease and treatment.[20] Medical men continued to be uneasy about the availability of patent medicines, chlorodyne in particular, after the failure of the 1884 Bill. Chlorodyne poisoning cases multiplied in the medical journals; and following the circulation of a memorandum asking for further legal controls on opium and morphine preparations by the chairman of the Parliamentary Bills Committee of the British Medical Association, to the Pharmaceutical and

Apothecaries Societies and the President of the General Medical Council in 1890, the attack on patent medicines and chlorodyne intensified.[21] Ernest Hart was editor of the *British Medical Journal* at this time, and it was his campaigning in that role and as Chairman of the British Medical Association's Parliamentary Bills Committee which brought action. Parliamentary questioning on the subject in 1891 evoked a non-committal response.[22]

In the same year, it was this Parliamentary Bills Committee which communicated with the Treasury Solicitor to ask him to institute prosecutions against chlorodyne and its manufacturer. The Treasury prosecution of J. T. Davenport in 1892 was successful in extending the 1868 Act to chlorodyne in particular and opiate-based patent medicines in general. Davenport was summoned before Mr Lushington at Bow Street Police Court to answer the charge that he had sold retail a mixture (chlorodyne) containing opium and chloroform without indicating the poisonous nature of the contents on the bottle. Davenport's defence was that the preparation was a patent one and hence exempt under Section 16 of the 1868 Act. Mr Lushington, however, took a stricter view of the term: a patent medicine he defined as one actually issued with a government patent rather than a remedy paying the medicine duty. The charge was held to be proved; and Davenport fined £5 with costs.[23] As a result chlorodyne and other patent medicines containing scheduled poisons had to be sold by a registered pharmacist and labelled 'poison'. The new policy was vigorously prosecuted and the council of the Pharmaceutical Society took action against offending dealers.[24]

It is difficult to estimate how far the professional 'scare' about expanding chlorodyne use was indeed justified. Chlorodyne was responsible for an increased number of deaths in the 1890s, even though actual death rates were steady. Collis Browne's sales, as its figures show, were not expanding rapidly; and the statistics of chlorodyne mortality may have to some extent mirrored public concern. For the highest mortality figures came after, not before, restriction.[25] Medical men to this extent magnified the 'problem' of chlorodyne use to justify their own control. Yet the 1892 decision certainly had a marked effect on the sale of chlorodyne. Collis Browne's sales figures were down by £6,200 in 1899 (around 20 per cent) from the 1891 level; and, at £25,000, were £3,000 lower than the total in 1871.[26] The campaign against patent medicines in general did not cease. Publications such as Health News's *Exposures of Quackery* (1895–6) devoted whole sections to 'chlorodyne, and other opiates and anodynes' and to the 'widespread system of home-drugging' which had resulted from the easy availability of opiate patent medicines.[27]

In America at the same time, the revelations of Samuel Hopkins Adams in *Collier's Magazine* were instrumental in the passage of a Federal Pure Food and Drugs Act in 1906.[28] But when the British Medical Association published its own famous investigations into the composition and profitability of patent medicines – *Secret Remedies* and *More Secret Remedies* in 1909 and 1912 – the talk was all of remedies once containing morphine or opium, but which had now dropped it from their formulae.[29] The investigations of the Privy Council Committee which considered the poisons schedule and reported in 1903 found just the same. Most of the children's soothing syrups no longer contained opium. Some cough mixtures - Kay's Linseed Compound, for instance, and Keatings' Cough Lozenges – still used it.[30] Others which had once included the drug now found commercial benefit in declaring that it was not present. Owbridge's Lung Tonic was one such; and Beecham's Cough Pills also declared that they did not contain opium. Liqufruita Medica guaranteed itself to be 'free of poison, laudanum, copper solution, cocaine, morphia, opium, chloral, calomel, paregoric, narcotics or preservatives ...'; it was basically a sugar solution. The frequency with which this type of claim was made on the wrapper was in itself testimony to the increasing alienation of the drug from popular, as much as from medical, usage.

PART SIX

The Professionals and Opium *c.* 1860 – 1900:
The Use of Opium and Its Alkaloids

12

Morphine and Its Hypodermic Use

Professional involvement in the question of opium use was not limited to the sale and availability of the drug. In the last few decades of the century doctors in particular became more closely involved in the way it was administered and used. Popular use of opium continued and the sale of 'non-medical' patent remedies was high, as the previous chapter has demonstrated. But the increased medical use of a new form of opium, its alkaloid, morphine, brought a closer medical concern both with hypodermic morphine-injecting addicts and, through them, with delineating new medical views of opium eating based on ideas of disease and treatment.[1] It is this involvement and the advent of the new hypodermic technology of administration which are considered in the following two chapters.

Although medical concern about hypodermic morphine use was only a feature of the last quarter of the nineteenth century, the isolation of morphine as the active principle of opium was made early in the century. Responsibility has traditionally been assigned to three men.[2] In 1803, Derosne, a French manufacturing chemist, produced a salt, his 'sel narcotique de Derosne'; this was the substance later known as narcotine, but it also contained some morphine. A year later, Armand Seguin read a paper before the Institut de France in which de described his isolation of the active principle of opium. His communication 'Sur l'opium' was not published until 1814. Meanwhile Frederick William Sertürner, a pharmacist of Einbeck in Hanover, working on Derosne's salt, had investigated the composition of opium more accurately than anyone before. He isolated a white crystalline substance which he found to be more powerful than opium. Calling the new substance 'morphium' after Morpheus, the god of sleep, he published details in the *Journal der Pharmazie*, in 1805, 1806 and 1811, although the significance of his breakthrough was not appreciated until he wrote again on the subject in 1816. In 1831, the Institut de France awarded him a substantial prize for 'having opened the way to important medical discoveries by his isolation of morphine and his exposition of its character'.

The isolation of morphine was part of a general systematization of remedies and discovery of alkaloids in line with the growth of toxicology as a science. Quinine, caffeine and strychnine were all isolated shortly after morphine. Other opium alkaloids were also discovered – narceine by Pelletier in 1832, and codeine by Robiquet in 1821 while examining a new process for obtaining morphine suggested by Dr William Gregory of Edinburgh. Morphine (sometimes still referred to as 'morphium') first became known in Britain in the early 1820s, in particular after publication of the English translation of Magendie's *Formulary for the Preparation and Mode of Employing Several New Remedies*.[3]

Morphine was manufactured on a commercial scale quite early on. It was produced by Thomas Morson, later a founder of the Pharmaceutical Society and one of its presidents. He had originally gone to Paris to train as a surgeon, and had picked up his pharmaceutical knowledge there. Morson took over a retail business in Farringdon Street on his return to England; and it was in the parlour behind the shop that morphine and other drugs were produced. Morson's first commercial morphine was produced in 1821, at about the time when Merck of Darmstadt also began production of wholesale morphine. The English variety sold at eighteen shillings per drachm, with the acetate and sulphate also selling at the same rate.[4] Macfarlan and Company of Edinburgh began to manufacture the alkaloid in the early 1830s, when Dr William Gregory (the son of James Gregory, of Gregory's Powder) devised a process for the production of morphia muriate. British opium collected by Mr Young in his initial experiments was used. The drug was later purified and more exact processes devised. In the early years of morphine production, Macfarlan's received opium from the London wholesale houses and returned them the muriate. The drug was still brown and formed a brown solution, for the process then used did not abstract the resin or colouring matter.

LIST

OF

New Chemical Preparations,

Employed as Medicines.

Sulph: Quinine.	...	40s. *per oz.*
Morphia.	... ...	18s. *per dram.*
Acetate of Morphia.	...	18s. *per do.*
Sulphate of Morphia.	...	18s *per do.*
Iodine.	... ...	7s. *per oz.*
Hydriodate of Potass.		9s. *per do.*
Strichnine.	... ...	25s. *per dram.*
Emetine.	... ...	10s. *per do.*
Brucine.	... ...	30s. *per do.*
Veratrine.	... ...	30s. *per do.*
Gentianine.	... ...	20s. *per do.*
Lupuline.		
Tr. of Lupuline.		
Tr. of Croton Tiglium.		
Oil of Croton Tiglium.		
Alchoholic Ext. of Nux Vomica.		
Extr. of Opium, deprived of Narcotine.		

T. MORSON.

65, *Fleet Market*, 1822.

Fig. 7. Thomas Morson's price list for 1822 showing some of his original morphine preparations.

When Macfarlan's produced a purer white substance, they had difficulty in persuading purchasers to accept it.[5]

There was little difficulty, however, in persuading medical men to use the new drug. The evidence suggests that by the late 1830s or early 1840s the drug was accepted, and often preferred, in medical practice. It found a place in the London Pharmacopoeia in 1836. By the end of the decade, medical men were discussing in some detail the dosage and form of administration they preferred. In King's College Hospital in London morphia was in routine use as early as 1840, mostly for sleeplessness. The stock of a Liverpool shop in the mid 1840s had seven ounces of morphia hydrochlorate (worth £3 4s. 10d.), two ounces of muriate and three and a half ounces of the acetate.[6]

The muriate, hydrochloride and acetate of morphia were all used in these early days; the two former preparations later became established as standard. Preparations such as bromide of morphine, bimeconate, morphine sulphate and morphine tartrate came on to the market later. The drug was recommended for almost as many conditions as opium. It was never even in these its early years administered solely by mouth. There were morphia suppositories – Dr Simpson's Morphia Suppositories, made of morphia and sugar of milk, dipped into white wax and lard plaster melted together, produced by Duncan and Flockhart of Edinburgh, were available. One surgeon was horrified to find that his dog had swallowed a batch of morphia suppositories made with mutton fat.[7] There was also the endermic use of the drug. Michael Ward, physician to the Manchester Infirmary, in his *Facts Establishing the Efficacy of the Opiate Friction* (1809), pointed out that opium through the skin had a different effect from opium administered by the mouth.[8] Opium was quite regularly used externally and the endermic method, whereby a section of the skin was removed, usually by blistering, and the powdered drug applied to the denuded spot, was particularly popular for morphine.[9] For instance, Mr Hanley, in Islington in 1865, was prescribed morphine hydrochloride in liquid form, also to be absorbed through the skin. He was to 'dip a little bit of soft lint into the lotion and lay it upon the most painful part occasionally'.[10]

At the same time as these perhaps crude and experimental attempts were being made to produce a more immediate drug effect, the hypodermic method of administration was developed.

Intravenous administration had a much longer history than hypodermic injection, which was a development of the mid-nineteenth century. Drugs, including opium, had been injected into both animals and man since the seventeenth century at least.[11] The method was desultorily used, and interest in it did not revive until the end of the eighteenth century. The new practice then of inoculation was a further stage in the evolution of the hypodermic method. Dr Lafargue of St Émilion, in a series of letters and papers in the 1830s, described his method for the inoculation of morphine. The point of a lancet was dipped into a solution of morphine, inserted horizontally beneath the epidermis, and allowed to remain there for a few seconds. But his researches eventually developed in a different direction. In the 1840s he was advocating the implantation of medicated pellets with a darning needle.[12]

Such methods were in a sense 'curtain raisers' for the true hypodermic method. Three men have the credit for its development: Dr Rynd of Dublin, Dr Alexander Wood of Edinburgh, and Dr Charles Hunter, a house surgeon at St George's Hospital in London. Rynd, working at the Meath Hospital and County Infirmary in Dublin in the 1840s, described how he had cured a female patient of neuralgia by introducing a solution of fifteen grains of acetate of morphine by four punctures of 'an instrument made for the purpose'. The patient recovered, as did others. Ten years later, Alexander Wood, apparently unaware of Rynd's earlier publication, described his own treatment of neuralgia. He had made several attempts to introduce morphia by means of puncture needles, and, in 1853, 'I procured one of the elegant little syringes constructed for the purpose by Mr Ferguson of Giltspur Street, London'. Experiments with the muriate on an elderly lady suffering from neuralgia proved the utility of the method. Papers published in 1855 and 1858 gave publicity to it.[13]

However, it was the use to which the new method was put by Dr Charles Hunter which revealed its true potential. Hunter had initially used Wood's hypodermic method purely as a local means of treating disease. Sepsis set in; Hunter was forced to use other sites for injection and quickly realized that the results obtained were as good. He became an advocate of the 'general therapeutic effect' of hypodermic medication, as distinct from the 'localization' supported by Wood and others.[14] What he called his 'ipodermic' (and later hypodermic) method led to a period of sustained and acrimonious debate between Wood and Hunter. Although the former had, in his 1855 paper, described the general effects of the method, it was Hunter who developed this aspect, while Wood clung tenuously to the belief that it was a local means of treating a local affection. The controversy created such interest that the Royal Medical and Chirurgical Society, to which Hunter had read a paper in 1865, appointed a committee to look into the question of hypodermic medication. Its report, published in 1867, came down strongly on Hunter's side. It concluded that 'no difference had been observed in the effects of a drug subcutaneously injected, whether it be introduced near to, or at a distance from the part affected'. Belief in the localization theory lingered on, but Hunter's method was more generally accepted.[15]

He had recommended the hypodermic use of morphine for its certainty in action and for more rapid absorption. Morphia injections he advocated as of benefit in melancholia, mania and delirium tremens, where it did away with the necessity for restraint. It was useful for chorea, puerperal convulsions, peritonitis, ague, uterine pain, tetanus, rheumatism and incurable diseases such as cancer. There were others in the medical profession as enthusiastic, but no one perhaps more so than Dr Francis Anstie. Anstie was editor of the *Practitioner* from its foundation in 1868 until his death in 1873 and his concern about working-class and opium use has already been mentioned. His particular interests lay in the areas of alcohol and neuralgia (on which he wrote sections for Dr Russell Reynolds's *System of Medicine*) as well as with opiates. His determined advocacy of new and apparently better methods was representative of that section of the medical profession which wished to develop more scientific, more 'professional' means of treatment, to elevate the status and develop the expertise of doctors as a body. In his opening remarks in the first issue of the new journal, he drew attention to the lack of proper analysis of remedies and the isolation of more exact means of treating disease.[16]

Anstie was correct in his belief that if the profession was to establish itself as such, and remain superior to and distinct from the mass of quacks, herbalists, patent-medicine vendors and manufacturers, it had to develop its own exclusive expertise, as well as a more scientific and exact means of treating disease. It was significant, then, that Anstie's warmest praise was reserved in the early years of the journal for the hypodermic method, and for its use with morphia in particular. His article of 1868, 'The hypodermic injection of remedies', marked the high point of unquestioning acceptance – 'of *danger*', he wrote

> there is *absolutely none* ... The advantages of the hypodermic injection of morphia over its administration by the mouth are immense ... the majority of the unpleasant symptoms which opiates can produce are entirely absent ... it is certainly the fact that there is far less tendency with hypodermic than with gastric medication to rapid and large increase of the dose, when morphia is used for a long time together.[17]

In this, Anstie was at one with the Committee on Hypodermic Injection which had recommended the method specifically for confirmed opium eaters, since smaller doses than those previously taken by mouth were requisite. In the late 1860s the group of 'new men' who formed a distinct medical group round Anstie were enthusiastic about the 'new remedy', hypodermic morphine. Clifford Allbutt, later Regius Professor of Physic at Cambridge and a noted writer on addiction, recommended the use of morphia to treat heart disease, although opium was generally forbidden in that type of condition. He was also using it to treat dyspepsia and 'hysteria'. There was much interest in and excitement about the new method. Hypodermic injections of morphia and aconite were reported in use for convulsions; there were morphia injections for chorea. Dr John Constable described how he had cured a case of hiccoughs by the subcutaneous method.[18]

Doctors were engaged in a more complex process than they realized. Advancing the barriers of scientific discovery, analysing and utilizing new and apparently safer or more reliable methods, they were at the same time involved in the process of establishing their own professional expertise at the expense of 'non-scientific', harmful or unreliable remedies. Enthusiasm for hypodermic morphine was generally accompanied by a denigration of opium; the 'medical' remedy was seen as more effective. But the profession was also creating its own problem by the advocacy of hypodermic usage, and it was not long before the first warnings of the increased incidence of addiction began to appear. The most influential in English medical circles was that of Clifford Allbutt in 1870.

Allbutt expressed the progress of his doubts in the *Practitioner*, in particular the case of nine of his patients who seemed as far from cure as ever despite the incessant and prolonged use of hypodermic morphia. 'Gradually ... the conviction began to force itself upon my notice, that injections of morphia, though free from the ordinary evils of opium eating, might, nevertheless, create the same artificial want and gain credit for assuaging a restlessness and depression of which it was itself the cause.'[19] He was not the first to draw attention to this attendant possibility, and warnings had been published as early as 1864.[20] Allbutt's warning was initially not generally accepted in the profession.[21] Even Anstie himself was unwilling to abandon the benefits of morphia because of the danger of addiction. He was in favour of a form of maintenance prescribing, of controlled morphine addiction on a lower dosage: 'Granting fully that we have ... a fully formed morphia-habit, difficult or impossible to abandon, it does not appear that this is any evil, under the circumstances.'[22] In hospital and general practice, the 1870s marked no particular dividing line; doctors still wrote enthusiastically to the medical journals of the good results they had obtained by using hypodermic morphine.

Yet there was a dawning realization that morphine injections on a repeated basis could have attendant dangers. Reports of the utility of the method were tinged with a certain wariness, in particular as details of the abuse of the drug on the continent and in America began to filter through. It was on the continent, too, that concern and a more exact definition of morphine addiction crystallized. Dr E. Levinstein of Berlin published in 1877 *Die Morphiumsucht nach Eigenen Beobachtungen*, translated into English the following year as *Morbid Craving for Morphia* (1878).[23] Levinstein's work was the first all-embracing analysis of the condition of morphine addiction to reach the English medical profession. (Dr Calvet had published an *Essai sur le Morphinisme aigu et chronique* in Paris in 1876 but this appears to have made no impact in Britain.) Levinstein's book was based on his own experiences in the institutional treatment of addiction in Berlin, and was instrumental in defining 'morphinism' as a separate condition or disease. As Levinstein himself remarked, others had seen it as 'Morphinismus', 'Morphia-delirium' or 'Morphia evil'. He was the first to define it as a disease with a similarity to dipsomania, although not a mental illness. Levinstein still saw addiction as a human passion 'such as smoking, gambling, greediness for profit, sexual excesses, etc. . . .'.

Disease theories were developing in many areas at this time; the elaboration of disease theories of narcotic addiction and the importance of Levinstein's work in this respect will be discussed in the following chapter. What was also important for the English medical profession, however, apart from the ideas contained in the book, was the interest in the subject which it stimulated. The 1878 book was widely reviewed and discussed. In 1879 came a request from Dr H. H. Kane of New York, anxious for information about British doctors' use of hypodermic morphia. He was particularly interested to learn if any cases of opium habit had been contracted in this way. His book, *The Hypodermic Injection of Morphia. Its History, Advantages and Dangers* (1880), was based on the experience of British as well as American physicians.[24] The work of another German expert, Dr H. Obersteiner, was published in the newly established *Brain*; and continental doctors were crowding thick and fast into this newly opened medical field.[25] British doctors themselves were increasingly aware of morphine addiction. Case histories which had appeared sporadically in the medical press in the 1870s were, by the end of the decade, greatly increased in quantity and prominence.[26]

A report on chloral produced by the Clinical Society of London in 1880 drew attention to the possibility of misuse not only of that drug, but of narcotics in general. The committee's report was in fact neutral as to the supposed deleterious effects of the long-continued use of chloral. But its publication was the occasion for comment on the apparent increase in addiction to all forms of narcotics, chlorodyne and morphine in particular. The dangers of hypodermic use were highlighted; there was a contribution in *The Times* from an addict who had re-used his original morphine prescription again and again.[27] The death of Mr Edward Amphlett, a nephew of Baron Amphlett and assistant surgeon at Charing Cross Hospital, who was revealed at the inquest in 1880 to have been accustomed for years to take chloral and morphia, confirmed fears of increased use.[28] In the Commons, Lord Randolph Churchill significantly compared Gladstone's oratory on Home Rule to 'the taking of morphia! The sensations . . . are transcendent; but the recovery is bitter beyond all experience . . .'[29]

Churchill's views were echoed in the medical presentation of morphine addiction. Dr Seymour Sharkey wrote on the treatment of 'morphia habitués', citing a case of his, a city manager, whose business gave him the facilities for getting as much morphia as he pleased and who had used the drug over a seventeen-year period. Sharkey later expanded, and to a certain extent sensationalized, his views in an article on 'Morphinomania' in the *Nineteenth Century* in 1887.[30] In 1889, Dr Foot led an extensive discussion of morphinism in a meeting of the Irish Royal Academy of Medicine. Ascribing a five-fold origin to the habit – for relief of pain, insomnia, melancholia, curiosity and imitation – he recognized that the possibility of cure was dependent on the duration of the habit, the persistence or not of the exciting cause and the physical or nervous constitution of the patient.[31]

In the 1880s doctors were as busy elaborating the dimensions of morphinism and delineating the outlines of the typical morphia habitué as they had once been in analysing those conditions where hypodermic usage was invaluable. Case histories of morphine addicts to a great extent replaced studies of morphine use in the medical journals. Continental and American influence was still noticeable. Dr Albrecht Erlenmeyer's work on morphine addiction, published originally in Germany in 1879, became known in its English version at the end of the 1880s.[32] The most persistent 'outside' influence on British medical thinking on morphine addiction towards the end of the century was the work of Dr Oscar Jennings. Jennings, an ex-morphine addict himself, was English, but the bulk of his working experience, and case histories, came from France. His ideas on the treatment of addiction led him into much controversy, yet the sheer volume of his published work – in books like *On the Cure of the Morphia Habit* (1890), *The Morphia Habit and its Voluntary Renunciation* (1909), *The Re-education of Self-control in the Treatment of the Morphia Habit* (1909), numerous articles and contributions to journals and conferences – made his name a force to be reckoned with.[33]

Well-defined views were held on the origin and incidence of the disease. Most accepted a stereotype whereby morphine addiction was vastly increased and increasing, where many addicts had acquired the habit through original lax medical prescription and through the eventual self-administration of the drug. Women were said to be peculiarly susceptible to morphinism; and not a few doctors recognized that the medical profession itself was also

highly prone to addiction. 'Morphinomania,' Dr H. C. Drury told
the medical section of the Irish Royal Academy in March 1899,
'is increasing with terrible rapidity and spreading with fearful
swiftness.' The 'recourse to injections under the skin' was according to the *Lancet* in 1882 'becoming general', while Dr S. A. K.
Strahan, physician to the Northampton County Asylum, agreed.
The 'vicious habit' was 'undoubtedly a growing disease'.[34] The
greatly increased general number of case histories and comments
on the subject gave substance to a feeling that an epidemic was
threatening.

Medical susceptibility to morphine addiction was established.
Drury, for instance, thought that morphinomania was particularly
prevalent among the medical profession, and a standard medical
text like Sir William Osler's *The Principles and Practice of Medicine*
(1894) saw doctors forming one of the main classes of addicts.[35]
Conventional ideas about the weakness of the female sex were also
soon linked with the spread of morphine use. As the *Lancet* put
it, 'Given a member of the weaker sex of the upper or middle class,
enfeebled by a long illness, but selfishly fond of pleasure, and determined to purchase it at any cost, there are the syringe, the
bottle, and the measure invitingly to hand, and all so small as to
be easily concealed, even from the eye of prying domestics.' Most
medical writings on the subject were united in seeing women peculiarly at risk.[36] Female susceptibility was linked with the iatrogenic
origin of most morphine addiction, and also with the idea of self-
medication. The apparent willingness of practitioners to hand over
control of injection either to a nurse or to the patient herself was
stressed, and this usurpation of the professional role of the doctor
was a continuing theme in discussions of morphine addiction. Dr
Macnaughton Jones told the British Gynaecological Society in
1895 that no patient should be allowed to inject herself. Levinstein, too, attributed the spread of the disease to the carelessness
of medical men in allowing patients to inject.[37]

These questions of the amount of increased usage of the drug
(and its hypodermic usage in particular), the numbers of addicts
at this period, and their social class and gender badly need more
extended examination if the reality of the picture presented in the
medical journals is to be assessed. In certain respects, it is clear that
the medical profession was myopically exaggerating the dimensions of a situation it had helped create. How much morphine

was actually being used in England at this time is difficult to estimate. To arrive at any picture of overall home consumption of morphine is almost impossible. Duty on imported opium ceased in 1860 and no actual 'home consumption' figures are available after that date. Estimates of home consumption of all narcotics, including morphine, after 1860 can only be obtained by subtracting the amount exported from that imported. This is an uncertain method of assessing anything but the most general trends in overall consumption. These moved upward for the first fifteen years after the abolition of duty in 1860, but decreased between the mid 1870s and the 1890s.[38] General trends reveal little about the production and home consumption of domestic morphine. Morphine was not separately incorporated into the trade statistics until 1911 (and then largely because of the demands of the 1911 Hague Convention for the collection and production of morphine and cocaine statistics). Until this date, it was included in the 'drugs, unenumerated' section and measured only in terms of financial value. The trade statistics are of little direct value in an examination of morphine production. Yet there was a widening post-1860 gap between imports and exports. This strongly suggests that much of the imported drug was being used to make morphine, since even the best Turkey opium would yield only around 10 per cent morphine. The general trend of home consumption also bore a strong relation to the business cycle. The connection with the onset of the 'Great Depression' of the 1870s was particularly marked, and consumption appears to have declined. Fluctuations like this again suggest a connection with the overall fortunes of the morphine industry.

Yet how much morphine Thomas Morson and Son, J. and F. Macfarlan and T. and H. Smith in Edinburgh were actually producing and exporting at this time remains uncertain. Wholesale business records show that morphine was popular, but no more so than other opium preparations and derivatives. The Society of Apothecaries for instance, one of the major wholesaling organizations, was producing large quantities of morphine preparations in the 1860s, but fewer a decade later. Yet the importance of morphine should perhaps not be overemphasized or singled out. The Society was still making large quantities of other opium preparations, too – it had twenty-six on its laboratory list in 1871. There were thirteen batches of paregoric, ten of laudanum, nine of powdered opium, and also of gall and opium ointment. Morphine at this wholesale level was only a part of the whole spectrum of opiate use.[39]

This is also the picture which emerges of 'grass-roots' usage in the second half of the century. In everyday medical and pharmaceutical practice morphine was in increased use. But there was nothing like the epidemic of rising consumption which the medical accounts suggested. Nor was everyday medical practice a matter of hypodermic injection alone. Morphine was used in many varied forms and there is little evidence of extensive self-administration of the hypodermic syringe. The evidence of prescription books shows that morphine was in quite regular use in the second half of the century, but that dispensing of the drug was not rapidly escalating. An Islington pharmacist, for instance, dispensed fifty-five morphine prescriptions in 1855 (from a total of 378), or 14.5 per cent of the whole number of opium-based remedies. By 1865, the number had risen to sixty-four (out of 316), or 20 per cent. But figures in 1875 and 1885 were lower.[40] Re-dispensing must be a matter of conjecture, since chemists noted only new prescriptions and did not re-enter a copy each time an old prescription was dispensed. Clearly, however, the picture of morphine prescribing at the level of general practice differed from the conventional stereotype. Doctors were likely to administer hypodermic injection themselves either in the surgery or on home visits. Yet if the self-injection which the medical accounts postulated were reality, some of it would have come to light through the dispensing of doctors' prescriptions by pharmacists. There is little sign of it. The poisons register for an Eastbourne pharmacist's practice, giving details of transactions under the Pharmacy Act in the 1880s and early 1890s, shows entries for morphia and ipecacuanha lozenges for cough, but only one entry in a six-year period between 1887 and 1893 for sol. morph. hypo, or hypodermic morphia.[41] Nevertheless cases where the hypodermic drug was recklessly prescribed are not hard to find. Alfred Allan, given hypodermic morphia 'very frequently' in King's College Hospital, was discharged in July 1870, partly at his own wish, partly because the 'Sisters got tired of him'.[42]

Even quite limited administration of the drug in this way, in unwise quantities or on an extended basis, could have resulted in a serious escalation of addict numbers. But there is little evidence that there were large numbers of morphine addicts in the late nineteenth century. One surprising omission in the welter of discussions on treatment methods, the origin of addiction and the characteristics of the addict was any serious consideration of how many of them there really were. It is only through examination of numbers of addicts admitted for treatment that some estimate can be made. An inebriates' home or a lunatic asylum were the two possibilities, and clearly only those whose habit was out of control would be admitted there. As Dr Robert Armstrong-Jones pointed out in 1902, it was difficult on that basis to calculate how large the class of addicts really was, since 'only the repentant sinner visits the consulting room'. Repentance must have been limited; for the numbers of admitted addicts were always very small. Jones himself reported eight admitted to the Claybury Asylum by 1902 (within an unspecified period). Four of these were taking morphia hypodermically and one by mouth; the others took opium in various forms. At Bethlem Royal Hospital, few addicts were admitted. There were only nine cases between 1857 and 1893, two of these taking morphia.[43] More cases were admitted to inebriates' homes. The Dalrymple Home at Rickmansworth took in addicts as well as alcoholics. Between 1883 and 1914, one hundred and seventeen drug cases had been admitted. Forty-six of these were taking morphia and fifteen both morphia and cocaine, a rate of admission of approximately two addicts a year.[44]

There were few signs of hypodermic usage of epidemic proportions here. Dr Armstrong-Jones was of the opinion that, for every case admitted to an asylum, there were probably scores outside with the habit whose mental and moral state was on the borderline of insanity. Yet he gave no evidence to support his assertion; and the low level of admissions, if not a guide to the general morphine addict population, at least indicated that only a small number were unable to lead some form of active life. Nor did the 'female' emphasis in medical writing bear much relation to reality. Prescription books show that as many men as women were initially prescribed morphine (although this does not take into account the possible sex bias of re-dispensing). Morphine was undoubtedly popular in the treatment of specifically female complaints – for period pains, in pregnancy and during labour – and also for those ailments such as neuralgia, sleeplessness and 'nerves' in general, which were considered to have a hysterical origin and so to be particularly common among female patients. There were well-known female addicts like G. B. Shaw's actress friend Janet Achurch.[45] Yet Jones's own case histories of 1902 were evenly divided between male and female; and whereas three of the four males used hypodermic morphia, only one of the females did so. The morphia cases admitted to Bethlem were all male.

The identifiable hypodermic morphine-using addict population at this date in fact appears to have had a medical or professional middle-class bias. There was no morphine-using drug sub-culture to parallel the beginnings of self-conscious recreational use of other drugs like cannabis and cocaine described in Chapter 16. Like the disease theory formulated to encompass addiction, the focus of morphine injection was very much a professional one. Virgil Eaton, in a study of opiate dispensing in Boston in the late 1880s, found the lowest proportion of morphine dispensed in the poorer quarters of the town. In England, too, morphia was always the more expensive drug and opportunities for addiction more easily available to better-off patients.[46] There undoubtedly was addiction to hypodermic morphine; and from this time forward hypodermic use of the drug was, in medical eyes, the major part of the 'problem' of opium use. Nevertheless part of the contemporary medical stereotype of the incidence and nature of the practice remains unproven. It is probable that, in numerical terms alone, morphine addicts bore no comparison to those dependent on opium. Much opiate consumption had always been outside the medical ambit of control, whereas morphine had always been primarily a 'medical' drug. The profession, by its enthusiastic advocacy of a new and more 'scientific' remedy and method, had itself contributed to an increase in addiction. The new technology of morphine use – the hypodermic method – did indeed create new objective problems in the use of the drug. The drug effect was more immediate, and smaller doses had a greater effect. But the profession showed a clear social bias in singling out this form of usage when there were still far larger numbers of consumers taking oral opium. The quite small numbers of morphine addicts who happened to be obvious to the profession assumed the dimensions of a pressing problem – at a time when, as general consumption and mortality data indicate, usage and addiction to opium in general was tending to decline, not increase.

13

The Ideology of Opium:
Opium Eating as a Disease

Morphine use and the problem, as medically defined, of hypodermic self-administration were closely connected with the medical elaboration of a disease view of addiction. Addiction is now defined as an illness because doctors have categorized it thus (current medical definitions of addiction or 'dependence' are described by Griffith Edwards in the Appendix). This was a process which had its origins in the last quarter of the nineteenth century. Disease entities were being established in definitely recognizable physical conditions such as typhoid and cholera. The belief in scientific progress encouraged medical intervention in less definable conditions. The post-Darwinian revolution in scientific thinking encouraged the re-classification of conditions with a large social or economic element in them on strictly biological lines. From one point of view, disease theories were part of late Victorian 'progress', a step forward from the moral condemnation of opium eating to the scientific elaboration of disease views. But such views were never, however, scientifically autonomous. Their putative objectivity disguised class and moral concerns which precluded a wider understanding of the social and cultural roots of opium use.[1]

De Quincey's *Confessions* and the Earl of Mar case have already indicated that such earlier medical discussions of addiction did not concentrate on the elaboration of its theoretical background or on the condition as an exclusively medical one.[2] Doctors were still very much on the periphery of the condition, not in control of it. It was the addict and not the doctor who defined the terms of the relationship. Doctors did treat opium eating in the early decades of the century, but not in a very systematic way.

Some doctors gave alcohol, reversing the traditional treatment for delirium tremens, which required opium; there were reports of bread pills soaked in poppy liquor and of maintenance on a lower dose. In many respects, however, the doctor acted very much upon the patient's wish. Some medical men reported instances of quite huge doses of opium regularly taken without considering it their prerogative to intervene. In other cases, the doctor was called in only to treat disturbing symptoms, not to rid the opium eater of the condition itself.[3] Decisions on treatment and medical intervention were, even in the middle of the century, often very much up to the patient, not the doctor.[4]

But in the last quarter of the century, medical men moved to the centre of discussions on the whole nature of opium-eating. As the discussion of hypodermic morphine has shown, the pioneers in this respect were mostly French and German; the European influence on disease theories was initially strong. The work of Levinstein and Erlenmeyer was known soon after publication in English medical circles. English specialists continued to take an interest in the reactions and investigations of their French and German counterparts. Perhaps more significantly for later developments, and a foretaste of the appraisal of American practice in the 1916–26 period, was the strong American influence which emerged around the turn of the century. America had a large 'drug problem' and works dealing specifically with drug addiction *per se*, as opposed to drink with drugs as a secondary subject, were first extensively published there. T. D. Crothers' *Morphinism and Narcomanias from Other Drugs* (1902) and J. B. Mattison's *The Mattison Method in Morphinism, A Modern and Humane Treatment of the Morphin Disease* (1902) joined Dr H. H. Kane's earlier work and the increasing notice being paid to American practice and legislative control of narcotic addiction.[5]

English experts and specialists were not, however, lacking. Most notable in the early period was the work of Dr Norman Kerr. Kerr, a member and at one stage chairman of the British Medical Association's Inebriates Legislation Committee, was closely involved in moves to secure the compulsory detention of alcoholic inebriates, which never, however, achieved complete success. His interest in narcotic addiction was an offshoot of his prime concern for alcoholic inebriety. Kerr's *Inebriety, Its Etiology, Pathology, Treatment and Jurisprudence* (1888) and his *Inebriety and*

Narcomania were important in defining an English version of disease theories.[6] Kerr was also instrumental in setting up the main debating forum in which medical elaboration of such theories took place. In 1876 he joined with a group of doctors in forming the Society for Promoting Legislation for the Control and Cure of Habitual Drunkards, of which he was elected president. In 1884 the Society, which had helped to press for the passing of the 1878 Habitual Drunkards Act, changed its title and re-emerged as the Society for the Study and Cure of Inebriety. Such early optimism proving unfounded, from 1887 the Society renamed itself as the Society for the Study of Inebriety. Its proceedings, later the *British Journal of Inebriety*, provided an arena for debate and for elaboration of disease theories; the Society's establishment emphasized the increasingly specialized nature of the whole question of addiction.

It was indeed a medical 'growth area' in the last decades of the century. No textbook was complete without its section on the 'morphia habit', 'morphinism' or 'acute and chronic poisoning by opium' (replacing the sections in earlier texts which had dealt with acute poisoning alone).[7] Addiction was a new medical specialism; and there were plenty of doctors willing to acquire and demonstrate the expertise. Jennings' numerous works derived in large part from his experience in practice in France (he was Paris correspondent of the *Lancet* for many years). There were medical experts in England, too, whose discussions were based on English practice. Clifford Allbutt, once the advocate of hypodermic morphine, was most prominent, along with the group of medical men he gathered round him, Humphrey Rolleston and W. E. Dixon most notably. Arthur Gamgee, Emeritus Professor of Physiology at Manchester University, Sir Dyce Duckworth of Bart's and Harrington Sainsbury, Senior Physician at the Royal Free, were important among the expanding numbers of specialists in the early 1900s. Directors of nursing and inebriates' homes and those doctors connected with lunatic asylums also figured largely at this time. Dr C. A. McBride, head of the Norwood Sanatorium, which specialized in alcohol and drug habits, wrote *The Modern Treatment of Alcoholism and Drug Narcotism* (1910); Sir Robert Armstrong-Jones, medical director of Claybury Asylum, Sir James Crichton-Miller, Lord Chancellor's Visitor in Lunacy, and Dr Thomas Clouston of the West Riding Lunatic Asylum also produced weighty contributions. The establishment of another 'expert' discipline was further confirmation of the expansion of the profession.

'Disease' was generally defined in terms of deviation from the normal. A hybrid disease theory emerged in which the old moral view of opium eating was re-formulated in 'scientific' form, where social factors were ignored in favour of explanations in terms of individual personality and biological determination. Most medical texts recognized that the majority of the addict case histories they cited were iatrogenic in origin. Medical administration of the drug, or self-administration by a patient unwisely given control of the hypodermic needle for an original painful condition, was a prime cause of addiction.[8] The physical dimensions of the disease were mentioned. Benjamin Richardson, Weir Mitchell and others were experimenting with opium (pigeons were in common use) to establish its effects on the human organism. The phenomenon of tolerance was recognized and commented on, along with the allied symptoms of withdrawal.[9] Levinstein's description of abstinence symptoms was particularly detailed, for, as he noted, 'although persons who suffer from morbid craving for morphia show different symptoms, some of them beginning to feel the effects of the poison after using it for several months, while others enjoy comparatively good health for years together, there is no difference between them as regards the consequences upon the partial or entire withdrawal of the narcotic drug.[10] His description of the restlessness, perspiration, palpitations and profound physical disturbance of the withdrawal period was particularly compelling.

Yet the straightforward physical side of addiction took increasingly second place to a strong psychological emphasis. Disease was defined not so much in physical as in mental terms. It was, according to Crichton-Miller, 'organismal and psychical', but the latter was generally of more interest. The two-fold distinction applicable to morphine addicts emphasized the difference. The morphinist wanted to be cured and would assist in a planned withdrawal of the drug; the morphinomaniac did not really want to be cured and had therefore to be treated as a lunatic. In the former, the habit was under control; in the latter, the craving was irresistible. Morphinomania was of most interest to the specialists, but in England the concept also formed part of the all-embracing analysis of 'inebriety'. The 'morphine disease' was less an entity in its own right, which it more definitely was in the specialist texts of continental origin. In England it was part of a more general consideration of alcohol, in which narcotic addiction formed a subsidiary part. Diffusion of the concept of inebriety owed much to the work of Norman Kerr and the Society for the Study of Inebriety. Its application to narcotic addiction was an offshoot of their work to apply medical criteria to what had previously been regarded as much a social problem as a vice. The Habitual Drunkards Act of 1878, confirmed and extended by the Inebriates Act ten years later, had established the beginnings of a medical framework and treatment structure. In less concrete terms, the work of the Society and of the British Medical Association committee had laid the foundations for a disease view of alcoholism. Narcotic addiction was caught up in the process, for, as Kerr explained, inebriety, 'an undoubted disease, a functional neurosis', could be classified with reference to the intoxicating agent. 'We thus have alcohol, opium, chloral, chloroform, ether, chlorodyne, and other forms of the disease.' Continental terminology was incorporated in the term – alcoholomania, opiomania, morphinomania, chloralomania and chlorodynomania were, Kerr told the Colonial and International Congress on Inebriety in 1887, all variants of this disease.[11]

The connection between alcohol and opium owed much to historic precedent, for in medical and social terms the two had long been linked. But the linking of opium with alcohol in the supposedly scientific concept of 'inebriety' meant that the drug, as much as alcohol, was viewed very much in the context of the temperance views which informed the work of medical men in this field. In England, the temperance and prohibitionist movement so dominated discussion of the drink problem that true scientific studies of alcoholism took place in the nineteenth century only on the continent.[12] It was perhaps significant in this connection that the toast at the first meeting of the Society for the Study of Inebriety should have been to 'The Temperance Organizations'. There were strong organizational links between the medical specialists in inebriety and morphinomania and the temperance movement. The connection with the developing anti-opium movement, campaigning on a primarily moral platform against Britain's involvement in the Indian opium trade with China, was equally marked. Many of the growing group of medical specialists moved easily between temperance, anti-opium and medical organizations studying inebriety. The moral and often absolutist views of the anti-opium movement were not transported wholesale into the medical arena. But there was considerable cross-fertilization. The organizational and conceptual links between the two will be more fully discussed in the following chapter. Specialists like Kerr recognized that there were difficulties in equating alcoholic with narcotic inebriety; organic lesions were, for instance, rare in the latter. But the temperance and anti-opium connection was a strong influence on the emergence of a hybrid medical and moral theory.

Despite the wish to move from the dark ages, when inebriates were (according to Kerr) 'vicious and depraved sinners', medical specialists in the subject found it difficult to accommodate the element of free will still apparent. Inebriety appeared to a great extent self-induced. In fact Dr Hill Gibson, giving a paper on 'Inebriety and Volition' to one of the first meetings of the S.S.I., could still conclude, against the medical view, that the condition was 'not a physical disease, but a moral vice'.[13] Moral values were inserted into this apparently 'natural' and 'autonomous' disease entity. Addiction, clearly not simply a physical disease entity, was a 'disease of the will'. It was disease *and* vice. The moral weakness of the patient was an important element in causation; the disease was defined in terms of 'moral bankruptcy', 'a form of moral insanity', terms deriving from similar formulations in insanity. According to Dr Thomas Clouston, both morphine addiction and alcoholism were the product of 'diseased cravings and paralysed control' – a paralysed control over a craving for drink, or opium, or cocaine, could be a disease as much as suicidal melancholia, he wrote.[14] Moral judgements were given some form of spurious scientific respectability simply by being transferred to a medical context. The moral emphasis in causation meant that symptoms were described in terms of personal responsibility, too. It was not the physical or even the mental dimensions of disease which were stressed, but the personal defect of the addict. Allbutt considered that 'plausibility and disorderliness' were symptomatic of the earlier stages. There was an utter disregard of time and no standards of truthfulness.[15]

This strong moral component ensured a disease theory which was individually oriented, where the addict was responsible for a condition which was somehow also the proper province for medical intervention. Opium eating was medicalized; but failure to achieve cure was a failure of personal responsibility, not medical science. Many of the specialists, Jennings perhaps most notably, placed great emphasis on the cultivation of self-control as part of the treatment regime. Health was equated with self-discipline. It was the 'voluntary renunciation' of the morphia habit and the 're-education of self-control' which were important. The will of the patient to be cured (already expressed in the morphinist/ morphinomaniac distinction) was what mattered. But the personal failings involved in the definition of the condition were also seen in quite clear social terms. It was the relationship between the 'diseased' individual and society which also concerned the doctors, the addicts' deviation from the norm and the social connotations of personal failings. Clouston saw as important the addicts' diminished volition, the impairment of a 'higher and finer sense of duty' and the desire for activity of any kind.[16] Crothers pointed out that he was rarely an innovator or leader in any department of work.

The strong element of free will and personal responsibility remaining in the disease of the will concept co-existed uneasily with its claimed medical and scientific basis. It was in illogical alliance, too, with the psychological influence within the disease theory, the classification of addiction as, if not a form of insanity, a type of mental disease of some more minor type. According to Kerr, the 'disease of inebriety resembles in many particulars the disease of insanity' (although Allbutt reported that he had not found insanity to be a consequence of morphinism). Physiological theories of mental functioning, the belief that insanity, like other disease entities, had its source in localized brain lesions, and that variations in mental and moral characteristics were a function of physical defects in the structure of the nervous system, helped addiction specialists to bridge the gap between moral and medical approaches. To Clouston, the lack of control which characterized addiction was indicative of malfunctioning brain structure. Despite the widespread use of the term 'morphinomania' (more commonly used than the milder 'morphinism'), the connection with more severe forms of mental illness was never fully established. Levinstein had maintained that it was not a 'mental alienation but a human passion ...'. And despite the clear parallels between treatment methods – the admission of narcotic inebriates to lunatic asylums, the establishment of inebriates' asylums – it was difficult to classify addicts as fully insane. What developed instead was a view of the condition as a functional rather than an organic abnormality. Addicts were 'abnormal' or 'neurotic' rather than insane. Their condition was a failure of the higher ethical brain according to Crothers, a 'toxic psycho-neurosis' in Jennings' words.[17] The belief in the addict's neurotic instability had, too, a strong moral focus. The addict was 'abnormal' in the literal sense that he deviated from generally accepted norms of conduct and thought.

The personal responsibility ascribed to the disease of addiction found expression in the idea of 'constitutional predisposition' with predisposing and exciting causes. It was the individual's own constitution which was directly responsible. Kerr, for instance, in the 1880s, had itemized sex, age, religion, race, climate, education, pecuniary circumstances, marriage relations, temperament, diet and a host of other possibilities as predisposing causes.[18] In later works, at a time of increasing concern in the wake of the revelations of physical standards at the time of the Boer War and of concern for 'national efficiency', the hereditary influence was stronger. Addicts were among the 'unfit', whose appearance in many areas presaged, it was thought, national decline. Criminality, insanity, homosexuality and poverty were among the conditions re-classified in this biologically determined way. The hereditary influence was also present in the analysis of addiction. Harrington Sainsbury's *Drugs and the Drug Habit* (1909) emphasized the necessity of good racial stock, of increased education and welfare provision, to prevent the spread of addiction.[19] Allbutt and Dixon, writing in the *System of Medicine* (1906) on 'Opium Poisoning and Other Intoxicants', pointed to a 'hereditary craving for intoxicants', with sometimes also nervous disease or insanity in the family tree of the neurotics who formed the bulk of addiction cases.[20]

By allocating such a large place to biological predestination, doctors confirmed the need for their intervention, as men of science, but abandoned any attempt at a wider understanding of the social and environmental roots of the condition. Addiction became seen as an exclusive condition rather than, as in the earlier discussions, a bad habit which anyone might fall into. The influence of 'constitutional' or 'hereditary' predisposition with predisposing and exciting causes substituted narrow individual perceptions couched in terms of personal failure for any extensive

analysis of the social roots of opium use. Like the eugenic movement itself, from which many of the biological arguments derived,
their bias was a professional one.[21] Formulation and application
were always limited to those addicts whom doctors were likely to
treat. The disease of narcotic inebriety, or morphinism, in medical
eyes at least, was very much class-based. According to a letter from
Dr J. St Thomas Clarke, medical attendant at Mrs Theobald's
Establishment for Ladies, in the *British Medical Journal* in 1882,
the better classes of society furnished a 'considerable proportion'
of morphine cases.[22] From this type of professional observation
came a disease theory applicable only to the middle-class patient.
Crothers' formulation, which saw physical and nervous exhaustion among 'hard working physicians, clergymen, active business
men, lawyers, teachers', who 'early became neurasthenic and cere-
brasthenic' as likely to lead to a generation of children who became
morphine addicts, was typical.[23] Jellinek, in discussing the dis-
semination of a new form of disease theory of alcoholism in post-
war America, has pointed out that recognition of the condition
as an illness was related to the extent of its occurrence in the upper
social classes.[24] In England, much the same spirit prevailed; and
the large number of doctors or those with some medical connection among those afflicted provided added impetus for establishing
a framework based on illness and disease.

The working-class addict appeared very little in the case histories; in the more extreme instances, the existence of any number
of addicts outside the professional class was denied. Sir Ronald
Armstrong-Jones of Claybury Asylum took a strictly materialist
view of class differences in the incidence of addiction. In his view,
morphine addicts were more numerous among the 'private class'
in Claybury, for

> ... there is generally a physical difference between the brains
> of those in the private and the rate-aided class ... not only is
> the brain-weight heavier, but there is also in the private class
> an added complexity of convolutional pattern, and these dif-
> ferences, of necessity, carry with them psychological and
> physiological concomitants, which mean a higher sensitiveness
> and a greater vulnerability.[25]

Few doctors saw addicts of this 'rate-aided' type and disease
theory was not formulated with them in mind. Working-class opi-

ate use was still a matter of continuing professional concern, as the moves against opiate-based patent medicines and the 'chlorodyne scare' in particular made clear. But this was a question of availability and the limitation of sale rather than of disease and treatment. For the middle-class morphine addict there was medical care and expensive in-patient treatment; working-class addiction was mostly a matter of curtailment of supply.

The idea of the exclusive addict denied, too, any possibility of alternative patterns of consumption. The existence of the moderate stable addict, the consumer who could exist without apparent personal or physical deterioration for years on the same level dose of the drug, had been accepted unquestioningly even by the earlier medical writers on the subject. In fact, the whole debate on opium eating and longevity had presupposed the existence of just such a class of addict. But disease theories encompassed the moderate as much as the uncontrolled addict. Allbutt himself, who had had a patient who took a grain of opium every morning and evening for the last fifteen years of his life and who was 'never ... so presumptuous as to endeavour to suppress' the habit, nevertheless concluded that 'the familiar use of opium in any form is to play with fire, and probably to catch fire'.[26]

Views like his were not unquestioningly accepted. Discussion of moderate addicts was conspicuous in debates over the Indo-Chinese opium trade; there is evidence that many doctors agreed with the opinion of Dr C. R. Francis in 1882. Dr Francis quoted the case of a friend who was a stable addict. 'Yielding to the popular prejudice against opium-eating, Mr A. has repeatedly endeavoured to break it off ... Doubtless he would succeed in time, as others have, but cui bono? He enjoys excellent health, is able to do a good day's work (mental as well as physical), and is entirely free from a variety of minor troubles having a nervous origin which used to annoy him before he began the opium.'[27] Moderate as much as uncontrolled addicts were equally diseased. Medical intervention was appropriate even if, as many of the case histories demonstrated, the addict lived a normal life in every other respect.

Disease theories, far from marking a step towards greater scientific awareness and analysis of the roots of dependence on narcotics, in many respects marked a closing of avenues, a narrower vision than before. The theories themselves were a hotch-potch of borrowings from developing medical science and established morality. The lack of definition of the term 'addiction' itself emphasized this. Even by the early years of the twentieth century, few specialists cared to use the term. Dr Huntley did so. Others still used 'inebriety', morphinomania, morphinism or opium eating; the morphia habit and morphia habitués were common. Drug or morphine addiction was not in wider usage until the years before the First World War. Specialists in inebriety disseminated a confused and illogical series of opinions masquerading as theory. A continuing belief in free will and individual responsibility coexisted uneasily with the model of disease and infection which doctors sought to impose. The condition could be self-induced and yet also be the result of hereditary defect; it was nevertheless somehow still, in medical eyes, a doctor's proper responsibility. Morality and medical science should apparently have been at odds; yet disease theory was very much a mixture of the two. The addict's sickness was mental; his 'neurosis' was in effect a deviation from the norms of established society, even though doctors rigorously excluded the social dimensions of addiction from their own disease formulation.

Disease theory had its effect, too, on methods of treatment. It was, in fact, the elaboration of such medical attitudes to addiction which, of necessity, entailed a parallel emphasis on control and cure of the addict. In the first half of the century, in the absence of any developed disease view, the question of treatment had barely been considered, although Christison and those who saw opium eating as compatible with longevity also saw nothing inhumane in abrupt and immediate withdrawal.[28] Categorization of the condition as a bad habit justified some degree of punishment; and the continuing moral element in developing disease theories ensured an increased emphasis on abrupt methods. This originated in the work of the continental experts – Levinstein's description, in his *Morbid Craving for Morphia*, of the addict's treatment, confined in a locked and barred room and guarded night and day by (preferably male) warder-nurses, was particularly memorable.[29] The abrupt method was originally much favoured by English addiction specialists; it became known in some circles as the 'English treatment'.[30] Ironically enough, those who presumed to deal with the condition within a framework of greater scientific objectivity and medical progress adopted methods entailing a fair degree of moral reprobation. The general move to abrupt withdrawal in fact implied a stricter moral reaction than the earlier treatment regimes. Dr J. Clarke of Leicester, recounting the case of a doctor's wife injecting twenty grains of morphine a day, from whom he had withdrawn the drug suddenly and abruptly, advised this procedure, even though the patient herself had wanted gradual withdrawal and had proved 'rebellious ... loading me with invective at each visit, asserting her increasing pain and exhaustion ...'.[31] The expanding group of doctors with an interest in treatment regimes agreed with him; the moral response was nowhere more plainly demonstrated.

Rapid reduction over two or three days was advocated by Erlenmeyer; gradual reduction over a longer period was also increasingly popular and was associated with Dr J. B. Mattison, Director of the Brooklyn Home for Narcotic Inebriates in New York, and with Dr Oscar Jennings. The abrupt method was never completely abandoned. In 1910, Dr C. A. McBride, Superintendent of the Norwood Sanatorium, still considered it 'the most satisfactory of all ... short, sharp and decisive'.[32] But it was increasingly recognized that such methods were usable only in cases where the habit was of recent origin, or the addict young and strong enough to bear them. Rapid, semi-rapid or gradual methods were more popular; and drug treatments widely used. Other disease entities involved drug regimes; and the search for a pharmacological antidote to the addiction disease was also under way. Addiction was often still seen in the medical texts as a form of poisoning – 'acute poisoning' described accidental or conscious overdosing, 'chronic poisoning' the establishment of dependence on opium or morphine. Drug treatments were therefore sometimes surprisingly close to methods of dealing with an opium overdose. Drs McBride and Mary Strangman, advocating atropine in the 1900s, were only adopting a commonly-used method of treating opium poisoning.[33]

The number and variety of alternative drug treatments increased considerably in the last decades of the century; the controversies between advocates of different regimes were intense and often acrimonious. Tedious and repetitive in detail as they sometimes were, grandiose in the claims advanced for rival methods, they nevertheless demonstrated a form of collective professional self-affirmation. The scientific nature of medical concepts was somehow underlined by increasing specialization and the emergence of different schools of thought. Many English specialists favoured the use of bromides. Norman Kerr, originally a devotee of abrupt methods, but a convert to gradual diminution over a period of a month or five weeks, used potassium and sodium bromide to subdue nervous irritability. Allbutt and Dixon recommended bromides with caffeine; Mattison used, for sleep, bromides, codeine and cannabis indica. Neil Macleod described in the 1890s how bromide poisoning had cured cases of opium addiction. Some doctors favoured cannabis as an alternative. Obersteiner thought coca a suitable treatment; Erlenmeyer favoured chloral. Even the newly discovered heroin found its place in treatment regimes. Methods rose and declined with surprising rapidity. Cocaine, much valued in the 1880s, was the subject of dire medical warnings by the early 1900s.[34]

That the subject could give rise to such heated debate was itself proof of its definition as a separate specialist entity and of the value of the medical contributions made within it. Yet the drug treatment for the addiction disease was accompanied, like the disease theory itself, by a continuing moral side. The analysis of the condition had emphasized the addict's deviation from acceptable social norms. Treatment, by way of reaction to this, placed emphasis on those same values of society. Self-control and self-help were consequently important. The patient's condition was seen to a large extent as the result of personal moral failure; cure should involve the cultivation of changes in personal characteristics. To this end, experts like Crichton Miller recommended treatment by the combined method, both medical and moral. Hypnotism enjoyed a vogue; and Kerr, too, emphasized the 'bracing-up' of self-control. The inebriate's conscience was to be approached by the inculcation of family and community duties. 'In opium inebriety,' as he noted, 'religion has wrought marvels.'[35] Jennings, too, favoured a moral as much as a medical approach. His writings were marked by an increasing emphasis on the personal qualities of the addict rather than on the purely medical drug treatment necessary. *The Morphia Habit and its Voluntary Renunciation* and *The Re-Education of Self-Control in the Treatment of the Morphia Habit* were his later works. Affirming that the success of therapeutic measures depended on the mentality of the patient, Jennings saw the restoration of will as most important. The 're-education of impulsivity' was what mattered. Sainsbury, too, emphasized the remoulding of character – 'first in order of treatment will be the personal appeal, by any and every means adapted to reach the higher nature of the sufferer, whose will-power, buried under a heap of collapsed intentions and broken purposes, must be dug out'.[36] The moral leadership of the specialist, too, was crucial in intractable cases. In the last resort 'scientific' treatment rested on moral concepts and the inculcation of self-control.

Treatment methods remained a mixture of the physiological and the psychological. Physical antidotes were recommended – it was not uncommon, for instance, for the removal of decayed teeth to be suggested, should the pain from them be an exciting cause of morphinism. Kerr proposed the wearing of flannel next to the skin, should the exciting cause be depression from exposure to cold. Many suggestions within the treatment regimes were social rather than medical. Activities which reflected acceptable social values were recommended. The values of air, exercise, cleanliness (Turkish baths in particular) and activity were recognized, together with 'very moderate and progressive cycling, or automobiling'.

There even remained a place for self-treatment and quack remedies. Commercial entrepreneurs devised saleable packages which continued the opium/alcohol connection. The 'Normyl' cure for Alcohol and Drug Addictions (twenty-four days' medicine in twenty-four bottles) was composed of 75 per cent alcohol with strychnine. The Teetolia Treatment ('After years of Drink and Drug Taking – cured in four days') had alcohol and quinine. There were the Keeley Cure and the St George Association for the Cure of the Morphia Habit, a cure itself based on morphia with a large amount of salicylic acid. The Turvey Treatment for Alcoholism and Narcomania – 'earning the gratitude of the nation, the support of the Ministry, the thankfulness of hundreds of our most successful business and literary men of the day' – offered a treatise together with a private consultation.[37] None quite matched the imaginativeness of Dr Kane who, in America, was publicizing his De Quincey home method.

Kane was a medical man with an established reputation in the discussion of disease theories and methods of treatment. In

England, too, on occasion the dividing line between quackery and mainstream medical science could still be unclear. Medical enthusiasm for 'quack remedies' was one example. There was Hopeine (morphia, coloured with oil of hops) and Argemone Mexicana. But in England, strongest medical interest was reserved for the Malayan anti-opium plant, or Combretum sundaicum. Interest was for a time intense. But, as Jennings pointed out, the only active principle contained in the leaves was a small amount of tannin; medical use of the drug seems to have died out as its inutility was demonstrated.[38]

McBride had hoped that the Malayan plant could be used in some form of out-patient rather than in-patient treatment. His hopes were disappointed; and the development of disease theory was in general accompanied by a strong institutional trend, a desire to segregate the addict which had its parallel in custodial treatment of the insane, criminals and the poor.[39] The only advocacy of greater control of the user of opium and some form of consistent professional intervention prior to the last quarter of the century had come from within the public health movement. Professor Alfred Taylor had suggested to the Select Committee on the sale of Poisons Bill in 1857 that those consumers who needed regular doses of opium should be issued with a certificate which would last for six months and would be used to obtain supplies from chemists in the neighbourhood. This view gained some support among other professional witnesses to the Committee, but was never at this stage put into practice. Control of the user of the drug in this way was a twentieth-century phenomenon. In the late nineteenth century, it was directly institutional control which was favoured. The German experts on addiction had recommended institutional confinement – Levinstein, for instance, had his own morphine institution in Berlin in the 1870s – and from the beginning of discussion of treatment methods in England there were moves towards confinement. Abrupt withdrawal on a long sea voyage was one procedure.[40] W. E. Gladstone's addicted sister Helen was sent to Germany as part of her cure. The necessity of physical confinement of the addict and disciplinary treatment were themes running through most discussions from the 1880s to the First World War. Addiction specialists were virtually unanimous in wishing to enlarge the area of medical control; it was rare to find one who argued against the use of retreats or asylums.

But efforts to extend this treatment advice into a full-scale system of established control met with some difficulty. Action under the Inebriates Acts and in particular attempts compulsorily to confine non-criminal addicts met with only a limited amount of success. Despite the textbook equation of alcoholic with narcotic inebriety, the legislative terms 'habitual drunkard' and 'inebriate' (the term established, largely at medical suggestion, by the 1888 Inebriates Act) covered only liquor which was drunk. Both the 1879 Habitual Drunkards Act and the 1888 Act provided for the voluntary detention of inebriates in retreats established under the Act and licensed by government-appointed inspectors. But the definition of 'intoxicating liquor' under the Act covered only that which was drunk, and not the injected drug. This was a point which became clear as the result of a number of cases in the 1890s. In 1893, for instance, it was established, as the result of a Liverpool case, that chlorodyne was included as an intoxicating liquor within the meaning of Section 3 of the Act.[41] It soon became clear that the injected drug did not. In 1889, Charles Park, a dentist from Morayshire, was admitted to High Shot House at St Margaret's Twickenham after requesting treatment for drug taking under the Inebriates Act. But Park was injecting morphia as well as cocaine. When he assaulted an attendant and broke out of the home, the Superintendent found it legally impossible to force his return.[42] Existing legislation certainly did not cover the intractable injecting addict who refused to accept the medical definition of the needs of his condition.

There had always been an element of compulsion within the system – although committal was voluntary, once the patient had entered the retreat, he was committed for quite a considerable period. Detention was never for less than six months. A year was said to be necessary in ordinary cases, and sometimes even two years if the habit was deeply rooted. If the addict (or alcoholic) escaped during that period, he could be brought back, as the Twickenham case demonstrated. There were attempts to strengthen this element of compulsion. The eugenic influence in general scientific thinking, and in disease theory in particular, brought with it a trend towards compulsory segregation, also manifested in the continuing contemporary discussion of the forcible segregation in labour colonies of the unemployed and 'undeserving' poor. Social Darwinist thought put forward policies of 'conscious social selection' to eliminate the unfit. From the late 1880s, British medical men were arguing for the establishment of compulsory committal under the Inebriates Act, and also for the extension of that term to cover injected drugs as well as those which were drunk. The Inebriates Legislation Committee of the British Medical Association and the Society for the Study of Inebriety were the main propagandist bodies, Norman Kerr the link between the two.

Throughout the 1890s and early 1900s, Kerr argued the case for compulsion and extension of definition before numerous official committees. The dimensions of the problem, as with hypodermic morphine, were never established. In 1892, the Inebriates Legislation Committee of the B.M.A. for the first time began to press for the inclusion within the Act of 'forms of intoxication other than the alcoholic form. Chloral, opium and other varieties of habitual drunkenness ...'.[43] The Committee, chaired at this time by Norman Kerr, presented evidence to the Departmental Committee on the Treatment of Inebriates in the following year which argued both for compulsory committal of habitual drunkards and for 'provision for the care and detention of inebriates in opium, morphine, chloral, chloroform, ether, cocaine or any other narcotic'.[44] Kerr, who had been in favour of compulsory detention since the 1880s, argued the case before the Committee and cited American experience in its favour. But only the principle of compulsion was accepted in the Committee's 1894 report; and compulsory committal for criminal inebriates alone was part of the subsequent Inebriates Act.[45]

It was left to a private member's Bill to make the first effort at inclusion of drug-taking. In 1901, an abortive Bill was introduced by Dr Farquharson, a member of the Inebriates Legislation Committee, which would have amended the term 'habitual drunkard' to include 'a person who, not being amenable to any jurisdiction in lunacy, is notwithstanding, by reason of habitual use of opium or any other drug, at times dangerous to himself or others, or incapable of managing himself and his affairs'.[46] The Bill was withdrawn, but the principles advocated by the medical profession were finally accepted by the 1908 Departmental Committee on the Inebriates Acts. This accepted that habitual drunkenness should cover drug-taking as well as drinking and suggested the establishment of a form of gradual compulsion. It was to be possible for an inebriate to make a voluntary application for the appointment of a guardian. The guardian would decide where the inebriate was to live, deprive him of intoxicants and warn sellers of drink and drugs against supplying him. In 1903 it had been considered whether the 1902 Licensing Act, which dealt with the sale of intoxicating liquor to habitual drunkards, could be applied to the sale of drugs to addicts. The matter had proceeded no further; but the proposal reappeared in the 1908 report, where supply after warning to any form of inebriate was to be an offence against the Act. If, too, in the guardian's opinion, his powers of control were insufficient, provision was to be made for compulsory measures to be taken.[47]

The proposal was an interesting one, to be unearthed again during the discussions of the Rolleston Committee on Morphine and Heroin Addiction, when Dr Branthwaite, a committee member and an ex-inspector under the Inebriates Acts, suggested the institution of a form of legal guardianship. But by 1908, the use of inebriates legislation to extend medical control in the area of drug taking was already a faint hope. Several inebriates Bills were introduced between 1912 and 1914 conferring both guardianship and gradual compulsion and extension of definition. None were successful; and the whole question of inebriety was, even before that date, being increasingly incorporated within the bounds of lunacy legislation. The idea of guardianship had in fact originated within the lunacy laws. It had long been possible to confine both drunkards and drug-takers made certifiably insane by their habits. Section 116 of the 1890 Lunacy Act had allowed a form of guardianship, too, which was on occasion applied to drug addicts. The Lord Chancellor's Visitor dealt with both lunatics found by inquisition and with those not so found. In either case, an order could be made for 'the commitment of the estate of the lunatic . . .'. The person dealt with, according to Section 116, did not have to be certifiable, but simply 'through infirmity arising from disease or age incapable of managing his affairs'.[48] Such provision had allowed for the control of the property of addicts; and in the 1900s, the British Medical Association began to press not simply for an extension of the Inebriates Acts, but for all this rather piecemeal legislation to be brought within the ambit of the lunacy laws. Legislative rationalization in part, this was also confirmation of the deviance of drug-taking already marked in disease theories.

The influence of the idea of 'moral insanity' continued to be strong. Dr James Smith Whitaker, Secretary of the British Medical Association (and later a member of the Rolleston Committee), recommending the extension of the duties of the Board of Commissioners of Lunacy to habitual inebriety and drug habits before the Royal Commission on the Care and Control of the Feeble-Minded in 1908, argued that drug habits could be classified as cases of unconfirmed mental disease and brought either under guardianship or compulsory committal – 'the whole procedure,' he considered, 'should be made analogous to that under the Lunacy Acts, with suitable modification in recognition of the fact that the persons in question are not insane, though suffering from moral infirmity'. The 1913 Mental Deficiency Act did indeed include 'any sedative, narcotic or stimulant drug or preparation' within the definition of 'intoxicant'. Such 'moral imbeciles' could be sent to an institution for defectives or placed under guardianship.[49]

This was a clear outcome of the custodial influence within the eugenic movement, the desire to control and regulate not just the demonstrably insane, but those whose 'feeble-mindedness' was in some cases demonstrated only by a refusal to conform to established values. Smith Whitaker had argued for the inclusion of drug-taking within the lunacy model on the grounds that this would do away with any possible compulsory criminal committal. Compulsion was in fact to be applied to all – but in his eyes, the medical certification required was adequate safeguard for the patient. The argument of possible criminal committal – of addiction dealt with within a penal model – was used to extend the area of medical control and to substitute a system of medical treatment little different in many respects from a prison regime.

Prison appears to have been in reality a very minor way of dealing with addicts. In 1896, for instance, the Scottish prison commissioners reported two cases treated in prison in Glasgow for the morphia habit.[50] Many addicts could have been sent to prison for offences unconnected with their condition. The absence of published medical comment on the incidence of prison confinement of addicts was an indication possibly of its relative rarity and, too, of lack of medical interest in the non-professional side of the question. It was mostly the working-class addicts who went to prison.

Confinement in lunatic asylums prior to 1914 was also quite rare.[51] Institutional confinement, for all practical purposes in this period, was limited to the voluntary facilities provided by the Homes for Inebriates Association and government-inspected by Home Office appointees under the Acts. Fourteen homes were licensed under the Acts by 1898, although not all took drug addicts. The Dalrymple Home at Rickmansworth, founded in 1884 after a public meeting at the Mansion House in 1882 had set up the Association of the Dalrymple Home for Inebriates (later the Homes for Inebriates Association), was the most important and took in the largest number of addicts.[52] Kerr, consulting physician at the Home, had argued strongly for it; his view was that inebriates should be treated in special homes, not in lunatic asylums. Theory and practice neatly coincided and the establishment of the Home gave added weight to medical views. Two of its medical superintendents, Dr Branthwaite and Dr Hogg, were influential not only in pre-war discussions of inebriety and lunacy, but later, too, in the 1920s, when they were prominent in the Rolleston deliberations. The regime of the Home had clear overtones of social control and the re-moulding of character and habits which had characterized the textbook discussions.[53]

Expanding private provision offered little for the narcotic addict without fairly substantial means. Like disease theory itself, treatment facilities were limited to professional people. Fees at the Dalrymple Home varied between two and five guineas a week, and an analysis of patients by social class (not, in this instance, limited to drug addicts) shows solicitors, doctors and actors with, at the very lowest, clerks and a tailor.[54] This was a matter of some concern to those involved in the Act's operation. Kerr, who saw the lack of provision for the poor as 'a national reproach', recommended the establishment of industrial homes for the treatment of inebriety, where the poor inebriate could be put to work while undergoing his cure.[55] The treatment and confinement of the working-class addicts evoked, as in Kerr's case, a harsher response; and the demands for compulsory committal derived part of their vigour from recognition of this lack in existing legislation. Medical control over such addicts was always limited in extent. Those who did enter homes found they could barely afford them. One case reported in the *British Medical Journal* in 1904 concerned a female chlorodyne addict in a home which cost her brother seven shillings a week.[56] But there was no public institution for the purpose apart from voluntary committal in a lunatic asylum or confinement in the workhouse. For the pauper addict, there was little alternative.

Disease theory was perceived by the expanding medical profession as a move to throw the light of scientific theory into an area characterized by outmoded moral judgements. Their medical ideology retained more than a trace of its moral ancestry. It excluded social in favour of individualist and biologically determinist explanations; yet in its operation and in the thinking of addiction specialists, it resolutely emphasized social values. It acted not simply as an agency of social control, but as one of social assimilation, in which symptoms were defined in terms of deviations from the norm and treatment involved inculcation in the values of conformity and self-help. Scientific theory and medical self-interest coincided in mediating social norms. The elaboration of theory and of treatment structures was also part of the process of class and professional self-affirmation. The addict was separated out as a distinctive type which only the medical profession was competent to treat. The reality of the condition was affirmed, but medical values were not scientifically autonomous; and the moral and class analysis which, reformulated, lay at the basis of disease theory justified increased medical intervention where the profession apparently even by the end of the century had little to offer.

PART SEVEN

The Eastern Dimension
and
British Opium Use *c.* 1860–1900

14

'Britain's Opium Harvest':
The Anti-Opium Movement

The 'opium wars' of the middle of the century have long been a familiar part of considerations of nineteenth-century opium use. But the most important Far Eastern influence on English opium use came not at this time, but in the last quarter of the century. The foundation of a fully fledged anti-opium movement in the 1870s opposing Britain's participation in the opium trade with China had its effect on perceptions of domestic opium use even though its primary focus was a Far Eastern and not an English one. The racial feeling aroused in anti-opium propaganda also found expression in the establishment of beliefs (largely erroneous) about opium smoking and opium 'dens' in the East End of London. It is with the shaping of attitudes towards domestic opium use by Far Eastern experience at the end of the century that Chapters 14 and 15 will deal.

The 'opium wars' and English opium use

Nevertheless, the domestic impact of the mid-century wars should at least be mentioned. For they initiated, at least in embryo, the connection between hostile reactions to opium use in the East and changed perceptions of opium in England. The opium wars were a development of a trading policy which received support from both the British and the Indian governments. The East India Company's monopoly of trade with China had ended in 1834. The Company maintained a virtual monopoly of the cultivation and sale of opium in India, but distribution of the drug in China was left in private hands. It had in this way perfected 'the technique of growing opium in India and disowning it in China'. It was the amount of opium entering China, the emperor's decision to make a strong stand, and British demands for free trade and diplomatic equality which led to the opium war of 1839–42, concluded by the Treaty of Nanking. A second opium war between 1856 and 1858 came to an end with the Treaty of Tientsin.[1] The two wars were prime examples of commercial imperialism, not only through the opening of the treaty ports but through British control of the Chinese customs which the 1842 Treaty established, and the continuing import of opium without restraint. They also saw the beginnings of an organized anti-opium agitation. Much early anti-opium feeling expressed itself in parliamentary terms. The debate on the war in 1840 led to condemnations of this 'pernicious article', opium; Gladstone was moved to an eloquent condemnation of the immorality of the trade.[2] But even the parliamentary opposition to opium was limited. A motion opposing the continuance of the trade and introduced by Lord Ashley in April 1843 was withdrawn when Sir Robert Peel assured him it would impede the negotiations in progress between the British and Chinese governments, and opposition did not revive until the time of the second opium war.[3] Ashley (now Lord Shaftesbury) presented a memorial on the subject to the Foreign Secretary in 1855. In 1857, he introduced the opium question in the House of Lords by asking for a judicial opinion on whether or not the trade was legal.[4]

In several ways the reactions and associations evoked by the wars were portents of the more developed anti-opium movement at the end of the century. It was at this time – when imports of opium into China were necessarily interrupted – that comment was made about the apparent increase in opium being brought into England and the consequent dangers of increased use of the drug, in particular among the working class. At the same time, too, the link between moral opposition to opium in the Far East and the medical ideology of opium use at home was forged. The longevity debate of the middle of the century owed much to Far Eastern evidence. Surgeon Little, who had attacked Sir Robert Christison's conclusions in the *Monthly Journal of Medical Science* in 1850, dealt exclusively with his experience of opium eating and smoking in Singapore; others who contributed to the longevity argument also deployed evidence of the effects of the drug taken from the East.[5] The disbelief in moderation and longevity and the division between legitimate medical and other non-medical use of the drug were already in the process of establishment.

Medical men involved in the English debate were also committed to the agitation against the Far Eastern trade. In 1843, Shaftesbury used the evidence of British medical men involved in the longevity debate to support his cause. Sir Benjamin Brodie, the noted surgeon, and twenty-four other medical men, including Sir Henry Halford, President of the Royal College of Physicians, and Anthony White, President of the Royal College of Surgeons, were of the opinion that:

> However valuable opium may be when employed as an article of medicine, it is impossible for any one who is acquainted with the subject to doubt that the habitual use of it is productive of the most pernicious consequences – destroying the healthy action of the digestive organs, weakening the powers of the mind, as well as those of the body, and rendering the individual who indulges himself in it a worse than useless member of society.[6]

The anti-opium trade movement was at this stage in its infancy, but moral opposition and medical justification for such views were already closely allied.

The anti-opium organizations in existence in England at the time of the opium wars were short-lived and without much public impact. An 'Anti-Opium Society' was responsible for the publication in 1840 of W. S. Fry's *Facts and Evidence Relating to the Opium Trade with China*. It was as chairman of a 'committee formed to sever all connections of the English people and its Government with the opium trade' that Shaftesbury presented the 1855 memorial.[7] The Society of Friends was turning its attention towards the contraband traffic in opium. Quakers were particularly prominent in the anti-opium movement of the late nineteenth century; as early as 1858 the Society appealed to Lord Derby, then Prime Minister, against legalization of the trade.[8] But the Treaty of Tientsin (1858) did establish its legality. The ground was cut away from under the movement's feet. An Edinburgh Committee for the Suppression of the Indo-Chinese Opium Traffic formed in 1859 received scant attention.[9] For all intents and purposes, the anti-opium question was in abeyance for the next decade.

The anti-opium movement 1874–1900

The question revived with vigour in the 1870s. In 1874, what was to be the main anti-opium organization, the Anglo-Oriental Society for the Suppression of the Opium Trade (the 'Anglo-Oriental' was later dropped), was founded. The Society owed its origin to the efforts of a group of Quaker anti-opium campaigners in Birmingham and to the unwavering support of the Pease family of Darlington, who were also Quakers. An anti-opium committee was originally formed in Birmingham in 1874 as the outcome of two public meetings held to protest against the trade. Edward Pease was a member of the Birmingham committee and it was he who suggested a competition whereby prizes were offered for essays on *British Opium Policy and its Results to India and China.* Storrs Turner, the ex-missionary who was to be the first secretary of the Society for the Suppression of the Opium Trade, was one of the prizewinners and his book was published under the same title in 1876. The Society transferred its offices to London – to King Street, Westminster, conveniently near both the Houses of Parliament and the India Office. In November 1874, the Anglo-Oriental Society was established as a national instead of a purely local organization.[10]

The early aims of the Society were in many ways a continuation of those of the mid-century organizations. Opium smuggling was no longer an issue since the Treaty of Tientsin. The main demands were now the abolition of the government monopoly of opium in India and the withdrawal of unfair pressure on the Chinese government to admit Indian opium. In these early days of its existence the Society's position was definitely a non-absolute one, and any emphasis on the distinction between medical and non-medical usage was notably absent.[11] The founder members and driving force behind the Society in its early years were almost without exception Quakers. Only Storrs Turner was not. Without the financial backing provided by the Pease banking family in particular the Society would never have remained in existence. But the Society broadened its support considerably during its early years. Lord Shaftesbury became its President in 1880 and its General Council contained representatives of the Church of England as well as nonconformists. Its executive retained a strong Quaker presence.[12]

The anti-opiumist cause won continuing support at this period most obviously because of the ten-year clause contained within the Treaty of Tientsin. The Treaty stipulated that there should be a revision of its tariff provisions every ten years. Opium, although imported by foreign merchants, could be carried into the interior of the country only by the Chinese. When it left the treaty ports, Chinese officials were at liberty to extract a heavy duty which was in itself a deterrent to increased import. The British government had been lobbying for some time before the treaty revision was imminent in order to facilitate the entry of Indian opium into China. In 1869, Sir Rutherford Alcock, British Minister in China, negotiated a revised Convention whereby additional import duties were to be paid on opium and on exported silk, and the British received commercial concessions in return. The Alcock Convention was never ratified. The Liberal government was deluged with memorials, not least from Sassoon & Co., the largest dealers in Indian opium, and the matter was left unsettled.[13]

The spotlight was once again on opium, however, as a result of these negotiations. In August 1869, when the Indian budget came before the Commons, several members, Sir Wilfred Lawson, the prominent temperance campaigner, among them, had condemned the opium trade. The next year, Lawson put forward a motion condemning 'the system by which a large portion of the Indian revenue is raised from opium'. It was thrown out by a majority of 104 (196 M.P.s voted). Lawson's motion and the debate upon it were the prototype of many to follow over the next quarter of a century and beyond. The terms in which they were couched might vary – that put forward by Mark Stewart, Conservative M.P. for Wigton and a member of the Council of the Society for the Suppression of the Opium Trade (S.S.O.T.), in 1875, for instance, envisaged the careful consideration of policy regulating the opium traffic between India and China 'with a view to the gradual withdrawal of the Government of India from the cultivation and manufacture of opium' (this too was lost by thirty-seven votes). But the arguments deployed on both sides varied little even if the wording on the order paper might alter.[14] The anti-opium cause was a continuing political issue from this time onward.

Economic considerations underlay the political agitation. Despite the importance of opium to the Indian budget, a peak in export of the drug was in fact reached in 1880. Signs of decline in the importance of opium as an Indian revenue item were already visible. The old-established opium firms, Jardine Matheson and Dent and Co. most obviously, were withdrawing from the market. China's own production of the drug was increasing; and the domestic product, although considered inferior to the Indian, was at least cheaper and easier to distribute, in particular clandestinely and without payment of internal dues. By 1885, China was probably producing just as much opium as she imported. Leading officials of the Chinese government still professed moral objections to the use of the drug; but since the chaos of the Taiping rebellion, local officials were often out of central control, if indeed there had ever been much direction. The Indian government in its turn tried to maintain a standard level of production and hence of prices by building up a reserve of opium. But other crops were also becoming profitable; and many peasants preferred to grow potatoes or tobacco rather than opium. In the 1890s, exports of Indian opium began to decline absolutely as well as relatively. Those who argued as part of the anti-opiumist cause that imports into China of British manufactured goods showed little increase because of the odium associated with the opium trade certainly had the statistics of manufactured goods on their side. British trade with China had increased hardly at all from the late 1860s to the late 1880s, while trade with Japan had tripled and even quadrupled in the same period.[15]

In the phase of late-Victorian imperialism just beginning in the 1870s, there were thus clear commercial arguments for replacing the importation of opium. The anti-slavery and anti-opium agitations had, in this economic sense, much in common. Alderman McArthur, M.P., in the chair at the S.S.O.T.'s inaugural meeting, emphasized the commercial argument that the opium trade was strangling other forms of commerce. 'When the ports were opened by treaty, we expected to do a large trade with China. Instead of doing the large trade we had anticipated, we sent to China, with its 400 millions of population, but six million pounds' worth of exports, while the Australian colonies, with four millions of people, took as much as fourteen millions pounds' worth of our goods.'[16] The poor Chinese were unwilling to buy British manufactured goods because of the odium associated with Britain's involvement in the opium trade – or unable to do so because

1.   The opium poppy, *Papaver somniferum*

2.   Poppy capsules grown in Britain

3.   The implements used by Mr Young in his experiments in Scotland. The poppy capsules were incised and the opium brushed into the container

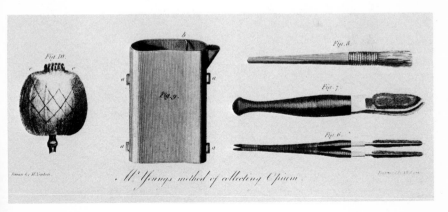

4.   Thomas De Quincey, 1785–1859, by Sir J. Watson Gordon

5.   Samuel Taylor Coleridge, 1772–1834

7.   Sir Robert Christison, 1797–1882, Professor of Materia Medica at Edinburgh, investigator of opium eating and advocate of the benefits of coca chewing

6.   Dr John Collis Browne, 1819–84, the first man to produce chlorodyne

8. Dr F. E. Anstie, 1833–74, editor of *The Practitioner* and advocate of new and more scientific remedies, including hypodermic morphine.

9. Sir Thomas Clifford Allbutt, 1836–1925, Regius Professor of Physick at Cambridge, and one-time enthusiast for hypodermic morphine. He later became a leading figure in the growing band of addiction specialists

10. Dr Norman Kerr, 1834–99, temperance advocate and founder of the Society for the Study of Inebriety which argued for the 'disease' view of addiction

11. Dalrymple House at Rickmansworth, the most important home taking both alcoholic and narcotic 'inebriates' for treatment in the 1880s and 1890s. Its establishment by the Homes for Inebriates Association symbolized the change to 'disease' views of addiction focused on the middle-class addict

12.   The female stereotype – women morphine addicts 'selfishly fond of pleasure'. The illustration, like much writing on morphine abuse, comes from France (*Le Petit Journal*), but the purported connection with middle-class women was also made in Britain

13.   Hunter's ipodermic or hypodermic syringe

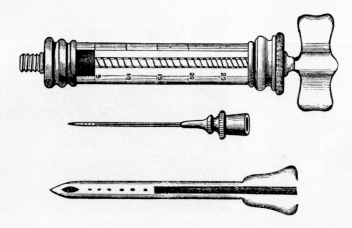

of the poverty to which smoking the drug had reduced them. Humanitarianism and economic self-interest coincided.

The S.S.O.T., which grew out of these conditions, was very much a pressure group of the classic Victorian type, conforming quite closely to the model established by the Anti-Slavery Society and, in the political sphere, by the Anti-Corn Law League. The Society's work as a pressure group initially had a dual focus – the creation of an educated public opinion opposed to the opium trade and the Indian government monopoly in particular, and parliamentary pressure to obtain definite political action. The support it attracted came in the religious sphere primarily from nonconformist and evangelical denominations, with the missionaries as a distinct and active grouping, increasingly so towards the end of the century.[17] The established church gave some support: the Bishop of Durham was one of the Society's earliest supporters. But there were reservations about the Society's activities in some parts of the Church of England.[18]

In the political sense, the Society drew its parliamentary support primarily from among the Radical, nonconformist wing of the Liberal Party, with Sir Joseph Pease, Liberal M.P. for Barnard Castle in Co. Durham, as its leading Commons spokesman. Despite the adherence of M.P.s who represented working-class constituencies, the anti-opium movement itself remained, unlike the Anti-Corn Law, or even the Anti-Slavery, agitations, obstinately elitist. It never attracted any significant body of working-class support.[19] The Society attempted to influence centres of opinion rather than to mobilize mass political and public support. Provincial political support was nevertheless important, and the Society adopted tactics commonly used by other contemporary pressure groups. The Rev. J. B. F. Tinling of Reading began work as a 'missionary' for the Society in 1876. His task was to establish local auxiliary committees throughout the country, but although he secured helpers in several towns and visited others, his task was not an easy one and meetings were often ill-attended. There is little evidence that the Society ever achieved any broadly based political lobbying organization in the provinces. Part of the reason for its failure to organize any extensive provincial support was its precarious financial position. In its early years its income barely reached £1,000 a year and much of this was due to the financial support given by the Pease family.

Although the agitation against the trade gathered pace, its income did not.

The public opinion it sought to create was not broad-based, but the opinion of influential élites in society. The Society attracted its greatest degree of public support in the early 1880s. Its main practical objective at this time was one on which many shades of anti-opium opinion could unite. This was the ratification of the Chefoo Convention of 1876. The Convention had been negotiated by Sir Thomas Wade, Alcock's successor as British Minister at Peking, as compensation for the death of Mr Margary, a young interpreter assassinated in 1875 in Yunnan when about to join a British exploration party from Burma. The British government used Margary's murder as the occasion for tidying up some outstanding trading matters, the import of opium among them. The Convention, instead of concentrating on the import duty on the drug, as was the case with the 1869 agreement, proposed instead to extend the area of internal taxation and prepared the way for an indefinite increase in the revenue which the Chinese government derived from import of the drug. It was not ratified for the next nine years because of pressure from opium merchants and the Indian government, both of whom feared that the Chinese would use it to impose prohibitory duties. The demand for its ratification thus became the major part of the anti-opiumist cause for almost a decade. The matter was repeatedly brought before parliament. In 1883, Pease presented a motion for an address asking that 'in all negotiations which take place between the Governments of Her Majesty and China, having reference to the Duties levied on opium under the Treaty of Tientsin ... the Government of China will be met as that of an independent state, having the full right to arrange its own import Duties.' Pease's motion was lost by a majority of sixty (192 M.P.s voted), and in a debate in 1881 no division was called.[20]

The anti-opiumist cause was a public issue in this period as it was not to be again until the 1900s. The Society's public activity expanded at an unprecedented rate. In 1880, election year, the Society placarded its election address which stressed commercial as well as moral arguments; and a pamphlet on the opium question was sent to every clergyman and nonconformist minister in the country.[21] A memorial signed by members of the Society and other public figures, 361 in all, urging extinction of the trade as now

conducted and 'the duty of this country to withdraw all encouragement from the growth of the poppy in India, except for strictly
medicinal purposes, and to support the Chinese government in
its efforts to suppress the traffic', was presented to Gladstone as
Prime Minister in 1882. Petitions poured into the Commons in
support. In the month prior to the debate on Pease's motion in
April 1883, petitions containing over 75,000 signatures had
arrived.[22] On 21 October 1881, the crowning public event of the
campaign took place – a meeting at the Mansion House in London
with the Lord Mayor in the chair and both the Archbishop of Canterbury and Cardinal Manning present as chief supporters. The
Lord Mayor made special note of the religious and political heterogeneity of the gathering. Moral and commercial heterogeneity
were also notable: it was the Archbishop who moved that 'the
opium traffic ... is opposed alike to Christian morality and the
commercial interests of this country'.[23] In the year 1882–3, there
were 180 meetings on the opium trade, three times as many as
in the previous year.[24]

Anti-opium propaganda material was produced in profusion.
The Society had its own series of tracts. There were publications
in book form such as Justin McCarthy's *The Opium War*. The
Society had its own journal, the *Friend of China*, published
monthly initially, bi-monthly from 1879 and monthly again in
1883. This published articles on the course of the agitation,
extracts from newspapers, both foreign and British, notes of meetings and analyses of every aspect of opium cultivation, trade and
revenue. It was the linchpin of the anti-opium agitation in these
years. Circulation figures were never released, but its influence
extended beyond what was most probably a limited one. The controversy spilled over into the public journals. The missionary
magazines were of course full of the matter; but anti-opium views
were also publicized among educated middle-class society as a
whole.[25]

There was no concerted pro-opium organization working on a
propaganda basis to compare with the Society for the Suppression
of the Opium Trade, and those who defended the cultivation of
opium in India, its import into China, or its medical and non-
medical use, did so often from a variety of disparate motives.
Some, like Sir George Birdwood and Dr W. J. Moore, had been
connected with the Indian government or in medical practice in

India (Moore was Deputy Surgeon-General of the Bombay Presidency), while others were in some way connected with the trade. Mr W. H. Brereton, whose lectures at St James' Hall in 1882 putting the case against the S.S.O.T. were later republished as *The Truth About Opium* (1882), was at one time a Hong-Kong solicitor and legal adviser to the opium farmers. Sir Robert Hart, Commissioner of the Imperial Maritime Customs in China, also issued a pamphlet in support of the opium trade in 1881.[26]

Perhaps the greatest renegade in the anti-opiumists' eyes was Sir Rutherford Alcock himself, whose apparent defection on the opium issue was the source of intense displeasure. Alcock's views had in fact changed little from the stand he had taken against the trade during his time in China. He simply maintained that the trade should be extinguished gradually and with as much good faith in the matter from the Chinese as from the English point of view. Nevertheless his earlier attacks on the opium trade, his evidence to the Select Committee on East Indian finance in 1871 in particular, were constantly quoted against him. His views were close to the way in which the trade was in fact ended after 1906, with both sides committed to reciprocal diminution of both import and cultivation. It was Alcock who was the leading speaker at a meeting of the Indian section of the Royal Society of Arts in 1882 which formed the main forum for the pro-opium response; it was his articles 'Opium and common sense' in *Nineteenth Century* in 1881 and 'The opium trade' in the *Journal of the Society of Arts* in the following year which received the brunt of the attack.[27] The evidence and arguments were bandied back and forth.

How far the strength of the agitation was responsible for settlement of the Chefoo question is uncertain. Lord Kimberley, Secretary of State for India, justified ratification of the Convention to the Indian government by reason of the strength of anti-opium feeling.[28] But most research on Victorian pressure groups suggests that they could do little but confirm government on a course of action on which it had already decided.[29] Certainly anti-opiumist parliamentary strength was too small and too divided between the parties to have constituted much of a political threat. The signing of an additional article to the Chefoo Convention in 1885 was thus only in part an outcome of the anti-opium agitation. India's opposition to its ratification had been withdrawn as early as 1881, and there was also Chinese pressure in its favour. In 1885, Britain signed an additional article whereby all opium on arrival at a Chinese port was to be placed in a bonded warehouse; on removal, an import duty was to be paid. Opium would thereafter be freed from all taxation in the interior of China. By agreeing to the Convention, the Chinese government had by one move obtained a larger share in the profits of the opium trade, and surrendered its claim to total prohibition. The anti-opium movement in England had received a severe setback; for it could hardly contend that Britain was forcing opium on China when the Chinese government had shown some eagerness to increase its share of the profits of the trade.

The year 1885 marked the apogee of the Society's fortune. Until the early 1890s, both its political and its public support decreased. Never again, even in the early 1900s when its political and parliamentary support was again rapidly increasing, was it to enjoy the sort of public acceptance demonstrated in the Mansion House meeting and the other gatherings which had taken place between 1881 and 1883. In 1886, a motion brought forward by Sir Joseph Pease dealing with the severance of the Indian government's connection with poppy cultivation, and the prohibition of such cultivation in India except for medical purposes, was a total failure. The House was counted out; and this was a serious check to the vigour of the anti-opium movement.[30] Early enthusiasm had waned; there were some internal difficulties within the Society and its financial support had died back.

The years after 1885 saw a considerable internal weakening of the anti-opium movement. Several different organizations came into being, partly because there was no longer an issue on which all could unite, and differences of opinion over future objectives came to the surface. The S.S.O.T. itself called a meeting of its council in January 1886 to decide whether it was even to continue in the same form, and whether a vigilance committee might not be more suitable for a less strident agitation. Differences of opinion over whether India or China should be the main focus of attention led in 1888 to the formation of another anti-opium society. This was the Christian Union for the Severance of the Connection of the British Empire with the Opium Traffic. It was closely identified with the missionary view of things, and missionary influence among its leadership and supporters was strong. The Union produced its own journal, *National Righteousness*, with a low circulation, irregularly published, and edited by Benjamin Broom-hall, secretary of the China Inland Mission, from 1888 until his death in 1911; the journal itself continued until 1915. Membership of the Union was, at around 3,000 by 1890, small and static.

Its focus continued to be a Chinese as well as an Indian one and it argued consistently that although Chinese domestic production was to be deplored, nevertheless India should unilaterally abandon her involvement in opium production and should prohibit the cultivation of opium for all but medical use.[31] There was in fact little difference in outlook on some issues between the S.S.O.T. and the Christian Union, and much overlapping in terms of personalities. There were close personal links, too, with the two other anti-opium organizations which also formed at this time. The Women's Anti-Opium Urgency League, established in 1891, had close links with the Christian Union. The Anti-Opium Urgency Committee was also set up in 1891; it was appointed by the National Christian Anti-Opium Convention held in London in March of that year.[32]

There was no concrete and accessible political issue on which all shades of anti-opium opinion could comfortably unite after 1885. There was a hardening of attitudes, an absolute response which shifted its emphasis from China towards India and other British possessions in the Far East. The campaign concentrated its efforts on the ending of the Indian opium monopoly and on the restriction of cultivation to the small amounts required for specifically medical purposes. In this absolute response, it was supported by the example of the United States, which in 1880 had signed an immigration treaty with China (not finally enforced by Congress until 1887) whereby both countries mutually forbade their subjects to import opium into each other's ports and Americans were prohibited from trafficking in it within China. Less well known was America's close involvement in the opium trade between India and China in the first half of the century. In the 1840s and 1850s two American companies were doing business in China in opium to the value of 2 million dollars a year, and Whitelaw Reed, U.S. Minister in China, was involved in attempts to obtain legalization of the trade. By 1880, American participation had virtually ceased; and the treaty could comfortably be signed in the knowledge that it did no harm to her trading interests.[33] In England, however, the reaction in anti-opium circles was an encouragement of demands for an absolute response, for prohibition rather than gradual diminution, for a sudden and final end to both cultivation and the trade in opium.

The Royal Commission on Opium

In this new phase of agitation, the anti-opium cause narrowed its basis of support. There was less of the sort of educated support of well-meaning liberal society of the early 1880s. Clergymen and missionaries now figured most prominently and the wider support which the movement could arouse through petitioning and public meetings came from members of nonconformist congregations. The new campaign reached its height between 1889 and 1893, in the years immediately preceding the appointment and work of the Royal Commission on Opium. The S.S.O.T. itself had emerged to some degree from the doldrums which had followed the signing of the additional article. A new secretary, J. G. Alexander, a Quaker barrister, managed to organize a revival of the agitation.[34] The Society's greatest success came in parliament. A motion in 1889 had been lost. But on 10 April 1891 Pease's motion in the Commons that the Indian opium revenue was 'morally indefensible', and that the Indian government should cease to grant licences for anything but the cultivation of the opium poppy for medical purposes and should stop the transit of Malwa opium across British territory, was won by 160 to 130 votes.[35]

The greatest hope of some success in moves against opium came in 1892 with the election of a Liberal government led by Gladstone. In 1891, many Conservative M.P.s had abstained on Pease's motion because of their unwillingness to vote against the government; most of its support had come from Liberal ranks. There were estimated to be around 240 supporters of the anti-opium cause in the new House of Commons. Known anti-opiumists in the government included Asquith at the Home Office, Campbell-Bannerman at the War Office, Sir Edward Grey as Foreign Secretary, and, perhaps most significantly, George Russell, Parliamentary Secretary at the India Office. Gladstone himself had not voted on Pease's motion in 1891, but his speeches during his Midlothian campaign had given the impression that he retained the sympathy with the anti-opium cause which he had shown as a young man.[36]

The Society's cause had much in its favour. But tactically it mismanaged the issue. Moves to amalgamate all the anti-opium groupings into one concerted organization failed, and the anti-opiumists met opposition in a divided and disorganized state. For the main stumbling block was opposition to ending the trade in the centres of power. Lord Kimberley, Secretary of State for India, was resolutely in favour of the opium trade and he received tacit encouragement from Gladstone. Pease and the S.S.O.T. were consistently outmanoeuvred. Kimberley's opposition destroyed all the Society's attempts to obtain a motion worded so that both the government and the anti-opiumists could agree on it.[37] The anti-opiumist motion as introduced by Alfred Webb moved for a Royal Commission, but one to inquire into the re-structuring of Indian revenue when the suppression of the opium trade had been carried out. The government amendment, on the other hand, left the question more open. The Commission was to inquire into the whole question of the production and consumption of opium in India, to see whether it should be prohibited except for medical purposes. Webb's motion was rejected and the government motion then adopted without a division. The anti-opiumists had not followed up the 1891 victory as well as they might.[38] But the S.S.O.T. had hopes that the Commission would in any case produce the sort of report which anti-opium opinion would like to see.

This did not happen; and the Report of the Royal Commission as published in 1895 has long been regarded as whitewashing the Indian opium question. In its initial composition there was little sign of this, for the Commission had a full complement of both anti-opium and pro-opium members. Presided over by Lord Brassey, it had among its members Indian notables, R. G. C. Mowbray, a Conservative M.P. opposed to interference with the trade, as well as Arthur Pease, brother of Sir Joseph, and a member of the General Council of the S.S.O.T., and Henry Wilson, M.P., representing the anti-opiumist cause. Sir J. B. Lyall, former Governor-General of the Punjab and also a member of the Commission, remarked in a letter to Lansdowne, the Viceroy, as it began its work, that its main purpose was the silencing of the anti-opium agitation. 'The facts of the case are all really well known enough, and the object appears to be to get an expression of opinion, of native opinion in particular, which will carry sufficient weight to enable the question to be shelved.'[39]

The Commission can hardly be accused of neglecting its duty. Beginning with sittings in London in September 1893, it travelled to India in November, early in December dividing in two, with one half visiting Burma. It travelled from Calcutta in the New Year to Patna, Benares, Lucknow and Delhi before reaching Bombay, and ended its public sittings on 22 February 1894. Having asked 29,000 questions of 723 witnesses and collected 2,500 pages of evidence, it produced a report which justified the existing situation. It found that the evil effects of opium eating in India had been greatly exaggerated, drew parallels between its moderate use and that of alcohol and claimed that the state monopoly established in India really amounted to restriction of cultivation, since this was confined to definite areas. The Commissioners also considered that the Indian revenue could not at present afford the financial loss entailed by prohibition, and put the burden of action on the Chinese government if it wished the importation of opium forbidden. It denied the connection which had been made between opiate use and crime, and refused to believe that the Indian government's connection with opium was any barrier to the spread of Christianity. It stood out for the continuing acceptance of what was an accepted part of Indian culture – 'opium is extensively used for non-medical and quasi-medical purposes, in some cases with benefit, and for the most part without injurious consequences. The non-medical uses are so interwoven with the medical uses that it would not be practicable to draw a distinction between them in the distribution and sale of the drug.'[40]

To an extent, the Commission was a whitewash. Its Indian sittings were carefully managed by the government of India. Staffing was provided by the Indian Civil Service and the Commissioners were conducted about the country by those in the employ of the government. Henry Wilson wrote a strongly dissenting minority report, and the Commission was subjected to detailed scrutiny by Joshua Rowntree, employed by the S.S.O.T.[41] In some respects, however, the anti-opium case had been defeated not by unfair stage management but by the realities of Indian experience. J. G. Alexander, who accompanied the Commissioners to India, himself pointed out while in Bombay that the time there had been 'in some respects discouraging, as we have heard from so many quarters where we should have expected sympathy, that the evil is greatly exaggerated...'. However, meetings with American missionaries, 'who have really gone below the surface in this matter', had 'confirmed prejudices'.[42] Wilson and Alexander worked hard at finding anti-opium testimony, but this proved difficult; Alexander Wilson, Henry's son, who accompanied them, himself noted how rarely the opium-besotted addict of the anti-opium tracts appeared in practice. The Earl of Elgin, who had succeeded Lansdowne as Viceroy while the Commission was sitting, wrote to Godley at the India Offfice in February 1894 that the anti-opiumists had admitted 'that the case in India has broken down'.[43] Striking testimony to this was the conversion of Arthur Pease, who signed the majority report and was asked to resign from the S.S.O.T. as a result.

The Commission was less of a cover-up than the anti-opiumists proclaimed, and succeeding analyses have been less than rigorous in their wholesale acceptance of the anti-opium point of view on the Royal Commission. The anti-opiumists had been outmanoeuvred at every turn; and the publication of the report in 1895 marked the beginning of a decade of stagnation for the movement. There was a hasty unification of anti-opium forces in 1894. The Representative Board of Anti-Opium Societies was set up under the chairmanship of Joshua Rowntree when it was realized that the Commission's report was likely to be pro-opium in its conclusions. But there was little anti-opiumists could do to disguise the defeat it represented. A motion introduced by Pease in May 1895 drawing attention to the report and seeking the ending of the opium trade was decisively defeated by 176 votes to 59; and increased resignations from the ranks of the Society testified to the feeling of its members.[44] The British anti-opium movement did not revive until the early 1900s. Not until change occurred in China, and in England a Liberal government fully committed to ending the trade came to power, did it recover the political and public initiative it had lost ten years before.

The anti-opium case and English experience

Many of the standard arguments expressed in this nineteenth-century campaign bore little relation to English experience. It was, for instance, hotly debated whether the British government had in fact forced opium on China, or whether the Chinese had known and used the drug long before the Indian trade in it began, whether the Chinese were sincere or not in their wish to suppress opium or whether the opium trade was injurious to British manufactured goods. The campaign nevertheless did have a significant domestic impact, in particular in contributing to changed perceptions of domestic opium use. There are obvious dangers in exaggerating the anti-opium cause as a public issue in England in the last quarter of the century. The vehemence of the anti-opiumist argument, the sheer volume of propaganda, the energy put into organizing public meetings, petitions and parliamentary motions, could and clearly did at some stages disguise lack of public interest and a failing financial base. But at certain periods the anti-opium movement clearly was of public importance and its arguments of domestic interest. Its arguments involved opium eating as well as opium smoking; and much time and energy were spent in discussing which was the most harmful (or harmless). Every variety of opinion on the subject was to be found. Some who favoured the continuance of the trade defended opium smoking by emphasizing the correspondingly greater danger of eating the drug. Sir George Birdwood put this point of view in a letter to *The Times* in 1881: 'The habitual eating and drinking of opium are altogether different.... Opium taken internally is a powerful and dangerous narcotic stimulant, but even so, it is no worse in the effects produced by excessive use than alcohol.'[45] In the 1890s, with greater interest in Indian opium use came increased emphasis on eating the drug. The anti-opiumists presented both as harmful – or opium smoking as less harmful than opium eating.

The debate was confused – Alcock for instance, in his discussion of the effects of smoking, blithely introduced evidence relating to opium eating without attempting to differentiate – but it continually referred to English experience. The question of the sale and availability of opium, whether for eating or smoking, and of the medical use of the drug was debated very much in the light of knowledge of English narcotic use. The example of the Fens was widely quoted by those who held that opium was valuable as a febrifuge and a prophylactic against malaria; and the examples of De Quincey, Coleridge and even Wilkie Collins were taken as illustrative of the effects of opium eating. The possibility of 'stimulant' opiate use among the English working class was indicative of the dangers of taking a tolerant attitude towards opiate use in China. The old bogey of working-class use found new life as part of the anti-opium cause.[46]

English experience with opium was at once both a warning and an example in the agitation against the Indo-Chinese trade. The anti-opiumists really tried to have the best of both worlds. For the legal position of opium in England was seen, at various times, as a model of restriction which the Indian government would do well to follow – or dangerously lax, and an argument for further domestic control. The latter argument was particularly popular in the first stage of the Society's existence.[47] The need for further domestic regulation was a continuing theme into the early 1880s. But the argument from domestic experience was also turned on its head. The restrictions, however lax, which applied in England were certainly an improvement on the open availability of the drug in India. The anti-opium organizations made great play of this differing legal reaction to the sale and availability of opium. A fable for children by Dr Emily Headland, *The Lady Britannia, Her Children, Her Step-children and Her Neighbours*, pointed the contrast. Lady Britannia, 'a loving mother', had found that many of her children had a fancy for opium, 'which she evidently thinks injurious, for she takes pains to prevent them from obtaining it. Anyone who sells it to them without its being labelled "Poison", meets with her severe condemnation.' With her step-children however, it was different. 'They had been badly brought up before she took them in hand; she now sends them tutors and Governors … and is in many respects a model step-mother. … It certainly is a strange thing, if she had any love for them, that she should let them buy this opium to their hearts content.'[48] This 'pharmaceutical imperialism' was heightened in the anti-opium campaign of the 1890s. Pease, introducing his 1891 motion, pointed out the need for the Indian system of sale to be brought in line with the English one; and a declaration supposedly signed by 5,000 medical men in 1892 made the same point. At the same time, the S.S.O.T. was agitating for a tightening-up of English poisons regulations. The end result was a greater general emphasis on the need for domestic as well as Indian restriction.

The anti-opium debate was in this way responsible for helping to create a climate of opinion which saw increased restriction as desirable and it began the tradition of relating the Far Eastern situation very specifically to domestic English experience. It also had a more precise influence. The moral ideology it expounded was linked with disease views of addiction. The supposedly 'scientific' basis of the disease point of view in many respects marked only the medical reformulation of anti-opium commonplaces. It was hardly surprising that, in a debate where opium was concerned, the medical profession should have played a considerable part. The medical inutility of opium was after all one of the planks of the anti-opium case and this naturally brought English medical men quite centrally into the debate, whether from a pro-opium or anti-opium point of view.[49]

The medical component in the anti-opium ranks was notable. The S.S.O.T.'s Council included medical men. Its election address in 1880 was signed by Risdon Bennett, President of the Royal College of Physicians and a Vice-President of the Society. The most clear-cut anti-opiumist medical influence, however, came through the small cadre of addiction specialists. The development of the anti-opium movement paralleled that of addiction as a medical specialism; and many of the doctors most active in formulating concepts of addiction were also active in the moral agitation. Benjamin Ward Richardson, who had been one of the first English doctors to write extensively about morphine addiction and its treatment, was a Vice-President of the Society, organizing for it in 1892 a conference on the medical aspects of the opium question. Brigade Surgeon Robert Pringle, another prolific writer and speaker on addiction, was in fact a paid official of the S.S.O.T. Pringle was equally at home addressing an anti-opiumist gathering, or one organized by the Society for the Study of Inebriety; he was a regular speaker at the latter's meetings.[50] Norman Kerr, a temperance advocate who had founded a total abstinence society while at university in Glasgow, was another addiction specialist who moved easily between the anti-opium and specialist medical worlds.[51] Professor Arthur Gamgee, too, Dean of the Medical School at Owen's College, Manchester, and a writer on addiction, was the main speaker at a meeting held in Manchester Free Trade Hall in 1882, delivering a strenuous rejection of Birdwood's letter in *The Times*.[52]

The involvement of such men in the moral campaign strengthened the moral bias within the medical concept of addiction. There were striking parallels between medical opinion and moral propaganda on the subject. The anti-opium movement was not simply the custodian of a 'vice' view of opiate use in contrast to medical disease terminology. There was considerable cross-fertilization between the two. Both adopted the fundamental distinction between medical and non-medical use of opium which was to inform the international control agreements and subsequent domestic narcotic policy. Theories of addiction, as formulated in the late nineteenth century, largely ignored those whose use of the drug was not iatrogenic in origin. There was little place for those whose habit arose from 'viciousness' or 'curiosity'. The anti-opium agitation constantly and consistently stressed this point, too. Whereas medical use of the drug was perfectly acceptable, non-medical usage was not. The motions brought before the Commons aimed at the prohibition of poppy cultivation in India, 'except to supply the legitimate demand of opium for medical purposes'. The views of the anti-opium movement supported the medical exclusiveness of disease theories. Both attempted to establish a form of medical uniformity which bore little relation to the actual usage of the drug in the Far East. There was in fact a close relationship between the use of the drug as a luxury and as a medicine. So far as perceptions of domestic English narcotics were involved, the medical/non-medical distinction bore more relation to reality. The use of opium was by the 1890s less of the everyday non-medical occurrence it had once been.

The anti-opiumists, like most medical specialists, saw moderate opiate use as impossible. Dosage was ever-increasing and addiction inevitable. The existence of a class of moderate opium users was one of the hardest fought issues in the whole opium debate.[53] This was a continuing theme in anti-opium as well as medical literature right from the start of the anti-opium campaign. The existence of such moderate users, if accepted, would undermine both the case for ending the cultivation of the poppy and the medical argument that all regular users of the drug were the proper concern of the profession. Doctors like Kerr and Richardson gave medical sanction to the denial of moderation.[54] Yet the opposed point of view again cited English as well as Indian experience, holding that moderate use was not just possible, but positively beneficial in certain circumstances. Dr Farquharson, in the course of the 1891 debate on Pease's motion, quoted the example of a friend of his, dying from consumption. At dinner,

> He got through the early part very well, but began to flag about the middle. He went out, and when he returned he said to me, 'Do you know what I went away for? I went away to give myself a subcutaneous injection of morphia.' When he came back he was cheerful, and was stimulated in a way I am sure no small dose of alcohol or a tonic could have stimulated him. I have not the least hesitation in saying that a moderate use of this stimulant preserved that poor man's life certainly for a year or two.[55]

The anti-opiumist description of the opium user, whether smoker, eater or injector of morphine, inevitably dealt with his moral as well as physical descent. Addiction was the cause not simply of bodily deterioration, but of lapsed moral sense as well.[56] English examples were quoted to make the point.[57] The medical declaration of 1892 saw the habit as morally as well as physically debasing. The anti-opiumist argument, like that of the addiction specialists, was essentially drug-centred and lacking a social dimension. Anti-opiumist propaganda considered opium smoking in China and eating the drug in India in isolation from the social and cultural factors which sustained it. Dr James Maxwell, for instance, speaking at the 1892 medical conference, stressed that the habit was far worse among poor than among wealthy opium smokers. It was among the Chinese working class 'that we see the evil effects of opium in an unmistakeable way'. English views of addiction displayed a similar social ignorance.

In fact the anti-opium movement was, in much of its propaganda, a form of justification for the medical control of opiate use currently being established. Anti-opiumists were well aware of the disease point of view (both Levinstein and Kane's works were publicized in the *Friend of China*); and the moral emphasis of the movement's own arguments was translated into scientific respectability through the medium of doctors active in both spheres. The anti-opium movement can hardly be said to have disseminated views hostile to opiate use throughout the British public even by the end of the century. Only in the early 1880s did it gain a wide degree of public support – and this did not extend very far down in society.

Although anti-opiumist arguments were by 1895 apparently defunct, they lived on in Britain at least through the views of a significant section of the medical profession. It was by means of the élite of medical specialists in addiction that the anti-opiumist standpoint was still effectively expressed.

15

The Myth of the Opium Den
in Late Victorian England

The most obvious public legacy of the anti-opium movement was the image of the opium 'den' and of Chinese opium smoking in the East End of London which it helped to form. This emerged at the end of the century and has remained very much of a popular stereotype. The creation of the myth of the mysterious threatening 'den' in the back streets of the East End had much to do with the moral campaign and the issues it raised.

The anti-opium campaign drew attention to what was an expanding yet curiously isolated alien community. There had been Chinese in Stepney as early as the 1780s. But there were only a handful at this period and throughout the first sixty years of the following century. The Chinese who came to this country were seamen, and their presence was transient.[1] Consciousness of the Chinese in England and of their opium smoking was related to increased Chinese immigration. It is clear that the number of Chinese settling in London began to expand quite rapidly in the 1860s. In 1861, there were an estimated 147 Chinese in the whole country, by 1881, 665. Another influx came just prior to the First World War. Most lived in London. In 1891, 302 China-born aliens out of a total of 582 were resident there. Many, in particular in the early years of permanent settlement, lived in the East End, in Stepney and Poplar. In 1881, 60 per cent of London Chinese lived in these two boroughs.[2] London's 'Chinatown' was a small area in comparison to its American counterparts. The Chinese who settled in England serviced Chinese seamen by establishing laundries, shops, grocers, restaurants and lodging houses. Their American counterparts were employed in railroad construction, company mining, farming or the manufacturing industries of San

Francisco.[3] The centre of English settlement lay in two narrow streets of dilapidated houses, now destroyed by bombing and redevelopment – Pennyfields and Limehouse Causeway. The Chinese formed a small, sealed community, isolated by culture, language and the transience of their stay from the surrounding neighbourhood.

Opium smoking as a domestic phenomenon never attracted attention until the last decades of the century, for even the longevity debate took its examples from the Far East. But descriptions of opium smoking as a domestic phenomenon did begin in the 1860s. This was a reflection of the greater numbers of Chinese actually settling in the country, and of the general fashion for investigation of 'darkest England', and East London in particular. The early presentations of opium smoking in the East End were notable for their calm descriptions of the practice. Attention was drawn to the growing alien community by the Prince of Wales's visit to East London in the 1860s; and among the first descriptions of domestic opium smoking was that in *London Society* in 1868 which described the den he had been to in New Court, off Victoria Street in Bluegate Fields. Here lived Chi Ki, a Chinese married to an English wife, who had played host to the Prince.[4] Such descriptions had an air of realism. The dens were 'mean and miserable', squalid and poor, but not mysterious or threatening. A visitor to another den found the Chinese company he kept a 'pleasant-looking, good tempered lot', while the room in which the smoking took place was clean and tidy. He admired the skill with which the opium was prepared for smoking, and wondered if the practice could be given wider application: 'It might be useful if the subject were investigated by medical men, to see if opium smoking might not be found a convenient way of administering the drug to patients who otherwise cannot take it without the stomach being upset'.[5]

Dickens' famous description of opium smoking in New Court in his unfinished *Mystery of Edwin Drood* (1870) marked the beginning of a more melodramatic presentation of the subject. The author and Fields, his American friend, had witnessed opium smoking in Bluegate Fields. In his fictional presentation of the subject, Dickens emphasized the links with mystery and evil, the degrading and demoralizing effect of the drug's use on both English and Chinese smokers, which became such a feature of later descriptions.[6] The den as a haunt of evil, the evil and cunning Chinaman wreathed in opium fumes had their origin as public images in the 1870s. In the popular press, in social investigations like Blanchard Jerrold and Gustave Doré's *London, A Pilgrimage* (1872), in fictional and literary presentations, the Sherlock Holmes stories, and perhaps most notably, Oscar Wilde's *The Picture of Dorian Gray* (1891), the practice of East End opium smoking was presented in a manner soon accepted as reality. Descriptions of the 'fantastic postures on the ragged mattresses. The twisted limbs, the gaping mouths, the staring lustreless eyes...' were commonplace. Those who read that 'Upon the wreck of a four-post bedstead ... upon a mattress heaped with indescribable clothes, lay, sprawling, a lascar dead-drunk with opium... It was difficult to see any humanity on that face, as the enormous grey dry lips lapped about the rough wood pipe and drew in the poison' were unlikely to remain sanguine about the practice.[7] Not all writers were so obviously hostile; yet from the 1870s an increasing tone of racial and cultural hostility was discernible.[8]

The question of the harmfulness and general effects of opium smoking was an important part of the anti-opium debate. Increased interest in the East End opium den paralleled the rise of the anti-opium movement; and the establishment of opium smoking in England as well as in China was weighty argument for the anti-opium point of view. It gave added substance and immediacy to arguments about the effects of the practice in China. Many of the arguments deployed in an Indo-Chinese context were also relevant to the domestic scene. East End Chinese, like their Far Eastern counterparts, should be 'saved' from the habit. Anti-opiumist moral feeling took little account of cultural differences – 'these ruinous dens' were full of poor Chinese, 'helpless slaves to this expensive indulgence'. England's duty was not only to China but to the Chinese in England – the 'Vile, unhabitable tenements, transformed into the homes of vicious, ruinous indulgence... constitute a pitfall and trap to many of those simple Easterns... Has England no duty here? Have those ill-paid servants no claim upon our care?'[9]

The anti-opium arguments used for China were also applied to the East End. The missionaries in China had encountered intense hostility at many levels of society, in part inspired by the privileges granted to them by the various treaties concluded between China and the foreign powers. The missionaries, how-ever, had used opium as a convenient explanation of their notable lack of success, and such arguments were also employed in a domestic context. A correspondent in the *London City Mission Magazine* in 1877 blamed the drug for the lack of enthusiasm for Christianity among the Chinese. 'The dirt, smoke, repulsive characters and sometimes the semblance of religion assumed to cover fraud and abominable sin, make the heart sick and the head ache; and I often feel how difficult it is to launch the life-boat in such a dangerous sea.'[10] The existence of English opium dens was of considerable propaganda importance; an anti-opium tract issued by the S.S.O.T. castigated the 'depraved appetite' and the 'weak and unmanly' nature of the Chinese East End opium smoker.[11]

The medical/anti-opium link was a strong one, as Chapter 14 makes clear. Many of the doctors who supported the anti-opium movement were also concerned with domestic opium smoking. In the 1890s Benjamin Ward Richardson spent some time visiting the London dens in an attempt to compare smoking with eating opium, or injecting morphia. He concluded that there were con-siderable differences between the various methods, but neverthe-less condemned opium smoking. Surgeon-Major Pringle agreed. He told the meeting of the British Medical Association in Nottingham in 1892 that the importance of getting rid of the 'opium smoking saloons' in London 'could not be overesti-mated'.[12] Domestic opium smoking, in the view of the growing group of doctors specializing in addiction, provided further sup-port for a view of narcotic use which was rapidly becoming accepted. Medical men concerned with domestic opium use, and those who argued against Far Eastern use of the drug, were both agreed that moderation was impossible, addiction inevitable and moral and physical decline the result. 'So powerful is its fascina-tion, so fatal its hold, that loss of time, deferred expectancy, the trouble of preparation, nothing can win from the irresistible crav-ing, which, once felt, so rarely loosens its grip.'[13]

Supporters of the anti-opium cause were also active in dissemi-nating the belief that opium smoking was somehow threatening in its implications for the indigenous population. The belief that the immorality of Britain's conduct towards China ('The Great Anglo-Asiatic Opium Curse') would somehow come home to roost appeared to be justified by the existence of opium dens and their effect on English people. A *Daily Chronicle* report in 1881 had described how a large proportion of the crew of the S.S. *Merionethshire* had been found disporting themselves in a Limehouse opium den when they should have been on board ship.[14] But the time when opium smoking could be a humorous matter was soon over. The opium dens run by 'cunning and artful Chinamen' were part of the racial stereotype which emerged. As an L.C.C. inspector, an ex-policeman, pointed out after his visit to the Chinese area and its opium dens in 1904, 'oriental cunning and cruelty ... was hall-marked on every countenance ... until my visit to the Asiatic Sailors' Home, I had always considered some of the Jewish inhabitants of Whitechapel to be the worst type of humanity I had ever seen...'. At the opium den itself, the 'loathsome apartment' where the drug was prepared led to smoking rooms where seamen lay, 'dazed and helpless, jabbering in an incoherent manner'.[15] Observers saw something menacing in the very passivity which smoking the drug induced. Dr Richardson thought that opium smokers were 'very dangerous under those circumstances ... they might rise up, and be mischievous to anyone who might perform an experiment upon them, however simple it might be'.[16]

The 'menace' of opium smoking lay not just in its effect on Chinese smokers in East London, but in the possibility of contamination of English people by such practices. There was some anxiety that the habit might spread among the working class in the East End, especially since, in the investigation of the 1840s, Dr Southwood Smith had pointed out the area as one where opium was consumed in large quantities by the local population. The evidence of a local inhabitant who frequented Limehouse Causeway at this period indicated that Chinese and English populations mostly kept their distance. The boys who ran errands for the Chinese lodging house keepers sometimes tried to smoke the drug. 'I only smoked it once... They always like to see you smoke opium, a Chinaman....'

But the amount of such smoking was minute.[17] The fear of pollution through opium smoking extended into a belief that opium smoking was spreading among the white middle-class population. The establishment of such a practice was thought to be an illustration of racial degeneracy. The classic theory of contagion was clearly related to the onset of economic decline, competition for jobs and class tensions in the period of late Victorian imperialism. Professor Goldwin Smith, speaking at an anti-opium meeting in Manchester in February 1882, had drawn attention to the large influx of Chinese into America, Canada and Australia, bringing with them a 'hideous and very infectious vice'.[18] Other writers on anti-opium matters made more specific links with the domestic effects. The Rev. George Piercy, an East End missionary and anti-opiumist, warned of the dangers. Drawing parallels with the spread of the practice in America, he condemned the habit: 'we really have a new habit, prolific of evil, springing up amongst us ... it is coming close to us with a rapidity and spring undreamt of even by those who have dreaded its stealthy and unseen step'.[19] The association with middle-class degeneracy was a particular feature of the late-nineteenth-century presentation of the opium den, most notable in fiction in Wilde's *Dorian Gray*. As C. W. Wood commented in 1897, in the course of a fictional presentation of the theme, 'very many of these celestials and Indians are mentally and physically inferior, and they go on smoking year after year, and seem not very much the worse for it. It is your finer natures that suffer, deteriorate and collapse. For these great and terrible is the ruin.'[20] There were tales of two prosperous 'opium establishments' in the East End, set up exclusively for a white clientele and patronized by Englishmen or 'society women seeking a new sensation'. Furnished in lavish style, entry to them was obtainable only by means of a password. The West End opium smoker, seeking after fresh thrills, was a new facet of the contemporary presentation of the opium den.[21] It was a particular illustration of the anti-opiumist argument which stressed the domestic retribution likely to be incurred through encouragement of the Indo-Chinese trade.

The image of the opium den associated with late-nineteenth-century London has remained so persistent that it is worth attempting to assess the reality of the practice. The hostile reaction evoked in anti-opiumist literature and in fiction appears on further examination to have disguised something much more prosaic. It is impossible to find out how much opium was being imported for smoking. Published import/export data, unlike their American counterpart, ignored prepared opium. The number of houses, however, where the practice took place appears to have been small in relation to the furore it caused. In 1884, even a hostile observer thought that there were only about half a dozen in the East End. Later inquiries elicited from the police only the information that there were thirteen Chinese boarding houses in the area. It was tacitly accepted that opium smoking would probably take place in a fair number of them. 'Opium smoking is a national habit with them, and they indulge in it in their bedrooms. The practice is rather on the decrease than otherwise.'[22] The 'den' was a shifting entity, changing its location almost as often as the floating population of seamen in the area. Miss Mary Elliott, whose father was Vicar of St Stephen's, Poplar, in the late nineteenth century, remembered the impermanent nature of the opium den. When the police raided a suspect house, they would find it empty, or fresh Chinese moving in who 'of course' knew nothing of the previous tenants.[23]

Nor was reaction to the practice so universally hostile as the accepted image of the opium den might suggest. Many of the more open-minded investigators of the practice came to the conclusion that there was really no such thing as an opium den at all. Opium smoking, along with gambling, was simply a relaxation enjoyed by many Chinese, and the rooms where it took place were something akin to a Chinese social club. A reporter sent by the *Morning Advertiser*, who had gone to the East End full of preconceived ideas about opium smoking, had to admit that 'it was not repulsive. It was calm, it was peaceful. There was a placid disregard of trivialities, politics, war, betting, trade, and all the cares, occupations, and incidents of daily life, which only opium can give'.[24] Several who visited the area came to conclusions which differed from the accepted stereotype. One such visitor smoked five pipes of opium in 'Chinatown' in the 1870s, and experienced hallucinations in which a centipede about four or five inches long with a chain round it was walking up his leg. 'This will not be my last trial,' he declared. 'As for the so-called "dens", they seemed to me simply poorly fitted social clubs, and certainly as free from anything visibly objectionable, as to say the least of it, public-houses of the same class.'[25] His last point was taken up by those who felt that to stigmatize opium smoking simply because it was an alien recreational practice was hypocritical when domestic alcohol consumption continued relatively unchecked.[26]

The reactions of those who lived in the area at the time and saw opium smoking at close quarters tend to agree with such moderate assessments. These are the best antidote to the opium den myth. In 1908, news that young boys had been mingling with the Chinese seamen in Limehouse was a cause for concern to the London County Council's Medical Officer.[27] One of those boys, living as an old man a few hundred yards from where he used to run errands for the seamen years before, disagreed sharply with the view of the den presented in late nineteenth-century fiction: '... you'd push a door open and you'd see them smoking ... I used to be in number 11, and in that house there on the second floor we had one bed, but on the ground floor, we had two, two beds. They were always there and as they walked in, and as they fancied a piece of opium....' There were no set houses reserved for opium smoking. It was simply a way in which Chinese seamen spent part of their leisure time while they were on shore:

> There was one or two houses, but, of course, it took place in most houses. In every house that I've been in, there's been a bed or two. It was quite natural for the people who lived in that house.... They're ordinary working people that come in here and have their pipe, because they're paid off from the shipping and they have their pleasure time in the Causeway as long as their money lasts.

Nor, in his eyes, was the image of the dazed, lolling opium smoker, caring for nothing but the drug, at all typical. Opium smoking was an aid to hard work, not a distraction from it, and smokers managed to combine their habit with a normal working existence. 'I've known them to get up at eight, seven or eight in the morning, smoke opium twice, two periods of opium, and then go and do their duty, do their work and they won't go to bed before eleven o'clock at night.'[28] In Liverpool at the same period, a City Council report on the Chinese settlements in the city revealed a similar reaction. The practice of opium smoking was limited; and even local police officers saw few harmful effects in it.[29]

The way the Limehouse resident saw opium prepared tallies almost exactly with the reports, shorn of their sensationalism, given by outside investigators. The preparation of the raw opium for smoking was a lengthy process, involving shredding the raw drug into a sieve placed over an ordinary two-pint saucepan containing water. This was simmered over a fire, and the essence, filtering through the sieve, fell to the bottom of the pot in a thin-nish treacle. Opium was often scraped out of the pipes in the house and added to the raw variety. The pot in which the essence landed would be constantly pushed and kneaded, although in some houses this was done in a different way. 'They got a long feather of a bird, a large bird, and they'll just skim the top of the opium, and until that opium is absolutely perfect without a bubble on it, and it's boiled to the amount that they've tested, and that's that....' The opium thus prepared was stored in lidded earthenware jars. Sometimes it was sold to outside customers; often seamen would buy it when going aboard ship. It was carried about in a hollowed-out lemon – the inside of the lemon taken out, the shell put over a broom handle and bound tightly with string until it was com-pletely dried out. Opium was weighed in this too.

> They bring out a great big quill from some gigantic bird ... with a little leaden weight at one end, with a nice silk coloured ribbon on it and a steelyard ... and they'll put your empty on first and they'll weigh your empty. They'll weigh it, dive down under the counter, put it in, like treacle, weigh it again then give it to you. And I've gone there for a cook and he's had 1s/6d ... they got a lot for 1s/6d.[30]

A special pipe, about eighteen inches long and often made of dark-coloured bamboo, was used for the actual smoking. One end, hollow and open, served as the mouthpiece. At the closed end, a tiny bowl 'made of iron and shaped like a pigeon's egg' was screwed in. Prior to smoking, a small quantity of prepared opium was taken on the point of a needle and frizzled over the flame of a lamp – 'twist it and twist it until it becomes sticky, a solid sticky substance...'. The opium pipe was then placed over the lamp and the opium inserted on the point of a needle through a small hole in the bowl of the pipe. The smoker would draw continually at the pipe until the substance was burnt out – 'the Chinaman ... took the bamboo fairly into his mouth, and there was at once emitted from the pipe a gurgling sound – the spirits of ten thou-sand previous pipe-loads stirred to life'.[31]

The interest aroused in the practice by the growth of the anti-opium movement had led to a corresponding period of medical experimentation with opium smoking. Smoking the drug was sug-gested for the treatment of tetanus; it was said to be 'an easy, inoffensive, and very efficacious mode of treating chronic and neuralgic affections ...'. An opium pipe (complete with 'all appurtenances, including lamp, vessel for oil, boxes for opium, etc.') was available for medical experimenters and others from Farmer & Rogers, in Regent Street, price 10/6.[32] Brereton's book on opium smoking and the publications of the defenders not only of the opium trade, but of opium's medical usage, encouraged such experimentation. A pamphlet dealing with *Opium Smoking as a Therapeutic Power According to the Latest Medical Authorities* was available from the 1870s – although its publication was discontinued in 1903 after strong protests from the *Lancet*.[33]

Medical usage had its parallels in social experimentation. Notably lacking at this period was any extensive narcotic-using drug sub-culture. But there were signs that the increasing deviance of opium use was beginning to be reflected in self-conscious 'recreational' use. Opium smoking as a distinctively different means of using the drug was the first form to experience this development. The drug began to be used for smoking among a small section of artistic society in the 1890s. 'Recreational' smoking of opium – and of other drugs such as cannabis and mescal – was largely confined to the 'radical Bohemia' of the avant-garde arts world and left-wing intelligentsia, small groups whose flouting of 'respectable' late-Victorian convention emphasized an interest in the spiritual, non-materialist side of life which encompassed both the occult and the effects of drugs.[34] Opium smoking was very much part of the developing drug 'scene'. Perhaps the most notable literary exponent in the 1890s was Count Eric Stenbock, the son of a Bremen family settled in England, but who had inherited estates in Estonia. Stenbock's practice of smoking opium was as notorious as his alcoholism. This homosexual occultist, accustomed to appear with a live snake encircling his neck, was truly 'a sort of living parody of Ninetyism'.[35] Yet opium smoking was also practised by other, less theatrically flamboyant members of the 1890s scene. The poet Arthur Symons described the experience in 'The Opium Smoker'.

> I am engulfed, and drown deliciously.
> Soft music like a perfume, and sweet light
> Golden with audible odours exquisite,
> Swathe me with cerements for eternity.

Time is no more, I pause and yet I flee.
A million ages wrap me round with night.
I drain a million ages of delight.
I hold the future in my memory.[36]

Oscar Wilde's description in *The Picture of Dorian Gray* (1891) and the revelations of the Sherlock Holmes stories were indicative of the milieu in which such use was acceptable. The reality was, however, sometimes more prosaic than its fictional presentation. The Limehouse resident who saw West End 'slummers' trying opium smoking in the early 1900s remarked that many had to give up because they could not keep the flame alight.

The reality of the practice was thus more prosaic, more narrowly circumscribed than the myth would suggest; the reaction of local people most in touch with it was tolerant; and the associations with white society limited. Yet opium smoking evoked a distinctly harsher legal response. In the early twentieth century, the legal controls imposed on the alien practice of opium smoking were to be an indication of the attempt which was to be made to introduce a generally absolute narcotic policy. But there was no distinct legislative response to Chinese opium smoking in England in the nineteenth century.[37] Moves against opium smoking in England first came at a local level and expanded at the time of the First World War into nationwide control.[38] The myth of the opium den was in the wider sense a domestic result of imperialism and the reaction to economic uncertainty. The Chinese and their opium use were a useful scapegoat. The cultural insensitivity which informed the reactions to Far Eastern opium use had its domestic counterpart; and the reaction to what was in reality only the customary relaxation of Chinese seamen illustrated both the structural tensions of late Victorian society and the changed place of opium within it.

PART EIGHT

The End of the Century

16

The Other 'Narcotics':
Caannabis and Cocaine

Two other drugs have long been thought of, along with opium, as 'dangerous narcotics'. The same problem framework was applied to cannabis and cocaine. Neither in fact can properly be called a narcotic drug. Cannabis is closer to the hallucinogens than to any other drug classification; cocaine is a stimulant. In the nineteenth century the drugs, both late arrivals on the scene, played a quite minor medical and social role in comparison to that of opium. They were nevertheless associated with that drug, not least in the discussions of the concept of addiction. They too had a part in the establishment of altered perceptions of 'narcotic' use.

Cannabis

Cannabis itself has a quite bewildering variety of derivations, variously named. The resinous exudation of the flowering tops and leaves is generally known as hashish; material derived by chopping the leaves and stalks is termed marijuana. But the variety of alternative terms in use was and is testimony to the drug's established place in the culture of many Eastern countries. Hashish was called esrat in Turkey (meaning simply a secret production or preparation), kif in Morocco, or madjun when it was made into a sweetmeat with butter, honey, nutmeg and cloves. It had been known to the Chinese several thousand years before Christ and the ancient Greeks and Romans had used it for both medical and social purposes.[1] In India, Persia, Turkey and Egypt it was in common use from quite remote times. The word 'assassin' supposedly derived from its use in Syria in the twelfth century to designate the followers of the 'Old Man of the Mountains' or Hasan-Ibn-Sabbah; they were called so because hashish was in frequent use among them. The term possibly owed its origin, too, to those Saracens who, intoxicated with the drug, were willing at the time of the crusades to go on suicidal expeditions into the enemy camp.

Cannabis was known in Europe well before the nineteenth century. In 1563, Garcia de Orta noted its use in India. Engelbert Kaempfer, the seventeenth-century German physician and botanist, had described the plant and its medical uses in an account of his travels in the Far East, *Amoenitatum Exoticarum Politico-Physico-Medicarum* (1712), known in England through the efforts of Sir Hans Sloane, president of the Royal College of Physicians.[2] Dr Robert Hooke brought it to the attention of Fellows of the Royal Society in 1689. Indian hemp, which 'seemeth to put a man into a dream', might, he thought, 'be of considerable use for lunatics'. Berlu in his *Treasury of Drugs* (1690) described its import from Bantam in the East Indies.[3] Such early accounts were, on present evidence, not followed up and the drug was not used in medical practice. Its popular usage was known. Pollen evidence indicates that hemp was cultivated in Western Europe before the birth of Christ; there is evidence of it in north-west England and southern Norway in Romano-British times. From around A.D. 500, hemp cultivation was more abundant, and persisted until quite recently. As contemporary court cases demonstrate, domestic cultivation of the plant is not impossible. Streets and districts in rural areas known as Hempfield are testimony to the former cultivation of the drug.[4]

Cannabis, like opium, had its popular uses which have been forgotten in the later medical emphasis. It was in the nineteenth century, however, that medical usage of the drug began in England. European, and particularly French, awareness of the intoxicating properties of the drug had been stimulated by the Napoleonic conquest of Egypt; the French administration of the country imposed heavy penalties for selling, using or trafficking in it. 'Travellers' tales' of the East, as in the case of opium, also served to publicize the drug.[5] Dr William O'Shaughnessy, an Edinburgh-educated Irishman, had a notable medical career. His studies of the blood in the English cholera epidemic of 1831, although controversial at the time, laid the foundations of intravenous fluid therapy, and his experiments with the electric telegraph while in India led to the establishment of an early telegraph network and a knighthood from Queen Victoria.[6] It was while he was out in India that O'Shaughnessy encountered the use of cannabis. His paper 'On the preparations of the Indian hemp, or gunjah (cannabis indica); their effects on the animal system in health, and their utility in the treatment of tetanus and other convulsive diseases' was published in 1842 in the *Transactions of the Medical and Physical Society of Calcutta.*[7]

O'Shaughnessy's careful survey of the uses of the drug led him to an advocacy of it as an 'anti-convulsive remedy of the greatest value'. While noting 'the singular form of delirium which the incautious use of the Hemp preparations often occasions ... the strange balancing gait ... a constant rubbing of the hands; perpetual giggling; and a propensity to caress and chafe the feet of all bystanders of whatever rank', he nevertheless recommended that both the extract and the tincture should be used by medical men.[8] Peter Squire of Oxford Street was responsible for converting cannabis resin into the extract and distributed it to a large number of the profession under O'Shaughnessy's directions. The extract and tincture both later appeared in the British Pharmacopoeia, and the Society of Apothecaries and other wholesalers included both in their wholesale production.[9] The drug was even cultivated commercially for a time near Mitcham.[10]

Cannabis appears to have been quite infrequently used in medical practice. Interruption of supply and uncertainty of action were the reasons given. Dr Russell Reynolds, in his textbook, recommended its use for sleeplessness (in particular in the treatment of delirium tremens), for neuralgia and dysmenorrhoea.[11] Seasickness and asthma also opened up possibilities for the use of the drug.[12] Cannabis indica was also in limited use as part of a possible treatment regime for opium eating, as that condition became considered as one suitable for treatment. Dr Mattison recommended the use of the fluid extract for the restlessness and insomnia consequent upon the withdrawal of opium.[13] But cannabis was never anything of a rival to opium; its medical acceptability was always far more limited.

In one sphere it did gain a foothold. The utility of cannabis in the treatment of insanity was seriously mooted in the last quarter of the century. Experimentation with the use of the drug for this purpose was initially a French interest. It was the work of Dr Jean Moreau at the Bicêtre Hospital in Paris and his publications of *Du haschish et de l'alienation mentale* in 1845, which drew attention in France to the possibilities of its use for the insane.[14] In England, trials of cannabis appear to have owed little directly to the French example. They were part of the elaboration of more extensive treatment and drug regimes at this time – and part, too, of the reaction away from opium as a standby. Dr Thomas Clouston, superintendent of the Cumberland and Westmorland Asylum at Carlisle, won the Fothergillian Gold Medal of the Medical Society of London in 1870 for his 'Observations and experiments on the use of opium, bromide of potassium, and cannabis indica in insanity, especially in regard to the effects of the two latter given together'.[15] Clouston's researches inclined him to favour the two latter and his conclusions attracted a fair amount of medical attention. Henry Maudsley himself, while enthusiastic about Clouston's denigration of opium, was less sure about the remedies he proposed to substitute. The question in his mind was 'whether the forcible quieting of a patient by narcotic medicines does not diminish the excitement at the expense of his mental power'. Maudsley had nevertheless used Clouston's method in a recent case, where he had seen a rapid recovery.[16]

But cannabis was also seen as a cause of insanity. The connection between cannabis use and mental illness, debated to this day, had its origin in English medical discussions and in Indian and Egyptian evidence at the end of the nineteenth century. The connection initially arose in observation of the form of intoxication which the drug's use could give rise to. What was seen as a form of poisoning was elaborated into a distinct variety of insanity. As early as 1848 frequent use of the drug was said to brutalize the intellect; it was in the 1870s that the argument was developed. W. W. Ireland, writing in the *Journal of Mental Science*, likened the condition following the use of the drug to the delirium of insanity. The alteration of notions of time and space and the illusions of sight also, where short distances appeared immense, were akin to the delusions of insanity.[17] The 'professionalization' of varieties of insanity had its effect in the area of cannabis use.

Since cannabis was so little used in England, it was evidence from the East which most effectively gave support to the view. It was through British doctors' reports on the Cairo Asylum in the 1890s that the connection between cannabis use and insanity was made in England. The colonial implications of the drug had significant domestic repercussions. But there was quite telling testimony which pointed to the absence of a connection. Parliamentary and governmental investigations on the East and India in the 1890s tended to cast doubt on any link.[18]

This was very much the conclusion reached, on the basis of a more scientific evaluation of the evidence, by the Indian Hemp Drugs Commission of 1893–4. The Commission, set up to examine the trade in hemp drugs, their effect on the social and moral condition of the people, and the desirability of prohibiting cultivation, has, in recent years, been rescued from obscurity. Its conclusions – that the physical, mental and moral effects of hemp drugs used in moderation were not adverse, that there was no evidence of cannabis use leading to addiction and that prohibition would be unworkable – appeared particularly relevant to the campaign to legalize cannabis in the 1960s, even though the blanket applicability of the Commission's findings has been disputed. There was little domestic discussion of the Commission's findings in the 1890s, partly because they appeared to have little relevance to English experience. There was no perceived problem of domestic cannabis use. What the Commission did succeed in doing, however, was to demolish the more facile medical belief in the connection of cannabis with insanity. Its detailed analysis of how those statistics connecting the two had been compiled decisively demonstrated the haphazard way in which conclusions had been drawn. Nine out of fourteen cases in the Dacca asylum attributed to hashish insanity, for instance, were shown not to have been so caused. The idea that hemp drugs were responsible for one third of all the cases of insanity in India had to be seriously revised. In many cases over-indulgence in hashish was not a cause, but merely a symptom of some underlying predisposition to insanity.[19] Nevertheless the insanity argument proved obstinately persistent. Dr Warnock, superintendent of the Cairo Asylum, published a report of his work there in 1895 which took no account at all of the findings of the Indian Commission.[20] Warnock's findings were taken up and incorporated within popular and medical belief; the analyses of the Hemp Drugs Commission were forgotten.

Discussion of hemp drugs and insanity was part of an increased medical interest in the drug and its effects in general in the 1890s. Part of the expanding medical examination of new and more effective remedies (which had led to the downgrading of opium) was an attempt to examine cannabis more scientifically and in particular to isolate an active principle. There had been attempts at this ever since the drug's introduction in the late 1830s, and there were a bewildering variety of products, which included cannabis, cannabene, cannabin tannin, cannabinine and others. But the active principle of the drug had still to be isolated. The unreliability of cannabis preparations remained a serious drawback to their general use in medicine. Cannabinol was isolated by Wood, Spirey and Easterfield in 1895. Research into the drug's effects was continued in the medical school at Cambridge.[21] The interest displayed in these years also helped make the reputation of a medical man to be an important force in the shaping of narcotic policy. Walter Ernest Dixon, a leading member of the Rolleston Committee on Morphine and Heroin Addiction in the 1920s and a public opponent of penal narcotics policy on the American model, worked on the pharmacology of cannabis indica while Salters Research Fellow in the 1890s. His conclusions were that activity would vary greatly according to the type of preparation used. The mode of ingestion had its different effect, too, and Dixon recommended smoking the drug if an immediate effect was desired. 'Hemp taken as an inhalation,' he decided, 'may be placed in the same category as coffee, tea, and kola. It is not dangerous and its effects are never alarming, and I have come to regard it in this form as a useful and refreshing stimulant and food accessory, and one whose use does not lead to a habit which grows upon its votary.'[22]

Research of this type under a medical imprint into the mental as well as the physical effects of cannabis use had a striking parallel in the establishment of a recreational hashish-using sub-culture at the same period. Use of the drug in literary circles in many ways simply transferred to a non-scientific setting the aims and methods of medical research into the drug. Cannabis became part of the same sub-culture which experimented with opium smoking. The doctrine of 'art for art's sake' which found expression in the drawings of Beardsley and the aestheticism of Oscar Wilde involved an emphasis on sensation and inner experience redolent of the Romantics. The 1880s and 1890s were a time of interest in the paranormal and in psychic phenomena. Spiritualism underwent a recrudescence; the Theosophical Society and the Society for Psychical Research were both founded in the 1880s. Interest in the occult and mystic phenomena were all part of the same tendency. It was among the members of a mystic order, the Hermetic Order of the Golden Dawn, and its literary associates, organized in 1891 into the Rhymers' Club which met in The Cheshire Cheese in the Strand, that recreational drug use was most common. It recalled the emphasis on experience and the inner life of the Romantic poets and writers; and indeed, Coleridge and Tom Wedgwood had tried a sample of 'bang' from India in 1803.[23]

William Butler Yeats, a member of both the 1890s groups, had smoked hashish while in Paris. He and Maud Gonne had experimented in extra-sensory communication, and she, while using cannabis for insomnia, had awoken one night to find herself apparently translated to the bedside of her sister Kathleen. Smoking hashish and drinking black coffee were reported to be among the more defiant and unconventional activities at the Rhymers' Club meetings; and several of the poets who congregated there toyed with the drug. Ernest Dowson had experimented while at Oxford, and did so again in the company of the writers Arthur Symons and John Addington Symonds and some of Symons' friends from the ballet one afternoon in Symons' rooms in Fountain Court, Temple. By the early 1900s, experimentation with the effects of drugs on consciousness seems to have been an accepted part of life in certain literary cum artistic milieux. Smoking opium and hashish were perhaps most commonly favoured, although Havelock Ellis (using Dowson and Yeats as guinea pigs) had been experimenting with mescal.[24] Drug-taking in this way was a quite minor part of the artists' experience; the sub-culture as a 'way of life' was at this period very much in the future.

Cocaine

Cocaine, perhaps surprisingly, was not an important part of the search for experience in literary circles at the turn of the century. As a separate alkaloid it had in fact only recently come into medical practice. The coca leaf itself, from which the alkaloid was derived, was, like cannabis, a nineteenth-century novelty in European medicine. The coca chewing of the Peruvian Indians had been known since the discovery of the Americas, but, unlike tobacco, the coca leaf was never introduced into European society. The attitude of the Spanish conquistadores of Peru was perhaps important; coca chewing, like other native customs, was regarded as a vice. The drug had been originally regarded by the Incas as a symbol of divinity, and it hence became known in Europe initially, as had cannabis and opium-eating, through the medium of 'travellers' tales' and later through more scientific description and investigation. Many of these descriptions were enthusiastic about the sustaining properties of the leaf. None was perhaps more so than Abraham Cowley, an English physician and poet who celebrated the virtues of coca in his *Book of Plants* (1662). Coca was:

> Endowed with leaves of wondrous nourishment, whose juice sucked in, and lo the stomach taken long hunger and long labour can sustain: From which our faint and weary bodies find more succour, more they cheer the dropping mind, than can your Bacchus and your Ceres joined.[25]

It was at about this time – in the late eighteenth and early nineteenth centuries – that a more scientific evaluation of coca began to prepare the way for its introduction into European medicine. Joseph de Jussieu, a botanist who had accompanied the French mathematician La Condamine to Quito in 1735, sent specimens to Europe for examination; through him the plant received the classification Erythroxylon coca. Poeppig, the German naturalist, Martius, Dr Weddell, a French botanist who went to South America in 1845, Clements Markham, von Tschudi, the Swiss naturalist, and the English botanist Richard Spriuce – all commented on the Indian use of coca. This examination of the drug was, like the experiments with British opium and interest in the alkaloids of that drug, another illustration of the growth of scientific inquiry and specialization in the early decades of the century.[26] The work of Dr Paolo Mantegazza was important in establishing the potentialities of coca for European medical use. Mantegazza, who had practised medicine for some time in Peru, on his return to Italy, published in 1859 *Sulle virtù igieniche e medicinali della coca*, in which, while describing the hallucinatory effects which the drug had had on him, he recommended it for a range of illnesses including toothache, digestive disorders and neurasthenia. It was about this time that the drug's active principle was isolated. The discovery of cocaine, the main alkaloid contained within the coca leaf, is generally attributed to Albert Niemann of Göttingen, although in 1855 Friedrich Gaedcke had produced from a distillate of the dry residue of an extract of coca a crystalline sublimate he called 'Erythroxylon'. It was Niemann who in 1860 isolated pure cocaine from leaves brought to Europe by Dr Scherzer. Wilhelm Lossen described its chemical formula in 1862; the isolation and description of other coca alkaloids followed later in the century.[27]

It was not cocaine, however, but the properties of the coca leaf which initially attracted most attention. The 1870s in England in particular were the time when most medical discussion took place; the coca leaf was part of the general increase of medical interest in new and apparently more scientific and exact remedies. Dr Anstie had mentioned the drug in his *Stimulants and Narcotics* in 1864; its moderate use seemed, he thought, 'to have an influence upon nutrition almost indistinguishable from that of ordinary food as to its ultimate results'.[28] The work of Dr Alexander Hughes Bennett of Edinburgh began more detailed investigations. The coca leaf was already in general use as a stimulant and tonic in a variety of diseases; Bennett's work with it, and with cocaine, a small quantity of which he obtained from Macfarlan's in Edinburgh 'after great difficulty', demonstrated the similarity of the physiological actions of coca, tea, coffee, guaranine and cocoa and of their active principles.[29] There followed a period of increased experimentation.[30]

In 1876, the American pedestrian, Weston, used the coca leaf in walking trials in London. He found the results disappointing; the leaves did not have the expected effect, but instead acted as an opiate. He came to the conclusion that the drug would in fact be detrimental in any trial of physical endurance.[31] Many medical men were, however, also trying the drug in the same way. Foremost among them was the veteran Sir Robert Christison, investigator of opium in the early decades of the century, and now, in his old age, an advocate of the advantages of coca chewing. Christison wrote in the *British Medical Journal* in 1876 how he had made two 'walking trials' with coca (or cuca) leaves, one in 1870, the other in 1875. His students at Edinburgh had experienced 'the removal of fatigue, and the ability for active exertion' through its use. Christison himself had been enabled to walk fifteen miles

without fatigue; and his two ascents of Ben Vorlich in the High-
lands were exceptional for a man of his age. He wrote:

> My companions ... were provided with an excellent luncheon
> ... but I contented myself with chewing two-thirds of one
> drachm of cuca-leaves ... I went down the long descent with
> an ease like that which I used to enjoy in my mountainous
> rambles in my youth. At the bottom, I was neither weary, nor
> hungry, nor thirsty, and felt as if I could easily walk home four
> miles...'[32]

For a time chewing coca became quite the rage among medical
men. Even Sir Clifford Allbutt took it with him on a walking tour
in the Alps in the hope of amazing his fellow climbers.

But there was still much disagreement about the general therapeutic possibilities of the coca leaf. Mr Graham Dowdeswell, for
instance, writing of his researches into its action in the *Lancet* in
1876, concluded that its effect was so slight as to preclude any
therapeutic or popular value.[33] Yet other medical men were not
averse to recommending it for what would now be more exactly
defined as non-medical usage. Dr William Tanner was reported
as praising it as a cure for bashfulness – 'it causes timid people,
who are usually ill at ease in society ... to appear to good
advantage ...'. A doctor-sportsman was full of admiration for its
effect in steadying his aim: 'Filling my flask with the coca tincture,
instead of with brandy ... down went the birds right and
left ...'[34]

It was not until the powers of the alkaloid as a local anaesthetic
were fully understood that the drug won complete medical acceptability. It was the early work of Sigmund Freud, and of his friend
and research colleague, Carl Koller, in Stricker's laboratory in
Vienna, which brought this about. Freud's use of cocaine is,
because of his own enormous fame, well-known. He first became
interested in the drug and its properties after reading a report of
how Dr Theodore Aschenbrandt, a German army physician, had
issued cocaine experimentally to some Bavarian soldiers during
autumn manoeuvres. The results were promising. Freud obtained
some cocaine for himself from Merck's of Darmstadt and began
to experiment. Fifty milligrams in a glass of water left him cheerful
and energetic. In May, influenced by American reports of the
drug's use as a cure for morphine addiction, he began to administer

cocaine to his friend Ernst von Fleischl-Marxow, who had become addicted to morphine to dull the pain of an amputated thumb. In his paper 'On Coca' ('Über Coca') published in July 1884, he produced the first major positive survey of the drug's therapeutic uses. Contending that it should be regarded as a stimulant rather than a narcotic, he blamed past failures on bad-quality preparations. From his own experience, he recommended the drug for a variety of illnesses and specially for symptoms such as fatigue, nervousness, neurasthenia and, most significantly, as a cure for morphine addiction.[35] Freud himself continued to experiment with the drug for several years; he published five papers in all on it, the last, 'Craving for and fear of cocaine', in 1887.

What can almost be termed Freud's love-affair with cocaine was an interesting episode in his career, albeit one which he preferred to disguise in later life. His enthusiastic advocacy owed something to his own personal circumstances, in particular the desire as a young medical researcher to establish a serious reputation and hence to be able to marry his fiancée Martha Bemays (to whom he wrote enthusiastically of the properties of cocaine) much earlier than he would otherwise have been able. It is possible, too, that his use of cocaine (which certainly continued to some degree after the last paper was published in 1887) may have mediated his change from physiological to mainly psychiatric interests. Certainly, as this change of emphasis began when he was working with Charcot in Paris in 1885 and 1886, Freud was still using cocaine regularly. Some interpretations relate his usage of the drug more specifically to the release of his creativity.

Of more long-term significance for medical usage of the drug, however, was the re-discovery of cocaine's anaesthetic properties made by Carl Koller. That the drug had this local anaesthetic effect had been known for some time. In 1862, for instance, a researcher called Schroff had noticed a numbing effect when he put some on his tongue; six years later, a Peruvian doctor, Thomas Moreno y Maiz, suggested that it might be a useful local anaesthetic. In the 1870s both Charles Faurel and von Anrep had noticed the anaesthetizing effect it had on the mucous membranes. Bennett, too, in his 1873 report had observed this property without fully realizing its significance.[36] Koller's application of it to surgery was made while working at Vienna with Freud. Koller had been concerned with finding a suitable anaesthetic for eye surgery; the

Richardson ether spray then in use was unsuitable for such delicate operations. The general narcosis which resulted prevented the patient's active co-operation, and the subsequent nausea and vomiting often damaged the work which had been carried out. As with many important discoveries much controversy surrounded this one – Freud later declared, for instance, that had he not left Vienna one weekend in September 1884, to see his fiancée, he too would have shared in the discovery; Koller denied that his discovery of the effect of cocaine on the eye was due to the fact that a drop fell into his own eye accidentally. In September 1884, he experimented with the drug on the eye of a frog and of a guinea-pig. 'I found the cornea and conjunctiva anaesthetic,' he reported, '... insensitive to mechanical, chemical, thermic and faradic stimulation. Afterwards, I repeated these experiments on myself, some colleagues and many patients.' Koller's paper on the subject and a practical demonstration of the experiment were given at the Heidelberg Ophthalmological Society in September 1884.[37]

The anaesthetic properties which Koller thereby disclosed were eagerly seized upon by a profession which had long sought an adequate and safe means of performing such delicate surgery. The use of the drug was extended into other areas. In New York in October 1885, Leonard Corning, a neurologist interested in local medication of the spinal cord, successfully anaesthetized the lower extremities by injecting cocaine between the eleventh and twelfth dorsal vertebrae. In 1889, August Bier of Kiel reported on six operations he had performed using spinal anaesthesia, and the method soon became quite common. Early experiments on nerve blocking or conduction anaesthesia, by injecting cocaine into the path of a sensory nerve trunk to anaesthetize the fibres of its peripheral distribution, were made by William Stewart Halsted in New York in the winter of 1884-5. Halsted's experiments were given little publicity; the method of nerve-block anaesthesia which he pioneered was only generally adopted around the turn of the century.

Even more extraordinary was the wave of popularity which cocaine enjoyed among the medical profession at large once Koller's discovery became known. In England in the mid-1880s, the pages of the medical journals were crammed with enthusiastic demonstrations of the uses of the drug; doctors flooded into print in its praise and each contribution purported to establish a different usage to which this wonder drug could be put. There were sixty-seven separate pieces about it in the first 1885 volume of the *British Medical Journal*. Its utility as a local anaesthetic in operations on the vagina and urethra, in dentistry, ophthalmic surgery, in vaccination, in operations on the nose and larynx, vomiting, mammary abscess, in cancer, scalds, circumcision, neuralgia, hay fever, senile gangrene and even in the removal of a needle from a foot were all canvassed. Nymphomania, sea-sickness – there seemed no limit to the possibilities. The usual medical controversies over the exact mode of action of the drug began.

The drug made its mark in a popular non-medical way, too; cocaine and coca were used as patent medicines. The name of Mariani was most commonly associated with coca products. W. Golden Mortimer even dedicated his *History of Coca 'The Divine Plant' of the Incas* (1901) to Angelo Mariani, the Parisian chemist and entrepreneur who was successfully selling coca extract not only as Vin Mariani, but also Elixir Mariani, Pâté Mariani, Pastilles Mariani and Thé Mariani (a non-alcoholic variety). Mariani's were not the only commercial coca products on the market. In 1888, Messrs Ambrecht, Nelson and Co. of Duke Street, London, had several varieties of coca wine, including sweet malaga (used by ladies and children) and a Burgundy coca wine for gouty and dyspeptic cases; there was also coca sherry and coca port. In 1894 there were at least seven firms producing coca wines for the domestic market.[38]

The medical disapproval of opiate-based patent medicines which had found expression even in the seventies and eighties did not initially extend to coca products. The *Lancet* was recommending them 'with confidence' in cases where a restorative was needed; their appearance and listing in medical journals betokened their general acceptability. The line of division between 'medical' and 'non-medical' products as well as usage was not closely defined. William Martindale, for instance, whose supplement on cocaine in the third edition of his *Extra Pharmacopoea* in 1884 had done much to advertise the uses of the drug as a local anaesthetic and much else besides, was producing his own brand of pastilles 'intended for the temporary relief of hunger, thirst, fatigue, exhaustion, distaste for food, or nervous depression and weak digestion'.[39] In the 1890s Burroughs Wellcome likewise had cocaine tabloids for what would now be regarded non-medical use. These 'voice tabloids', composed of cocaine, chlorate of potash and borax, were said to 'impart a clear and silvery tone to the voice. They were easily retained in the mouth while singing and speaking ... used by the leading singers and public speakers throughout the world.'[40]

But medical approval began to wane in the 1890s. Commercial coca products were separated from their previous semi-medical status and were incorporated in the general medical and pharmaceutical campaign against the availability of all patent medicines.[41] This was part of a remarkable medical *volte-face* on the use of cocaine in general. The euphoria of 1884–5 was soon replaced by an appreciation of the dangers which such unrestrained use could give rise to. The use of cocaine to treat morphine addiction was strongly called in question. Freud had praised the drug for its utility in this way. Fleischl, to whom he had administered the drug, himself became dependent on it in place of morphine.[42] The whole pattern of events was very similar to the earlier medical enthusiasm for, and subsequent partial rejection of, hypodermic morphine. With cocaine, the process was completed in a very much shorter time. By 1887, the *British Medical Journal* could comment that the 'undeniable reaction against the extravagant pretensions advanced on behalf of this drug had already set in'.[43] The work of Dr J. B. Mattison in New York was noted in the British medical press; he had warned that there was a genuine danger of replacing an opium or morphine with a cocaine habit if the drug was used in this way. Dr Albrecht Erlenmeyer, too, who at the height of the cocaine craze had himself reported on his use of cocaine to treat eight persons addicted to morphia, was by 1888 warning against the method and melodramatically categorizing cocaine as the 'third scourge of mankind', after alcohol and opium.[44] Soon such warnings came thick and fast. The dependence on the drug of Halsted, pioneer of its anaesthetic use, was not known in England.[45] Nevertheless a close connection was established between morphine and cocaine by warnings against the treatment of morphine addiction with cocaine. Cocaine's subsequent classification as a narcotic owed much to this early connection as well as to the later international implications of cocaine abuse.

The 'cocaine habit' was, through the connection with morphine, incorporated within the general disease view of addiction.

But the lack of physical symptoms associated with use and withdrawal from the drug engendered a harsher medical response. Disease theories were always notable by the reformulation of moral views in scientific form; and the 'vice' categorization was strongly applied to cocaine. To Allbutt, it was 'slavery worse than that of morphine'; bondage was a hopeless matter. This appears to have been the almost universal reaction of the addiction specialists.[46] Cocaine, it is now recognized, engenders no physical addiction or abstinence sickness. What was particularly worrying to the medical writers on the cocaine habit in the nineteenth century was the greater element of free will, of pleasure rather than pain, in the use and withdrawal from the drug. Crothers noted that no other narcotic made such a pleasing impression on the brain – it was 'a foretaste of an ideal life'.[47] The cocaine user seemed more of an autonomous, non-medical personality than the morphinist or opium addict; and the medical response was harsh. Treatment methods retained a punitory aspect after cocaine had been abandoned for morphine addiction. Abrupt and immediate withdrawal was more generally acceptable for cocaine. Numbers of users were in any case small, and few underwent treatment, since the cocaine addict was, like the morphine injector, not covered by the terms of the Inebriates Acts.

But the non-medical cocaine user was quite a rarity at the turn of the century. Recreational cocaine use was spreading in the United States and Europe in the 1890s. In England, it was cannabis and opium smoking which were favoured. Cocaine was apparently confined to even more limited circles. Conan Doyle's famous (and often-quoted) portrayal of Sherlock Holmes's use of the injected drug – the '7 per cent solution' – was indicative more of the medical use of it which Conan Doyle (and through him, Watson), as a doctor himself, had encountered. It was noticeable, too, that references to the great detective's use of cocaine (and possibly morphine, too) became steadily more disapproving as time went on. In *A Scandal in Bohemia* (1886), at a time when cocaine was still in favour as a 'wonder-drug', and in *The Man with the Twisted Lip*, in the following year, Holmes's use of the drug was treated with a certain amount of levity. Holmes, according to Watson, was 'alternating from week to week between cocaine and ambition ...'. But through *The Five Orange Pips*, *The Yellow Face* and *The Sign of Four*, Watson's attitude grew steadily more disapproving, until in *The Missing Three-quarter* (1896) Holmes himself could refer to the hypodermic syringe as 'an instrument of evil', while Watson spoke of a 'drug mania' which had threatened his friend's career. Conan Doyle's portrayal of his character's cocaine use was a good indication of changed medical attitudes to the drug; but it was no index of recreational cocaine use.[48]

In America at this period, such use was spreading down through the social scale; cocaine was becoming a drug with a dubious social reputation. There was less of this in England. Lower-class usage was not at all noticeable until the First World War.[49] There was less of a domestic 'scene' at this time. The drug use of Aleister Crowley and of his friend and mentor, Allan Bennett, are perhaps the only examples of self-conscious recreational cocaine use in the 1890s. Crowley, at this time living in Chancery Lane, with Bennett, who had been trained as an analytical chemist, was initiated to the Order of the Golden Dawn in 1898. Both men experimented with many drugs, cocaine among them, at this time. Crowley later wrote of Bennett, who suffered acutely from asthma, that 'his cycle of life was to take opium for about a month, when the effect wore off, so that he had to inject morphine. After a month of this he switched to cocaine, which he took until he began to "see things", and was then reduced to chloroform.' It was Bennett's wholehearted devotion to the consciousness-expanding potential of drugs (he later became a Buddhist monk in Ceylon) which led Crowley to a life-long advocacy of their use, especially cocaine and heroin, in the pursuit of ritual and sexual magic.[50] Crowley apart, the cocaine 'scene' was almost non-existent.

17

Opium at the End of the Century

By the end of the century opium was no longer so central to medical practice, nor did it occupy its former place in popular culture. The 'opium of the people' had been taken over by the medical profession; the established division between medical and non-medical usage was recognition that the previous widespread diffusion of opium use in society was declining.

Medical practice itself was changing. New drugs like chloral, quinine and the bromides were replacing opium as a time-honoured standby in fever and sleeplessness. The opiate 'composing draught' at night was replaced by a dose of chloral, as many prescription books indicate. Some medical men of the 'old school' lamented the change. Dr Samuel Wilks, Consulting Physician to Guy's Hospital and long an opponent of a headlong change to new and often untried drugs (he had attacked the unwise use of chloral as early as 1871), commented in 1891 on the general medical 'ignorance of the best properties of opium' and

> with some medical men an actual dread of it, some ill-defined fear of its excessive harmfulness so as to make it a drug to be avoided by all possible means, and that every substitute should be thought of in its stead ... For my own part, I have seen more evil results from the long continued use of chloral and bromides than from opium.[1]

A few consultants like Wilks continued to defend the drug's use, but theirs were isolated voices. W. B. Cheadle, Physician at St Mary's and Lecturer on Clinical Medicine at the medical school there, even launched a full-scale attempt at rehabilitation in 1894. Recommending treatment by opium in a range of illnesses from goitre through to heart disease, bronchitis, ulcer, whooping cough, colitis, dysentery, diarrhoea, peritonitis, gall stones and diabetes, he lamented that in general the use of opium was becoming 'more and more narrow and routine'.[2] But his was a losing cause. As a means of easing pain or procuring sleep, or as a suppository, or in small doses for coughs and diarrhoea – these were by then about the limit of its accepted usefulness. Continuous and systematic treatment with the drug was by this time rarely seen.

Wilks and Cheadle appear to have been correct in their assessment of the decline in use, at least as far as hospital practice went. At King's, opium was being used from the 1870s primarily to deal with pain and sleeplessness and in the treatment of diabetes. William Osler's classic *Principles and Practice of Medicine* (1894) recommended the drug only in a limited number of conditions. He counselled hypodermic morphine rather than opium in rheumatism, rabies, tetanus and stomach ailments. Squire's *Companion* listed only a reduced number of sixteen opium preparations in its 1899 edition.[3] In general practice, opiates seem to have remained reasonably popular, for not all local doctors would be conversant with the most up-to-date medical opinion, and patients could continue to have prescriptions, as their own property, redispensed. In Islington, 15.5 per cent of all prescriptions dispensed in 1885 were still opium-based.[4] The opiates which were used were changing too. Old-established preparations like laudanum and syrup of white poppies were less popular; doctors were tending to prescribe more morphine and paregoric, the camphorated tincture. It would be unwise to conclude that there was a considerable decline in the medical use of opium by the end of the century. At the top of the profession this was the case, but the drug, in varied forms, still retained popularity in everyday medical practice.

Its popularity for self-medication was becoming more limited. Giving opium to babies remained quite common in working-class areas until the early decades of the twentieth century. A few drops of laudanum in a baby's bottle of milk continued to be acceptable. But mortality ascribed to the administration of such drugs was decreasing. The under-five death rate was in permanent decline after 1868. Twenty infants died from the effects of opiates in 1885, only ten in 1898. A rate of 4.8 per million population for the under-fives in 1890 had dropped to 3.2 by 1900 and 1.8 by 1907 (Table

4, p. 276). The practice still continued, but opium was less central to working-class child care. Elderly women still remember young babies being given laudanum on sugar, and chemists whose experience dates back to the 1900s still prepared quantities of Godfrey's and 'babies' carminatives'.[5] But the chemists' preparations had become an ancillary rather than a central part of child care. Investigations by the British Medical Association into patent remedies in the 1900s found that opium had been dropped from the formulae of those products still on the market. It was sometimes doubtful if the new recipe was an improvement. Mrs Winslow's Soothing Syrup had jettisoned morphine in favour of potassium bromide, alcohol and sugar.[6] And this period of declining child mortality from opium demonstrated conclusively that opium had not been a major cause of infant mortality. For the general infant mortality rate was, at 163 per 1,000 live births in 1899, at its highest ever.

Opium was less important, too, for adult use. Old practices, on occasion, still continued. At the turn of the century in North Kensington, for instance, an unqualified 'horse doctor' also acted as doctor to the people of the neighbourhood. Opium and red lavender was his usual remedy for coughs and diarrhoea. His young daughter was sent to the local chemist to buy the pennyworths of laudanum and opium much as the children of factory operatives had gone on similar errands fifty years before.[7] But opium was used for a more limited range of complaints. Pharmacists in practice at the time remember that most of their regular customers for the drug were elderly – old women who called in on a Saturday night, for instance, for a few drops of 'lodlum' to help them with their coughs and sleeping.[8] Few young people took the drug in any extensive quantity. That this was the case is borne out by generally declining levels of mortality and of home consumption of the drug (so far as this can be measured). Estimates of home consumption indicate that it rose after the abolition of import duty in 1860, but that the trend took a downward turn between the mid 1870s and the 1890s (Table 3, p. 275). A permanent decline in overall narcotic death rates began at the end of this decade, too, and continued in the early years of the twentieth century. A rate of 6.5 per million living in 1894 had fallen to 4.9 per million in 1903.[9]

The deviance of regular opium use was by no means universally accepted; addicts still found ready acceptance in their communities and among those pharmacists who sold the drug to them. 'Nobody noticed addiction and everyone had laudanum at home,'[10] commented one. The limited nature of the recreational drug sub-culture at the turn of the century was in itself testimony to a continuing overall cultural acceptance of drug use. For the sub-culture encompassed only the use of those drugs which were outside medical practice – smoking opium and cannabis most obviously. Drug taking for its participants was subsidiary to their rejection of literary convention; it was certainly never, at this stage, a way of life in itself.

Nor, indeed, did every 'medical' addict even accept the new definition of his condition. Injecting addicts who refused to conform to the model of disease and treatment were a continual source of official anxiety to those concerned with the Inebriates Acts. The case of one addict, the son of a leading South Wales physician, was put by the family solicitor in 1905. This 'drug-ebriate' was refusing

> to go to any sort of retreat. He is not a drunkard ... and he cannot be certified to be insane ... After the effects of the drug are over he is mentally well. If he were insane he could of course be taken to an Asylum ... but not being a drunkard nor insane and refusing voluntarily to go to any 'Home', the problem is what to do with him ...[11]

But at an official professional level, opium use was clearly set within a new paradigm by this time. The ethic of professional control replaced the general social use of opium of the earlier decades. Restriction under the legitimizing 'expert' control of the medical and pharmaceutical professions was by this time central to any consideration of opium use. The medical moves to establish control of the redispensing of prescriptions, and in particular those containing morphine (prescriptions were at this date still the patient's own property and redispensable at will), which began in the last decades of the century, underlined the changing balance in the relationship between doctor and patient.[12] The restrictions of the 1908 Pharmacy and Poisons Act which placed opium and all preparations containing more than 1 per cent morphine in Part One of the poisons schedule (cocaine was also added to Part One) demonstrated continuing reliance on pharmaceutical expertise.

More important than the practical ways in which professional control continued to be extended was the ideological shift which had taken place. The disease view of addiction with its implicit notions of constitutional or hereditary predisposition established an individualistic, privatizing ideology, nominally value-free. Medical concepts reinforced and reflected existing social structures. A distinct area of ideological terrain had been won. The alliances which, on this basis, went on to shape narcotic policy in the twentieth century were already at this stage present in embryo. They foreshadowed the collaboration between the medical profession and the civil service, between government and doctors, which was established as the basis of policy in the 1920s. There were links between the strong medical contingent in the public health movement, campaigning against the open availability of opium, and the government statisticians who provided the data on which much of this case was based. There was the connection, too, between doctors involved in the operation of the Inebriates Acts and the civil servants who administered them. Policy in the twentieth century would be formulated and controlled through the interaction of these influential élites. The 'medical model' of addiction would be placed at the centre of policy formation.[13]

These medical perceptions of disease and treatment are implicitly criticized in the analysis of nineteenth-century opium use in England. It is not simply backward-looking to draw attention to the popular non-medical use of opium which undoubtedly existed; and indeed, in many respects popular and medical cultures of opium use intermingled. The parallel 'medical' and 'popular' uses of opium indicate that the transmission of such knowledge was not simply a one-way, top-to-bottom, process. Nor is a more rigorous approach to the historical roots of medical perceptions a denial that there was indeed something to worry about. People did die unnecessarily from accidental overdoses; babies were doped by their mothers. But the social situation out of which such events arose was as important.

Nevertheless, the contemporary implications of the historical perspective are less obvious than some might wish. Historically in this century, the alternatives to medical concepts in the area of narcotic use have been penal ones. This alone has been sufficient to secure continuing adherence to a more humanitarian means of control. Yet, as the nineteenth century shows, even this approach has always had its limits. There was even then a more overtly repressive response for addicts outside the middle class. Limitation of sale or admission to the workhouse were the working-class addicts' equivalent of the medical categories of disease and treatment. Medical and penal approaches are not as mutually exclusive as they are often posited to be.

But to argue on this basis, as some critics of the medical perspective have done, for a return to liberal individualism, man as 'a responsible agent, subject to temptations which he may resist or to which he may yield', is to miss the complexities of the historical situation.[14] Those who argue that, because controlled and moderate opium use has been possible without any form of restriction, it should be so again are misjudging the issue. Open sale and availability of opium did not lead to the rapidly escalating levels of use one might expect; and the problems attributable to it had their wider context. But the re-creation of such a situation is another matter. For if the present societal reaction to, and reality of, narcotic use is very much the outcome of its nineteenth-century and early twentieth-century past, it is also in another sense a victim of it. As Griffith Edwards also points out in Chapter 18, the nineteenth century cannot be taken out of context as a simple model for the present.

This is not to argue that the changing attitudes towards opium in nineteenth-century society have no relevance at all. The medical response to opium which was established was almost inevitable given the type of social and structural changes at work in society at that time; the re-classification of poverty, homosexuality and other conditions along similar lines is indicative of that. But the history of opium and other narcotics in nineteenth-century society does provide a vantage point from which the assumptions of both the 'penal' and the 'medical' models (so far as these can be separately identified) can be analysed. Above all it demonstrates that the concepts, the reactions, the structures of control which are now taken for granted are not fixed and immutable. The division between 'medical' and 'non-medical' use, the categorization of what is 'legitimate' or 'illegitimate' drug use, addiction as a sickness, or even as an exclusive condition, are not timeless concepts, but historically specific and laden with implicit assumptions. Contemporary attitudes towards narcotics are not simply an arbitrary figment of man's unreason for which history provides some whigg-ishly relevant insights. They are the product of a social structure and the social tensions of that time. Michael Ignatieff has com-mented in a recent study of the establishment of the prison in the early nineteenth century that no proper discussion of reform or change can take place as long as the participants still use concepts and perceptions which arise out of a past which they ostensibly deny.[15] Discussions of the historical relevance of opium and its contemporary implications have suffered from much the same deficiency. But through an awareness of the dynamics of the 'problem' of opium use, of the social roots of medical ideas, of the developing links between medicine and the state, can come a questioning of our present-day assumptions and contemporary pretensions to control.

PART NINE

The Nineteenth Century
in Relation to the Present

18

Changes of Scene

If Dr Anstie or Sir Arthur Pease, De Quincey or some nameless back-street seller of laudanum, or some others of the great range of relevant nineteenth-century actors were today to return to earth and inspect the current production of the play in which they had once performed, how strange or familiar to their expectations would they find the present scene? For a start, they would certainly be chagrined to discover how little most people even in specialist circles read or remembered the writings, the debates and the campaigns, or the back-street shops. Only De Quincey could expect a familiar greeting. Here and there some of them would uncover pleasing little reminders that they had indeed once trodden the same ground – the Society for the Study of Addiction still exists as monument, and the *British Journal of Addiction*, which under an earlier name reported their scientific deliberations, moves forward towards its hundredth year of publication. The phrase 'Chinese Heroin' would catch attention, and a previously distrusting view of the Oriental would be reinforced by the news that the Triad gangs had moved into the heroin import and distribution business – a small but poetic vengeance for the opium wars. The growing of British opium is forgotten, although the keen home cultivator may produce his few plants of cannabis at risk of prosecution, while the market stalls in the Fenlands are innocent of any memory of opium pills. The question of 'infant doping' in the meaning familiar to the nineteenth-century reformers might not appear to be completely dead when they discovered the vast prescribing in America (and to a lesser extent in Britain) of amphetamines to the 'overactive child'. They would, of course, be fascinated by the progress of science, and particularly by the astonishing recent discovery that the body produces its own opiate-like substances.

But beyond the little assurances of sameness and the many little evidences of change, there would soon dawn on these visitors the large and central fact that a concern with drugs and with addiction was still enormously with us. The market stalls or the chandler may no longer be selling opium, but tranquillizers are multinational business. Concern over how we are to co-exist with drugs, far from having faded away, has become a continuing and major source of societal anxiety. The definition of drug taking as a problem – the whole 'problem framework' which began hesitantly to emerge in the nineteenth century – remains now as a dominant and usually unquestioned legacy.

So far as the prevalence of addiction is concerned, what would most surprise the nineteenth-century actors would be that a matter which had seemed for decades to be under control in this country – a success story for their reforming endeavours and the control system whose foundations they laid – had broken through again in the 1960s. Behind the actual upsurge in numbers would, on closer inspection, be seen the emergence of a prevalent type of addict which the nineteenth century had not envisaged. The drug problem has become dominantly a problem of young people: roughly twice as many men as women are now affected, and prevalence has in recent years shown an even social class spread. Heroin and cocaine were the drugs of choice at the start of the new epidemic, although a wide variety of other substances were soon in use too. Multiple drug use is now the order of the day: drugs are being injected intravenously. The source of supply for heroin and cocaine may initially have been the over-prescribing of a handful of doctors, but soon a situation arose where drugs were obtained from many sources – lax prescription, pharmacy breaking, thefts from warehouses, illicit manufacture of amphetamines and so on – and then circulated through a system of large or petty blackmarket dealings. Drug users were drawn together for supply and mutual support: they began to use the same jargon, to assume a sub-cultural identity. The ugly and denigrating American word 'junkie' began to be heard. Drug use and crime inevitably became associated because illegal possession of drugs, and their 'supply', were crimes by definition; because pharmacy breaking and forged prescriptions became common; and because the prior petty criminal involvement of many of the adolescents drawn into this drug world came to be mixed with their drug taking. In America the young 'street addict' came to be seen as at the very centre of the problem of law and order, and as he stole and robbed to support his habit, he re-cycled the wealth of New York or Chicago. Some intimations of the potential for drug-taking to stimulate the formation of sub-cultures had been seen in the nineteenth century. But cannabis-taking among British artistic circles of that period had, for instance, never even faintly become a centrally cohesive activity in the way that the seeking and use of heroin became an organizing activity for groups of young city dwellers in the twentieth century.

Looking at our contemporary drug scene, the nineteenth-century visitor might therefore at first conclude that, although drug misuse was still with us, the nature of the phenomenon was so different in social terms that we were not now talking about the same happening. The stereotype of the middle-class woman injecting the morphia which her doctor has unwisely given her is replaced by the image of the addict as the drop-out, the delinquent adolescent, the fringe member of society. However, on close inspection, the junkie himself might be seen as the fullest incarnation of nineteenth-century fears of the 'stimulant' use of opium – here indeed is the stereotype of addiction for fun and indulgence, for what the nineteenth century feared in the rumoured uses of opium in the mill towns. There is a parallel between our fear of the pleasure-seeking rebellion of youth and the previous century's terror of the working classes getting out of hand.

Important strands in the total nineteenth-century story of opium use of course included, besides addiction, the fundamental themes of opium as self-medication and opium in medical practice, that is, the place of the drug in therapeutics. In looking at the ways in which nineteenth-century themes carry through to the present, it is important therefore to stress that the totality of the story is not encompassed simply by addiction and drug *problems*. What current manifestations of therapeutics are the heirs of opium as medicine?

Under that heading, it would soon be evident to the inquiring visitor that Britain still has a vast and rich tradition of self-medication, which is not today a matter of opium but of many other substances. And even as medical prescribing and folk traditions of self-medication merged in the nineteenth century and the use of opium for symptomatic treatment of illness shaded off with no clear demarcation into drug-taking for pleasure, or relief of anomie, so today there are similar mergings affecting the drugs which are employed in place of opium. As regards present rates of self-prescribing, Karen Dunnell and Ann Cartwright[1] found in a community survey that over a two-week period the ratio among adults of self-prescribed to prescribed medicines was roughly two to one. Two-thirds of adults had in fact taken a self-prescribed medicine over the previous two-week period, while about 41 per cent of the sample had taken 'aspirin or other pain killers' during that time. Nineteen per cent of babies had been given 'an indigestion remedy or gripe water'. All the reasons which formerly made opium so popular for symptomatic medication are still society's common pains and tribulations, but with a variety of drugs now taking a role in different areas – analgesics in particular in place of opium for pain relief or ill-defined malaise, varieties of cough medicine where opium was previously the sovereign remedy, and tranquillizers and anti-depressants as present-day substitutes on a huge scale for opium's role as a psycho-active drug for the relief of nervous tribulations and the stress of life. In 1968 a piece of research showed that diazepam (Valium), a minor tranquillizer, is now the most frequently prescribed of any single drug in Britain.[2] One may well suspect that diazepam is taken as much for relief of anomie as for any diagnosable medical condition, and for the young mother living in the tower block its role is closely similar to that of opium in the nineteenth-century slums. Other work has shown that 8.6 per cent of adults in the U.K. will, during a twelve-month period, have taken anxiety-relieving drugs continuously for four weeks at a stretch. The multiple heirs to opium are self-prescribed, sometimes on the doctor's advice, obtained on medical prescription, swapped around the family, or given as a free sample by a drug firm and generously passed on by the doctor to his patient.

What might then cause surprise to ghostly visitors would be the discovery that in our contemporary and drug-laden society the most vocal manifestation of reforming public concern over drugs has been directed not at bringing substances under stricter control, but at the legalization of cannabis. A remarkable reversal in the attachments of liberal sentiment in one sense has come about. In the nineteenth century, men and women of good conscience and middle-class self-assurance were worrying about the opium use of the working classes and the quietening syrups which the mother in the industrial town gave to her baby: the contemporary middle-class reform movement has argued that cannabis use should be left to personal choice and claims that drug laws are applied with discrimination against working-class black youths in Brixton. Without discussing the factual basis for concern, there is some reminder here of the arbitrariness of what counts as a liberal cause, although it could be argued that closer analysis might show less of a paradox than surface inspection suggests. Today's reform movements have a philosophy which borrows much from nineteenth-century liberalism and J. S. Mill's emphasis on the individual's right of choice. The surface causes may suggest a turnabout, but the philosophy is continuous.

Evidence of the seriousness with which drug misuse is viewed today and the status which the problem has achieved might then be picked up in terms of the scope of government responses, the institutes and the international meetings and proliferation of learned journals, the committees and reports, the ramifications of the United Nations' control apparatus and the international treaties, the flow of Western money towards eradication of opium-growing or crop-substitution programmes in the East.[3,4] The listing (and the costing) of this range of happenings, and comparison with nineteenth-century equivalents, could be seen as the real measure of the growth and institutionalization of social action. Nineteenth-century concern with the opium trade between India and China was basically an unofficial and uninstitutionalized response made by moral reformers, who sought the leverage to move governments and forced their anxieties on to parliament; their activities are now the formal business of the United Nations. It is an analysis of the pounds and dollars spent, the offices given over to these activities, the number of policemen, bureaucrats and customs officers directed to such ends, which gives the true picture of change. Governments now operate where previously only the amateurish societies for Improvement were at work. The small but generous benefactions of good Quaker bankers are replaced by the multi-million dollar U.N. Special Fund on Drug Abuse Control (U.N.F.D.A.C.).

Opiates still have particular symbolic meaning for national

activity and for international crusade, but the concerns and activities of control now spread much more widely, and there were
already hints of this in the nineteenth century, with cocaine, cannabis and chloral entering the arena. The U.N. Single Convention
of 1961 dealt essentially with opiates, cocaine and cannabis, but
the Convention on Psychotropic Substances of 1971 aims to
spread the net far more widely, and at the international level reflects the anxieties which many countries are experiencing over the
misuse of synthetic stimulants such as the amphetamines, and
depressants such as the barbiturates and other sedatives, and the
minor tranquillizers. Many of the nineteenth-century activists
were concerned with the problems of alcohol as well as opiates,
but the extent to which the two movements have come together
has been limited, despite the promulgation by the World Health
Organization of the 'Combined Approach'. And cigarette smoking, although an aspect of the addiction problem which is increasingly acknowledged as constituting in most countries a far greater
threat to health than the traditional substances of concern, tends
to be dealt with through social mechanisms separate from either
drugs or alcohol. There can be no doubt that the historian of the
future will find fascinating material in our present fumbling toward policies to deal with smoking, our ability so sanguinely to
accept smoking as a drug habit which in this country perhaps kills
100,000 people each year, and the contrast with the massive concern over opiates, which evidently do so much less harm.

To look at the present in terms of how it might be perceived
by any of the key figures from the nineteenth century's opium
debates is not just a device for stringing together a series of
images. Unless one is reading history for history's sake, the
account of the previous century's engagement with drugs given
in earlier chapters inevitably invites introspective and self-regarding concern as to the continuities and the contrasts which can be
detected, and the insights which may be gained into our own pre-
dicament. We look at the past not simply for the fun of it, but
with the hope that we may better understand the present.

Superficial attempts to read 'lessons from history' can only mis-
lead. Britain is dealing now with many of the same drugs as a century ago, but the society within which drugs are used and controlled, and related problems defined, has radically changed.

The analytical approach which guides this chapter rests on the belief that the very facts of changing social context which make nonsense of the attempt to write history as homily are also exactly the difficulties which, if met rather than ignored, render this process of extrapolation meaningful. By taking due note of the changing nature of *context* one can then see more clearly the continuing *themes*, with their true underlying continuity in no way diminished by the fact that their expression will be very much shaped and altered by the context of changing times. For instance, one theme which can be traced is that of society's image of the heavy drug user: 'bad habit' is replaced by 'addiction', and in different contexts the word addiction itself has then certainly changed in meaning and implication. The complex theme of social control is also very important, and given that concept as an organizing idea, it is possible to relate the many different strategies of informal and formal control which society has employed over the decades.

The ways in which society thinks about and handles drugs could indeed be read as a set of markers which when properly comprehended offer important ways into understanding the nature and processes of the particular society which thinks and handles.

For the professional historian, the question of how and to what extent history is to be taken as addressing the present is a familiar debate. Parallel arguments also concern the anthropologist, who must be immensely aware of the dangers of the type of over-simple reading of anthropological material which seeks in Western-oriented ways to slant and demean the interpretation of primitive cultures toward instructive fables and pretty analogies for our own times.

This introductory section to the present chapter has attempted to set out in brief form some of the wide range of issues on which comparison could be made between past and present – a catch-up note for the nineteenth-century visitor, or in reality a checklist for ourselves. The potential themes are many and others could certainly be identified beyond those which will be touched on here.

Having thus set the scene, we shall select a few of the themes and attempt to go rather deeper.

Medicalization as organizing idea

The account given in this book of a progressive medical dominance in society's ways of thinking about and responding to drugs identifies a theme which runs through to the present day and to modern sociological debate. The nineteenth century was a period during which the basis was laid for a disease theory of addiction. The social consequences were seen in the addict being defined as patient, the design of treatment methods and treatment facilities which would now deal with this illness, and the emergence of medical specialists who had the continuing right to define the realities. The medical profession certainly at times became an instrument of control as well as of treatment. Opiates were literally taken away from the people and became in large measure the property of the doctors. Both practically and conceptually (and in the broadest sense politically), drugs became *medicalized*. Later in this chapter, aspects of medicalization will be taken up under a number of headings. The influences of medical thinking in this field have gradually become so protean that it is indeed difficult to find a theme which is not in some way related to this idea. While leaving detailed consideration of medical influence within particular themes till later, it is useful here to look briefly at some general questions relating to medicalization.

Conspiracy theory is a simple-minded approach which seemingly offers instant answers to all these questions. The basic thesis was many years ago economically stated by Bernard Shaw – 'Every profession is a conspiracy against the laity'. It is this idea which finds its elaboration in the writings of Szasz[5] or Laing,[6] or in the polemics of Illich.[7] It is also an idea which at times influences formal sociological studies of professionalism, studies which despite their claimed objectivity reveal a paranoid tinge. Medicine is portrayed as out to grab as many monopoly rights as possible, and arbitrarily but with value-laden judgements to delineate which deviations from accepted behaviour are to be called sick. Witch-hunting and case-finding are deemed then to be synonymous activities. The profession claims the right to control the stigmatized individual in the name of treatment, and supports or engages in widespread repressive social action in the name of public health. The essential device which is supposed to legitimize this whole packet of medical interference is the doctor's claim that the behaviour in question is illness or disease. With drug-taking behaviour, this analysis therefore suggests that the essential piece of legerdemain was the medical promulgation of addiction as a disease – the discovery of a circumscribed and diagnosable medical condition where previously there had only been 'bad habit'.

To what extent though is the medical profession ever usefully to be seen as an autonomous social organization, an entity moved entirely by its own intent and volition?[7] This is certainly not the argument of the historical chapters of this book; but the influence of the conspiracy theory interpretation is certainly important in contemporary polemics which surround drug issues, especially in the United States. In conspiracy theory, medicine is a foreign power lodged dangerously within the body of the state, and potentially subversive of the state's true interests. Opium is taken into medical ownership because the doctors are expansionist – the doctors are not of society but against society. A very different view is that medicine is the product of society, and is in fact often no more than its agent or mere catspaw. Furthermore, the profession is not a once-and-for-all product, but an organization continually reflecting and influenced by the society without which it has no meaning or existence. If this is correct, then far from society having to guard against the medical conspiracy, medicine will have to be wary of the risk of society's conspiracy to turn the profession into its too obedient servant – the danger is that doctors will agree to incarcerate addicts or otherwise act as agents of control, because society wants addicts incarcerated or otherwise controlled and will subvert the profession. It must, however, be remembered that the word 'society' is only shorthand for a vastly complex organization which is very far from being unitary, while the medical profession also has many different groupings and attitudes within it. The analysis might of course be taken much further by considering what part of the profession has at which time held what sort of two-way relationship with which other segments and interest groups within the larger society. Perhaps the story of drugs suggests that neither extreme – medicine as the autonomous conspirator, or as society's poodle – is accurate. Medicine in certain contexts and at certain stages of history may, on occasion (for better or for worse), generate its own initiatives – it may make a grab at opium control in the interests of its own prestige, but even then society as a whole is evolving in a manner which leads to this and other professionalisms. In different contexts and in other stages of development medicine appears to have done little more than passively connive: doctors were not in general particularly keen to set up the drug clinics of the 1960s but were in effect ordered to do so by the government. Most often the roots of action on any drug issue appear to be mixed, with influences which interact and mutually amplify.

We are here of course doing no more than touch on the surface of the type of analysis which drug problems require if we are to understand fully the role and function of a profession *within* a society. Enough has though been said on this issue to suggest that historical interpretation within the simple framework of conspiracy theory is likely to betray the real subtleties. Medicine is no more a conspiracy against the laity than society is a conspiracy against an otherwise altruistic and disinterested profession. Their relationship is symbiotic.

Addiction

The supplanting of the simple idea of *bad habit* by addiction during the latter part of the nineteenth century has been described in Chapter 13. Here is an apparently straightforward example of the medicalization of society's perceptions.

The concept of addiction is not just still very much with us, but permeates society's ideas on drug use. Addiction is written into legislation and it is the person *addicted* to designated drugs who must be notified to the Home Office.

National Health Service treatment of drug misuse focuses on treatment of addicts. The word suffuses official documents, the treatment world, the research literature both nationally and internationally, media discussion and ordinary conversation on these topics.

The scientific world to some extent agrees to use the term *drug dependence* as a latter-day replacement for addiction, but one often has the feeling that the speaker at the scientific meeting is likely to stumble and correct himself as the new word is rather uneasily substituted for the old, with 'drug-dependent person' a desperate circumlocution for 'addict'. The concept of dependence was introduced by the World Health Organization[8] in 1964. The term was defined thus:

a state, psychic and sometimes also physical, resulting from the interaction between a living organism and a drug, charac-

terised by behavioural and other responses that always include
a compulsion to take the drug on a continuous or periodic basis
in order to experience its psychic effects, and sometimes to
avoid the discomfort of its absence. Tolerance may or may not
be present. A person may be dependent on more than one drug.

The purpose of this exercise in redefinition appears largely to
have been to get away from the stereotyped view of addiction in
terms of the opiate picture alone, and to substitute varieties of
dependence pictures, each related to a group of drugs. Between
these pictures there would be commonalities as well as dissimilari-
ties. In so far as the aim was to produce a nomenclature more in
accord with what is actually to be seen, the move achieved a useful
purpose – for instance, it invited people to look closely at the alcohol picture rather than simply to ask whether alcoholism was or
was not a 'real addiction', with its reality tested only by the extent
to which it accorded with the morphine picture. More covertly
the influence may have been to spread the net of medicalization
even further – the seriousness with which heavy use of barbiturates, non-barbiturate hypnotics, amphetamines and of course
alcohol would be viewed could in some way be enhanced. From
drug use of these types being seen as giving rise to rather uncertain or second-class varieties of addiction – *habituation* was a
shadowy and intermediate concept – they now each had their own
dependence syndrome. Although no one seems to have realized
it at the time the promulgation of dependence was in many ways
the rediscovery of *inebriety*, with its drug-specific sub-types. Inebriety had been an idea which held a wide group of substance
concerns together, and dependence could meet the same purpose.
For the sake of simplicity we shall continue this discussion in
terms of the meanings which are today given to addiction, with
due awareness that in scientific circles it is sometimes the word
dependence which is being used instead, and that a fine-grained
analysis would have to look at the shades of difference between
the meanings given these two words. The terms *drug misuse* and
drug abuse are also in circulation, often with no very precise definition except the latent meanings of social disapproval. But it is
undoubtedly addiction rather than dependence or any other
rephrasing which is the word still to be heard in conversation
at the bus stop, the person uttering it having no thought of

its origin in nineteenth-century medicalization of the popular vocabulary.

What meanings in our present twentieth-century context are attached to addiction, and what are the influences and consequences of this word? One approach to that question is to look at statements which can be culled from medical and scientific writing. The attempt to delineate professional views on addiction by picking out a particular series of quotations could though be misleading – the process is inevitably selective and even with the best endeavours selection may be biased. No one view or brief selection of views can accurately characterize the position of a whole profession. But to tap what we are searching for it is reasonable to look both at a few texts written for specialists and at books written by drug experts who seek to inform a general audience. It would indeed be difficult to find many relevant major texts of recent years which have not felt compelled to tackle this question of whether addiction is a disease, the nature of this putative disease, and the social implications of giving addiction this disease status.

One might wonder whether the repetitiveness with which authors return to this issue and the lack of any finality itself speaks to some fundamental unease and uncertainty whether medicine has become lumbered with a metaphysical debate rather than a scientific discussion capable of closure.

Is addiction in current thinking still seen as a disease and, if so, in what precise terms? Here is a quotation which shows that at least in some quarters the disease theory in its most primitive and somatic guise is still very much alive:

> When biochemical abnormalities are discovered in addicts (as I am sure they will be someday), a new era of clinical research will open. Will these abnormalities appear in all persons exposed to narcotics, or only in some? Can they be replicated in animals? Can treatment restore the change to normal? Can addiction be considered a metabolic disorder, like diabetes, and its progress followed with a chemical index? These are exciting questions, and are the ones that investigators will be asking in the future.[9]

That passage, written in 1978, comes from Dr Vincent Dole, one of the most distinguished American authorities on drug addiction.

If Dole's Position can be seen as a direct lineal descendant of the more organic nineteenth-century views of addiction, the 'moral insanity' view, or addiction as impairment of will, finds equally direct recent expression in the same volume of conference proceedings:

> An obvious advantage with the disease concept of addiction is that it may be of assistance in persuading patients to submit to a sensible treatment programme. When we speak of illness, they realize that we are not moralizing over their situation but understand that they happen to have fallen into a situation in which they have lost normal voluntary control.[10]

Loss of 'normal voluntary control' is easily recognizable as the descendant of Dr Thomas Clouston's 'diseased cravings and paralysed control'. And as was the case a century ago, the disease formulation directly legitimizes the 'sensible treatment programme'.

Here next is a passage from a popular book on drug addiction by Dr James Willis, a British psychiatrist specializing in treatment of addicts:

> Thus to regard dependence on alcohol and on drugs as a kind of disease does constitute a humane and a practical approach in our efforts to understand a very complex area of human behaviour... Drug addicts and alcoholics are, after all, continuously damaging themselves with toxic substances, and to act in this way is, to say the least, an abnormal way of carrying on.[11]

The disease concept is again seen both as humane and as 'practical' or pragmatic. And there is in addition the appeal to common sense – surely people who behave in this wrong-headed way just can't be normal? The postulate that we may as well look upon odd behaviour as ill behaviour is tentatively and almost apologetically put forward.

Ambivalence as to whether drug taking is disease or moral delinquency, the attempt to wrap the two ideas into one package as addiction, the legitimization of treatment by the concept of addiction – quotations from contemporary twentieth-century sources suggest the continuation of a debate which has been in the same state of confusion for many decades.

Another important theme can be picked up in an extract from a book published in 1975 by an American psychiatrist:

> The failure to recognize that drug abuse and addiction are

symptomatic of an underlying psychiatric disorder and psychological conflict ... has the effect of a self-fulfilling prophecy ... Parents, for example, should take firm stands and insist on medical treatment when they discover drug abuse behaviour in their children.[12]

Moral insanity is here re-interpreted as *underlying* psychiatric disorder, but there is the same axiomatic implication that treatment is needed, that the doctor is the man immediately to be called in. Here is medicine directly caught in the act of attempting to influence popular images.

A further variant on the theme of underlying disorder, with the same treatment implications, is that of personality deviancy. Here is a fairly typical formulation of this type, given by a British doctor, Dr George Birdwood, in 1969:

Voluntary treatment puts the responsibility for his care on the addict himself, thus imposing a strain that he is ill-fitted to bear. It ignores the widely accepted fact that he is an immature and inadequate person ... To expect such a person to summon-up sufficient will-power to break his habit permanently is patently absurd.[13]

'Disease of the will' is clearly a formulation which still thrives, but with the idea subtly translated into underlying 'immaturity and inadequacy', which then predicate the need for compulsion. A personal view unsupported by review of evidence is given the status of 'widely accepted fact'. An absolute explanation of addiction is offered that then speaks very directly in support of an absolutist solution. The doctor is not only again telling the people what to think, but in this instance is also telling the government what it ought to do.

Searching the contemporary drug literature offers rather the same pleasures and excitements as browsing in an antique shop where there is the chance of picking up a good piece of Victoriana. As this series of quotations indicates, many of the nineteenth-century ideas on addiction as disease are undoubtedly still in currency, often in mint condition. As a further source, we may take the two-volume handbook, *Drug Addiction*, which has a German publisher but an American editor and largely American contributors. It was published in 1977. The following quotation comes from the scene-setting opening chapter, written by Dr W. R. Martin, a distinguished and widely respected medical scientist with a lifetime's experience of work on opiates. He writes:

> Although it is argued by some that drug abuse is caused by social deprivation and assimilation into deviant sub-cultures, an alternative hypothesis is that drug abusers share with other social deviants a disorder in their thinking processes characterized by impulsivity, immaturity, egocentricity, hypophoric and increased need states. It is proposed that this disorder may have a hereditary basis or be a consequence of or exacerbated by drug abuse and may be biologically transmitted ... Although psychopathy is probably the most prevalent and most costly of all mental illnesses, it has received only modest attention from the psychiatric and medical community ... Although the United States government is making a large commitment to drug abuse, only a small portion of the funds are committed to basic research whose purpose is to understand the disease and treat it. In order to develop psychotherapeutic agents for the treatment of psychopathy, a concerted effort must be made to synthesize and test new agents for their efficacy. There is every reason to be optimistic about the development of drugs for the treatment of psychopathy.[14]

Not so much a statement as a manifesto. Psychopathy, described in intensely moralistic terms, is an 'illness', or indeed in a later passage a 'disease'. Social explanations of drug addiction are discounted, and psychopathy (as biological condition) is seen as the underlying disorder. These postulates legitimize drug treatment of drug addiction. Furthermore, a platform is created from which to call for priority funding of a particular type of biological medical research: in a cost-conscious society the way to build the climate for research backing is firstly to introduce a panic factor and underline the costliness of psychopathy – 'the most costly of all mental illnesses'. The expectation is then held out to government agencies that research money can deliver exciting goods – 'there is every reason to be optimistic'.

Here perhaps is a particularly revealing example of how the same process runs through time, identical in its fundamentals but with different manifestations in different social and temporal contexts: medicalization in the twentieth century goes on to become a vital strategy for the winning of research funds – as long ago as 1972 the total annual U.S. federal budget for addiction research ran at $42,218,000.[15] The social implications of the need to sell your particular image of drug addiction and thus to foster your own institution's research budget may go beyond the immediate influence on the research world and budgetary allocations. For the process inevitably means the lobbying of government. Successfully winning round a government agency such as Washington's National Institute of Drug Abuse to a particular view for the sake of research gain may then leave behind a mark on that agency of much more pervasive influence. Research within a particular mould has ripples of influence as it becomes the training ground for the best young scientists, attracted to the prestigious and well-funded laboratory. The government agency has to justify both to the public and its political masters the type of research which it has backed, and the implicit definitions of what should be society's priority concerns are thus further reinforced. The distinguished researcher in his white coat is also often the man whom the media interview, so that his image of addiction further influences the public's awareness.

Images of addiction are in fact consistently and relentlessly marketed – in the nineteenth century to make opium the property of the medical profession, in the twentieth century to justify the position of enforcement agencies or the international control apparatus, or to win tomorrow's research budget. Images compete, and in the process the marketing becomes even more aggressive. The medical and scientific images feed and change the public, administrative and political view, and in return these perceptions give the doctors and scientists the needed support. Processes become circular and reinforcing. The most far-reaching consequences of the medicalization of images are not what happens within the strictly medical sphere – the hospitals and research laboratories – but the wider influences on societal perceptions and national and international policies.

But far more subtle and socially sensitive images of addiction are to be found in some scientific writing than is conveyed by the selection of quotations given above. A recent American research monograph on heroin[16] reviews a range of models and the objective evidence supporting particular views, showing, for instance, the scientific difficulties which still beset efforts to determine whether the seeming prevalence of personality disorder among addicts is cause or consequence of drug-taking. The research reported in that monograph was itself conducted and interpreted within a learning theory model, and it is interesting to see how the latter-day psychologist's view of addiction as learnt behaviour is in a way the rediscovering of 'bad habit'. Indeed, the psychologist in this regard brings the word *habit*, used now in a strict technical sense, back into circulation.

It would be a major research undertaking to determine precisely which images of addiction – addiction as biological disorder, as 'disease of will', as evidence of underlying mental illness or personality disorder, or as aberrant learning – have in different countries and at different times been the most influential on different sectors of society. We are not talking about just one type of model, or about potential influence on a society in undifferentiated terms – the real interest would come when one could document in detail which models influenced this or that committee, what assumptions lay behind a named piece of legislation, what was the idea at large in a particular suburb when the residents opposed the placing of a drug rehabilitation hostel in their midst.[17] It seems possible that it is the sophisticated and carefully qualified view of things that often remains in the monographs, while it is the scientist who entertains no doubt whose views most readily generate the wider influence. What views the drug user himself entertains of his condition have seldom been thought worth investigation – certain drug sub-cultures might even be the last repository of the folk belief in bad habit, unforgiving and strangely unmedicalized.

The meaning of treatment

The nineteenth-century discovery that the addict is a suitable case for treatment is today an entrenched and unquestioned premise, with society unaware of the arbitrariness of this come-lately assumption. People may debate the future direction of the National Health Service's Drug Treatment Clinics, but any suggestion that the current model is fundamentally mistaken in its assumption, that the treatment enterprise should be closed down and people with bad habits left to their own devices, would be dismissed only as outrageous and bizarre.

But although there are a number of reasons for believing that the basic postulate that addiction is a condition to be treated is the direct descendant of the last century's evolution in thinking, much else in regard to the meaning of treatment has changed.

In essence, the nineteenth century evolved the treatment of addiction as a method of dealing with the individual who in some way offended society's idea of what was decent and orderly. It was not as if anyone could put forward evidence that the condition was particularly life-threatening or damaging to the health of the individual himself, nor was there much evidence that the social demand for treatment was generated in any large measure by the belief that the addict caused great trouble to family and friends, or to other members of society. In the late nineteenth century the *leading* image of the addict was of the middle-class patient (often a woman) indulging in a self-regarding act which was mildly damaging to health and perhaps a little bit of a nuisance. The historical evidence given in Chapter 12 suggests that this image of the class and sex characteristics of the addict was badly out of focus, while even at the height of concern about morphine addiction, remarkably few addicts were actually being admitted to hospitals or nursing homes. The extent of learned debates on therapeutic methods which were conducted in the medical journals was out of balance with the actual treatment demands.

In so far as treatment had a manifest clinical purpose it was therefore to save the individual from his own behaviour, although the latent social purpose of correcting unacceptable deviance must have been of equal or greater importance. If opiates had produced compulsive drug-seeking without physical withdrawal symptoms, the medical profession might not have had such a ready opening for promulgation of disease theories, while if alcoholism treatment had not provided a contemporary parallel and a base for medicalization, treatment of opiate addiction might not have become such a socially accepted idea. Without alcoholism, there would certainly have been no Society for the Study of Inebriety.

For the twentieth century up to the mid 1960s, the British medical view on the worth and necessity of treatment for opiate addiction settled down to something more tempered than in the 1890s. The professional attitude was now in the main that addicts were best left on their drugs unless they wanted assistance to do otherwise, in which eventuality nursing-home help would be arranged and a regime put into operation not unlike the medico-moral treatment of former days. There was still a lingering debate on the virtue of abrupt versus gradual withdrawal and every now and then a resurgence of interest in introduction of compulsory care. But behind the seeming sameness, two new elements had during these years been added to the social meaning of treatment.

There was firstly the birth of the belief that treatment was an *alternative* to criminal handling of the addict. This, of course, came about only after 1920, when the first Dangerous Drug Act made illegal possession of opiates a criminal offence. From then onward, treatment could award itself the accolade of being not only benign in itself, but much more benign than the alternative model of response which might otherwise have been chosen in Britain, and which was to be established as the dominant response to addiction over many decades in the U.S.A. Indeed, Britain only narrowly averted treading the American path when in 1926 the Rolleston Committee[18] ruled that it was acceptable practice for a doctor to maintain an addict on his drugs if the patient could not otherwise function healthily, or for the practitioner to prescribe diminishing doses to other patients in a process of weaning. The Committee accepted the illness model. Any absolutist intentions that the Home Office may earlier have entertained were defeated, and the doctors won the day. They were able to do so with authority because they could still count on the doctor's right to define the nature of addiction, which had been secured in the nineteenth century. Not only opium but the addict was to remain medical property. It may, though, be an inadequate reading of the significance of Rolleston to make an interpretation simply in terms of a battle between the profession as the force of righteousness, and the Home Office. Also to be taken into account is that this committee marked the beginning in Britain of an alliance in the drug area between 'experts' and the bureaucracy of control which goes forward to today's Home Office Advisory Council on the Misuse of Drugs. The profession's championship of the illness model might certainly in this instance be seen as being as much rooted in a determination to protect the doctor's right to prescribe and his freedom from bureaucratic interference as in any desire to protect the freedom of the drug user.

The second assumption which became attached to treatment

during this period was what might be called the doctrine of *competitive prescribing*.[19] British doctors did not themselves initially promulgate this view of the function of treatment, but the idea came from American commentators.[20] These commentators drew inferences from the fact that America prohibited opiate prescribing to addicts and had a large-scale and intractable drug problem sustained by a criminally organized black-market, and a problem unresolved by an expensive and punitive enforcement programme. They pointed out that Britain, with a largely medical response, appeared on the other hand to contain the problem at a vastly lower prevalence level and to have no significant black-market. The inference was that prescribing undercut the black-market and hence, as well as its being a measure for dealing with the individual, it also constituted a magically effective public health measure.

The degree to which these two evolutions in the perceived function of treatment were justified by the facts deserves scrutiny, again for the moment taking the question as bearing only on the period from Rolleston up to the mid-1960s, when the heroin drug epidemic marked a general shake-up in balances. As regards the idea that treatment was operating as a benign alternative to punitive response, this contention was in principle well founded: addicts who in America would have been prosecuted were in England free of penal entanglement. The British addict who forged a prescription or stole drugs might on occasion come before the courts and likewise there may have been some exceptions to the national approach in America, but the contrast between the two national modes of response holds good. It must though be remembered that the British had the advantage of having to deal with a much lower addiction prevalence. As regards the contention that competitive prescribing was responsible for there being only negligible black-market activity, this question has been discussed at length elsewhere[21] and the conclusion must be drawn that this postulate was based on faulty inferences and a flattering American mis-reading of the British scene. The reasons why Britain had, over this period, a lesser drug problem than America related most importantly to enormously different social conditions in the cities of the two countries – different patterns of poverty, urban decay, ethnic underprivilege and entrenched criminal organization. The relaxed and gentlemanly British way of responding to drugs was witness to the small scale of the problem rather than the cause of that scale.

But the idea that prescribing was an effective prevention policy was put into circulation, and when the 1960 heroin epidemic exploded in Britain it was an idea which loomed large in importance for policy makers. The pervasive fear was that the British epidemic would lead to a situation where our cities might, before long, be faced with problems so sadly familiar to America – endemic and intractable illegal narcotic use particularly among young people, a drug sub-culture and a criminal black-market. The debates and documents of the time amply chronicle the acute official and public anxiety in this regard, and the determination to avoid any move which by driving the addict into the hands of the criminal dealer would 'invite in the Mafia'. The nineteenth century had seen addiction treatment as person-directed: the Second Brain Committee report[22] of 1965, the Dangerous Drug Act of 1967 and the system of Drug Treatment Centres which went into operation in 1968[23] may seemingly still have been about treating the individual, but they marked a shift in emphasis towards official belief in the social function of treatment as preventive strategy. What was to happen to the individual even became in some ways now of secondary importance. The Drug Unit in Cambridge had the courage of its convictions, and named itself a Containment rather than a Treatment Unit. Giving a patient injectable heroin in the name of treatment might be in the patient's best interests, or it might not. There was a tricky and highly responsible decision to be made every time a patient came to a clinic demanding to be 'registered'. It would be wrong to suggest cynicism or any betrayal of medical ethics on the part of the doctors concerned, but the fact is that the treatment system as it had evolved in 1968 subtly pressurized doctors into a position of conflict. They were running a prescribing system probably for the good of their patients, but they were now also operating as agents of a system designed not only for individual good but aiming also to avert the spread of a criminal black-market. What had previously been the speculative American interpretation now became the root of British policy. This development in the inner meaning of treatment and the consequent role accepted by the medical profession provide an illustration of the imperfections of explanations which see the profession as autonomous, and for ever generating its own motivations as the independent state within a state. Here was the control system covertly making the profession its instrument of policy. That the doctors concerned now worked for a National Health Service may in some ways have made the profession more amenable to being cajoled, if not directed.

In the 1960s the social meaning of treatment also evolved two other new implications. One of these was the idea that giving a prescription would in a certain sense control the individual:[24] he would be brought out from under cover, be in contact with an agency of society, counted, discouraged from criminality, got into gainful employment, and generally cleaned up. Again, such aspects of treatment could be seen as in the patient's best interests, and for that very reason the profession would be easily moved into this role. The other new element in the treatment was that for the first time cogent reasons existed for believing that opiate addiction, in the pattern of injected drug use which had evolved, was profoundly dangerous to life and health. Addicts were dissolving their heroin tablets in any dirty water that came to hand and injecting themselves without regard for sterile precaution. The common result was varieties of septicaemia, and the sharing of syringes led to the spread of virus hepatitis. Deaths from injection complications or overdose were frequently being reported, and such tragedies were all the more horrifying because of the youth of the population involved. It was a long way from a little quiet tippling of laudanum: the longevity debate was supplanted by studies of coroners' courts, which showed about 3 per cent of young drug addicts dying in any one year.[25] Whatever the other and more covert elements in the meaning of treatment, traditional concern for preservation of life and prevention of illness seemed therefore to demand energetic medical commitment. Whether in the event the treatment offered achieved those traditional goals remained an unanswered question. We do not know whether prescribing drugs to this new wave of addicts, a group so different from the patients known to Rolleston, averted or even heightened the long-term likelihood of tragedy.

Thus the fundamental conclusion to be drawn here is that in different contexts there has remained within society's repertoire of concepts something called treatment of addiction. Study of the nineteenth century offers insights into the origins of this treatment movement, and a preliminary view of the inner complexity of the meanings and social motivations. As that theme is followed forward, so the meanings shift and the complexities multiply.

Has anything other than the word itself remained the same in treatment? In fact, rather like finding a few fossil animals remarkably alive and well and even capering, it is possible to find some aspects of nineteenth-century ideas of treatment still very much with us and infecting our perceptions and policies. Such a direct follow-through is evident in the ambiguous perception of addiction as both moral defect and disease. The moral view forms the basis for the therapeutic community movement. The disease concept, in traditional medical terms, then continues to call for a therapeutic attack on the 'physical illness' itself. This latter aspect of perception might be seen as contributing to faith in methadone maintenance treatment programmes.

To substantiate those contentions, let us look first at some of the evidence on therapeutic communities. In America there has been enormous investment in establishment of such facilities for treatment of addicts. Quoting again the available but rather outdated figures, there were in 1970 about 4,000–5,000 addicts in the U.S.A. resident in these houses.[25] Britain, with a smaller drug problem, has never mounted a therapeutic community programme on that scale, but since the 1960s a number of communities have been active and have received government, local government and charitable support. And the direct flow from underlying concept of addiction to the actualities of treatment can be seen in the following description of the Phoenix House programme in New York by Dr Mitchell Rosenthal:

> What Boorstein has stated for the offender in general, I would re-emphasize for the addict population. At the present time, the only approach to the problem which can deal with the numbers involved and the ego defects present is the Therapeutic Community ... To take it one step further, I believe the therapeutic community to be the treatment of choice in the vast majority of cases of addicts, regardless of the availability of other methods.

Dr Rosenthal then continued:

> Addictive or character disorders suffer from a lack of identity, which can be considered a deficiency syndrome ... Moral values

are taught ... In a Phoenix House the teaching of socialization and its consequent morality is made both explicit and emphatic ... We regard antisocial, anti-military, amoral and acting-out behaviour as 'stupid'.[26]

In considerable degree, the American concepts have been the ideas with which the British houses have operated. In 1970, Phoenix House was established in London. The idea of self-responsibility has been emphasized by Mr David Warren-Holland, a previous director of Phoenix, London:

> The concept of self-help is vitally important to this process. We believe it is essential the ex-addict be given ample opportunity to help himself in his own recovery and to assume responsibility for his life. Treatment of the ex-addict as helpless and incapable deprives him of this opportunity and panders to his manipulative and irresponsible behaviour.[27]

So far as the therapeutic community is concerned, one may therefore wonder whether nineteenth-century concepts have in this instance been transformed, or whether in this movement they still find their original expression in unaltered and pristine form. Jennings, with his *The Re-education of Self-Control in the Treatment of the Morphia Habit*, sounds entirely modern. But there can be no doubt that in both the U.S.A. and the U.K. controlled opiate prescribing is quantitatively the much larger treatment investment than therapeutic communities or any other approach. The roots of maintenance clearly go back to the nineteenth century, and Dr Anstie's writings of 1871 on controlled morphine addiction at low dosage provide a ready text for today's drug clinics – 'Granting that we have ... a fully formed morphia-habit, difficult or impossible to abandon, it does not appear that this is any evil, under the circumstances' (see p. 142).

We have already argued in this chapter that the prescribing of drugs to the addict in today's context has multiple meanings, but the more biological views of the nature of addiction may be expected to have their follow-through in the justification of drug treatment of drug addiction. And such a connection has been given very direct expression by champions of maintenance. Methadone is seen as correcting some sort of defect state, and a protagonist such as Dr Vincent Dole will argue that psychopathological theories of addiction are ill-founded: for him the seeming psycho-pathology is consequence rather than cause of addiction, as witnessed by the psychopathic behaviour fading away once his patients are maintained on methadone. By the same token, Dole would not see psychiatric treatment for addicts as commonly needed. He specifically rejects the view of the 'moralists', and seeks to establish a view of addiction as illness, in terms of a disease model which would have been in accord with much nineteenth-century thinking.[9]

Strategies for control

Another important theme which must be traced out is the developing story of society's attempt to control drug use and drug users. The story can be seen as a process of continuing shift from reliance on informal controls to belief in the need for varieties of formal controls.

By *informal control* is meant a subtle and complex apparatus comprising a host of manners, conventions, traditions and folkways, with attendant systems of disapprobation for infringement of these rules and expectations, and approbation for their observation, which together will make known and felt what society expects of the individual in relation to opiate use or anything else. As regards nineteenth-century opium there would have been regional differences and variations in rules according to age and sex and other definitions of social position, rather than a universal norm. The norms which society proposed would be internalized by the individual so that 'he believed' that it was right to take opium for his toothache, but wrong to drink laudanum like a De Quincey or a Coleridge. Practices and beliefs in a stable society would be transmitted through the generations – the grandmother would tell the young mother what was the right use of poppy-head tea for the sick child.

At the beginning of the nineteenth century it was informal controls – alone and unaided – which regulated society's use of opium. The control of drug use was embedded in culture and was no more legislated or formally controlled than is at present the eating of peas.

Exactly the same reliance on informal controls can be seen today among, for instance, the opium-growing hill tribes of Northern Thailand, and the anthropological literature is redolent with descriptions of Central American and South American cultures which have unanxiously employed potent hallucinogens such as peyote and mescaline, within systems of informal control.[28] In our own society, aspirin provides a living example of drug use left in the hands of the people, while with alcohol we are betwixt and between – manners and conventions, but also licensing laws.

But so far as opiates were concerned, our society slowly and inexorably moved from reliance on informal controls to a complex, rigid, anxious, punitive and absolute system of formal control – the Dangerous Drugs Acts, imprisonment for illegal possession, the addict notified to the Home Office, opiates the property of the medical profession with the doctors themselves increasingly controlled, and control in many respects internationalized by treaty. The story of the origins of this astonishing shift is what much of this book is about.

What are the reasons for the shift? One explanation might be attempted by looking at the general disruption of society and culture brought about by the Industrial Revolution in nineteenth-century England. Many aspects of the subtle and informal apparatus which controlled the individual's behaviour by expectation and precept must have been smashed or put into disarray. The existence of an apparatus which is otherwise un-noted and taken for granted only becomes apparent when it is overwhelmed by rapid socio-economic change. The same processes can be seen today in many parts of the Third World, exemplified by breakdown in age-old informal controls over drinking practices in the anomie of the squatter compounds, the shanty towns, the *villas miseras*.[29] Drinking in many primitive cultures has been closely controlled by custom, and the African village where everyone in all his doings is intimately responsive to cultural behest provides a setting where there is no need for laws to regulate drinking. Go to the slums of Lusaka, and less than a generation onwards people fall down drunk in the road as they spill out of the beer halls. That country will now inevitably move towards formal controls over drinking as a poor but inevitable substitute for the disapprobation of the village elders.

A possible argument here is therefore that what happened in regard to the shift from informal to formal control of opiates in the nineteenth century was witness to fundamental changes in the relationship between individual and society, and it is tempting to stigmatize these changes as the *impoverishment* of culture. In terms of this argument our stringent contemporary controls bear witness to a profound distrust of the strength and quality of our own culture. It can then be argued that the process becomes circular, and that the more we legislate and the greater the number and the more intense the stringency of formal controls, the more certainly will informal cultural processes wither and fade. The analogy with aspirin can be deployed to carry this point. Make aspirin a dangerous drug tomorrow (the analogy runs), ban it from the supermarket and make it available only on prescription (with due entry of that prescription in the doctor's records on pain of prosecution), and within a generation or two the present traditions of aspirin self-medication would have gone without trace. Moves to put aspirin back in the supermarket would then be certain to give rise to appalled protest.

What has been said here about the weakening of culture, essentially by influences related to industrialization, is in line with a type of analysis that is today's conventional wisdom. To this conventional analysis is then usually added a more or less passionate lament, a yearning for a pre-industrial type of culture such as the townsman's fantasies of the rose-covered cottage in which he has never lived and in which he would in fact be singularly uncomfortable. The 'proper lesson from history' is not that we should yearn for the past, but rather that having acknowledged that the balance between informal and formal controls which any society applies to drugs is symptomatic of the cultural state of that society, we should see that the total package of drug controls cannot be dreamed up in terms of some absolute and disembodied ideal – the controls must be congruent with the strengths and resources of the society in question and the moment.[30] It may well be that the way people live and order their relationships in a complex and multiple industrial society will quite inevitably mean a heavier reliance on formal and external controls. On the other hand, one should be willing to question whether the present system of stringencies is indeed truly congruent with society's needs, or whether it is to an extent an anachronism, something which developed in a different context, an apparatus nicely in tune with the past which gave it birth rather than with the present which suffers its excesses.[31] Religious tolerance may not have been appropriate when there were fears of a Popish plot, but we have successfully got rid of disenfranchisement on religious grounds. Are our formal controls on drugs partly a lumber of the past? Those who seek a radical solution to the drug problem would certainly so contend, and would see the answer in a return to the right personally to choose one's drugs as freely as to choose one's religious faith.

How could the likely consequence of such a total removal of controls be tested, other than by daringly making the experiment? Inevitably those who would champion such an approach will be tempted to use the historical evidence which has been laid out in previous chapters to bolster their case – they will argue that when opium was freely available not much harm resulted. Even if one believes that temporal differences in social context, and injected drug use, make nonsense of an over-simple attempt to slant nineteenth-century experience of uncontrolled supply towards an argument for decontrolling twentieth-century supply, historical evidence as to what happens to population drug use in uncontrolled conditions must surely have some relevance to general understanding of drug ecology when the equilibrium is allowed to balance itself out without too much tampering. It is worth looking factually at the historical evidence while holding over the question of the relevance of that evidence to the present context until a little later.

What then were the dimensions of population opiate use and related problems with opiates which were experienced during the nineteenth-century equilibrium period? Quantitative evidence of a quality to satisfy the demands of the modern epidemiologist is lacking, but nonetheless there are sufficient clues to allow a number of important conclusions to be drawn. Firstly, the opium import figures suggest that we are indeed justified in using the word 'equilibrium'. As noted in Chapter 3 the data show that between 1830 and 1869 average home consumption of opium per thousand population varied between two and three pounds of opium per head. Given the imperfections in the way in which the statistics were gathered, some of that variation may be reporting error, although it is equally possible that occasional larger variations may have been masked. But it is reasonable, despite due qualifications, to take as a conclusion that consumption under conditions of free supply in effect plateaued out – there was certainly no continuing steep escalation of the sort initially seen between 1820 and 1840 when home consumption had risen from 21,000 lb. to a total of 47,000 lb. annually, even given the rise in base population.

The second conclusion relates to the actual level of the plateau. Three pounds avoirdupois amount approximately to 1.36 kg. The average consumption per person at 3 lb. per 1,000 population would therefore have been 1,360 mg. of opium annually. A recommended single-dose level for opium is today 60 mg. (containing about 6 mg. of morphine). This would imply that between 1830 and 1860 the average user – man, woman and child – was consuming in terms of today's judgements roughly 127 therapeutic doses of opium each year. It is fair to conclude therefore that the plateau represented a very high level of population experience with this drug.

There has recently, as regards population alcohol consumption, been much interest among epidemiologists in how use levels are distributed within the population, with the prediction that the distribution curve will usually be skewed and with a long low upper tail, rather than being represented by the familiar inverted U of the normal distribution curve.[32] The data are not available to reconstruct how opium consumption would have been distributed, but obviously the average alone does not tell us all we want to know – many people would have been consuming less than the average, and equally certainly a proportion would here have been consuming much more, and some people very much more.

The third conclusion to be drawn from the historical evidence is that the distribution of drug use was uneven over the country. The Fens provide the obvious example of particularly high usage rates, as borne out both by contemporary impressionistic accounts and the poisoning figures.

What cannot be satisfactorily reconstructed is an absolutely coherent picture of the prevalence of addiction, or of harm resulting from opium use. Poisoning and suicide figures are the only indices to hand, but there is no available way of quantitatively estimating the prevalence of social problems such as secondary poverty from diversion of wages, the influence on work capacity, the impact on family and interpersonal relations, or the number of accidents occurring under the influence of opium. A subtler form of epidemiology would have been required than the sort of social inquiry which was then practised. And it would be equally presumptuous to suppose that such unmeasured problems were either frequent or, because they were not adequately assessed, rare – we do not know with confidence whether 'opium sots' were common and commonly a social burden, or whether they were uncommon and untroublesome. The hint is though that incapacity from use of opium was not seen as a problem of such frequency and severity as to be a leading cause for social anxiety. The prime image of the opium user was dissimilar to that of the wastrel and disruptive drunkard. Opium users were not lying about in the streets, or filling the workhouses, or beating their wives. It seems fair to conclude that at the saturation level which the plateau represented, opium was not a vastly malign or problematic drug in terms of its impact on social functioning. But the conclusion must at the same time also be accepted that opium when freely available was, indeed, a drug which could at the population level give rise to certain definite health risks. The impact on infant mortality cannot be quantified, and as has already been argued in Chapter 9 opium would often have interacted with disease and malnutrition to produce an unhappy result, when no single factor could be held solely to blame.

So much then for a tentative set of conclusions. In a particular historical period and in the social context of a particular country, and with opium as a drug available only in oral form, we can begin to see the outline nature of the equilibrium reached between the society and the drug – a plateau at a high general level of usage and with regional variation, no persuasive evidence of large-scale social incapacity, but with associated mortality levels which, though not too disastrous when matched against certain modern drug experiences, were nonetheless cause for concern.

Exactly the same question concerning the nature of the equilibrium between a society and drug use in conditions of uncontrolled availability may be approached by looking at certain recent accounts from special settings. For instance, Dr Charas Suwanwela and his colleagues, writing in 1978,[33] provided a view of opium use and addiction among the hill tribes of Northern Thailand. They found that varied and varying patterns of use existed:

It is impractical to separate the occasional users into experimenters, occasional and habitual users as in some reports dealing with urban populations because of the hill tribe situation:

a single person may shift from one to another pattern depending on illness and other factors. The distinction between frequent users and addicts is also not very precise. A person who was not using opium every day, requested to be detoxified. On the other hand, addicts who personally accepted their undesirable status were using variable amounts of opium with variable frequency.

There is the inference here that counting addicts might not have been a logically very satisfactory exercise in nineteenth-century England.

Nonetheless, Dr Suwanwela managed to design an operational definition of addiction for his survey purposes, basing it on daily use and experience of withdrawal symptoms. Within those terms, he found that addiction rates varied greatly from village to village – from 16.8 per cent of population aged ten years and over among the Hmong tribe of Ban Khun Wang, to 6.6 per cent among the Lisu people of Doi Sam Mun. And here in microcosm is a restatement of one of the conclusions which has just been drawn from the historical material – given free availability, use patterns will be a patchwork rather than a uniformity. Social and cultural context as well as supply will influence the plateau which is achieved.

As regards the social effects of addiction, the Tai report is largely dealing with smoked opium rather than eaten opium, although some opium is eaten by these villagers. The following passage conveys the complexity of the situation:

> When addicts were asked to recall their ability to work before and after the condition, most stated that they were less productive afterwards. Some, however, could not work at all previously and opium kept them going. For example, a 39-year-old Meo male was addicted for three years because of swelling of both legs and generalized weakness . . . [after detoxification] he could not work adequately. He decided to go back on opium, and has since been able to earn a living as a farmer and as the village silversmith.

Some addicts are said to be 'rather lazy', and they 'sleep late and work only periodically'. No one, says this report, would want his daughter to marry an addict. Addiction is disapproved, except among the elderly. But it is also reported that 'it is not unusual to see a villager who has been addicted for 30 or 40 years actively working. These are indeed productive members of the household.' The authors sum up the question of opium's impact on social functioning by saying that there are 'two extremes with many in-between'.

As ever, there is need to underline the point that different contexts will mean different consequences. But there are inviting two-way analogies to be drawn between endemic smoked opium in Thai villages and endemic British patterns of opium eating in the nineteenth century. The conjecture that nineteenth-century opium use, particularly in rural and agricultural settings, would not have caused widespread social disability is strengthened. One begins more closely to sense the possible *texture* of the problem, the fine-grained detail of ordinary lives which history cannot by itself reconstruct – multiple and shifting patterns of use rather than absolutes of addicted versus not addicted, a bit of late-lying in the morning, extremes and betweens. How many Fenland labourers may there have been who were able to work only because of their opium?

One might also argue that the nineteenth-century British opium experience has something to say to the contemporary problems and policies of the East. Even with advancing industrialization, with growing cities such as Bangkok, opium is a drug with which a reasonable equilibrium might be expected to be established, even with minimal formal controls. Twentieth-century Bangkok and nineteenth-century Manchester are different contexts, motor traffic and horse trams set different problems, smoked opium and opium pills or laudanum may bring different consequences, but one might at least conclude that endemic opium use in the developing world should not be cause for panic, or for repressive measures which upset the balanced ecology with consequences worse than the original situation.[34] We are back to rediscovering the Royal Commission on Opium of the 1890s[35] – what they told us about India, what history tells us about nineteenth-century Britain, or what the latter-day epidemiologist has to say about Thailand all point to the likelihood that, with opium, a society left to find its natural balances comes to no great harm. If secondary poverty is the problem, this might be met by making opium cheaper rather than by a prohibition which drives up the price.

Unfortunately such a conclusion regarding the possibilities of sustaining a reasonably unworried equilibrium with opium came in many ways too late. Post-war international drug policy has been recklessly insensitive to such considerations, and old patterns of opium use in countries such as Thailand, Burma, Singapore, Hong-Kong, Iran and Turkey have been attacked with crusading zeal. Possession of an opium pipe becomes an offence, and in some countries the drug user has faced the death penalty. Insensitivity has not been an accident, but the order of the day, and it is obvious that policies have often been instigated which are not related to the interest of the countries concerned, but are motivated primarily by the interests of Western states which wish to suppress the opium cultivation which fed the illicit heroin supplies primarily of the United States. So far as large tracts of the East are concerned, suppression of opium use has encouraged its substitution by heroin because lesser bulk means easier surreptitious handling. There is also a logistic attractiveness in heroin because the technique of sniffing this drug is speedy and simple, and it does not require a pipe or the other paraphernalia of opium smoking. It is also sometimes stated that the mere fact that heroin use does not involve the detectable smell of smoked opium makes the drug preferable where there are alert police patrols.

To contend that banning opium in the East has given birth to domestic heroin use in those countries as a direct and simple consequence, and with no other factors involved, would be too simple. But there can be little doubt that the sudden insult to old balances often contributed to bringing about a worse situation than the original. In addition to the effect which post-war policies may have had on actual patterns of indigenous drug use, new images of 'the drug problem' have certainly led in some traditional opium-using cultures to damaging criminalization of the user and to some diversion of health care resources. In one or two countries, such as Pakistan and India, special gifts of resistance have allowed the Western pressures in some measure to be withstood, and the opium addict may still, without fuss or bother, collect his drug each day from the licensed vendor.

Let's now though take the discussion back to a consideration of whether the nineteenth-century and twentieth-century evolution of British drug control policies and the movement from informal to formal control is to be seen as careless insult to ecology, as witness to 'impoverishment of culture', or as something to be understood more sympathetically.

Movement in drug control in Britain during the nineteenth century was a slow evolution, much debated, at times much contested – an outcome from manoeuvring between factions as well as the product of larger social movements. The industrial revolution had upset an older ecology but an equilibrium was restored. The movement towards formal control was not an alien and insensitive imposition, but related to society's increasing background concern with health and a willingness to interfere in health matters, together with the availability of a newly confident medical profession which was both self-seeking and the servant of society's behests. Much of our present and more stringent formal control system might be seen in similarly sympathetic terms: unsterile intravenous injections make nonsense of easy comparison with opium eating, young addicts who readily draw others into their habits demand a control response quite different from the stay-at-home morphine addict of the 1890s, the reality as well as the threat of black-market enterprise is with us, and one would be hard put to argue that the dangers to health could be remedied by removing all controls.

But at the same time, it is reasonable to interpret the evidence as also supporting a rather conflicting conclusion. Ecologies can indeed be upset by clumsy interference. The Dangerous Drugs Act of 1920 was not part of a smooth historical evolution, but a sharp and imposed change, even given that war-time regulations and DORA 40B may have paved the way for this change. This is not the place to go into the history of that period in detail, but there is the immediate feeling of contrast with the movement which led, say, to the 1868 Pharmacy Act. Put simply, the Pharmacy Act was the slow outcome of national debates and manoeuvrings, while the 1920 Act although having internal elements in its genesis reflected for the first time the influence of international pressures.

Since 1920 there must be the uneasy feeling that there are elements within the total system which have not developed in tune with need, or which no longer serve the real needs. These remarks are directed particularly to aspects of drug legislation which offer heavy penalties for possession or supply of opiates. The young addict found with a supply of heroin on him for personal use, can in theory be liable to a prison sentence of seven years. If he were caught in Piccadilly selling some of his surplus, he could in theory be liable to up to fourteen years' imprisonment. In practice, sentences of this severity are never in these circumstances handed down, and the upper range of sentencing is reserved for large-scale and professional dealing. Furthermore, the possibility of a prison sentence for the addict may be benignly used to move him towards probation and social help. The fact is, though, that no one knows exactly how this penal system is working in practice, and an unknown number of addicts are going to prison to no one's real advantage. The control system is not here responding to context, but has in some sense itself gone out of control.

It is easy to forget the extent to which informal controls still operate – for every adolescent who accepts the opportunity to use a drug there are many who refuse. The value and richness of such informal mechanisms is neglected or insulted by 'Health Education' which attempts superficially to instruct from outside and from a position of cultural ignorance. Research too very easily neglects these informal processes as too elusive for the habits of thought of investigators (and fund givers) who are willing to persevere with a type of epidemiology which is concerned only with the counting of cases. History itself must not of course be misused as simple-minded Health Education for very different times, but the history of opium use does at the very least repeatedly and remarkably point up the fact that there are different ways of seeing things and doing things, and thus lead to self-questioning. So far as our own times are concerned, our vision of drug control has become too frightened and too mechanistic.

TABLES

Table 1: The Sources and Quantities (in lbs.) of England's Opium Imports 1827–1900

YEAR	TURKEY	%	INDIA	%	CHINA	%	PERSIA	%	EGYPT	%	FRANCE	%	REST	%
1827	109,921	97.2	—	—	—	—	—	—	—	—	—	—	3,219	2.8
1828	78,402	93.1	57	0.1	—	—	—	—	—	—	546	0.6	5,181	6.3
1829	42,804	91.8	36	0.1	—	—	—	—	—	—	2,243	4.8	3,551	6.2
1830	192,136	91.9	—	—	—	—	—	—	—	—	—	—	6,459	8.1
1831	8,884	89.1	28	0.3	—	—	—	—	2	<0.1	—	—	1,261	10.5
1832	65,475	95.8	—	—	—	—	—	—	—	—	—	—	1,687	4.2
1833	72,020	67.4	—	—	—	—	—	—	9,699	9.1	11,508	10.8	13,605	12.7
1834	12,438	25.8	15	<0.1	—	—	—	—	21,464	44.5	2,563	5.3	11,736	24.3
1835	77,986	91.2	84	0.1	902	1.1	—	—	—	—	3	<0.1	6,506	7.5
1836	119,929	91.7	22	<0.1	821	0.6	—	—	623	0.5	3,045	2.3	6,354	4.8
1837	70,099	88.0	—	—	—	—	—	—	3,768	4.7	1,118	1.4	5,618	5.9
1838	80,554	84.1	580	0.6	124	0.1	—	—	12,895	13.5	102	0.1	1,577	1.6
1839	177,651	90.5	6,358	3.2	—	—	—	—	4,673	2.4	6,204	3.2	1,357	0.7
1840	50,746	65.2	19,125	24.6	—	—	—	—	5,879	7.5	1,350	1.7	782	1.0
1841–52							FIGURES NOT AVAILABLE							
1853	154,017	96.7	—	—	—	—	—	—	15,027	15.4	1,651	1.7	5,295	3.3
1854	76,703	78.8	—	—	—	—	—	—	6,712	5.9	431	0.4	4,007	4.1
1855	102,373	90.7	2,080	1.8	326	0.3	—	—	2,958	3.6	890	1.1	943	0.9
1856	74,914	91.9	—	—	—	—	—	—	3,014	2.2	—	—	2,762	3.4
1857	125,022	91.6	—	—	—	—	—	—	3,668	3.8	988	1.0	8,387	6.2
1858	90,397	92.5	—	—	—	—	—	—	2,410	1.7	—	—	2,642	2.7
1859	136,695	96.8	—	—	—	—	—	—	11,296	5.4	—	—	2,063	1.5
1860	195,366	92.6	—	—	—	—	—	—	6,831	3.1	—	—	4,205	2.0
1861	279,393	98.4	—	—	—	—	—	—	—	—	—	—	4,612	1.6
1862	212,280	95.9	—	—	—	—	—	—	4,632	1.8	—	—	2,270	1.0
1863	247,111	97.2	—	—	—	—	—	—	4,479	1.8	—	—	2,571	1.0
1864	244,019	97.6	—	—	—	—	—	—	—	—	—	—	1,542	0.6
1865	394,313	98.2	—	—	—	—	—	—	—	—	—	—	7,258	1.8
1866	194,393	98.1	—	—	—	—	—	—	—	—	—	—	3,830	1.9
1867	258,862	94.6	—	—	—	—	—	—	—	—	—	—	14,660	5.4
1868	317,333	98.5	—	—	—	—	—	—	—	—	—	—	5,176	1.5

Year														
1869	203,546	92.7					9,154	2.5			6,796	3.1	9,135	4.2
1870	275,838	74.2			11,002	3.0	21,894	3.7	50,868	13.7	11,559	3.1	13,244	3.5
1871	492,855	83.3	6,636	1.1	7,140	1.2			22,005	3.7			40,936	7.0
1872	325,572	91.4	1,061	0.3	13,853	3.5	73,807	14.3	9,636	2.7			19,942	5.6
1873	355,363	88.7	7,296	1.8	37,011	7.2	36,606	6.8	6,260	1.6	11,339	2.2	17,697	4.4
1874	348,074	67.7	24,117	4.7	34,182	6.4	51,165	12.8					20,024	3.9
1875	381,631	71.2	25,861	4.8	5,660	1.4	56,284	9.3					94,617	10.8
1876	315,624	78.8	13,390	3.3			37,160	6.6					65,629	3.7
1877	530,870	87.4	5,696	0.9			47,240	8.3					14,512	2.4
1878	511,535	91.5					45,258	11.3					10,145	1.9
1879	499,351	87.2			34,699	8.7	21,012	2.6					25,820	4.5
1880	288,764	72.1					54,442	11.4					31,653	7.9
1881	717,534	90.5					91,680	11.8					56,600	6.9
1882	359,560	75.1			34,347	7.2	41,573	8.5					30,275	6.3
1883	617,272	79.7	18,906	2.4	17,756	2.3	37,040	5.2	2,419	0.3	13,220	1.7	12,816	1.8
1884	412,528	84.1	4,910	1.0	4,065	0.8	83,656	16.1	8,269	1.7	10,653	2.2	8,677	1.7
1885	657,686	92.6	5,786	0.8	3,758	0.5	123,704	18.9	3,012	0.4			2,817	0.4
1886	405,761	77.9	12,420	2.4	3,948	0.8	8,451	1.4	5,337	1.0	4,613	0.9	5,389	0.9
1887	391,717	59.9	81,038	12.4	27,161	4.2	19,570	4.0	4,223	0.6	6,098	0.9	20,181	3.0
1888	549,848	93.6	7,715	1.3			30,035	6.7			3,320	0.6	18,031	3.1
1889	428,495	87.1	14,832	3.0			52,238	10.2			15,715	3.2	13,503	2.7
1890	360,963	80	9,223	2.0	5,598	1.1	59,712	11.1	3,543	0.8	33,704	7.5	13,725	3.0
1891	367,468	71.9	15,758	3.1	122	0.1	22,658	6.1	2,395	0.5	61,626	12.1	6,191	1.0
1892	431,299	80	10,261	1.9			44,008	9.9			26,249	4.9	11,567	2.0
1893	247,071	67	43,577	11.8			3,890	1.0	5,176	1.4	16,890	4.6	26,781	9.0
1894	365,581	81.6	7,829	1.8	16,070	3.3	84,040	17.2	4,760	1.1	12,552	2.8	12,852	2.8
1895	362,572	94.7	8,240	2.2	5,880	1.3	60,770	13.7			3,180	0.8	5,184	1.3
1896	364,827	74.6	15,470	3.2	1,260	0.3	72,710	17.1					8,828	1.7
1897	349,945	79	14,070	3.2			26,212	4.4	1,120	0.3	6,104	1.4	5,280	1.0
1898	284,871	66.9	33,296	7.8	3,317	0.4	36,640	4.4	1,755	0.4	17,850	4.2	14,300	3.3
1899	409,363	68.6	72,720	12.2					2,260	0.4	61,302	10.3	24,679	4.0
1900	619,292	74.3	96,397	11.6							39,751	4.8	37,933	4.5

Table 2: Import and Home Consumption of Opium 1827-60

Year	Actual home consumption in 1,000 lb.	Actual home consumption in lb. per 1,000 population	Estimated home consumption[1] in lb. per 1,000 population
1827	17	1.31	1.95
1828	21	1.54	−0.36
1829	24	1.76	0.35
1830	23	1.64	2.82
1831	26	1.85	−1.08
1832	30	2.14	3.45
1833	35	2.47	3.76
1834	28	1.96	1.14
1835	31	2.12	0.77
1836	39	2.61	4.02
1837	37	2.48	0.81
1838	30	1.99	5.42
1839	42	2.68	11.99
1840	47	2.97	2.67
1841	39	2.46	5.93
1842	48	2.97	−3.36
1843	32	1.97	−4.70
1844	33	1.98	3.11
1845	40	2.38	1.28
1846	35	2.05	−0.61
1847	46	2.67	2.90
1848	61	3.52	6.96
1849	44	2.51	−0.44
1850	42	2.38	2.19
1851	50	2.80	2.25
1852	62	3.44	5.69
1853	67	3.64	3.88
1854	61	3.30	1.56
1855	56	2.98	3.33
1856	42	2.23	1.58
1857	56	2.92	4.82
1858	54	2.78	0.80
1859	61	3.11	3.15
1860	11[2]	3.39	5.67

1. Estimated home consumption is obtained by subtracting the amount of opium exported from that imported.
2. Up to March 1860 only. Actual home consumption per 1,000 population based on an extrapolation for the whole year.

SOURCE: Parliamentary Papers: *Annual Statistics of Trade, Imports and Exports of Opium 1827–1860.*

Table 3: Narcotic Deaths 1863–1910

YEAR	TOTAL NARCOTIC DEATHS No.	Per million population	ACCIDENTAL NARCOTIC DEATHS No.	Per million population	NARCOTIC SUICIDES No.	Per million population
1863	126	6.1	106	5.1	19	0.9
1864	134	6.4	102	4.9	28	1.3
1865	120	5.7	98	4.6	22	1.0
1866	114	5.3	92	4.3	18	0.8
1867	138	6.4	110	5.1	28	1.3
1868	140	6.4	104	4.7	35	1.6
1869	100	4.5	83	3.7	17	0.8
1870	90	4.0	62	2.8	27	1.2
1871	97	4.3	86	3.8	11	0.5
1872	102	4.4	81	3.5	21	0.9
1873	108	4.6	66	2.8	42	1.8
1874	103	4.3	77	3.2	25	1.1
1875	116	4.8	80	3.3	36	1.5
1876	111	4.6	81	3.3	30	1.2
1877	110	4.5	78	3.2	32	1.3
1878	130	5.2	94	3.8	35	1.4
1879	144	5.7	100	3.9	43	1.7
1880	131	5.1	95	3.7	36	1.4
1881	144	5.5	105	4.0	40	1.5
1882	128	4.9	96	3.6	32	1.2
1883	136	5.1	103	3.9	32	1.2
1884	120	4.5	73	2.7	47	1.7
1885	162	6.0	107	3.9	53	1.9
1886	137	5.0	93	3.4	42	1.5
1887	156	5.6	104	3.7	52	1.9
1888	177	6.3	108	3.8	65	2.3
1889	149	5.2	99	3.5	48	1.7
1890	164	5.7	97	3.4	65	2.3
1891	173	5.9	116	4.0	56	1.9
1892	163	5.5	104	3.5	59	2.0
1893	174	5.8	107	3.6	67	2.3
1894	196	6.5	111	3.7	85	2.8
1895	193	6.3	119	3.9	74	2.4
1896	177	5.7	110	3.6	67	2.2
1897	206	6.6	139	4.5	64	2.1
1898	159	5.0	97	3.1	62	2.0
1899	169	5.3	95	3.0	74	2.3
1900	169	5.2	95	2.9	72	2.2
1901	138	4.2	75	2.3	62	1.9
1902	151	4.6	88	2.7	63	1.9
1903	164	4.9	102	3.1	61	1.8
1904	162	4.8	81	2.4	80	2.4
1905	162	4.8	67	2.0	92	2.7
1906	152	4.4	83	2.4	64	1.9
1907	148	4.3	80	2.3	67	1.9
1908	129	3.7	61	1.7	66	1.9
1909	119	3.4	66	1.9	51	1.4
1910	101	2.8	57	1.6	44	1.2

SOURCE: Registrar General's Reports: *Violent deaths 1863–1911.*

Table 4: Narcotic Deaths by Age 1863–1908

YEAR	All narcotic deaths					Deaths/1 million living				Opium				Laudanum			
	0–1	1–4	5–19	20–34	35+	0–4	5–19	20–34	35+	0–4	5–19	20–34	35+	0–4	5–19	20–34	35+
1863–7	236	56	23	63	254	20.5	0.7	2.5	7.8	2.3	0.1	0.5	2.1	13.3	0.5	1.9	5.3
1868	46	11	5	20	58	19.3	0.7	3.9	8.6	4.1	0.1	1.2	0.7	12.2	0.6	2.5	6.8
1869	30	9	4	11	46	13.0	0.6	2.1	6.7	3.7	0.3	0.2	2.8	8.0		1.7	3.7
1870	24	5	4	12	45	9.6	0.4	2.3	6.5	2.3		0.4	1.7	5.9	0.4	1.5	4.5
1871	31	8	3	16	38	12.7	0.4	3.0	5.4	2.0		0.7	1.7	9.1	0.1	1.9	3.6
1872	29	11	4	8	50	12.8	0.5	1.5	7.1	3.2	0.1	0.4	1.6	6.7	0.4	0.9	4.4
1873	23	4	1	15	65	8.5	0.1	2.7	9.1	0.9		0.2	2.4	6.3	0.1	2.4	6.3
1874	27	9	1	18	48	11.2	0.1	3.2	6.6	4.5		0.5	1.5	5.6	0.1	2.2	4.1
1875	31	8	3	16	58	12.0	0.4	2.8	7.9	2.8	0.1		1.8	7.1	0.3	2.7	5.7
1876	22	8	3	18	60	9.1	0.4	3.1	8.1	2.7			1.9	4.2	0.3	2.4	5.5
1877	20	6	3	18	65	7.8	0.4	3.1	8.7	0.9	0.2	0.7	2.0	3.6		1.9	5.3
1878	28	6	3	22	71	10.0	0.4	3.7	9.4	1.5		0.5	2.9	4.4	0.4	2.9	5.5
1879	28	8	2	25	82	10.5	0.2	4.2	10.7	2.9	0.1	1.3	2.6	5.0	0.1	1.8	6.3
1880	28	4	6	27	66	9.2	0.7	4.5	8.5	1.7		1.0	1.9	6.3	0.6	2.3	5.3
1881	25	9	2	20	88	9.7	0.2	3.3	11.2	6.8	0.2	2.9	10.8				
1882	18	3	2	20	85	6.0	0.2	3.2	10.7	4.0	0.2	3.1	10.2				
1883	23	7	2	20	84	8.5	0.2	3.2	10.4	7.1	0.2	2.7	9.6				
1884	14	6	6	29	66	5.7	0.7	4.5	8.1	4.0	0.6	4.4	7.7				
1885	20	4	7	18	113	6.8	0.8	2.8	13.7	5.9	0.7	2.6	12.0				
1886	15	10	3	16	93	7.1	0.3	2.4	11.1	5.7	0.3	2.3	10.5				
1887	17	5	5	24	105	6.2	0.5	3.6	12.4	5.4	0.5	3.5	11.7				
1888	15	6	4	34	117	5.9	0.4	5.0	13.7	5.6	0.4	4.7	12.6				
1889	17	5	4	27	95	6.2	0.4	3.9	11.0	4.8	0.4	3.8	10.1				
1890	13	4	3	35	109	4.8	0.3	5.0	12.5	3.9	0.3	4.6	11.4				

YEAR	Soothing syrups				Chlorodyne				Morphine				Cocaine			
	0–4	5–19	20–34	35+	0–4	5–19	20–34	35+	0–4	5–19	20–34	35+	0–4	5–19	20–34	35+
1891	0.6			0.1			0.3	1.4								
1892	1.1						0.3	0.9							0.1	0.1
1893	0.8			0.1	0.3			1.5								
1894	0.3				0.3		0.3	1.0							0.1	0.1
1895	0.5				0.3		0.7	1.2							0.1	
1896	0.5				0.3		0.6	1.8							0.1	0.1
1897					0.3	0.3	0.4	1.9							0.1	0.3
1898							0.4	0.5						0.1	0.1	
1899	0.3				0.3		0.2	0.9								0.1
1900					0.3		0.1	0.7						0.1		
1901	0.8					0.1	0.2	0.5							0.4	0.1
1902	0.3						0.4	1.5							0.2	0.2
1903	0.3						0.5	1.3							0.2	
1904							0.3	0.9		0.5		0.1			0.1	0.1
1905							0.3	0.2								
1906							0.2	0.8							0.2	0.1
1907							0.1	0.4								0.3
1908								1.0							0.1	0.3

Appendix

The Nature and Significance of Addiction

Addiction is the word which is popularly in use to describe compulsive drug taking. In scientific writing the word (and the underlying concept) has to an extent been supplanted by the phrase *drug dependence*. Here though the complexities of scientific nomenclature need not be gone into, and it seems better to retain the older and slightly less cumbersome term.

The opiates are drugs of addiction. There are variations in individual susceptibility, but anyone who takes an opiate for a long enough period and in sufficient dose will become addicted. What is the nature of this condition which trails with it so many fears and stereotypes, and which seems often to be thought of almost as possession rather than as intelligible happening? This question is very relevant to an understanding of the problems which society encountered over that long period when opium was so readily available that it could provide the conditions where addiction must have been common and endemic.

Opiates are drugs to which the individual's central nervous system will, on repeated exposure, develop a high degree of *tolerance* – a much bigger dose of the drug is then required to produce the same and desired effect in the tolerant than in the naïve subject. There is therefore in the drug's intrinsic properties a ready and in-built invitation to escalate the dose. If the drug was taken for, say, a chronic neuralgia, its effectiveness would at first be very evident and much valued, but if it was to go on being of use to the person purchasing his laudanum from the corner grocer's shop, he would soon find that to produce the original effects he was having to take the laudanum in larger quantities. But every addict sooner or later finds his plateau dose, and there is considerable variation in levels and patterns of use. Many reach a fairly moderate dose level which suits them, and stick to it. This is what nineteenth-century writers on addiction were referring to when they cited cases of 'moderate addicts' who showed no tendency to continuing escalation.

Tolerance is then intimately linked to the onset of *withdrawal symptom* experience and *physical dependence*. The tolerant individual begins to find that some hours after his last dose he feels restless, that he develops goose pimples and begins to yawn, that his eyes are watering and his nose running, and that he is generally uncomfortable. With increasing dependence more severe withdrawal symptoms will be experienced, and if this person is then deprived of his drug for twelve or more hours he risks an agonizing withdrawal experience characterized particularly by great restlessness and anxiety, severe abdominal cramps and profuse diarrhoea. Appalling though the experience may then be, the condition is not life-threatening unless there is some severe intercurrent illness or infection. The patient recovers. Lesser degrees of addiction carry risks only of lesser withdrawal symptoms, and like the drug effect itself the withdrawal experience is much influenced by set and expectation.

Addiction to opiates may best be pictured as both a psychological and biological condition, characterized by a desire to continue taking the drug in high dosage, a salience of this drug-seeking drive over other life considerations and a tendency to relapse. It seems likely that repeated experience of the powerful euphoriant effect of the drug contributes to the initiation of addiction: in simple terms a habit is built up because it is intensely pleasurable. But what also very importantly contributes to the enhancement of this 'learnt drive' is the repeated experience of withdrawal and the concomitant experience of repeated and wonderfully reassuring relief which is afforded by the next drug dose. The addict is *conditioned* to crave that next dose. Such a view of addiction can, however, be criticized for placing too great an emphasis on the drug itself and its user's experience in isolation from environmental determinants which initiate and sustain drug use, and which give the drug its symbolic meaning and the user his social role. The pharmacological qualities cited here and the psychological experience of the users are important, but it is difficult to see how, on their own, they can provide a coherent idea of a condition called addiction or dependence. Here can be seen very plainly what is meant by the need to integrate different levels of explanation.

So much for the nature of addiction. What about its significance, and in particular its significance for nineteenth-century society? The threat which is posed by addiction to *oral* preparations of opiates is much less than the dangers of addiction to the drug in *injected form*, and it was of course the latter type of addiction which characterized the British 'heroin epidemic' of the 1960s, and characterizes the large-scale contemporary drug problem in the U.S.A. The special dangers of injected drug use include the ease of accidental overdose and the risks of accidental infection caused by a dirty needle. Today's picture of injected heroin use must therefore not be allowed too easily to colour any assumptions as to what would have been the familiar picture, in the nineteenth century, of addiction to opium or opium preparations taken by mouth. There would have been risks of overdose, sometimes as a result of the unreliable strength of many of the available commercial preparations, but the risks would be nothing like so great as those encountered by the twentieth-century heroin addict who injects the drug directly into his veins. What proportion of overdose cases in the nineteenth century were occurring among addicts and what proportion among casual users is unknown, but certainly the contemporary concern with self-poisoning did not simply equate overdosing with addiction. The problem of accidental infection is then irrelevant to oral use. Another possible medical implication of addiction which received nineteenth-century attention was the general question of whether habitual opium use shortened life, but here too the problem was conceived in terms of the fact of high usage rather than the underlying fact of the addiction. On the longevity issue the present judgement would probably be that opiates themselves produce no directly damaging or life-shortening effect on the body and that addiction itself is not a physically damaging condition.

The problems which the nineteenth century encountered with addiction were therefore presumably more in the social than the medical sphere. Opium may have been cheap, but a heavily tolerant individual might well build up to such a dose as to involve a weekly cash outlay to embarrass the family's finances in a working-class household where every penny counted. The drive towards continued drug use would mean that the family's welfare easily became neglected. There might also be other social complications – neglect in child care, for instance, or impairment of working capacity. Such possible social complications do not seem much to have caught the nineteenth-century eye, although there were occasional references to matters of this sort. Indeed, the fact that addiction itself was not sharply conceptualized for the larger part of the century, in many of the relevant debates and social movements, meant that the addict did not suffer the sort of secondary social damage which comes from labelling and stigma, and which has been so much part of the present-day reaction of the Western world to drug-taking and the drug-taker.

Addiction to drugs other than opiates has features specific to each drug group. Cocaine can produce an intensely compulsive drive towards continued drug use, despite the absence of withdrawal symptoms. Depressant substances such as chloral can also induce addiction, with a well-marked withdrawal picture. Psychomimetic substances in general do not give rise to addiction, and if cannabis has any addictive potential this was certainly not an issue with the sort of doses and preparations which the nineteenth century encountered.

Far from the physical attributes of the drugs in question being a side-issue or something quite separate from the main business, an understanding of the extraordinary subtlety and potency of the actions of these substances on the human mind and body helps not only to make intelligible the social processes which were the game evolved around them, but re-inforces one's sense also of the astonishing subtlety and potency of accidental and informal, or formal and purposive social processes, which allow society at different phases in history to live on terms with these strange mind-acting chemicals.

Reference

A very useful general source book on pharmacology is L. S. Goodman and A. Gilman, *Pharmacological Basis of Therapeutics*, 5th edn (New York, Macmillan, 1975).

References

Introduction

1. P. Laurie, *Drugs. Medical, Psychological and Social Facts* (Harmondsworth, Penguin Books, 1974), gives a good introduction to present-day use of and attitudes towards drugs.
2. The war-time 'emergency' leading to the introduction of the first stringent controls is analysed in V. Berridge, 'War conditions and narcotics control: the passing of Defence of the Realm Act Regulation 40B', *Journal of Social Policy*, 7, No. 3 (1978), pp. 285–304.
3. This section on the nature of the drugs has been contributed by Professor Edwards.
4. This section is based, among other works, on C. E. Terry and M. Pellens, *The Opium Problem* (Montclair, New Jersey, Patterson Smith, 1970; first published 1928); L. Lewin, *Phantastica. Narcotic and Stimulating Drugs, Their Use and Abuse* (London, Kegan Paul, 1931); M. Goldsmith, *The Trail of Opium* (London, Hale, 1939); A. Hayter, *Opium and the Romantic Imagination* (London, Faber and Faber, 1968); D. Macht, 'The history of opium and some of its preparations and alkaloids', *Journal of the American Medical Association*, 64 (1915), pp. 477–81; and R. S. France, 'An Elizabethan apothecary's inventory', *Chemist and Druggist*, *172* (1959), p. 50.
5. For examples of this approach, see D. Musto, *The American Disease. Origins of Narcotic Policy* (New Haven and London, Yale University Press, 1973); and T. Duster, *The Legislation of Morality* (New York, Free Press, 1970). B. Inglis, *The Forbidden Game. A Social History of Drugs* (London, Hodder and Stoughton, 1975), analyses English drug use, although his book is not based on any substantial original research. J. L. Himmelstein, 'Drug politics theory: analysis and critique', *Journal of Drug Issues*, 8 (1978), pp. 37–52, adopts a usefully critical approach to some of the historical/polemical analyses of U.S. drug policy.

6. T. Szasz, *Ceremonial Chemistry. The Ritual Persecution of Drugs, Addicts and Pushers* (London, Routledge and Kegan Paul, 1975).

7. P. Thane, Introduction, pp. 11–20, in P. Thane, ed., *The Origins of British Social Policy* (London, Croom Helm, 1978).

8. See the paper by E. Lomax, 'The uses and abuses of opiates in nineteenth-century England', *Bulletin of the History of Medicine*, 47 (1973), pp. 167–76.

9. Social control has been criticized as an analytical tool because of its associations with functionalism and a static, not class-antagonistic social model, in particular by G. Stedman-Jones, 'Class expression *versus* social control?', *History Workshop*, 4 (1977), pp. 163–70.

10. M. Foucault, *The Birth of the Clinic. An Archaeology of Medical Perception* (London, Pantheon Books and Tavistock Publications, 1973), p. 32. Anyone working in the area of medically defined deviance must be influenced by Foucault's ideas and my debt to him in certain chapters will be obvious.

11. Earlier brief surveys of the main issues are in V. Berridge, 'Opium and the historical perspective', *Lancet*, 2 (1977), pp. 78–80; and V. Berridge, 'Victorian opium eating: responses to opiate use in nineteenth century England', *Victorian Studies*, 21, No. 4 (1978), pp. 437–61.

1: The Import Trade

1. 'W.B.E.', *A Short History of Druggs and Other Commodities, the Produce and Manufactory of the East Indies* (London, eighteenth century, exact date uncertain), p. 47.

2. 'Meeting of the Westminster Medical Society', *London Medical Gazette*, 3 (1828–9), pp. 712–13.

3. Parliamentary Papers (P.P.), for example 1887, LXXX: *Accounts and Papers. Imports and Exports of Opium*, show the increase in quantities of opium from the 'East Indies' (Bombay and Scinde). In 1886, over 12,000 lb. were imported into England. (See Table 1, p. 272.)

4. J. Ince, 'Prescriptions for examination', *Pharmaceutical Journal*, n.s. *11* (1869–70), pp. 684–5. Many other pharmacists were also enthusiastic about the new variety, as, for example, in 'Persian opium', *Pharmaceutical Journal*, 3rd ser. *3* (1872–3), p. 31, and F. A. Fluckiger and D. Hanbury, *Pharmacographia. A History of the Principal Drugs of Vegetable Origin, Met with in Great Britain and British India* (London, Macmillan, 1879), p. 49.

5. The description of opium growing and the opium market in Asia Minor owes much to the descriptions given in, for example, Landerer, 'On the preparation of Smyrna opium', *Pharmaceutical Journal*, *10* (1850–51),

pp. 474–5; S. H. Maltass, 'On the production of opium in Asia Minor', *Pharmaceutical Journal*, *14* (1854–5), pp. 395–400; E. R. Heffler, 'Notes on the culture of and commerce in opium in Asia Minor', *Pharmaceutical Journal*, n.s. *10* (1868–9), pp. 434–7; P. L. Simmonds, 'Supplies of opium and scammony from Turkey', *Pharmaceutical Journal*, 3rd ser. *2* (1871–2), pp. 986–7.

6. Landerer, op. cit., pp. 474–5.

7. Descriptions of the appearance of the various varieties of opium are given in Landerer, op. cit., pp. 474–5; J. Murray, *A System of Materia Medica and Pharmacy* (Edinburgh, Adam Black, 6th edn 1832), p. 82; and 'Opium', *Household Words*, *16* (1857), pp. 104, 181.

8. Although there are no reliable import figures for the earlier centuries, there is evidence that opium was available in England in the late sixteenth century. R. S. France, op. cit., p. 50, shows that Zacharie Linton, the apothecary in question, had half an ounce of opium among his drugs in 1593.

9. The decline of European staging posts can be traced in the published import/export data. 1857 was the last year in which any notable amounts of opium came other than direct from Turkey; see P.P. 1857–8, LIV: *Accounts and Papers. Imports and Exports of Opium*, p. 89.

10. Greater London Record Office, Records of Smith Kendon Ltd 1865, statements about the S.S. *Crimean*, Ms B/SK/26. The listing of cases of opium along with bales of madder and bags of gum indicated the normality of the trade.

11. P.P. 1808, XII: *Accounts and Papers. Trade: Imports and Exports of Opium*, pp. 50–51, 88–9.

12. I. S. Russell, *The Later History of the Levant Company, 1753–1825* (unpublished University of Manchester Ph.D. thesis, 1935); A. C. Wood, *A History of the Levant Company* (London, O.U.P., 1935).

13. Herring's evidence on this point was given to P.P. 1854–5, VIII: *First Report from the Select Committee on the Adulteration of Food, Drink and Drugs*; see also G. E. Trease, *Pharmacy in History* (London, Bailliere, Tindall, and Cox, 1964), p. 156.

14. J. H. Heap, 'The commerce of drugs', *Pharmaceutical Journal*, n.s. *16* (1903), p. 529.

15. P.P. 1854–5, op. cit.

16. *Robsons London Directory* (London, William Robson, 12th edn 1832), p. 155; *Post Office London Directory* (London, Kelly, 1855).

17. P.P. 1854–5: *Report from the Select Committee on Adulteration*, op. cit.

18. Evidence given by Professor Thomas Redwood to the Select Committee on Adulteration, P.P. 1854–5, op. cit., q. 1762–5. See also 'The opium robbery', *Pharmaceutical Journal*, n.s. *4* (1862–3), pp. 327–8.

19. Information on prices is taken from London Price Current, 1819–1820, Pharmaceutical Society Ms. 12381; and for example P.P. 1860, LXIV: *Accounts and Papers. Imports and Exports of Opium.*

2: The Cultivation of Opium in Britain 1790–1820

1. E. J. Hobsbawm, *Industry and Empire* (Harmondsworth, Penguin Books, 1969), pp. 98–9.

2. J. Ball, 'English opium', *Transactions of the Society ... of Arts, 14* (1796), pp. 253–70.

3. C. Alston, 'A dissertation on opium', *Medical Essays and Observations, 5*, part 1 (1742), pp. 110–76. See also T. Arnot, 'A method of preparing the extract and syrup of poppies', *Medical Essays and Observations, 5,* part 1 (1742), pp. 105–9.

4. J. Kerr, 'The culture of the white poppy and preparation of opium in the province of Bahar', *Medical Observations and Inquiries, 5* (1776), pp. 317–22.

5. W. Woodville, *Medical Botany* (London, James Phillips, 1793), vol. 3, p. 506. See also S. Crumpe, *An Inquiry into the Nature and Properties of Opium* (London, G. G. and J. Robinson, 1793), p. 18.

6. T. Jones, 'English opium', *Transactions of the Society ... of Arts, 18* (1800), pp. 161–94; see also J. Burnby, 'Medals for British rhubarb', *Pharmaceutical History, 2* (1971), pp. 6–7; and *John Sherwen and Drug Cultivation in Enfield: A Re-examination,* Edmonton Hundred Historical Society occasional paper, n.s. No. 23, 1973.

7. A. Duncan, 'Observations on the preparation of soporific medicines from common garden lettuce', *Memoirs of the Caledonian Horticultural Society, 1* (1814), p. 160; J. Howison, 'Essay on the preparation of opium in Britain', ibid., p. 365.

8. J. Young, 'English opium', *Transactions of the Society ... of Arts, 37* (1820), pp. 23–39; 'The Winslow opium', *Pharmaceutical Journal,* 4th ser. *160* (1948), pp. 106, 151. See also, for other experiments, G. Swayne, 'On the manufacture of British opium', *Quarterly Journal of Science, Literature and the Arts, 8* (1820), pp. 234–40; *9* (1820), pp. 69–80; and J. W. Jeston, 'English opium', *Transactions of the Society ... of Arts, 41* (1823), pp. 17–31.

9. J. Cowley and Mr Staines, 'English opium', *Transactions of the Society ... of Arts, 40* (1823), pp. 9–29; *41* (1823), pp. 15–16, and 'On the cultivation of the white poppy and on the preparation of English opium', *Technical Repository, 7* (1825), p. 145.

10. J. Cowley and Mr Staines (1825), op. cit.

11. 'Cultivation of opium in England', *London Medical Repository, 24* (1825), p. 93.

12. J. Young, op. cit., pp. 23–39.

13. J. Ball, op. cit., pp. 267–70; T. Jones, op. cit., pp. 190–93.

14. J. Cowley and Mr Staines, op. cit., *40* (1823), pp. 9–29.

15. As, for example, in the comments made on its production in 'The narcotics we indulge in', *Blackwood's Edinburgh Magazine*, *74* (1853), pp. 605–28; 'Opium', *Penny Magazine*, *3* (1834), p. 397; 'Poppy oil and opium', ibid., *13* (1844), pp. 46–8; J. Pereira, *Elements of Materia Medica* (London, Longman, Orme, Browne, Green and Longmans, 1839–40), vol. 2, p. 1276; A. Ure, 'Observations on opium and its tests', *London Medical Gazette*, 6 (1830), pp. 73–6.

16. F. Fluckiger, 'What is opium?', *Pharmaceutical Journal*, n.s. *10* (1868–9), pp. 208–11; J. Hood, 'Notes on the cultivation of the opium poppy in Australia', ibid., 3rd ser. *2* (1871–2), pp. 272–4.

17. The Western European trials are described in, for instance, 'Opium from French poppies', *Pharmaceutical Journal*, *17* (1857–8), p. 28; C. Harz, 'Opium production in Europe', ibid., 3rd ser. *2* (1871–2), pp. 223–5.

18. The Mitcham market is described in A. S. Taylor, *On Poisons in Relation to Medical Jurisprudence and Medicine* (London, John Churchill, 1848), p. 607; and J. Stephenson and J. Churchill, *Medical Botany* (London, John Churchill, 1831).

3: Open Sale and Popular Use

1. 'Messrs Morson give up the retail', *Chemist and Druggist*, *57* (1900), p. 650; A. Duckworth, 'The rise of the pharmaceutical industry', ibid., *172* (1959), pp. 127–8; J. K. Crellin, 'The growth of professionalism in nineteenth century British pharmacy', *Medical History*, *11* (1967), pp. 215–27.

2. All these wholesale druggists gave evidence to the First Select Committee Enquiry into Adulteration in 1854.

3. Society of Apothecaries, Laboratory mixture and process book, 1868–72, Guildhall Library Ms. 8277.

4. W. Allen and Co., Inventories of drugs, 1810–11, Pharmaceutical Society Ms. 22008. There is information about prices and preparations also in Allen and Hanbury, Price book of drugs, 1846–66, Pharmaceutical Society Ms. 22006; and Sales Ledger of a wholesale druggist, 1847–58, Wellcome Library Ms. 833.

5. A. Duckworth, op. cit., pp. 127–8; R. S. Roberts, 'The early history of the import of drugs into Britain', pp. 165–83, in F. N. L. Poynter, ed., *The Evolution of Pharmacy in Britain* (London, Pitman, 1965).

6. Dicey and Sutton, Drug invoice, 1838, Pharmaceutical Society Ms.

12177, shows Thomas Harvey of Leeds buying drugs, including opium, from Dicey and Sutton in Bow Church Yard, London.

7. W. Kemp and Son, *Monthly Price List of Specialities* (Horncastle, no publisher, 1890); G. Meggeson, Price list of medicated lozenges, *c.* 1850, Pharmaceutical Society Ms. 1232–4.

8. D. N. Phear, 'Thomas Dover, 1662–1742. Physician, privateering captain, and inventor of Dover's Powder', *Journal of the History of Medicine and Allied Sciences, 9* (1954), pp. 139–56.

9. Public Record Office, Home Office papers, H.O. 45, 7531, 1865: Letter from Edward Foster to Sir George Grey.

10. P.P. 1857, XII (sess. 2): *Report from the Select Committee of the House of Lords on the Sale of Poisons etc. Bill*, q. 852. There is also evidence of this type of informal restriction in P.P. 1834, VIII: *Report from the Select Committee on Inquiry into Drunkenness*, q. 1793; *British Medical Journal, 1* (1868), p. 637.

11. 'Alleged child poisoning', *Pharmaceutical Journal*, 3rd ser. *6* (1875–6), pp. 596–7; R. C. Ellis, 'Short notes of a fatal case of poisoning by opium', *Lancet, 2* (1863), p. 126. Both reports show how shops selling opiates were kept by factory workers' wives.

12. Prescription book of a Scarborough chemist, *c.* 1875, Wellcome Library Ms. 3994.

13. *Morning Chronicle*, 15 November 1849; Home Office papers, H.O. 45, 5347, 1854: Letter from Hull coroner to Home Secretary.

14. 'Poison shops', *Lancet, 1* (1858), p. 486.

15. W. Bateman, *Magnacopia* (London, John Churchill, 1839).

16. Clay and Abraham, Stock list of a Liverpool shop, Pharmaceutical Society Ms. 40619. A Peterborough shop had sixteen opium preparations in stock: R. Bright, Memorandum of the valuation of stock taken 1 November 1854 at 29 Broad Street, Peterborough, Pharmaceutical Society Ms. 9987.

17. Reminiscences date back to the early 1900s, but it can be assumed that practices would have changed little over the previous fifty years. Indeed, where procedures can be directly compared, there seems to be no difference. This section is based on information from H. Cook, E. W. Frost, W. E. Hollows and other retired pharmacists. See also P.P. 1843, XV: *Children's Employment Commission: Second Report of the Commissioners on Trade and Manufactures*, Appendix to the Second Report, part 2, q. 30.

18. S. Flood, 'On the power, nature and evil of popular medical superstition', *Lancet, 2* (1845), p. 203.

19. T. Hardy, *The Trumpet-Major* (London, Smith, Elder and Co. 1880), p. 274. I am grateful to Meta Zimmeck for this reference.

20. P.P. 1857: *Select Committee on Sale of Poisons ...*, op. cit., *1*, 852.

21. 'Register of the sales of opium and laudanum in Stockton-on-Tees', *Pharmaceutical Journal*, *17* (1857–8), p. 165.

22. W. Armitage, Chemist's prescription book, 1847–99, Wellcome Library Ms. 978.

23. 'Memories of the "jug and bottle" trade. By an octogenarian', *Chemist and Druggist*, *167* (1957), pp. 164–5; 'Sale of poisons', *Lancet*, *1* (1870), p. 92; the Hoxton reminiscence was collected by Anna Davin.

24. This section is again based partly on pharmacists' memories and also on 'Poisoning by laudanum', *British Medical Journal*, *2* (1878), p. 889; P.P. 1857: *Select Committee on Sale of Poisons . . .*, op. cit., q. 1195; 'Suicides by laudanum', *Pharmaceutical Journal*, new ser. *3*, 1861–2, pp. 628–9; 'Opium as a daily transaction', ibid., *207* (1971), p. 215.

25. J. Parkinson, *Medical Admonitions to Families, Respecting the Preservation of Health, and the Treatment of the Sick* (London, H. D. Symonds, 1801), p. 157.

26. W. Rayner, Workhouse medical officers' order book, 1840, Stockport Local History collection, Ms. B/EE/3/21, describes how opium pills were given to some workhouse inmates at night.

27. G. H. Rimmington, retired pharmacist, personal communication, 1975.

28. *Pannell's Reference Book for Home and Office* (London, Granville Press, 1906), pp. 480–81, and J. Parkinson, op. cit., pp. 326–7, both describe this usage.

29. For example the chemists' recipe book of Mr Lloyd Thomas (1879–1900), which contains a recipe for 'pauverine' cough mixture, a cheap variety especially for poor customers. I am grateful to the late Mr G. Lloyd Thomas for lending me his father's book.

30. 'Poisoning by laudanum', *Pharmaceutical Journal*, 3rd ser. *10* (1879–80), p. 599; P.P. 1839, XXXVIII: *Returns from the Coroners of England and Wales of All Inquisitions Held by Them During the Years 1837 and 1838, in Cases where Death was Found by Verdict of Jury to Have Been Caused by Poison*, p. 431. See also 'On toothach' (sic), *The Doctor*, *2* (1833–4), p. 206; T. L. Brunton, 'The influence of stimulants and narcotics on health', pp. 183–267 in M. Morris, ed., *The Book of Health* (London, Cassell, 1883).

31. W. Buchan, *Domestic Medicine* (London, A. Strahan, 18th edn 1803), pp. 294, 297, 304, 335, 337, 361, 399, 410–11, 415, 660, 663–4, 670, 675, 685.

32. *Morning Chronicle*, 1 November 1849; P.P. 1857, XII: *Report . . . on the Sale of Poisons*, op. cit., q. 276.

33. 'Poisoning by opium and gin . . .', *Lancet*, *1* (1862), p. 326; P.P. 1839, XXXVIII: *Returns from the Coroners . . .*, op. cit., p. 435; *The Times*, 5 January 1870; 'The sale of laudanum', *British Medical Journal*, *1* (1891), pp. 363–4.

34. The drawbacks of mortality data are discussed in B. W. Benson, 'The nineteenth century British mortality statistics: towards an assessment of their accuracy', *Bulletin of the Society for the Social History of Medicine*, *21* (1977), pp. 5–13.

35. J. Jeffreys, 'Observations on the improper use of opium in England', *Lancet*, *1* (1840–41), pp. 382–3; and 'The Sale of Poisons', *Pharmaceutical Journal*, *9* (1850), pp. 163, 205–10, 590–91.

36. These data are discussed in more detail in V. Berridge and N. Rawson, 'Opiate use and legislative control: a nineteenth century case study', *Social Science and Medicine*, *13A* (1979), pp. 351–63. The establishment of the domestic morphine industry should also be taken into account in assessing the rise in home consumption (see Chapter 12).

37. R. Christison, 'On the effects of opium eating on health and longevity', *Lancet*, *1* (1832), pp. 614–17; G. R. Mart, 'Effects of the practice of opium eating', ibid., *1* (1832), pp. 712–13; see also V. Berridge, 'Opium eating and life insurance', *British Journal of Addiction*, *72* (1977), pp. 371–7.

38. *Annual Reports of the Registrar General* (London, H.M.S.O., 1867), pp. 176–9. For an example of one regular user who did exceed the limit of his tolerance by mistake, see Inquisition at Whitechapel on Samuel Linistram, 28 November 1820, Middlesex Record Office Ms. MJ/SPC E 1130.

39. 'Prison chaplain's register. 1854', Buckinghamshire Record Office, MSQ/AG/27.

40. *Reynolds's Newspaper*, 1 October 1854. For other examples, see 'The estate of pauperism and laudanum-drinking', *Lancet*, *1* (1878), p. 325; letter from J. D. Phillips, *British Medical Journal*, *1* (1884), p. 885.

41. P.P. 1894, LXI. *Minutes of Evidence of the Royal Commission on Opium*, q. 3387.

42. F. E. Anstie, *Stimulants and Narcotics* (London, Macmillan, 1864), p. 149.

4: Opium in the Fens

1. H. C. Darby, 'Draining the Fens', in L. F. Salzman, ed., *Victoria History of the County of Cambridge and the Isle of Ely* (London, University of London, Institute of Historical Research, 1948), pp. 75–6, and H. C. Darby, *The Draining of the Fens* (Cambridge, 2nd edn 1956), p. 65.

2. L. M. Springall, *Labouring Life in Norfolk Villages* (London, G. Allen and Unwin, 1936), p. 59; D. W. Cheever, 'Narcotics', *North American Review*, *95* (1862), pp. 375–415. V. Berridge, 'Fenland opium eating in the nineteenth century', *British Journal of Addiction*, *72* (1977), pp. 275–84, discusses the question of the Fens in greater detail.

REFERENCES

3. C. Lucas, *The Fenman's World. Memories of a Fenland Physician* (Norwich, Jarrold and Sons, 1930), p. 52.

4. E. Gillett and J. D. Hughes, 'Public health in Lincolnshire in the nineteenth century', *Public Health,* no volume number (1955), pp. 34–40, 55–60; local figures are also quoted in P.P. 1864, XXVIII: *Sixth Report of the Medical Officer of the Privy Council, 1863,* Appendix 14, 'Report by Dr Hunter on the excessive mortality of infants in some rural districts of England', p. 459.

5. Dr Hunter's report, op. cit., p. 459.

6. G. Rayleigh Vicars, 'Laudanum drinking in Lincolnshire', *St George's Hospital Gazette, 1* (1893), pp. 24–6.

7. W. Lee, *Report to the General Board of Health on a Preliminary Inquiry into the Sewerage, Drainage, and Supply of Water, and the Sanitary Condition of the Inhabitants of the Parish of Holbeach* (London, W. Clowes and Sons, 1849), p. 14; 'Opium eating in England', *British Medical Journal, 2* (1858), p. 325; W. Waterman, retired pharmacist, personal communication, 1977.

8. *Morning Chronicle,* 26 December 1850; W. Lee, *Report to the General Board of Health on ... the parish of Ely* (London, W. Clowes and Sons, 1850), pp. 18–19.

9. P.P. 1894, LXII: *Royal Commission on Opium,* q. 24706.

10. 'Notes on Madras as a winter residence', *Medical Times and Gazette,* n.s. *14* (1857), p. 426.

11. Quoted in M. Llewelyn Davies, ed., *Life As We Have Known It* (London, 1931, Virago reprint 1977), pp. 113–14.

12. C. Kingsley, *Alton Locke* (London, 1850, Everyman edn 1970), p. 130.

13. G. H. F. Nuttall, L. Cobbett and T. Strangeways-Pigg, 'Studies in relation to malaria. I: The geographical distribution of anopheles in relation to the former distribution of ague in England', *Journal of Hygiene, 1* (1901), pp. 4–44.

14. T. Joyce, 'The Pharmacy Act and opium eaters', *Lancet, 1* (1869), p. 150.

15. C. Marlowe, *Legends of the Fenland People* (London, Cecil Palmer, 1926), p. 134; 'Increased consumption of opium in England', *Medical Times and Gazette,* n.s. *14* (1857), p. 426; G. Ewart-Evans, personal communication, 1975 and 1976. The high level of laudanum use for animals was still notable in the area in the 1920s: Home Office papers, H.O. 45, 11932.

16. P.P. 1867, XVI: *Children's Employment Commission: Sixth Report of the Commissioners on Organized Agricultural Gangs ...* p. 183; P.P. 1867–8, XVII: *First Report of the Commission on the Employment of Children, Young Persons and Women in Agriculture,* p. 131.

17. *Morning Chronicle,* 27 September 1850.

18. Evidence on the apparent female preponderance is in E. Porter, *Cambridgeshire Customs and Folklore* (London, Routledge and Kegan Paul, 1969), pp. 13, 26; M. Llewelyn Davies, op. cit., pp. 113–14; Parliamentary Debates (*Hansard*), *352* (1891), col. 314.

19. T. Hood, *Reminiscences*, quoted in H. A. Page, *Thomas De Quincey: His Life and Writings* (London, John Hogg, 1877), pp. 233-4.

20. G. Rayleigh Vicars, op. cit., pp. 24–6.

21. L. M. Springall, op. cit., p. 59; P.P. 1860, LXIV: *Accounts and Papers. Imports and Exports of Opium.*

22. Evidence on quantities sold is in the *Morning Chronicle*, 26 December 1850; *The Times*, 23 September 1867; A. Calkins, *Opium and the Opium Appetite* (Philadelphia, J. Lippincott, 1871), p. 34.

23. *Morning Chronicle*, op. cit.

24. *Medical Times and Gazette*, n.s. *14* (1857), p. 426

25. 'General Medical Council. Pharmacy', *Medical Times and Gazette*, *2* (1868), pp. 51–2; 'Report of the Pharmacy Bill committee to the General Medical Council', *British Medical Journal*, *2* (1868), p. 39.

26. The later history of Fenland opium use is discussed in V. Berridge, op. cit., pp. 275–84.

5: Opiate Use in Literary and Middle-Class Society

1. For an example of this tendency, see R. E. Reinert, 'The confessions of a nineteenth century opium eater: Thomas De Quincey', *Bulletin of Menninger Clinic*, *16* (1972), pp. 455-9.

2. E. Schneider, *Coleridge, Opium and Kubla Khan* (University of Chicago Press, 1953), p. 17.

3. A. Knight, 'The milk of paradise in the patent remedy: a study of the uses of opium in eighteenth century English society and literature', unpublished typescript, c.1971, argues that 'stimulant' effects of the drug were experienced by eighteenth-century writers. I am grateful to Judith Blackwell for loaning me this typescript.

4. A. Hayter, *Opium and the Romantic Imagination* (London, Faber and Faber, 1968, paperback edn 1971), p. 335.

5. Quoted by A. Hayter, op. cit., p. 107.

6. T. De Quincey, *Confessions of an English Opium Eater* (London, Taylor and Hessey, 1822, Penguin edn 1971), p. 71.

7. W. C. B. Eatwell, 'A medical view of Mr De Quincey's case', appendix 1, in A. H. Japp, *Thomas De Quincey: His Life and Writings* (London, John Hogg, 1890).

8. J. Gillman, *The Life of Samuel Taylor Coleridge* (London, William Pickering, 1838), vol. I, p. 245.

9. Some of De Quincey's criticisms of Coleridge are in 'Samuel Taylor Coleridge', pp. 93–4; and 'Coleridge and opium eating', pp. 71–111 in *The Works of Thomas De Quincey*, vol. 2 (Edinburgh, Adam and Charles Black, 1862).

10. J. D. Campbell, *Samuel Taylor Coleridge. A Narrative of the Events of His Life* (London, Macmillan, 1894), p. 122.

11. M. Lefebure, *Samuel Taylor Coleridge: A Bondage of Opium* (London, Victor Gollancz, 1974), p. 44, 199–200, 251; E. L. Griggs, 'Samuel Taylor Coleridge and opium', *Huntington Library Quarterly*, *17* (1954), pp. 357–8.

12. J. Gillman, op. cit., p. 245.

13. Anon., *Advice to Opium Eaters* (London, W. R. Goodluck, 1823), preface.

14. H. A. Page, *Thomas De Quincey: His Life and Writings, with Unpublished Correspondence* (London, John Hogg, 1877), pp. 271–2.

15. Baron de Tott, *Mémoires du Baron de Tott, sur les Turcs et les Tartares* (Amsterdam, no publisher, 1784), pp. 158–9.

16. M. Elwin, ed., *Confessions of an English Opium-Eater, in Both the Revised and the Original Texts with its Sequels, Suspiria de Profundis and The English Mail Coach, by Thomas De Quincey* (London, Macdonald, 1956), Introduction.

17. H. A. Page, op. cit., pp. 237–8.

18. 'Confessions of an English Opium Eater', *The British Review and London Critical Journal*, *20* (1822), pp. 474–88.

19. 'Confessions of an English Opium Eater', *Medical Intelligencer*, *3* (1822), pp. 116–18.

20. 'Noctes Ambrosianae', *Blackwood's Edinburgh Magazine*, *14* (1823), pp. 485–6; 'A recent confession of an opium-eater', ibid., *80* (1856), pp. 629–36.

21. E. L. Griggs, op. cit., pp. 360 and 364–78.

22. J. Cottle, *Reminiscences of Samuel Taylor Coleridge and Robert Southey* (London, Houlston and Stoneman, 1847), pp. 360–61; J. D. Campbell, op. cit., p. 200.

23. J. Cottle, op. cit., pp. 348–9; Cottle's 'wretched reminiscences' of Coleridge's opium eating were heavily criticized in the *Quarterly Review*, *59* (1839), pp. 1–33.

24. 'Coleridge and opium', *British Medical Journal*, *2* (1884), p. 1219, and ibid, *1* (1885), pp. 109, 210.

25. 'Opium eating and opium smoking', *Friend of China*, *11* (1890), pp. 138–40; P.P. 1894, LXI: *Minutes of Evidence of the Royal Commission on Opium*, q. 16872.

26. This circle of opium users and addicts is described in M. Lefebure, op. cit. pp. 61–2, and in A. Hayter, op. cit., pp. 27–8.

27. L. A. Marchand, *Byron, a Biography* (London, John Murray, 1957),

vol. 2, p. 559; P. Quennell, ed., *Byron, a Self-Portrait. Letters and Diaries, 1798–1824* (London, John Murray, 1950), vol. 2, p. 566.

28. T. L. Hood, ed., *Letters of Robert Browning* (London, John Murray, 1933), pp. 223–4; R. Holmes, *Shelley, The Pursuit* (London, Weidenfeld and Nicolson, 1974), pp. 111, 113, 115 and 391–2.

29. A. Hayter, op. cit., pp. 306–28. I am grateful to Robert Gittings for the information about Keats' suicide plans.

30. A. Hayter, op. cit., p. 293.

31. W. Gerin, *Branwell Brontë* (London, Thomas Nelson, 1961), pp. 159, 289.

32. Quoted in P. Haining, ed., *The Hashish Club* (London, Peter Owen, 1975), pp. 66–8.

33. W. Collins, *The Moonstone* (London, 1868, Penguin edn 1966), p. 430.

34. G. Pickering, *Creative Malady* (London, Allen and Unwin, 1974), pp. 262–4; A. Hayter, *Mrs Browning. A Poet's Work and Its Setting* (London, Faber and Faber, 1962), pp. 58, 60–62, 67–8; A. Hayter, *Opium*, op. cit., pp. 278-9.

35. W. Monk, ed., *The Journals of Caroline Fox* (London, Elek, 1972), p. 171; A. Hayter, *A Sultry Month* (London, Faber and Faber, 1965), p. 156; L. and E. Hanson, *Necessary Evil: The Life of Jane Welsh Carlyle* (London, Constable, 1952), pp. 388, 439 and 516.

36. J. Pollock, *Wilberforce* (London, Constable, 1977), p. 79.

37. S. G. Checkland, *The Gladstones. A Family Biography 1764–1851* (Cambridge University Press, 1971), pp. 290–91, 351 and 377–80; M. R. D. Foot and H. C. G. Matthew, eds., *The Gladstone Diaries* (Oxford, Clarendon Press, 1974), vol. 3, p. 487.

38. C. Beaton and G. Buckland, *The Magic Image* (London, Weidenfeld and Nicolson, 1975), p. 74.

39. Mrs A. Tweedie, ed., *George Harley* (London, Scientific Press, 1899), pp. 174–6. I am grateful to Mr L. M. Payne for drawing this reference to my attention.

40. H. Walpole, *Selected Letters* (London, Dent, 1926), p. 111; A. Calkins, *Opium and the Opium Appetite* (Philadelphia, J. Lippincott, 1871), p. 139.

41. G. Pickering, op. cit.

42. H. Davy, *Fragmentary Remains, Literary and Scientific* (London, John Churchill, 1858), pp. 42–3.

43. Duke of Wellington, *Wellington and His Friends* (London, Macmillan, 1965), pp. 69–70; R. W. Chapman, ed., *Jane Austen's Letters to her Sister Cassandra and Others* (London, O.U.P., 1952), p. 26; V. Dickinson, ed., *Miss Eden's Letters* (London, Macmillan, 1919), p. 132.

44. J. Bryson and J. C. Troxell, eds., *Dante Gabriel Rossetti and Jane Morris: Their Correspondence* (Oxford, Clarendon Press, 1976), pp. 131–2.

45. D. I. Macht and N. L. Gessford, 'The unfortunate drug experiences of Dante Gabriel Rossetti', *Bulletin of the Institute for the History of Medicine*, 6 (1938), pp. 34–61.

46. P. Brendon, *Hawker of Morwenstow. Portrait of a Victorian Eccentric* (London, Jonathan Cape, 1975), pp. 194–7, 200, 212, 224.

6: Opium in Medical Practice

1. For the position of the medical profession in the first half of the nineteenth century, see, for example, N. and J. Parry, *The Rise of the Medical Profession. A Study of Collective Social Mobility* (London, Croom Helm, 1976), pp. 109–31; I. Inkster, 'Marginal men: aspects of the social role of the medical community in Sheffield, 1790–1850', pp. 128–63 in J. Woodward and D. Richards, eds., *Health Care and Popular Medicine in Nineteenth Century England. Essays in the Social History of Medicine* (London, Croom Helm, 1977); and M. J. Peterson, *The Medical Profession in Mid-Victorian London* (Berkeley, University of California Press, 1978).

2. For an example of an early pharmacopoeia, see Royal College of Physicians, London, *Pharmacopoeia* (London, G. Woodfall, 3rd edn 1815). *British Pharmacopoeia* (London, Spottiswoode, 1858), and a later edition of 1885, also list standard opium preparations in medical use. See also P. Squire, *A Companion to the Latest Edition of the British Pharmacopoeia* (London, J. and A. Churchill, 14th edn, 1886).

3. J. Murray, *A System of Materia Medica and Pharmacy* (Edinburgh, Adam Black, 6th edn 1832), p. 94.

4. *Notes and Queries*, 2nd ser. *3* (1857), p. 445.

5. G. Young, *A Treatise on Opium Founded on Practical Observations* (London, A. Mular, 1753); C. Alston, 'A dissertation on opium', op. cit., pp. 110–76; S. Crumpe, *An Inquiry into the Nature and Properties of Opium* (London, G. G. and J. Robinson, 1793).

6. J. Brown, *The Elements of Medicine* (London, J. Johnson, 1795); the influence of Brown's ideas on Beddoes and the literary and scientific circles at Bristol is described in A. Hayter, op. cit., pp. 27–8; and M. Lefebure, op. cit., pp. 61–2.

7. S. Crumpe, op. cit., pp. 190–91.

8. R. Christison, *A Treatise on Poisons* (Edinburgh, Adam Black, 2nd edn 1832), p. 617; M. Ward, *Facts Establishing the Efficacy of the Opiate Friction* (London, C. Wheeler, 1809), p. 55.

9. F. E. Anstie, op. cit., p. 79; T. C. Allbutt, 'Opium poisoning and other intoxications', pp. 874–920 in his *System of Medicine* (London, Macmillan, 1897), vol. 2.

10. F. Robinson, 'On the utility of a knowledge of the temperaments in

connexion with the diagnosis and treatment of disease', *Lancet*, *1* (1846), p. 360.

11. 'The action of opium', *Medical Times and Gazette*, *12* (1845), pp. 165–6.

12. J. Pereira, op. cit., vol. 2, p. 1301.

13. Any medical journal of the period can give a multitude of examples of the reliance placed on opium. For the use of opium in the conditions mentioned here, see, for example, G. B. Wood, *A Treatise on Therapeutics* (Philadelphia and London, J. B. Lippincott and H. Bailliere, 1856), pp. 739–44, 745, 748, 750–58 etc. Also the articles on gout, rheumatism, convulsions, neuralgia, obstruction of the bowels, etc. in J. Russell Reynolds, ed., *A System of Medicine* (London, Macmillan, 1866–79), vols. 1–5.

14. 'Review of Dr Griffin's *Medical and Physiological Problems*', *British and Foreign Medical Review*, *21* (1846), pp. 105–7.

15. For O'Shaughnessy, see N. Howard-Jones, 'Cholera therapy in the nineteenth century', *Journal of the History of Medicine and Allied Sciences*, *27* (1972), pp. 373–96. For examples of cholera treated with opium, see *British and Foreign Medico-Chirurgical Review*, *40* (1867), pp. 9, 18, 26, 36. 'Cholera mixtures' based on camphor, turpentine and laudanum, sometimes with the addition of brandy or 'best Irish whiskey', are often to be found in prescription books of this period.

16. F. W. Pavy, 'Report of a case of diabetes mellitus successfully treated by opium', *Transactions of the Clinical Society of London*, *2* (1869), pp. 44–56. Pavy's researches were widely publicized in the leading medical journals. See also Royal College of Physicians, King's College Hospital case notes, 'Case of Maurice Ward, labourer with diabetes mellitus', Dr Yeo, vol. 79, and W. Osler, *The Principles and Practice of Medicine* (London, Y. J. Pentland, 1892), p. 304.

17. For some discussion of the use of opium in childbirth, see F. A. B. Bonney, 'On the effect of opiates upon labour and after pains', *Lancet*, *2* (1844), pp. 71–2; E. Murphy, 'Lectures on the mechanism and management of natural and difficult labours', ibid., *2* (1845), p. 29; J. Craig, 'On the use of opium in uterine haemorrhage', ibid., *2* (1846), pp. 10–12. Case notes also provide illustrations of its use: e.g. 'Case of Anne Hoskins', 1827, Greater London Record Office, General Lying-In Hospital case notes (GLI/B19).

18. Ideas of female ill-health are discussed in L. Duffin, 'The conspicious consumptive: woman as an invalid', pp. 26–56 in S. Delamont and L. Duffin, eds., *The Nineteenth Century Woman: Her Cultural and Physical World* (London, Croom Helm, 1978). The sex variation of mortality statistics is discussed in V. Berridge and N. Rawson, 'Opiate use and legislative control: a nineteenth century case study', *Social Science and Medicine* (1979).

19. J. Ferriar, *Medical Histories and Reflections* (London, Cadell and Davies, 2nd edn 1810), pp. 136–7.

20. J. Connolly, 'Clinical lectures on the principal forms of insanity', *Lancet*, *2* (1845), p. 526.

21. W. Smith, 'Practical observations on the treatment of insanity', *Medical Times and Gazette*, *20* (1849), pp. 197–9.

22. H. Maudsley, 'Opium in the treatment of insanity', *Practitioner*, *2* (1869), pp. 1–8.

23. T. S. Clouston, 'Observations and experiments on the use of opium, bromide of potassium and cannabis indica in insanity, especially in regard to the effects of the two latter given together', *British and Foreign Medico-Chirurgical Review*, *46* (1870), pp. 493–511; *47* (1871), pp. 203–20.

24. F. E. Anstie, 'On certain nervous affections of old persons', *Journal of Mental Science*, *16* (1870–71), pp. 31–41; 'Psychological medicine', ibid., *20* (1874–5), pp. 224–35.

25. J. C. Mackenzie, 'The circulation of the blood and lymph in the cranium during sleep and sleeplessness, with observations on hypnotics', *Journal of Mental Science*, *37* (1891), pp. 18–61.

26. J. Pereira, op. cit., p. 1304.

27. 'Case of Thomas Jones', 1850, Dr Todd's cases, King's College Hospital case notes.

28. T. Laycock, 'Clinical illustrations of the pathology and treatment of delirium tremens', *Edinburgh Medical Journal*, *14* (1858–9), pp. 289–305; G. Johnson, 'On delirium tremens, its symptoms, pathology and treatment', *Lancet*, *1* (1866), pp. 419, 449, 607, 712.

29. F. E. Anstie, 'Alcoholism', p. 88 in J. Russell Reynolds, op. cit., vol. 2 (1868).

30. 'Cambridge Medical Society', *Lancet*, *1* (1882), p. 65.

31. These conclusions are based on an analysis of prescription books from London, Manchester and Yorkshire. Prescription book of an Islington chemist, Wellcome Library Mss. 3875–3993; Manchester prescription book, Wellcome Ms. 6471; Prescription book of George Daniel, chemist of Holloway Road, Wellcome Ms. 2033; Prescription book of William Armitage, Wellcome Ms. 978.

7: 'A Peculiar Sopor': Opium Poisoning and the Longevity Debate

1. P.P. 1834, VIII: *Select Committee ... on Drunkenness*, op. cit., q. 325; P.P. 1842, XXVII: *On the Sanitary Condition of the Labouring Population*, Local reports for England and Wales (Irish University Press, 1971), vol. 3, p. 212.

2. P.P. 1844, XVII, *First Report of the Commissioners for Inquiring into*

the State of Large Towns and Populous Districts, qs. 943–5. Other reports to the Commission, in particular the Rev. J. Clay's piece on Preston and John Ross Coulthart's on Ashton-under-Lyne, also brought up the issue of opium.

3. M. W. Flinn, ed., *Introduction to Chadwick's Sanitary Condition of the Labouring Population of Great Britain* (Edinburgh University Press, 1965), p. 21, notes the involvement of the profession in social questions. P.P. 1862, XXII: *Fourth Report of the Medical Officer of the Privy Council*, Appendix 5, 'Dr Greenhow's report on the circumstances under which there is an excessive mortality of young children among certain manufacturing populations', p. 659; and P.P. 1864, XXVIII: *Sixth Report of the Medical Officer of the Privy Council*, and Appendix 14, 'Report by Dr Henry Julian Hunter on the excessive mortality of infants in some rural districts of England', pp. 459–64.

4. P.P. 1864, op. cit., *Sixth Report of the Medical Officer of the Privy Council*, Appendix 16, 'Professor Alfred S. Taylor's report on poisoning and the dispensing, vending and keeping of poisons', pp. 754–5; P.P. 1857, XII: *Report ... on the Sale of Poisons ...*, op. cit., q. 778 and qs. 852–8; P.P. 1865, XII. *Special Report from the Select Committee on the Chemists and Druggists Bill and Chemists and Druggists (No. 2) Bill*, q. 63.

5. M. W. Flinn, op. cit., p. 31, notes the use of statistics in this way.

6. P.P. 1857, op. cit., q. 791.

7. *Annual Reports of the Registrar General*, op. cit. (London, H.M.S.O., 1867), pp. 176–9. See B. W. Benson, 'The nineteenth century British mortality statistics; towards an assessment of their accuracy', *Bulletin of the Society for the Social History of Medicine*, *21* (1977), pp. 5–13, for discussion of the limitations of the Registrar General's reports.

8. The accident figures could have been inflated, for it was well known that coroners would do much to avoid the stigma of a suicide verdict. The opium mortality rates are discussed in V. Berridge and N. Rawson, op. cit., pp. 351–63.

9. *The Times*, 4 March 1834.

10. J. H. Sprague, 'On the most efficacious means of remedying the effects of opium', *London Medical Repository*, *18* (1822), pp. 125–9; 'Decease of Mr Augustus Stafford, M.P.', *Pharmaceutical Journal*, *17* (1857–8), pp. 339–41.

11. W. Buchan, op. cit., p. 445.

12. 'Death from opium', *Pharmaceutical Journal*, n.s. *7* (1865–6), p. 37

13. W. Ryan, 'Delirium tremens – poisoning by laudanum – erysipelas – recovery', *Lancet*, *2* (1845), pp. 475–7.

14. R. Christison, *Treatise*, op. cit., p. 600.

15. L. J. Bragman, 'The case of Dante Gabriel Rossetti', *American Journal of Psychiatry*, *92*, part 2 (1935–6), pp. 1111–22; D. I. Macht

and N. L. Gessford, 'The unfortunate drug experiences of Dante Gabriel Rossetti', *Bulletin of the Institute of the History of Medicine, 6* (1938), pp. 34–61.

16. 'Poisoning with opium', *Lancet, 2* (1828–9), p. 764.

17. W. Howison, 'On the medical and moral treatment of young women who have swallowed laudanum in large quantity', *Edinburgh Medical and Surgical Journal, 18* (1822), pp. 49–62. J. Tweddale, letter, *Lancet* (1826), p. 245.

18. For further discussion of this, see V. Berridge and N. Rawson, op. cit., pp. 351–63.

19. 'Large doses of opium', *Pharmaceutical Journal*, n.s. *2* (1860–61), p. 386; A. Calkins, op. cit., p. 127.

20. P.P. 1857, op. cit., qs. 468–97.

21. P.P. 1834, VIII: *Select Committee ... on Drunkenness*, op. cit., q. 7; Metropolitan Police papers, Mepol 2/1698 1916, Sir Edward Henry, Metropolitan Commissioner of Police, to Sir Francis Lloyd, General Officer Commanding the London District.

22. R. Christison, *Treatise*, op. cit., p. 601. See also *Blackwood's, 80* (1856), op. cit., pp. 629–36; 'Abuse of opium in Scotland', *London Medical Gazette, 4* (1829), p. 249; 'Attempt to poison witnesses on a trial', *Pharmaceutical Journal, 16* (1857), pp. 293–4; and R. Richardson, 'A dissection of the Anatomy Act', *Studies in Labour History, 1* (1976), pp. 1–14 for other examples of opium used for criminal purposes.

23. Cumberland Record Office, Lowther Mss. Stray Letters, 1827.

24. An Act for the Better Prevention of Offences, 1851, 14 and 15 Vict. ch. 19; Offences against the Person Act, 1861, 24 and 25 Vict. ch. 100.

25. A. J. Coulthard, 'Arthur Devereux: chemist and poisoner', *Journal of Forensic Medicine, 6* (1959), pp. 178–88, describes the case of a chemist who murdered his wife and children with morphia in 1900.

26. For example, Baroness Orczy's story 'The Woman in the Big Hat' (1910) where the fatal morphia is administered in a cup of chocolate. Reprinted in H. Greene, ed., *The Rivals of Sherlock Holmes. Early Detective Stories* (London, Bodley Head, 1970), p. 270.

27. *Medical and Physical Journal, 49* (1823), p. 119; see also S. Wray, 'Cases illustrating the decided efficacy of cold affusion', *London Medical Repository, 18* (1822), pp. 26–9.

28. 'Poisoning by opium', *Medico-Chirurgical Review, 2* (1825), p. 235.

29. W. T. Iliff, 'On a case of poisoning by opium, and its successful treatment by electro-galvanism', *Lancet, 1* (1849), pp. 314–15, and *2*, pp. 574–5.

30. J. Hughes Bennett, 'Antagonism between sulphate of atropia and meconate of morphia', *British Medical Journal, 2* (1874), pp. 518–20, 547–8 and 581–3; J. Harley, 'The Gulstonian Lectures, Lecture 3: On the physiological action and thereaputic use of henbane, alone and in

combination with opium, and on the combined operation of opium and belladonna', *Medical Times and Gazette*, *1* (1868), p. 376; A. G. Burness, 'Strychnine as an antidote to opium poisoning', *Medical Press and Circular*, *18* (1874), p. 333.

31. Review of Dr Moor's book, *British Medical Journal*, *1* (1900), p. 200.
32. Surveyed in V. Berridge, 'Opium eating and life insurance', op. cit.
33. R. Christison, 'On the effects of opium eating on health and longevity', *Edinburgh Medical and Surgical Journal*, *37* (1832), pp. 123–35; also R. Christison, *Lancet*, op. cit., pp. 614–17.
34. G. R. Mart, op. cit., pp. 712–13.
35. R. Little, 'On the habitual use of opium', *Monthly Journal of Medical Science*, *10* (1850), pp. 524–8.
36. J. Pereira, op. cit., p. 1293.

8: The Adulteration of Opium

1. A. Normandy, *Commercial Hand-Book of Chemical Analysis* (London, George Knight, 1850), p. 438.
2. J. Burnett, *Plenty and Want. A Social History of Diet in England* (Harmondsworth, Penguin Books, 1968), pp. 100–101.
3. See, for example, S. W. F. Holloway, 'The Apothecaries' Act 1815; a reinterpretation', *Medical History*, *10* (1966), pp. 107–29 and 221–36 which criticizes the old view of the Act as a progressive, reforming measure which allowed the apothecaries greater powers of inspection. See also his 'Medical education in England, 1830–58: a sociological analysis', *History*, *49* (1964), pp. 299–324, for an analysis of developing organizational and structural changes in the medical profession.
4. See S. W. F. Holloway, *History*, op. cit., for the advent of Parisian medicine and toxicology; also R. H. Shyrock, 'Medicine and society in the nineteenth century', *Journal of World History*, *5* (1959), pp. 116–46. Some of the earlier toxicology lectures are reported in the *Lancet*, e.g. A. Cooper, 'Of vegetable and mineral poisons', *Lancet*, *2* (1826), pp. 169–73.
5. Anon., *Deadly Adulteration and Slow Poisoning Unmasked, or Disease and Death in the Pot and Bottle* (London, Sherwood, Gilbert and Piper, 1830), p. 134; J. R. McCulloch, *Dictionary of Commerce* (London, Longman, 1832), pp. 798–800.
6. A. Normandy, op. cit., p. 438.
7. P.P. 1854–5, VIII: *First Report from the Select Committee on the Adulteration of Food, Drink and Drugs*, qs. 455–470. See also P.P. 1854–5, op. cit., q. 117; and 'Evidence of Dr R. D. Thomson on the adulteration of drugs before the Select Committee on the Poor Law Amendment Act', *Lancet*, *1* (1838–9), pp. 797–801.

8. A. Normandy, op. cit., pp. 60–66.

9. F. Accum, *A Treatise on Adulterations of Food and Culinary Poisons* (London, Longmans, 1820), p. 205; *Deadly Adulteration*, op. cit., p. 55; and Anon., *The Tricks of the Trade in the Adulteration of Food and Physic* (London, David Bogue, 1856), p. 99.

10. J. Burnett, op. cit., p. 266.

11. R. D. Thomson, *Lancet*, op. cit., pp. 797–801.

12. J. Bell, 'On the adulteration of drugs', *Pharmaceutical Journal*, *1* (1841–2), pp. 253–62.

13. R. Christison, *Observations on the Adulteration of Drugs* (Edinburgh, Adam Black, 1838), p. 13.

14. 'The Analytical Sanitary Commission', *Lancet*, *1* (1853), pp. 64, 116–17, 251–3; *2* (1853), pp. 555–6; *1* (1854), pp. 10–14, 51–4, 77–81, 107–8, 165–8.

15. P.P. 1854–5, VIII: *First Report*, op. cit.; P.P. 1856, VIII: *Report from the Select Committee on the Adulteration of Food Drink and Drugs*; A. H. Hassall, *Adulterations Detected: or Plain Instructions for the Discovery of Frauds in Food and Medicine* (London, Longman, 1857).

16. W. J. Bell, *The Sale of Food and Drugs Acts, 1875 to 1907*, 5th ed by Charles F. Lloyd (London, Butterworth, 1910), p. 9.

17. J. F. Liverseege, *Adulteration and Analysis of Food and Drugs* ... (London, J. and A. Churchill, 1932), pp. 501–2; H. H. L. Bellot, *The Pharmacy Acts, 1851–1908* (London, Jesse Boot, 1908), p. 45; 'Sale of paregoric deficient in opium', *Pharmaceutical Journal*, 3rd ser. *20* (1889–90), p. 925.

9: Opium and the Workers: 'Infant Doping' and 'Luxurious Use'

1. As for example in M. Hewitt, *Wives and Mothers in Victorian Industry* (London, Rockliff, 1958), pp. 141–52; E. Lomax, 'The uses and abuses of opiates in nineteenth century England', *Bulletin of the History of Medicine*, *47* (1973), pp. 167–76; and A. E. Roberts, 'Feeding and mortality in the early months of life; changes in medical opinion and popular feeding practice, 1850–1900' (University of Hull Ph.D. thesis, 1973), Chapter 8.

2. A. C. Wootton, *Chronicles of Pharmacy* (London, Macmillan, 1910), vol. 2, pp. 177–8.

3. J. K. Crellin and J. R. Scott, 'Pharmaceutical history and its sources in the Wellcome collections. III. Fluid medicines, prescription reform and posology, 1700–1900', *Medical History*, *14* (1970), p. 151.

4. 'Godfrey's Cordial', *Pharmaceutical Journal*, *11* (1851–2), p. 237.

5. 'Onward from Galen; a current causerie', *Chemist and Druggist*, *167*

(1957), pp. 164–5; 'Poisoning by Godfrey's Cordial', *Pharmaceutical Journal*, 3rd ser. *10* (1879–80), pp. 746–7.

6.   P.P. 1843, XIII: *Children's Employment Commission: Second Report of the Commissioners on Trade and Manufactures*, q. 30, qs. 73–4, q. 81.

7.   See the evidence on all this presented, for instance, to P.P. 1844, XVII: *First Report of the Commissioners for Inquiring into the State of Large Towns and Populous Districts*, op. cit., Rev. J. Clay, 'Report on the sanatory [sic] condition of the Borough of Preston', p. 46, and J. R. Coulthart, 'Report on the sanatory condition of Ashton under Lyne', pp. 77–80. Also P.P 1845, V: *Second Report of the Commissioners for Inquiring into the State of Large Towns and Populous Districts*, Appendix 2, 'Lyon Playfair's report on the sanatory condition of large towns in Lancashire', pp. 365–71.

8.   P.P. 1834, XIX, op. cit., pp. 538–9.

9.   P.P. 1864, XXVIII: *Sixth Report*, op. cit., p. 34. Most of Simon's reports have something on child drugging and the use of Godfrey's.

10.   *Annual Reports* (London, H.M.S.O., 1867), op. cit.; also V. Berridge and N. Rawson, op. cit.

11.   Parliamentary Debates (*Hansard*), 3rd ser. 77 (1845), cols. 449–50.

12.   Manchester and Salford Sanitary Association, *Annual Reports*, 1856–7, 1861, 1864; Ladies Sanitary Association, *Annual Reports*, 1881, 1882.

13.   'The details of woman's work in sanitary reform', *Englishwoman's Journal*, *3* (1859), p. 223.

14.   P.P. 1857, XII, op. cit., *Sale of Poisons*, qs. 860–62; A. S. Taylor, *On Poisons*, op. cit., pp. 586–7; see also, for example, J. Elder Cummings, 'The neglect of infants', *Transactions of the National Association for the Promotion of Social Science*, *1874* (London, Longmans, Green, 1875), p. 723.

15.   For example, G. Rosen, 'Disease, debility and death', in H. J. Dyos and M. Wolff, eds., *The Victorian City* (London, Routledge, 1973), vol. 2, p. 650.

16.   P.P. 1871, VII: *Select Committee on the Protection of Infant Life*, q. 374.

17.   As for example fictionally in B. Disraeli, *Sybil, or The Two Nations* (London, 1845; Longmans, Green, 1881), p. 113.

18.   Evidence of this is in I. Pinchbeck, *Women Workers and the Industrial Revolution*, *1750-1850* (first edition 1930, reprinted London, Frank Cass, 1969), p. 197; R. B. Litchfield, 'The family and the mill; cotton mill work, family work patterns, and fertility in mid-Victorian Stockport', pp. 180–96 in A. S. Wohl, ed., *The Victorian Family. Structure and Stresses* (London, Croom Helm, 1978); M. Anderson, *Family Structure in Nineteenth Century Lancashire* (Cambridge University Press, 1971), pp. 71–2.

19. A. Wohl, 'Working wives or healthy homes?', *Bulletin of the Society for the Social History of Medicine, 21* (1977), pp. 20–24.

20. P.P. 1843, XIV: *Children's Employment Commission; Appendix to the Second Report of the Commissioners* (Trades and Manufactures), part I, 'Report by R. D. Grainger on the employment of children and young persons in the manufactures and trades of Nottingham, Derby, Leicester, Birmingham and London ...' f. 61–2. See also F. Engels, *The Condition of the Working-class in England* (London, 1892, Panther edn 1969), p. 135.

21. M. Hall, 'The effects of the habit of giving opiates on the infantine constitution', *Edinburgh Medical and Surgical Journal, 12* (1816) pp. 423–4.

22. Quoted in Lyon Playfair's report to the commission on Large Towns and Populous Districts, 1845, op. cit., p. 366.

23. Review of Dr West's book in *British and Foreign Medico-Chirurgical Review, 20* (1845), p. 551.

24. Prescription book of an Islington chemist, op. cit.

25. T. Bull, *The Maternal Management of Children, in Health and Disease* (London, Longman, 1840), pp. 110–12.

26. For examples of such cases, see *The Times*, 12 November 1857; Macclesfield Infant Mortality Committee, *Infant Mortality in Macclesfield. Report of a Special Committee of the Town Council* (Macclesfield, Swinnerton and Brown, 1877), p. 11.

27. J. B. Curgenven, *The Waste of Infant Life* (London, Faithfull and Head, 1867), p. 4; Home Office papers, H.O. 45, 8040, 1867, Recommendations of Harveian Society on infanticide; and 'Report of the Infant Mortality Committee', *Transactions of the Obstetrical Society of London, 11* (1869), pp. 132–49, and *12* (1870), pp. 388–403.

28. P.P. 1871, VII: *Select Committee on the Protection of Infant Life.*

29. See I. Pinchbeck and M. Hewitt, *Children in English Society* (London, Routledge and Kegan Paul, 1973), vol. 2, pp. 596, 613.

30. T. De Quincey, op. cit., p. 31.

31. M. Lefebure, op. cit., p. 59.

32. Mrs E. Gaskell, *Mary Barton. A Tale of Manchester Life* (London, Chapman and Hall, 1848, Penguin edn 1970), p. 219.

33. J. Pereira, op. cit. (London, Orme, Brown, Green and Longmans, 1854–7), vol. 3, p. 623. For other examples, see P.P. 1844, op. cit., q. 943, and 'The factory system', *Quarterly Review, 57* (1836), pp. 396–443.

34. Westminster Medical Society, 'The opium trade', *Medical Times and Gazette, 1* (1840), pp. 162–3.

35. *Morning Chronicle*, 15 November 1849.

36. P.P. 1834, XIX: *Factories Inquiry Commission*, op. cit., pp. 538–9.

37. P.P. 1857, op. cit., qs. 218–31 and qs. 852–8.

38. 'Noctes Ambrosianae', *Blackwood's Magazine*, *28* (1830), p. 391.
39. 'Medicus', 'Teetotalism and opium taking', *Lancet*, *1* (1851), p. 694.
40. B. Harrison, *Drink and the Victorians* (London, Faber and Faber, 1971), pp. 107–26.
41. R. Christison, *Lancet*, op. cit., pp. 614–17.
42. P.P. 1839, XLII: *Hand Loom Weavers*, 'Report with Appendices of the Assistant Commissioners on Southern and Eastern Scotland and Several Countries in Continental Europe', p. 52. See also P.P. 1840, XI: *Report from the Select Committee on the Health of Towns*, q. 1086.
43. J. Jeffreys, 'Observations on the improper use of opium in England', *Lancet*, *1* (1840–41), pp. 382–3.
44. J. Jeffreys, *The Traffic in Opium in the East* (London, Longman, 1858), pp. 18–19.

10: The 1868 Pharmacy Act

1. W. J. Reader, *Professional Men* (London, Weidenfeld and Nicolson, 1966), p. 2.
2. For analyses of this process, see J. Bell and T. Redwood, *Historical Sketch of the Progress of Pharmacy in Great Britain* (London, Pharmaceutical Society, 1880), pp. 108–19, p. 208.
3. E. S. Turner, *Call the Doctor* (London, Michael Joseph, 1958), p. 154; C. Newman, *The Evolution of Medical Education in the Nineteenth Century* (Oxford University Press, 1957), p. 190; F. N. L. Poynter, 'The influence of government legislation on medical practice in Britain' in F.N.L. Poynter, ed., *The Evolution of Medical Practice in Britain* (London, Pitman, 1961), pp. 11–12; I. Waddington, 'General practitioners and consultants in early nineteenth century England; the sociology of an intra-professional conflict', *Bulletin of the Society for the Social History of Medicine*, *17* (1976), pp. 11–12, and M. J. Peterson, op. cit.
4. J. K. Crellin, op. cit., p. 215. See also 'The Pharmacy Act 1868, and the rights of the general practitioner', *Medical Times and Gazette*, *2* (1868), pp. 508–9.
5. J. Bell and T. Redwood, op. cit., pp. 300, 328, 336, 340; H. Linstead, *A Guide to the Provisions of the Pharmacy and Poisons Acts, 1852 to 1933, and the Dangerous Drugs Acts, 1920 to 1932* (London, Pharmaceutical Press, 1936), pp. 1–4; also W. J. Uglow Woolcock, 'Historical sketch of the Pharmaceutical Society of Great Britain', *Pharmaceutical Journal*, 4th ser. *22* (1906), pp. 58–9, 193–4, 252, 342, 374–5, 438–9.
6. P.P. 1865, op. cit.
7. 31 and 32 Vict. ch. 121, 1868: An Act to Regulate the Sale of Poisons, and Alter and Amend the Pharmacy Act 1852.

8. P.P. 1864, XXVIII, Appendix 16, op. cit., and P.P. 1857, op. cit., qs. 860–62.

9. P.P. 1857, XII: *Sale of Poisons*, op. cit., q. 91; Home Office papers, H.O. 45, 6431, 1857, Sale of Poisons Bill, correspondence and draft of Bill.

10. P.P. 1857, XII, op. cit., qs. 85-8, q. 91 and qs. 282-8.

11. Parliamentary Debates (*Hansard*), 3rd ser. *152* (1859), col. 209.

12. 'Draft of Bill to regulate the sale of poisons', *Pharmaceutical Journal*, new ser. *8* (1866–7), p. 671.

13. 'Report of the Pharmacy Bill Committee to the General Medical Council', *British Medical Journal*, *2* (1868), p. 39. See also 'General Medical Council – Pharmacy', *Medical Times and Gazette*, *2* (1868), pp. 51–2.

14. *British Medical Journal*, op. cit., p. 39. For details of discussion of opium during the passage of the Bill, see Parliamentary Debates (*Hansard*), *192* (1868), col. 1556; *House of Lords Journal*, *100* (1867–8), p. 463; Chemist and Druggist, *The Pharmacy and Poison Laws of the United Kingdom* (London, Chemist and Druggist, 1892), p. 53.

15. 'Proceedings on the Pharmacy Bill', *Pharmaceutical Journal*, n.s. *10* (1868–9), p. 59.

16. The effects of the Act are discussed in further detail in V. Berridge and N. Rawson, op. cit.

17. Privy Council Office papers, P.C. 8, 153, 1869, 'Pharmacy Act 1868. Law Officer's opinion'.

18. 'Sale of Poisons', *Pharmaceutical Journal*, n.s. *10* (1868–9), pp. 500–502. See also 'The Privy Council and Pharmacy Act', *Lancet*, *1* (1869), p. 469, where the journal commented: 'public safety will be better secured by a limited construction of the words "poison" and "preparations"'.

19. 'Supply of laudanum by an unqualified person', *Pharmaceutical Journal*, 3rd ser. *19* (1888–9), p. 985.

20. This conclusion is based on a survey of the prescription books already mentioned in Chapter 6.

11: The Patent Medicine Question

1. For 'professional' opposition to patent medicines, see 'Petition from Royal College of Physicians, Edinburgh to House of Commons ...', *Lancet*, *1* (1859), p. 294.

2. 'Patent and secret narcotic preparations', *British Medical Journal*, *2* (1890), p. 639; Health News, *Exposures of Quackery* (London, The Savoy Press, 1895), vol. 1, pp. 24–6; L. G. Matthews, *History of Pharmacy*

in Britain (Edinburgh and London, E. and S. Livingstone, 1962), p. 366; P.P. 1914, IX: *Report from the Select Committee on Patent Medicines*, p.v.

3. A. C. Wootton, op. cit., pp. 172–3.
4. 'Quack medicines', *The Doctor*, 6 (1876), p. 37.
5. 'Squire's Elixir', *Lancet*, *1* (1823–4), p. 38; *Chemist and Druggist*, *167* (1957), op. cit., pp. 164–5, 274, 298 and 322.
6. Quoted in P.P. 1914, op. cit., p. vi.
7. Health News, op. cit., p. 34.
8. For example, the correspondence in *The Times* on 10 January 1880, which dealt in general with the abuse of narcotics, but also brought up the question of chlorodyne. See also Privy Council Office papers, P.C. 8, 310, 1884, 'Notes on the Sale of Poisons Bill'.
9. Privy Council Office papers, P.C. 8, 273, 1882, 'Memorandum on the Pharmacy Act'; P.C. 8, 283, 1883, 'Objections to the Pharmacy Bill'; P.C. 8, 299, 1883, 'Pharmacy Bill. Sale of poisons', P.C. 8, 364, 1886, 'Poisons Bill', and P.C. 8, 310, 1884, op. cit.
10. P.C. 8, 283, 3 March 1883, letter to Home Secretary from Society of Chemists and Druggists.
11. See details of the Bill and its failure in *Pharmaceutical Journal*, 3rd ser. *14* (1883–4), pp. 746, 763; *British Medical Journal*, *1* (1882), p. 760; Home Office papers, H.O. 45, 9605, 1881–6, 'Sale of poisonous patent medicines ...'; and *Hansard*, 3rd ser. *286* (1884), col. 801, where its second reading was deferred for six months in the expectation of a government Bill which never materialized.
12. J. P. Entract, 'Chlorodyne Browne: Dr John Collis Browne, 1819–84', *London Hospital Gazette*, *5–73*, no. 4 (1970), pp. 7–11; and J. Collis Browne, *Practical Instructions for the Treatment and Cure of Cholera and Diarrhoea by Chlorodyne* (London, n.d.), pp. 15–16.
13. See, for example, the advertisement in *News of the World*, 11 May 1862.
14. 'Formula for chlorodyne', *The Doctor*, *2* (1872), p. 173; 'Composition of chlorodyne', *Lancet*, *1* (1870), p. 72.
15. Correspondence from Squire and Davenport on chlorodyne, *Lancet*, *2* (1869), pp. 74 and 152.
16. E. S. Turner, *The Shocking History of Advertising* (London, Michael Joseph, 1952), pp. 66–7.
17. C. D. Wilson, managing director of J. T. Davenport and Co., personal communication, 1975.
18. 'Postal services and traffic', *Pharmaceutical Journal*, *210* (1973), p. 115.
19. 'Poisoning by chlorodyne', *Pharmaceutical Journal*, 3rd ser. *20* (1889–90), p. 1035. See also H.O. 45, 10454, 1893, 'Letters on the question of chlorodyne and the Habitual Drunkards Act, 1879'.

20. Norman Kerr did, however, recognize 'chlorodynomania' as a disease entity, but few other English specialists followed his lead. N. Kerr, *Inebriety, its Etiology, Pathology, Treatment and Juridsprudence* (London, H. K. Lewis, 2nd edn 1889), p. 115.

21. 'Memorandum by the chairman of the parliamentary bills committee of the B.M.A.', *British Medical Journal*, 2 (1890), pp. 973–5.

22. 'The consumption of chlorodyne and other narcotics', *British Medical Journal*, 1 (1891), p. 817.

23. 'Important decision under the Pharmacy Act 1868', *Pharmaceutical Journal*, 3rd ser. 22 (1891–2), pp. 928–40.

24. H. H. Bellot, op. cit., p. 36; 'The Irregular Sale of Poisons', *British Medical Journal*, 1 (1892), p. 978.

25. See V. Berridge and N. Rawson, op. cit. Also *Annual Reports of the Registrar General* (London, H.M.S.O., 1889–99).

26. C. D. Wilson, op. cit.

27. Health News, op. cit., p. 35; also R. Hutchinson, *Patent Foods and Patent Medicines* (London, Bale, Sons and Danielsson, 2nd edn 1906).

28. S. H. Holbrook, *The Golden Age of Quackery* (New York, Macmillan, 1959), p. 26.

29. British Medical Association, *Secret Remedies, What They Cost and What They Contain* (London, B.M.A., 1909), pp. 12–13, 14–18; and *More Secret Remedies, What They Cost and What They Contain* (London, B.M.A., 1912), p. 77, 148.

30. H.O. 45, 10059, 1888–1903, 'Departmental Committee to consider Schedule A of the Pharmacy Act, 1868', p. 548; R. Hutchinson, 'Patent medicines', *British Medical Journal*, 2 (1903), p. 1654.

12: Morphine and Its Hypodermic Use

1. G. Sonnedecker, 'Emergence of the concept of opiate addiction', *Journal Mondiale Pharmacie*, No. 3 (1962), pp. 275–90, and No. 1 (1963), pp. 27–34, deals with the emergence of the use of hypodermic morphine, but the articles are marred by an automatic acceptance of a 'problem' framework deriving closely from current concerns.

2. Details of the process of discovery are in W. R. Bett, 'The discovery of morphine', *Chemist and Druggist*, 162 (1954), pp. 63–4; J. Grier, *A History of Pharmacy* (London, Pharmaceutical Press, 1937), p. 93; A. C. Wootton, *Chronicles of Pharmacy*, op. cit., p. 244.

3. For an early notice of it, see 'Morphia, or morphine', *Lancet*, 1 (1822–3), pp. 67–8.

4. 'Messrs Morson give up the retail', *Chemist and Druggist*, 57 (1900), p. 650; A. Duckworth, 'The rise of the pharmaceutical industry', ibid., 172 (1959), p. 128; 'Letter about the manufacture of morphine', *Phar-*

maceutical Journal, 4th ser. 5 (1897), p. 19; T. Morson, 'List of new chemical preparations, 1822', Pharmaceutical Society Pamphlet 8745.

5. W. Bett, op. cit., pp. 63–4; W. Gregory, 'On a process for preparing economically the muriate of morphia', *Edinburgh Medical and Surgical Journal*, 35 (1831), pp. 331–8.

6. Examples of the early use and availability of the drug are in 'Professor Brande on vegetable chemistry', *Lancet*, 2 (1827–8), pp. 389–90; King's College Hospital case notes, op. cit., 1840; Clay and Abraham, 'Stock of a Liverpool shop', 1845 Pharmaceutical Society Ms. 40619; W. Bateman, *Magnacopia*, op. cit., pp. 33–4.

7. 'Dr Simpson's morphia suppositories', *Medical Times and Gazette*, new ser. 14 (1857), p. 141; 'Apomorphia', *Lancet*, 1 (1883), p. 577.

8. M. Ward, op. cit., p. vii; see also the standard article on the development of the hypodermic method, N. Howard-Jones, 'A critical study of the origins and early development of hypodermic medication', *Journal of the History of Medicine*, 2 (1947), pp. 201–49.

9. Review of Dr Ahrenson's book, *British and Foreign Medical Review*, 5 (1838), p. 348.

10. Islington prescription book, op. cit., 1865 entry.

11. Details of experiments by Christopher Wren are given in D. I. Macht, 'The history of intravenous and subcutaneous administration of drugs', *Journal of the American Medical Association*, 1916, p. 857.

12. M. Martin-Solon, 'Review of a report on the inoculation of morphine, etc. proposed by Dr Lafargue', *British and Foreign Medical Review*, 4 (1837), p. 506; N. Howard-Jones, op. cit., pp. 203–4.

13. See N. Howard-Jones, op. cit., and 'The evolution of hypodermics', *Chemist and Druggist*, 159 (1953), p. 607.

14. Letter from Charles Hunter in *Medical Times and Gazette*, 2 (1858), pp. 457–8, cited in N. Howard-Jones, op. cit., p. 222.

15. Hunter was in fact right, for the drug's essential pain-relieving action is on the central nervous system. From the injecting site, it is absorbed into the blood stream and carried to the brain. C. Hunter, 'On the ipodermic/hypodermic treatment of diseases', *Medical Times and Gazette*, 18 (1859), pp. 234–5, 310–11, 387–8; C. Hunter, *On the Speedy Relief of Pain and Other Nervous Affections by Means of the Hypodermic Method* (London, John Churchill, 1865).

16. F. E. Anstie, Editorial, *Practitioner*, 1 (1868), pp. i–iii; for further details of Anstie, see his entry in the *Medical Directory* (London, J. Churchill, 1874), p. 48, and H. L'Etang, 'Anstie and alcohol', *Journal of Alcoholism*, 10 (1975), pp. 27–30.

17. F. E. Anstie, 'The hypodermic injection of remedies', *Practitioner*, 1 (1868), pp. 32–41.

18. Examples of medical enthusiasm for the hypodermic method are in T. C. Allbutt, 'The use of the subcutaneous injection of morphia in

REFERENCES

dyspepsia', *Practitioner*, *2* (1869), pp. 341–6; 'Review of the West Riding Lunatic Asylum Medical Reports', *Journal of Mental Science*, *17* (1871–2), p. 559; J. Constable, 'Case of persistent and alarming hiccough in pneumonia, cured by the subcutaneous injection of morphia', *Lancet*, *2* (1869), pp. 264–5.

19. T. C. Allbutt, 'On the abuse of hypodermic injections of morphia', *Practitioner*, *5* (1870), pp. 327–31.

20. T. C. Allbutt, 'Opium poisoning and other intoxications', in his *System of Medicine* (London, Macmillan, 1897), vol. 2, p. 886.

21. G. Oliver, 'On hypodermic injection of morphia', *Practitioner*, *6* (1871), pp. 75–80, is one example of a dissentient from Allbutt's views.

22. F. E. Anstie, 'On the effects of the prolonged use of morphia by subcutaneous injection', *Practitioner*, *6* (1871), pp. 148–57.

23. E. Levinstein, *Morbid Craving for Morphia* (*Die Morphiumsucht*) (London, Smith, Elder, 1878).

24. H. H. Kane, *The Hypodermic Injection of Morphia. Its History, Advantages and Dangers* (New York, Chas. L. Bermingham, 1880). For Kane's inquiries in the English medical journals, see 'Hypodermic injection of morphia', *Lancet*, *2* (1879), p. 441.

25. H. Obersteiner, 'Chronic morphinism', *Brain*, *2* (1878–80), pp. 449–65; and 'Further observations on chronic morphinism', ibid., *5* (1884–5), pp. 323–31.

26. Both the *British Medical Journal* and the *Lancet* had much discussion and correspondence on hypodermic morphine addiction and its treatment at this time; e.g. J. St T. Clarke, 'The sudden discontinuance of hypodermic injections of morphia', *Lancet*, *1* (1879), p. 70; C. Murchison, 'The causes of intermitting or paroxysmal pyrexia', ibid., *1* (1879), p. 654.

27. *The Times*, 30 January 1880; editorial comment in *Lancet*, *1* (1880), p. 100.

28. Amphlett's death was reported in the *British Medical Journal*, *2* (1880), p. 484.

29. *Hansard* 3rd ser. *304* (1886), col. 1343.

30. S. Sharkey, 'The treatment of morphia habitués by suddenly discontinuing the drug', *Lancet*, *2* (1883), p. 1120; and his 'Morphinomania', *Nineteenth Century*, *22* (1887), pp. 335–42.

31. Foot's discussion was widely reported in the medical journals, for example 'Royal Academy of Medicine in Ireland', *Lancet*, *2* (1889), p. 1336.

32. There was also continuing American influence through the work of Drs Crothers and Mattison, as in T. D. Crothers, *Morphinism and Narcomanias from Other Drugs. Their Etiology, Treatment and Medico-Legal Relations* (Philadelphia and London, W. B. Saunders, 1902); and J. B.

308

Mattison, *The Mattison Method in Morphinism. A Modern and Humane Treatment of the Morphin Disease* (New York, 1902). Mattison also spoke and wrote for the Society for the Study of Inebriety.

33. Jennings' works and papers are too numerous to be listed comprehensively here. See, for example, O. Jennings, *On the Cure of the Morphia Habit* (London, Bailliere, Tindall and Cox, 1890); 'On the physiological cure of the morphia habit', *Lancet*, 2 (1901), pp. 360–68; *The Morphia Habit and its Voluntary Renunciation* (London, Bailliere, Tindall and Cox, 1909).

34. H. C. Drury, 'Morphinomania', *Dublin Journal of Medical Science*, *107* (1899), pp. 321–44; 'Reckless use of hypodermic injections', *Lancet*, *1* (1882), p. 538; S. A. K. Strahan, 'Treatment of morphia habitués by suddenly discontinuing the drug', *Lancet*, *1* (1884), pp. 61–2.

35. W. Osler, op. cit., p. 1005. Osler's conclusion was not universally held. Ronald Armstrong-Jones, medical superintendent at Claybury Asylum, openly disagreed with it: R. Armstrong-Jones, 'Notes on some cases of Morphinomania', *Journal of Mental Science*, 48 (1902), pp. 478–95. There were some notable doctor addicts, for example George Harley, Professor of Practical Physiology at University College Hospital: A. Tweedie, ed., *George Harley, F.R.S.* (London, Scientific Press, 1899), p. 174.

36. T. D. Crothers, op. cit., p. 87. For examples of supposed female susceptibility, see W. A. F. Browne, 'Opiophagism', *Journal of Psychological Medicine*, n.s., *1* (1875), pp. 38–55, and W. S. Playfair, 'On the cure of the morphia and alcoholic habit', *Journal of Mental Science*, *35* (1889), pp. 179–84. J. L'Esperance, 'Doctors and women in nineteenth century society: sexuality and role', in J. Woodward and D. Richards, eds., op. cit., pp. 105–27, analyses how the medical profession validated women's position in society. See also *The Times*, 12 January 1880; T. C. Allbutt (1897), op. cit., p. 895. Allbutt did however later revise his ideas about the female preponderance among morphine addicts; Armstrong-Jones also doubted the validity of the stereotype.

37. H. C. Drury, op. cit., p. 327.

38. The difficulties of using trade statistics to arrive at home consumption data are discussed in V. Berridge and N. Rawson, op. cit., p. 355. Comparison of published home consumption figures prior to 1860 calculated per 1,000 population, with estimated figures derived from subtracting the amount of opium exported from that imported, show that estimated home consumption after 1860, then the only statistic available, can be used only to indicate general trends.

39. Information derived from analysis of the Society of Apothecaries laboratory process book, op. cit.

40. Islington prescription book, op. cit.

41. Poisons Register, *c.*1886–93, Pharmaceutical Society Ms.

42. King's College Hospital case notes.

43. R. Armstrong-Jones, op. cit. (1902); and his 'Drug addiction in relation to mental disorder', *British Journal of Inebriety*, *12* (1914), pp. 125–48. Bethlem Admission Registers 1857–1893, Bethlem Royal Hospital.

44. Homes for Inebriates Association, *Thirtieth Annual Report*, 1913–14, p. 13, P.P. 1884–5, XV: *Fifth Annual Report of the Inspector of Retreats under the Habitual Drunkards Act, 1879*, p. 32. A breakdown of cases admitted shows not one had an associated narcotic habit.

45. G. B. Shaw, *Collected Letters, 1874–97*, ed. Dan. H. Laurence (London, Max Reinhardt, 1965), pp. 503, 581.

46. V. G. Eaton, 'How the opium habit is acquired', *Popular Science Monthly*, *33* (1888), pp. 663–7.

13: The Ideology of Opium: Opium Eating as a Disease

1. The question of the social rooting of medical ideology is discussed in K. Figlio, 'Chlorosis and chronic disease in nineteenth-century Britain: the social constitution of somatic illness in a capitalist society', *Social History*, *3* (1978), pp. 167–97.

2. See also Anon., *Advice to Opium Eaters*, op. cit., written by an ex-addict.

3. For details of the different modes of treatment, see, for instance, Basham, 'Case of delirium tremens from opium-eating; improved general health, but terminating in dementia', *Lancet*, *1* (1846), pp. 254–6; also ibid., *1* (1838–9), p. 680; and J. Vaughan Hughes, 'An opium eater', *Lancet*, *2* (1859), p. 439.

4. W. Whalley, 'Confessions of a laudanum drinker', *Lancet*, *2* (1866), p. 35, where the patient's family decided on maintenance doses. A similar case was reported to the Select Committee on Drunkenness, P.P. 1834, VIII, op. cit., q. 1288.

5. T. D. Crothers, op. cit.,; and J. B. Mattison, op. cit.

6. N. Kerr, *Inebriety, its Etiology, Pathology, Treatment and Jurisprudence* (London, H. K. Lewis, 2nd edn 1889).

7. A typical example is the section on 'morphinism' by Thomas Stevenson in R. Quain, ed., *A Dictionary of Medicine* (London, Longmans, 1894), vol. 2, p. 157.

8. T. C. Allbutt (1897), op. cit., p. 886; J. White 'The habit of opium-taking as induced by hypodermic injections', *British Medical Journal*, *1* (1887), p. 627.

9. As in 'Tolerance of large doses of morphine', *British Medical Journal*, *1* (1888), p. 449.

10. E. Levinstein, op. cit., p. 107.

11. N. Kerr, op. cit., p. 64; N. Kerr, 'Opening address to the Colonial and International Congress on Inebriety', *Proceedings of the Society for the Study of Inebriety, 13* (1887), pp. 1–3.

12. Brian Harrison makes this point about the influence of temperance thinking on disease views of alcoholism in his *Drink and the Victorians* (London, Faber and Faber, 1971), p. 371. W. F. Bynum's 'Chronic alcoholism in the first half of the nineteenth century', *Bulletin of the History of Medicine, 42* (1968), pp. 160–85, also makes the point that most scientific studies were continental in origin. See also H. G. Levine, 'The discovery of addiction; changing conceptions of habitual drunkenness in America', *Journal of Studies on Alcohol, 39* (1978), pp. 143–74.

13. 'Inebriety and volition', *Proceedings of the Society for the Study and Cure of Inebriety, 1* (1884), p. 40.

14. T. S. Clouston, 'Diseased cravings and paralysed control: dipsomania; morphinomania; chloralism; cocainism', *Edinburgh Medical Journal, 35* (1890), pp. 508–21, 689–705, 793–809, 985–96.

15. T. C. Allbutt (1897), op. cit., pp. 889–90. See also B. W. Richardson (1883), op. cit., p. 1194.

16. T. S. Clouston, op. cit., p. 793.

17. T. D. Crothers, op. cit., p. 110; O. Jennings, *The Morphia Habit and its Voluntary Renunciation*, op. cit., p. 5. See also R. Armstrong-Jones (1915), op. cit., p. 54.

18. N. Kerr (1889), op. cit., p. 149.

19. H. Sainsbury, *Drugs and the Drug Habit* (London, Methuen, 1909), p. 260.

20. T. C. Allbutt and H. D. Rolleston, eds., *A System of Medicine* (London, Macmillan, 1906), vol. 2. See also P.P. 1908, XXXV: *Royal Commission on the Care and Control of the Feeble-minded*, q. 3983.

21. G. R. Searle, *Eugenics and Politics in Britain, 1900–1914* (Leyden, Noordhoff Publishing Co., 1976), p. 59, notes that it was the professional middle class which was the prime concern of the eugenics movement.

22. J. St Thomas Clarke, Letter, *British Medical Journal, 2* (1882), p. 540.

23. T. D. Crothers, op. cit., p. 60.

24. E. M. Jellinek, *The Disease Concept of Alcoholism* (New Haven, Connecticut, Hill House Press, 1960), p. 193.

25. R. Armstrong-Jones, 'Drugs of Addiction', *Morning Post*, 10 June 1914.

26. T. C. Allbutt (1897), op. cit., p. 884. See also W. Huntley, 'Opium addiction: is it a disease?', *Proceedings of the Society for the Study of Inebriety, 50* (1896), pp. 1–12; T. S. Clouston (1890), op. cit., p. 796, for similar views.

27. C. R. Francis, 'On the value and use of opium', *Medical Times and Gazette, 1* (1882), pp. 87–9 and 116–17. This process has its similarities

to the definition of other 'exclusive' conditions, prostitution for instance. See J. and D. Walkowitz, 'We are not beasts of the field: prostitution and the poor in Plymouth and Southampton under the Contagious Disease Acts', in M. Hartman and L. W. Banner, eds., *Clio's Consciousness Raised* (New York, Harper and Row, 1974); also J. Weeks, 'Sins and diseases: some notes on homosexuality in the nineteenth century', *History Workshop*, *1* (1976), pp. 211–19.

28.   R. Christison (1850), op. cit., p. 538.

29.   E. Levinstein, op. cit., pp. 110–18.

30.   According to Allbutt (1897), op. cit.

31.   J. St Thomas Clarke, op. cit., p. 540.

32.   C. A. McBride, *The Modern Treatment of Alcoholism and Drug Narcotism* (London, W. Rebman, 1910), p. 280.

33.   M. S. P. Strangman, 'The atropine treatment of morphinomania and inebriety', *Journal of Mental Science*, *54* (1908), pp. 727–33.

34.   Some of these varied drug 'antidotes' are described in N. Macleod, 'Morphine habit of long standing cured by bromide poisoning', *British Medical Journal*, *2* (1897), pp. 76–7; C. A. McBride, op. cit., p. 334. J. Kramer, 'Heroin in the treatment of morphine addiction,' *Journal of Psychedelic Drugs*, *9* (1977), pp. 193–7, casts doubt on whether heroin was in fact ever much used for this purpose in American medical practice. See also 'The use of cocaine in the morphia habit; a warning', *Lancet*, *2* (1907), p. 811.

35.   N. Kerr (1889), op. cit., p. 295; H. Crichton Miller, 'The treatment of morphinomania by the "combined" method', *British Medical Journal*, *2* (1910), pp. 1595–7.

36.   H. Sainsbury, op. cit., p. 285.

37.   These cures were surveyed and criticized in the two British Medical Association reports on patent remedies, British Medical Association (1909), op. cit., pp. 166–8, and (1912), op. cit., pp. 137, 140. The Turvey Treatment was regularly advertised in *The Times*, e.g. on 6 October 1914.

38.   There were reports on the plant in all the leading professional journals, e.g. 'Combretum sundaicum', *Pharmaceutical Journal*, 4th ser. *25* (1907), p. 566; also C. A. McBride, op. cit., p. 366.

39.   For similar processes at work in other areas of 'deviance', see D. Rothman, *The Discovery of the Asylum: Social Order and Disorder in the New Republic* (Boston, Little, Brown, 1971); G. Steadman Jones, *Outcast London. A Study in the Relationship between Classes in Victorian Society* (Oxford University Press, 1971); and A. T. Scull, 'Museums of madness; the social organization of insanity in nineteenth century England' (unpublished Princeton Ph.D. thesis, 1974). R. M. MacLeod, 'The edge of hope; social policy and chronic alcoholism, 1870–1900', *Journal of the History of Medicine and Allied Sciences*, *22* (1967), pp. 215–45, sur-

veys the developments in inebriates legislation and institutional confinement from the point of view of alcohol. See also M. Ignatieff, *A Just Measure of Pain. The Penitentiary in the Industrial Revolution 1750–1850* (London, Macmillan, 1978).

40. 'Hospitals for morphinism', *British Medical Journal*, *1* (1885), pp. 55, 266.

41. Home Office papers, H.O. 45, 10454.

42. H.O. 45, 9989.

43. 'Report of the Inebriates Legislation Committee', *British Medical Journal*, *2* (1892), p. 190.

44. P.P. 1893–4, XVII: *Report from the Departmental Committee on the Treatment of Inebriates*, Appendix 2, 'Memorial from the Inebriates Legislation Committee of the B.M.A.'. Norman Kerr's evidence to the Committee also made this point.

45. H.O. 45, 10225, Home Office memorandum on 1898 Bill, and 61 and 62 Vict. ch. 60, 1898: An Act to Provide for the Treatment of Habitual Inebriates. Deputations from the B.M.A. and the S.S.I. had seen the Home Secretary in 1894 and 1895 asking for the inclusion of all drug-takers, and evidence on this point was also given to the 1895 Committee on Habitual Offenders.

46. P.P. 1900, II: *A Bill to Amend the Inebriates Act, 1879 to 1899, and to Make Further Provision for the Control and Cure of Habitual Inebriates.*

47. H.O. 45, 10454, contains discussion of the possible use of the 1902 Licensing Act. See also P.P. 1908, XII: *Departmental Committee on the Inebriates Act*, pp. 830–32.

48. 1890 Lunacy Act, 53 and 54 Vict. ch. 5, Sect. 108(3) and Sect. 116(1) (d).

49. P.P. 1908, XXXV, op. cit., pp. 707–8, and 3 and 4 Geo. V ch. 28., 1913 Mental Deficiency Act.

50. Quoted in P.P. 1896, XLIV: *Eighteenth Report of the Prison Commissioners for Scotland*, p. 858. Published prison statistics, however, did not generally itemize such cases separately. Only where the prisoner was classified as insane and in need of treatment was a drug habit revealed.

51. This is demonstrated by the small numbers admitted in Bethlem Royal Hospital. See Bethlem Admission Registers, 1857–93, and R. Armstrong-Jones (1902), op. cit., pp. 491–5, and (1915) op. cit., pp. 42–53.

52. Described at its inception in *British Medical Journal*, *1* (1881), p. 594.

53. Homes for Inebriates Association, *Annual Report*, 1885–6, p. 19.

54. P.P. 1890–91, XIX: *Report of the Inspector of Retreats under the Habitual Drunkards Act, 1879.*

55. N. Kerr (1889), op. cit., p. 387.

56. 'Treatment of the chlorodyne habit', *British Medical Journal*, *1* (1904), p. 932.

14: 'Britain's Opium Harvest': The Anti-Opium Movement

1. For details of the opium trade, and the opium wars, see M. Greenberg, *British Trade and the Opening of China, 1800–1842* (Cambridge University Press, 1951); M. Goldsmith, *The Trial of Opium* (London, Hale, 1939); L. P. Adams II, 'China: the historical setting of Asia's profitable plague', pp. 365-83 in A. W. McCoy, *The Politics of Heroin in South East Asia* (New York, Harper and Row, 1972); H. Morse, *The International Relations of the Chinese Empire* (London, Longmans, Green, 1910–18); and D. E. Owen, *British Opium Policy in China and India* (New Haven, Yale University Press, 1934).
2. *Hansard 53* (1840), cols. 743, 855–6 etc.
3. *Hansard 68* (1843), col. 362 onward.
4. *Hansard* 3rd ser. *144* (1857), col. 2027 onward.
5. R. Little, op. cit., pp. 524–38.
6. *Hansard* (1843), op. cit., cols. 400–401. There was also a Society for Suppressing Opium Smuggling.
7. Some publications of the Society are held in the Braithwaite Collection, Society of Friends, Ms. vol. 207. See also R. Alexander, *The Rise and Progress of British Opium Smuggling* (London, 3rd edn, Judd and Glass, 1856).
8. Details of the appeal are in the Braithwaite Collection, already cited. The appeal was made on 10 September 1858.
9. It was mentioned in the *Medical Times and Gazette, 19* (1859), p. 387.
10. For details of the origin and early activities of the Society see the early issues of its journal, the *Friend of China*, in particular *1* (1875), pp. 3–7, *2* (1875), p. 72, and *6* (1875), pp. 206–7. There are also details in H. G. Alexander, *Joseph Grundy Alexander* (London, Swarthmore Press, 1920); M. J. B. C. Lim, 'Britain and the termination of the India-China opium trade, 1905–13' (unpublished London Ph. D. thesis, 1969), pp. 24–6; P. D. Lowes, *The Genesis of International Narcotics Control* (Geneva, Librairie Droz, 1966), pp. 58–63; and F. S. Turner, *British Opium Policy and its Results to India and China* (London, Sampson Low, 1876). B. Johnson, 'Righteousness before revenue: the forgotten crusade against the Indo-Chinese opium trade', *Journal of Drug Issues, 5* (1975), pp. 304–26, gives a survey of its activities.
11. 'Introductory address', *Friend of China, 1* (1875), p. 5.
12. Details of the Society's membership, executive committee etc. were regularly listed inside the front cover of the *Friend of China*.
13. Details of the Treaty of Tientsin, the revised 1869 Convention and the negotiations are in M. J. B. C. Lim, op. cit., p. 19; and D. E. Owen, op. cit., pp. 242–6.
14. Some of the motions put forward, and debates on them, are in *Hansard*, 3rd ser. *201* (1870), col. 480 onward; 3rd ser. *225* (1875), col. 571

onward; 3rd ser. *230* (1875), col. 536 onward; 3rd ser. *252* (1880), col. 1227; 3rd ser. *277* (1883), col. 1333.

15. Details of the trading relations between India and China are in D. E. Owen, op. cit., pp. 281, 291, 309–10, and M. B. Morse, op. cit., vol. 3, pp. 438–9. I am grateful to Dr Kato Yuzo for showing me unpublished trade statistics he has collected. These confirm the decline in relative importance of the Indo-Chinese opium trade as an item of Indian revenue in the 1880s and 1890s.

16. The anti-opium and anti-slavery movements also had some organizational and personal overlap. The two Sturge brothers, Edmund and Joseph, founders of the British and Foreign Anti-Slavery Society, were also members of the S.S.O.T.'s Executive Committee. Alderman McArthur's comment was reported in *Friend of China*, *1* (1875), p. 6.

17. *Friend of China*, *3* (1877), pp. 67 and 71–5.

18. Lambeth Palace Library, Tait papers, vol. 210, ff106–7, shows Archbishop Tait's reservations about associating himself with the Society.

19. *Friend of China*, *2* (1877), p. 159; *11* (1890), p. 340.

20. The matter was brought before the Lords in 1878 by the Earl of Aberdeen and in 1879 by the Earl of Carnarvon, and in 1880, 1881 and 1883 in the Commons by Sir Joseph Pease. *Hansard* 3rd ser. *252* (1880), col. 1227; 3rd ser. *277* (1883), col. 1333.

21. Details of these lobbying and pressure group activities are to be found in *Friend of China*, *3* (1877), p. 67; *4* (1880), pp. 90–92, 143; *4* (1881), pp. 252, 367–9.

22. Lambeth Palace Library, Tait papers, vol. 286, ff228–31; H.G. Alexander, op. cit., pp. 59–61; *Hansard* (1883), op. cit., col. 1333.

23. The meeting appears as a high point in most reminiscences of the campaign, e.g. B. Broomhall, *The Truth about Opium Smoking* (London, Hodder and Stoughton, 1882), p. 5; R. Alcock, 'Opium and common sense', *Nineteenth Century*, *10* (1881), pp. 854–68.

24. *Friend of China*, *6* (1883), pp. 168–87.

25. As, for instance, in a series of articles written by Edward Fry, a High Court judge and anti-opium supporter: E. Fry, 'China, England and opium', *Contemporary Review*, *27* (1875–6), pp. 447–59; *30* (1877), pp. 1–10; and *31* (1877–8), pp. 313–21.

26. W. H. Brereton, *The Truth about Opium* (London, W. H. Allen, 1882).

27. R. Alcock, op. cit., and 'The opium trade', *Journal of the Society of Arts*, *30* (1882), pp. 201–35. Even a leading Chinese anti-opiumist like Li Hung-Chung, who supported the Society's agitation, condoned the cultivation of opium in his own province; Alcock's demand for a reciprocal guarantee was hardly excessive. Among other contributors to this debate were A. J. Arbuthnot, 'The opium controversy', *Nineteenth Century*, *11* (1882), pp. 403–13; B. Fossett Lock, 'The opium trade and Sir Rutherford Alcock', *Contemporary Review*, *41* (1882), pp. 676–93;

and F. Storrs Turner, 'Opium and England's duty', *Nineteenth Century*, *11* (1882), pp. 242–53.

28. P. D. Lowes, op. cit., p. 65.
29. N. McCord, *The Anti-Corn Law League* (London, George Allen and Unwin, 1958), pp. 203–4, makes this point about the eventual effect of the activities of that pressure group.
30. *Hansard*, 3rd ser. *305* (1886), col. 278.
31. Details of the discussions over strategy and tactics are in Braithwaite Collection, op. cit., Ms. vol. 207; and *National Righteousness*, no. 1 (1887) and other issues, published irregularly in 1889 and 1890.
32. Further details are in Braithwaite Collection, op. cit., and *National Righteousness*. Rachel Braithwaite, secretary of the Women's Anti-Opium Urgency League, was sister of J. Bevan Braithwaite, chairman of the Christian Union. There were many similar personal links between the anti-opium organizations.
33. A. H. Taylor, *American Diplomacy and the Narcotics Traffics 1900–39* (Durham, N.C., Duke University Press, 1969), pp. 12, 16, 18–19.
34. H. G. Alexander, op. cit., p. 63; Braithwaite Collection, vol. 207; and *Friend of China*, *11* (1889), pp. 59–63.
35. *Hansard*, 3rd ser. *352* (1891), col. 285; see also W. T. Wu, *The Chinese Opium Question in British Opinion and Action* (New York, Academy Press, 1928), p. 126.
36. *Friend of China*, *12* (1891), p. 84; and *National Righteousness*, no. 9 (1892), p. 14.
37. Details of the manoeuvring between the government and the S.S.O.T. are in the Society's Executive Committee minutes 1891–3, Temp. Mss 33/2, Society of Friends Library. Archbishop Benson had also been privately lobbying for a Royal Commission: Benson papers 189, vol. 99, ff61–4 and 69–71; vol. 109, ff366–7 and 368–9; vol. 110, ff49–50 and ff51–4, Lambeth Palace Library.
38. *Hansard*, 4th ser. *14* (1893), col. 591 onward; *National Righteousness*, no. 14 (1894), p. 3.
39. Quoted in M. J. B. C. Lim, op. cit., p. 32.
40. P.P. 1895, XLIII: *Final Report of the Royal Commission on Opium*, p. 133.
41. J. Rowntree, *The Imperial Drug Trade* (London, Methuen, 1905), pp. 152, 163.
42. H. G. Alexander, op. cit., p. 66.
43. Quoted in M. J. B. C. Lim, op. cit., p. 35.
44. *Hansard*, 4th ser. *34* (1895), cols. 278–324; Society for the Suppression of the Opium Trade Executive minutes, 1894–5; *The Times* 23 May 1895.
45. *The Times*, 6 December 1881.
46. As for example in F. W. Chesson, 'The opium trade', *Fortnightly*

Review, n.s. *10* (1871), pp. 351–7; J. Dudgeon, 'Opium in relation to population'. *Edinburgh Medical Journal*, *23* (1877), pp. 239–50; P. Hehir, *Opium: Its Physical, Moral and Social Effects* (London, Bailliere, Tindall and Cox, 1894), pp. 307, 322–3.

47. In 1879, after a Lincolnshire chemist had asked for advice on how one of his customers could leave off her habit, the *Friend of China* urged stricter safeguards on the sale of poisons in England. The Japanese model, by which the government alone could sell opium, was favoured. See 'Opium Eating in England', *Friend of China*, *3* (1879), pp. 314–16.

48. E. Headland, *The Lady Britannia, Her Children, Her Stepchildren, and Her Neighbours* (1892), Braithwaite Collection, Ms. vol. 207; *Friend of China*, *13* (1892), pp. 164–5.

49. Most of the polemical literature produced in the anti-opium campaign contained some consideration of the medicinal value of opium; e.g. L. Arnold, ed., *The Opium Question Solved by Anglo-Indian* (London, S. W Partridge, 1882), pp. 15–16; G. H. M. Batten et al., 'The opium question', *Journal of the Society of Arts*, *40* (1892), pp. 444–94.

50. Richardson's conference was reported in a supplement to the *Friend of China*, *13* (1892); Pringle's appointment as a lecturer is discussed in the Society's Executive minutes for 1893. His contributions to the S.S.I. included R. Pringle, 'Opium – has it any use, other than a strictly medicinal one?', *Proceedings of the Society for the Study of Inebriety*, *39* (1894), pp. 3–16; and 'Acquired insanity, in its relation to intemperance in alcohol and narcotics', ibid., *57* (1898) p. 2.

51. For Kerr's involvement, see *Friend of China*, *11* (1889), pp. 67–70; and 'Medical Debate in London', ibid., *16* (1896), pp. 129–31.

52. *Friend of China*, *5* (1882), pp. 36, 56, 58.

53. See for example J. Dudgeon, 'The opium traffic from a medical point of view', *Friend of China*, *2* (1876), pp. 12–17.

54. Supplement to the *Friend of China*, *13* (1892), op. cit. See also 'An Opium Experience', anti-opium tract, Leaflet series no. 8, Braithwaite Collection, Ms. vol. 207.

55. *Hansard* (1891), op. cit., col. 313.

56. J. Dudgeon (*Friend of China*), op. cit., p. 13.

57. *Friend of China*, *6* (1883), pp. 127–8.

15: The Myth of the Opium Den in Late Victorian England

1. The following chapter is in part based on V. Berridge, 'East End opium dens and narcotic use in Britain', *London Journal*, *4*, No. 1 (1978), pp. 3–28. See also, for the Chinese in London, P.P. 1814–15, III: *Report*

on Lascars and Other Asiatic Seamen; and P.P. 1816, X: *Correspondence ... Relative to the Care and Maintenance of Lascar Sailors during their Stay in England.*

2. Figures are taken from K.C.Ng, *The Chinese in London* (London, Institute of Race Relations, 1968), pp. 5–11.

3. J. Helmer and T. Vietorisz, *Drug Use, The Labor Market and Class Conflict* (Washington, D.C., Drug Abuse Council, 1974), pp. 3-7, details the position of immigrant Chinese in the U.S.A. See also J. Helmer, *Drugs and Minority Oppression* (New York, Seabury Press, 1975), pp. 31–2.

4. Anon., 'East London opium smokers', *London Society, 14* (1868), pp. 68–72.

5. Anon., 'What opium smoking feels like. By one who has tried it' (1870, unattributed), John Burns collection, Greater London Record Office.

6. J. Forster, *Life of Charles Dickens* (London, Chapman and Hall, 1874), vol. 3, p. 488, describes how the visit to the opium den took place. The scene is in C. Dickens, *The Mystery of Edwin Drood* (London, Chapman and Hall, 1870, Penguin edn 1974), pp. 37–9, 77.

7. G. Doré and W. B. Jerrold, *London, A Pilgrimage* (London, Grant, 1872; New York, Dover edn 1970), pp. 147–8; see also O. Wilde, *The Picture of Dorian Gray* (London, Ward Lock, 1891, Penguin edn 1966), pp. 207–8.

8. See, for example, R. Rowe, *Picked Up in the Streets* (London, W. H. Allen, 1880), pp. 38–42; J. Platt, 'Chinese London and its opium dens', *Gentleman's Magazine, 279* (1895), pp. 274–5; and 'London opium dens. Notes of a visit to the Chinaman's East-End haunts. By a Social Explorer', *Good Words, 26* (1885), pp. 188–92. Others are cited in V. Berridge, op. cit., p. 24.

9. *Good Words*, op. cit., pp. 188–92.

10. 'Opium smoking in London', *Friend of China, 3* (1877), pp. 19–20, originally in the *London City Mission Magazine*.

11. 'The Chinese in London. No. 4. An opium den', Tract in the Braithwaite Collection, op. cit., Ms. vol. 207.

12. 'The medical aspect of the opium question', supplement to *Friend of China, 13* (1892), op. cit., and 'Report of the British Medical Association Annual Meeting at Nottingham', *British Medical Journal, 2* (1892), p. 258.

13. *Good Words*, op. cit.

14. *Daily Chronicle*, 17 October 1881, quoted in *Friend of China, 5* (1882), p. 28.

15. 'Opium dens in London', *Chambers' Journal, 81* (1904), pp. 193–5.

16. *Friend of China*, supplement *13* (1892), op. cit.

17. Interview with W. J. C., Limehouse, 1976.

18. A. J. Arbuthnot, 'The opium controversy', *Nineteenth Century, 11*

(1882), pp. 403–13. Publicity given to H. H. Kane's 'American opium smokers', *Friend of China*, *14* (1881), pp. 440–44, also tended to the same conclusion.

19.   G. Piercy, 'Opium smoking in London', *Friend of China*, 6 (1883), pp. 239–42, originally published in the *Methodist Recorder*.

20.   C. W. Wood, 'In the night watches', *Argosy*, *65* (1897), p. 203.

21.   *East London Advertiser*, 28 December 1907.

22.   *Friend of China*, 7 (1884), p. 220; Public Record Office, Foreign Office papers, F.O. 371, 423, 1908, 'Report on Chinese opium dens by Commissioner of Police'; also P.P. 1909, CV: *Correspondence Relative to the International Opium Commission at Shanghai*, pp. 307–9.

23.   *East End Herald*, 30 December 1955.

24.   *Friend of China*, 7 (1884), p. 220. See also W. Besant, *East London* (London, Chatto and Windus, 1901), pp. 205–6.

25.   Anon., John Burns Collection, op. cit.

26.   *The Times*, 25 and 28 November 1913.

27.   *Hansard*, *14* (1893), col. 1704. This is also mentioned in Papers presented to the Public Health Committee, 21 May 1908, and Minutes of the Public Health Committee, 5 November 1906 and 21 May 1908, London County Council Records, Greater London Record Office.

28.   Interview with W. J. C., Limehouse, 1976.

29.   *Report of the Commission Appointed by the (Liverpool) City Council to Inquire into Chinese Settlements in Liverpool* (1907), p. 7. J. P. May, 'The Chinese in Britain, 1860–1914', pp. 111–24 in C. Holmes, ed., *Immigrants and Minorities in British Society* (London, George Allen and Unwin, 1978), quotes similar evidence for Birkenhead in the 1900s.

30.   Interview with W. J. C., op. cit.

31.   There are descriptions of the process in, amongst others, J. Greenwood, *In Strange Company* (London, Henry S. King, 1873), pp. 229–38; *Notes and Queries*, 8 (1896), p. 129; Anon., 'A night in an opium den', in G. Cotterell, ed., *London Scene from The Strand* (London, Strand Magazine, 1974), pp. 76–9; and *Daily Graphic*, 14 February 1908.

32.   See discussion on the medical utility of opium smoking in *Medical Times and Gazette*, 2 (1868), p. 704, and *1* (1869), pp. 26–7 and 320.

33.   'A dangerous pamphlet', *Lancet*, 2 (1903), pp. 330–31.

34.   For a more extensive consideration of the drug sub-culture and its structural roots, see V. Berridge, 'The origins of the English drug "scene"', in J. Kramer, ed., *Drugs and the Arts* (California, 1979).

35.   R. Croft-Cooke, *Feasting with Panthers. A New Consideration of Some Late Victorian Writers* (London, W. H. Allen, 1967), pp. 250, 253–4; J. Adlard, *Stenbock, Yeats and the Nineties* (London, Cecil and Amelia Woolf, 1969), pp. 45 and 64–5; and E. Rhys, *Everyman Remembers* (London, J. M. Dent, 1931), pp. 28–9.

36. A. Symons, 'The opium smoker', in *Poems* (London, Heinemann, 1902), vol. 1, p. 3.

37. State laws against the practice were being enacted in the U.S.A. at this time; see D. F. Musto, *The American Disease. Origins of Narcotic Control* (New Haven and London, Yale University Press, 1973), pp. 3–6, 244–5.

38. See V. Berridge (*London Journal*), op. cit., pp. 3–23.

16: The Other 'Narcotics': Cannabis and Cocaine

1. Details of the several varieties and products of the plant are in A. B. Garrod and E. B. Baxter, *The Essentials of Materia Medica and Therapeutics* (London, Longman, 9th edn 1882), pp. 360–62; and 'Preparations of Indian Hemp', *Pharmaceutical Journal*, 3rd ser. *4* (1873–4), pp. 696–7. For its early history, see I. Hindmarch, 'A social history of the use of cannabis sativa', *Contemporary Review* (1972), pp. 252–7; and T. Brunner, 'Marijuana in ancient Greece and Rome? The literary evidence', *Bulletin of the History of Medicine*, 47 (1973), pp. 344–55.

2. J. P. Dolan, 'A note on the use of cannabis sativa in the seventeenth century', *Journal of the South Carolina Medical Association*, 67 (1971), pp. 424–7.

3. Quoted in R. Hunter and I. MacAlpine, *Three Hundred Years of Psychiatry 1535–1860* (O.U.P., 1963), pp. 216–17; F. A. Fluckiger and D. Hanbury, *Pharmacographia. A History of the Principal Drugs of Vegetable Origin, Met With in Great Britain and British India* (London, Macmillan, 1879), pp. 547–8.

4. H. Godwin, 'The ancient cultivation of hemp', *Antiquity*, *41* (1967), pp. 42 and 137–8, examines evidence for the cultivation of the drug. See also E. Porter, op. cit., pp. 44–5 and 375, and *Notes and Queries*, *181* (1941), p. 119.

5. See, for instance, S. Morewood, *A philosophical and statistical history of the inventions and customs of ancient and modern nations in the manufacture and use of inebriating liquors; with the present practice of distillation in all its varieties: together with an extensive illustration of the consumption and effects of opium, and other stimulants used in the East, as substitutes for wine and spirits* (Dublin, W. Curry and W. Carson, 1838), p. 115.

6. His career is described in J. B. Moon, 'Sir William Brooke O'Shaughnessy – the foundations of fluid therapy and the Indian telegraph service', *New England Journal of Medicine*, 276 (1967), pp. 283–4.

7. W. B. O'Shaughnessy, 'On the preparations of the Indian hemp, or gunjah; their effects on the animal system in health and their utility in the treatment of tetanus and other convulsive diseases', *Transactions*

of the Medical and Physical Society of Calcutta, 8 part 2 (1842), pp. 421–61. O'Shaughnessy's work was also noted in the British medical press in 1839, e.g. W. B. O'Shaughnessy, 'New remedy for tetanus and other convulsive disorders', *Lancet, 2* (1839–40), p. 539.

8. W. B. O'Shaughnessy (1839–40), op. cit.

9. P. Squire, *A Companion to the Latest Edition of the British Pharmacopoeia* (London, J. and S. Churchill, 1864), p. 45. Society of Apothecaries Laboratory mixture and process book, 1868–72, op. cit., Ms. 8277. The Society was making extract of cannabis in 1868 and both extract and tincture in 1871.

10. *Pharmaceutical Journal, 6* (1846–7), pp. 70–72.

11. J. Russell Reynolds, 'On some of the therapeutic uses of Indian hemp', *Archives of Medicine, 11* (1861), pp. 154–60; and J. Russell Reynolds, ed., *A System of Medicine,* op. cit., vol. 2, pp. 88, 91, 749, vol. 5, p. 740.

12. See, for instance, its recommendation in R. Greene, 'Cannabis indica in the treatment of migraine', *Practitioner, 9* (1872), pp. 267–70; F. F. Bond and B. E. Edwards, 'Cannabis indica in diarrhoea', ibid., *39* (1887), pp. 8–10; and R. Greene, 'The treatment of migraine with Indian hemp', ibid., *41* (1888), pp. 35–8.

13. J. B. Mattison, 'Cannabis indica in the opium habit', *Practitioner, 35* (1885), p. 58.

14. This also led through the collaboration of Moreau and Théophile Gautier to the foundation of the Club des Haschischins for the non-medical experimental use of the drug. See P. Haining, ed., *The Hashish Club* (London, Peter Owen, 1975), vol. 1.

15. T. S. Clouston, 'Observations and experiments on the use of opium, bromide of potassium, and cannabis indica in insanity, especially in regard to the effects of the two latter given together', *British and Foreign Medico-Chirurgical Review,* 46 (1870), pp. 493–511, and 47 (1871), pp. 203–20.

16. H. Maudsley, 'Insanity and its treatment', *Journal of Mental Science, 17* (1871–2), pp. 311–34. See also T. W. McDowall, 'Cases in which mental derangement appeared in patients suffering from progressive muscular atrophy', ibid., *18* (1872–3), p. 390.

17. W. W. Ireland, 'On thought without words, and the relation of words to thought', *Journal of Mental Science, 24* (1878–9), p. 429.

18. Reported in P.P. 1893–4, LXVI: *East India (Consumption of Ganja),* pp. 88, 158–62; see also J. H. Tull Walsh, 'Hemp drugs and insanity', *Journal of Mental Science, 40* (1894), pp. 21–36; also pp. 107–8. See also *British Medical Journal, 2* (1893), pp. 630, 710, 813–14, 868–9, 920, 969, 1027, 1452.

19. Indian Hemp Commission. For an analysis of its conclusions, see O. J. Kalant, 'Report of the Indian Hemp Drugs Commission, 1893–94:

a critical review', *International Journal of the Addictions*, 7 (1) (1972), pp. 77–96.

20. Quoted in T. S. Clouston, 'The Cairo Asylum: Dr Warnock on hashish insanity', *Journal of Mental Science*, 42 (1896), pp. 790–95.

21. C. R. Marshall, 'The active principle of Indian hemp', *Lancet*, 1 (1897), pp. 235–9. There were further attempts at this in the early 1900s, surveyed in *Pharmaceutical Journal*, n.s. 15 (1902), pp. 129–32 and 171.

22. W. E. Dixon, 'The pharmacology of cannabis indica', *British Medical Journal*, 2 (1899), pp. 1354–7.

23. R. B. Litchfield, *Tom Wedgwood, The First Photographer* (London, Duckworth, 1903), p. 135; and J. Cottle, *Reminiscences of Samuel Taylor Coleridge and Robert Southey* (London, Houlston and Stoneman, 1847), p. 463.

24. Cannabis use among this circle is more fully described in V. Berridge, op. cit.; see also S. Levenson, *Maud Gonne* (London, Cassell, 1976), pp. 80–81 and 85; V. Moore, *The Unicorn. William Butler Yeats' Search for Reality* (New York, Macmillan, 1954), p. 25; A. Symons, *Studies in Prose and Verse* (London, J. M. Dent, 1964), p. 265; H. H. Ellis, 'Mescal: a new artificial paradise', *Contemporary Review*, 73 (1898), pp. 130–47. The painter Augustus John describes some of his drug-taking experiences in this artistic milieu in A. John, *Chiaroscuro* (London, Jonathan Cape, 1952), pp. 177–9.

25. Quoted in W. Golden Mortimer, *History of Coca, 'The Divine Plant' of the Incas* (1st edn 1901; San Francisco, Fitz Hugh Ludlow Memorial Library edn, 1974), pp. 26–7.

26. For details of the early scientific evaluation of the coca leaf, see R. Ashley, *Cocaine: Its History, Uses and Effects* (New York, St Martin's Press, 1975), pp. 4–6; W. R. Bett, 'Cocaine, divine plant of the Incas. Some pioneers – and some addicts', *Alchemist*, 21 (1957), pp. 685–9; 'Cocaine', *Chambers' Journal*, 63 (1886), p. 145.

27. L. Grinspoon and J. B. Bakalar, *Cocaine. A Drug and its Social Evolution* (New York, Basic Books, 1976), pp. 19–20.

28. F. E. Anstie (1864), op. cit., p. 144.

29. A. H. Bennett, 'An experimental inquiry into the physiological actions of theine, guaranine, cocaine and theobromine', *Edinburgh Medical Journal*, 19 (1873), pp. 323–41; see also 'The physiological action of coca', *British Medical Journal*, 1 (1874), p. 510.

30. For example, E. H. Sieveking, 'Coca, its therapeutic use', *British Medical Journal*, 1 (1874), p. 234; A. Leared, 'The use of coca', ibid., p. 272; J. A. Bell, 'The use of coca', ibid., p. 305.

31. Weston's use of the drug was reported in *British Medical Journal*, 1 (1876), pp. 271, 297–8, 334–5, and *Lancet*, 1 (1876), pp. 447, 475.

32. R. Christison, 'Observations of the effects of the leaves of erythroxylon coca', *British Medical Journal*, 1 (1876), pp. 527–31.

33. G. Dowdeswell, 'The coca leaf', *Lancet*, *1* (1876), pp. 631–3, 664–7.

34. 'Cuca for bashfulness', *Doctor*, *7* (1877), p. 113; 'A new use for Coca', *Lancet*, *2* (1876), p. 449.

35. For Freud and cocaine, see W. R. Bett, op. cit., pp. 685–9; W. Golden Mortimer, op. cit., pp. 413, 428; L. Grinspoon and J. B. Bakalar, op. cit., pp. 32–3; R. Ashley, op. cit., pp. 21–8; and C. Koller, 'Historical notes on the beginning of local anaesthesia', *Journal of the American Medical Association*, *90* (1928), pp. 1742–3; S. Freud, *The Cocaine Papers*, R. Byck, ed. (New York, Stonehill, 1974), reprints Freud's writings on cocaine.

36. W. F. van Oettingen, 'The earliest suggestion of the use of cocaine for local anaesthesia', *Annals of Medical History*, n.s. *5* (1933), pp. 275–80.

37. This sequence of events is reported in many sources, e.g. B. P. Block, 'Cocaine and Koller', *Pharmaceutical Journal*, *180* (1958), p. 69; C. Koller (1928), op. cit., pp. 1742–3; H. K. Becker, 'Carl Koller and cocaine', *Psychoanalytic Quarterly*, *32* (1963), pp. 309–73; and G. Sharp, 'Coca and cocaine studied historically', *Pharmaceutical Journal*, *1* (1909), pp. 28–30.

38. Reported in *British Medical Journal*, *2* (1888), p. 1344, and *2* (1894), p. 1052.

39. 'Coca pastils', *Lancet*, *2* (1884), p. 1078.

40. Advertisement in *Everybody's Pocket Cyclopaedia* (London, Saxon, 1893).

41. See, for example, R. Hutchison, 'Patent medicines', *British Medical Journal*, *2* (1903), p. 1654.

42. *British Medical Journal*, *1* (1885), p. 1183.

43. 'Cucaine habit and cucaine addiction', *British Medical Journal*, *1* (1887), p. 1229; A. Erlenmeyer, 'Cocaine in the treatment of morphinomania', *Journal of Mental Science*, *31* (1885–6), p. 427.

44. A. Erlenmeyer, 'The morphia habit and its treatment', ibid., *34* (1888–9), p. 116.

45. Halsted's dependence on cocaine was in fact translated to a physical addiction to morphine.

46. N. Kerr (1889), op. cit., p. 122; T. S. Clouston (1890), op. cit., pp. 1806–9; W. Lawton, 'Stimulants and narcotics and their users and abusers', *Pharmaceutical Journal*, *1* (1908), pp. 268–9, 544–6 and 569–70.

47. T. D. Crothers, op. cit., p. 282.

48. Cited in A. Conan Doyle, *The Complete Sherlock Holmes Short Stories* (London, John Murray, 1928, 1976 reprint).

49. V. Berridge, 'War conditions and narcotics control: the passing of DORA Regulation 40B', *Journal of Social Policy*, *7* (1978), pp. 285–304.

50. A. Crowley, *The Confessions of Aleister Crowley*, ed. J. Symonds and F. Grant (London, Jonathan Cape, 1969), p. 180, and J. Symonds, *The Great Beast. The Life and Magick of Aleister Crowley* (London, Macdonald, 1971), pp. 17, 23–4.

17: Opium at the End of the Century

1. S. Wilks, 'On the vicissitudes of opium', *British Medical Journal, 1* (1891), pp. 1218–19.
2. W. B. Cheadle, 'A lecture on the clinical use of opium', *Clinical Journal, 4* (1894), pp. 345–51.
3. W. Osler, op. cit., pp. 33, 58, 98, 124, etc.; and P. Squire, *Companion to the Latest Edition of the British Pharmacopoeia* (London, J. and A. Churchill, 1899), pp. 448–9.
4. Islington prescription book, op. cit.
5. Most of the pharmacists I have spoken to, or corresponded with, remember this to a limited extent; e.g. interviews with Mr Ive, 1978, Mr Hollows and the late Mr Lloyd Thomas.
6. British Medical Association (1912), p. 147.
7. Interview with Mrs Cooper, Kilburn, 1978.
8. G. H. Rimmington, personal communication, 1975.
9. Home consumption of opium is difficult to assess after the abolition of import duty on opium in 1860. Home consumption figures prior to 1860 had not been directly associated with the variation in imports and exports (Table 2, p. 274). Subtracting exports from import figures gives a poor estimate of home consumption; it corresponded only very generally with *actual* home consumption data prior to 1860. After that date, estimated consumption is the only figure available, but it can only be used to indicate a very general trend, which is demonstrated in Figure 3 (p. 35). For further discussion of this point, see V. Berridge and N. Rawson, op. cit.
10. Miss I. Robertson, personal communication, 1975.
11. Home Office papers, H.O. 45, 10454 1905, 'Case of a drug addict not covered by the Inebriates Acts'.
12. W. Gadd, 'The ownership of medical prescriptions', *Lancet, 2* (1910), p. 1030; 'Prescriptions of opium and morphine', *British Medical Journal, 2* (1904), p. 78.
13. V. Berridge, 'The making of the Rolleston Report, 1908–1926', *Journal of Drug Issues, 10* (1980), pp. 7–28, surveys this further stage in the evolution of policy.
14. T. Szasz, op. cit., p. 170.
15. M. Ignatieff, *A Just Measure of Pain*, op. cit., p. 220.

18: Changes of Scene

1. K. Dunnell and A. Cartwright, *Medicine Takers, Prescribers and Hoarders* (London, Routledge and Kegan Paul, 1972).
2. 'Benzodiazepine withdrawal' (editorial), *Lancet*, *1* (1979), p. 196.
3. K. Bruun, L. Pan and I. Rexed, *The Gentlemen's Club: International Control of Drugs and Alcohol* (The University of Chicago Press, Chicago, 1975).
4. L. Pan and K. Bruun, 'Recent developments in international drug control', *British Journal of Addiction*, 74 (1979), pp. 141-60.
5. T. Szasz, op. cit.
6. R. Boyers and R. Orrill, eds., *Laing and Anti-Psychiatry* (Harmondsworth, Penguin Books, 1972).
7. I. Illich, *Medical Nemesis: The Expropriation of Health* (London, Calder and Boyars, 1975).
8. World Health Organization, *Technical Report Series*, No. 407 (Geneva, W.H.O., 1967).
9. V. P. Dole, 'A clinician's view of addiction', in J. Fishman, ed., *The Bases of Addiction* (Berlin, Dahlem Konferenzeii, 1978), pp. 37-46.
10. D. N. Nurco (rapporteur), 'Sociology and epidemiology of addiction, group report', in *The Bases of Addiction*, op. cit., pp. 441-62.
11. J. H. Willis, *Drug Dependence* (London, Faber and Faber, 1969).
12. A. Kiev, *The Drug Epidemic* (New York, Free Press, 1975).
13. G. Birdwood, *The Willing Victim* (London, Secker and Warburg, 1969).
14. W. R. Martin, 'General problems of drug abuse and drug dependence', in W. R. Martin, ed., *Drug Addiction*, vol. 1 (Berlin, Dahlem Konferenzeii, Springer-Verlag, 1977).
15. J. V. De Long, 'Treatment and rehabilitation', in *Dealing with Drug Abuse, a Report to the Ford Foundation* (London, Macmillan, 1972).
16. R. E. Meyer and S. M. Mirin, *The Heroin Stimulus. Implications for a Theory of Addiction* (New York, Plenum Press, 1979).
17. A. Kosviner, 'Unwanted neighbors', *International Journal of the Addictions*, 8 (1973), pp. 801-8.
18. Ministry of Health, *Report of the Departmental Committee on Morphine and Heroin Addiction* (London, H.M.S.O., 1926).
19. G. Edwards, 'Drug problems U.K./U.S.A.', in R. A. Bowen, ed., *Anglo-American Conference on Drug Abuse* (London, Royal Society of Medicine, 1973), pp. 2-6.
20. E. M. Schur, *Narcotic Addiction in Britain* (London, Tavistock, 1962).
21. G. Edwards, 'Some years on: evolutions in the "British System"', in D. J. West, ed., *Problems of Drug Abuse in Britain* (Cambridge, Institute of Criminology, 1978), pp. 1-45.

22. *The Second Report of the Interdepartmental Committee* (London, H.M.S.O., 1965).

23. G. Edwards, 'The British approach to the treatment of heroin addiction', *Lancet, 1* (1969).

24. G. V. Stimson, 'Treatment or control? Dilemmas for staff in drug dependency clinics', in D. J. West, ed., *Problems of Drug Abuse in Britain*, op. cit., pp. 52–70.

25. A. H. Ghodse, M. Sheehan, B. Stevens, C. Taylor and G. Edwards, 'Mortality among drug addicts in Greater London', *British Medical Journal, 2* (1978), pp. 1742–4.

26. M. S. Rosenthal, 'The Phoenix House Therapeutic Community: an overview', in H. Steinberg, ed., *Scientific Basis of Drug Dependence* (London, Churchill, 1969), pp. 395–409.

27. D. W. Holland, 'The development of "Concept Houses" in Great Britain and Southern Ireland, 1967–1976', in D. J. West, ed., op. cit., pp. 125–32.

28. P. T. Furst, ed., *Flesh of the Gods: The Ritual Use of Hallucinogens* (London, Allen and Unwin, 1972).

29. G. Edwards, *Alcohol Problems in Developing Countries* (Mimeograph, W.H.O., Geneva, 1978).

30. G. Edwards and A. Arif, *W.H.O. Study on Drug Dependence in Socio-Cultural Context: Guidelines for Programme Planning* (W.H.O., Geneva, 1980).

31. G. Edwards, *Unreason in an Age of Reason* (London, Royal Society of Medicine, 1971).

32. S. Lederman, *Alcool, alcoolisme, alcoolisation*, Institut National d'Études Démographiques, Travaux et Documents, Cahier no. 29 (Paris, Presses Universitaires de France, 1956).

33. C. Suwanwela, V. Poshyachinda, P. Tasanpradit and A. Dharmkrong-At, 'The hill tribes of Thailand, their opium use and addiction', *Bulletin on Narcotics, 30* (1978), pp. 1–19.

34. J. Westermeyer, 'The pro-heroin effect of anti-opium laws', *Archives of General Psychiatry, 33* (1976), pp. 1135–90.

35. *Royal Commission on Opium* (1894–5), op. cit.

Bibliography

Manuscript collections

1. *Public Record Office*
   Home Office papers, H.O. 45 series. Dealing with the sale of poisons, patent medicines, and the operation of the inebriates acts.
   Privy Council Office papers, P.C. 8 series. Dealing with the 1868 Pharmacy Act and the sale of poisons.

2. *Wellcome Institute for the History of Medicine*
   Chemists' prescription books.
   Wholesale druggists' sales ledgers
   Trade account books.

3. *Pharmaceutical Society*
   Allen and Hanbury collection: inventories and price books of drugs.
   Stock valuations for pharmacists' shops.
   Catalogues of drugs.
   Price lists.
   Poisons registers.

4. *Greater London Record Office*
   General Lying-In Hospital case notes.
   By-laws relating to seamen's lodging houses.
   London County Council minutes.
   Proceedings of, and papers presented to, Public Health Committee.
   John Burns Collection.
   Records of Smith Kendon about the import of opium.
   Records of Whiffen and Company, manufacturing chemists.

5. *Tower Hamlets Local History Library*
   Collection of material on the Chinese community in Limehouse.

6. *Royal College of Physicians*
King's College Hospital case notes.

7. *Bethlem Royal Hospital*
Admission registers and case notes.

8. *Friends' House*
Braithwaite Collection. Anti-opium tracts and resolutions, 1850s–1914/
15.
Society for the Suppression of the Opium Trade. Executive Committee
minutes, 1891–7.

9. *Lambeth Palace*
Papers of Archbishop Tait, 1875–82.
Papers of Archbishop Benson, 1891–2.
Papers of Archbishop Davidson, 1892.
Bishops' meetings minutes, 1893–1908.

10. *Guildhall Library*
Society of Apothecaries laboratory mixture and process book, 1868–72.

11. *Middlesex Record Office*
Coroners' inquisitions in East London in the 1820s.

12. *National Library of Scotland*
Edinburgh Life Assurance Company minutes, 1828–33.

13. *Stockport Local History Library*
Workhouse medical officer's order book, 1840.

Unpublished theses

M. J. B. C. Lim, 'Britain and the termination of the India-China opium
trade, 1905–13', London Ph.D., 1969.
A. C. Roberts, 'Feeding and mortality in the early months of life: changes
in medical opinion and popular feeding practice 1850–1900', Hull University Ph.D., 1973.
I. S. Russell, 'The later history of the Levant Co. 1753–1825', Manchester
University Ph.D., 1935.

Parliamentary papers

1. *Import/Export Statistics* in Accounts and Papers as follows:
P.P. 1808, XII; 1829, XVII; 1830, XXVII; 1831, XVII; 1831-2,
XXXIV; 1834, XLIX; 1835, XLVIII; 1836, XLV; 1837, L; 1838,

XLV; 1839, XLVI; 1840, XLIV; 1841, XXVI; 1842, XXXIX;
1843, LII; 1844, XLV; 1845, XLVI; 1846, XLIV; 1847, LIX;
1847–8, LVIII; 1850, LII; 1851, LIII; 1852, LI; 1852–3, XCVIII;
1854–5, LI; 1856, LVI; 1857, XXXV; 1857–8, LIV; 1859,
XXVIII; 1860, LXIV; 1861, LX; 1862, LVI; 1863, LXV; 1864,
LVII; 1865, LII; 1866, LXVIII; 1867, LXVI; 1867–8, LXVII;
1868–9, LVIII; 1870, LXIII; 1871, LXIII Part II; 1872, LVI;
1873, LXIII; 1874, LXIV; 1875, LXXIII; 1876, LXXII; 1877,
LXXX; 1878, LXXI; 1878–9, LXVIII; 1880, LXXI; 1881,
LXXXVII; 1882, LXIV; 1882, LXVIII; 1883, LXX; 1884,
LXXVIII; 1884–5, LXXV; 1886, LXIV; 1887, LXXX; 1888,
XCVII; 1889, LXXV; 1890, LXXII; 1890–91, LXXXII; 1892,
LXXVII; 1893–4, LXXXVIII; 1894, LXXXIV; 1895, XCV;
1896, LXXXIII; 1897, LXXXVII; 1898, XCI Part I; 1899, XCV;
1900, LXXXVI

2.   *Reports etc.*

P.P. 1834, VIII: *Report from the Select Committee on Inquiry into Drunkenness.*

P.P. 1834, XIX: *Factories Inquiry Commission: Supplementary Report of the Central Board ...*

P.P. 1839, XXXVIII: *Returns from the Coroners of England and Wales of All Inquisitions Held by Them During the Years 1837 and 1838, in Cases where Death was Found by Verdict of Jury to Have Been Caused by Poison.*

P.P. 1839, XLII: *Hand Loom Weavers. Reports with Appendices ...*

P.P. 1840, XI: *Report from the Select Committee on the Health Of Towns.*

P.P. 1842, XXVII: *Report on the Sanitary Condition of the Labouring Population.*

P.P. 1843, XIII: *Children's Employment Commission: Second Report of the Commissioners on Trades and Manufactures.*

P.P. 1843, XIV: *Children's Employment Commission: Appendix to the Second Report, Part I.*

P.P. 1843, XV: *Children's Employment Commission: Appendix to the Second Report Part II.*

P.P. 1844, XVII: *First Report of the Commissioners for Inquiring into the State of Large Towns and Populous Districts.*

P.P. 1845, V: *Second Report and Appendix.*

P.P. 1852, XIII: *Report from the Select Committee on the Pharmacy Bill.*

P.P. 1854–5, VIII: *First and Second Reports from the Select Committee on the Adulteration of Food, Drink and Drugs.*

P.P. 1856, VIII: *Report from the Select Committee on the Adulteration of Food, Drink and Drugs.*

P.P. 1857, XII: *Report from the Select Committee of the House of Lords on the Sale of Poisons etc. Bill.*

P.P. 1860, XXIX: *Second Report of the Medical Officer of the Privy Council; with Appendix, 1859.*

P.P. 1862, XXII: *Fourth Report of the Medical Officer of the Privy Council*, with Appendix 5, 'Dr Greenhow's report on the circumstances under which there is an excessive mortality of young children among certain manufacturing populations'.

P.P. 1864, XXVIII: *Sixth Report of the Medical Officer of the Privy Council*, Appendix 14, 'Report by Dr Henry Julian Hunter on the excessive mortality of infants in some rural districts of England'; Appendix 16, 'Professor A. S. Taylor's report on poisoning, and the dispensing, vending, and keeping of poisons'.

P.P. 1865, XXVI: *Seventh Report of the Medical Officer of the Privy Council*, Appendix 9, 'Report by Dr Hunter on the sanitary state of Crickhowell'.

P.P. 1865, XII: *Special Report from the Select Committee on the Chemists and Druggists Bill and Chemists and Druggists (No. 2) Bill.*

P.P. 1867, XVI: *Children's Employment Commission: Sixth Report of the Commissioners on Organised Agricultural Gangs, Commonly Called 'Public Gangs' in Some of the Eastern Counties.*

P.P. 1867–8, XVII: *First Report of the Commission on the Employment of Children, Young Persons, and Women in Agriculture.*

P.P. 1870, XXXVIII: *Twelfth Report of the Medical Officer of the Privy Council, 1869.*

P.P. 1871, VII: *Report of the Select Committee on the Protection of Infant Life.*

P.P. 1872, IX: *Report from the Select Committee on Habitual Drunkards.*

P.P. 1884–5, XV: *Fifth Annual Report of the Inspector of Retreats under the Habitual Drunkards Act, 1879.*

P.P. 1893–4, LXVI: *East India (Consumption of Ganja).*

P.P. 1893–4, XVII: *Report from the Departmental Committee on the Treatment of Inebriates.*

P.P. 1894, LX, LXI, LXII; and 1895, XLII: *Reports, and Minutes of Evidence of the Royal Commission on Opium.*

P.P. 1904, XXXII. *Report of the Inter-Departmental Committee on Physical Deterioration.*

Acts

24 and 25 Vict. ch. 100, 1861: Offences against the Person Act

31 and 32 Vict. ch. 121, 1868: Act to Regulate the Sale of Poisons and Alter and Amend the Pharmacy Act 1852 (1868 Pharmacy Act)

42 and 43 Vict. ch. 19, 1879: Habitual Drunkards Act
51 and 52 Vict. ch. 19, 1888: An Act to Amend the Habitual Drunkards
Act 1879 (Inebriates Act)
53 and 54 Vict. ch. 5, 1890: Lunacy Act
8 Edw. 7 ch. 55, 1908: Poisons and Pharmacy Act

Newspapers, Periodicals, Annual Reports

Archives of Medicine
Argosy
Asclepiad

Blackwood's Magazine
Brain
British and Foreign Medical Review, 1836–48
British and Foreign Medico-Chirurgical Review, 1848–77
British Medical Journal

Chambers' Journal
Chemist and Druggist
Clinical Journal
Contemporary Review

The Doctor, 1833–4
The Doctor, 1871–8

Edinburgh Medical Journal
Edinburgh Medical and Surgical Review

Fortnightly Review
Friend of China

Hansard (Parliamentary Debates)

Illustrated London News

Journal of the Institute of Actuaries
Journal of Mental Science (Asylum Journal of Mental Science, 1855-7)
Journal of Psychological Medicine
Journal of the Society of Arts
Journal of the Statistical Society of London

The Lancet
London Medical Gazette
London Medical Repository

Medical and Physical Journal
Medical Intelligencer

Medical Press and Circular
Medical Times and Gazette
Medico-Chirurgical Review
Monthly Journal of Medical Science
Morning Chronicle 1849–50

National Righteousness
News of the World
Nineteenth Century
Notes and Queries

Pharmaceutical Journal
The Practitioner
Proceedings of the Society for the Study of Inebriety
Public Health

Quarterly Review

Reynolds's Newspaper

The Times
Transactions of the National Association for the Promotion of Social Science
Transactions of the Obstetrical Society of London
Transactions of the Society of Arts

Contemporary books, articles, pamphlets etc.

Accum, F., *A Treatise on Adulteration of Food and Culinary Poisons* (London, Longmans, 1820).

Alcock, R., 'Opium and common sense', *Nineteenth Century*, *10* (1881), pp. 854–68.

'The opium trade', *Journal of the Society of Arts*, *30* (1882), pp. 201–35.

Alexander, J. G., 'Lotus eating and opium eating', *Contemporary Review*, 66 (1894), p. 337.

Alexander, R., *The Rise and Progress of British Opium Smuggling* (London, 3rd edn, Judd and Glass, 1856).

Allbutt, T. C., 'The use of the subcutaneous injection of morphia in dyspepsia', *Practitioner*, *2* (1869), pp. 341–6.

'On the abuse of hypodermic injections of morphia', *Practitioner*, *5* (1870), pp. 327–31.

'Opium poisoning and other intoxications', pp. 874–920 in T. C. Allbutt, ed., *A System of Medicine* (London, Macmillan, 1897), vol. 2.

and Dixon, W. E., 'Opium poisoning and other intoxications', pp. 937–88 in T. C. Allbutt and H. D. Rolleston, eds., *A System of Medicine* (London, Macmillan, 1906), vol. 2.

Alston, C., 'A dissertation on opium', *Medical Essays and Observations*, *5*, part 1 (1742), pp. 110–76.

Analytical Sanitary Commission, *Lancet*, *1* (1853), pp. 64, 116–17, 251–3; *2* (1853), pp. 555–6; and *1* (1854), pp. 10–14, 51–4, 77–81, 107–8, 165–8.

Anon., *Deadly Adulteration and Slow Poisoning Unmasked, or Disease and Death in the Pot and Bottle* (London, Sherwood, Gilbert and Piper, 1830).

  The Tricks of the Trade in the Adulteration of Food and Physic (London, David Bogue, 1856).

  Advice to Opium Eaters (London, W. R. Goodluck, 1823).

Anstie, F. E., *Stimulants and Narcotics* (London, Macmillan, 1864).

  'The hypodermic injection of remedies', *Practitioner*, *1* (1868), pp. 32–41.

  'On the effects of the prolonged use of morphia by subcutaneous injection', *Practitioner*, 6 (1871), pp. 148–57.

Arbuthnot, A. J., 'The opium controversy', *Nineteenth Century*, *11* (1882), pp. 403–13.

Armstrong-Jones, R., 'Notes on some cases of morphinomania', *Journal of Mental Science*, 48 (1902), pp. 478–95.

Arnold, L., ed., *The Opium Question Solved, by Anglo-Indian* (London, S. W. Partridge, 1882).

Arnot, T., 'A method of preparing the extract of syrup of poppies', *Medical Essays and Observations*, *5*, par. 1 (1742).

Baines, M. A., *Excessive Infant Mortality: How Can It Be Stayed?* (London, John Churchill & Sons, *c*. 1861–2).

Ball, J., 'English opium', *Transactions of the Society . . . of Arts*, *14* (1796), pp. 253–70.

Bateman, W., *Magnacopia; A Chemico-Pharmaceutical Library of Useful and Profitable Information for the Practitioner, Chemist and Druggist, Surgeon-Dentist, etc.* (London, John Churchill, 1839).

Batten, G. H. M., et al., 'The opium question', *Journal of the Society of Arts*, 40 (1892), pp. 444–94.

Bell, J. and Redwood, T., *Historical Sketch of the Progress of Pharmacy in Great Britain* (London, Pharmaceutical Society, 1880).

Bennett, A. H., 'An experimental inquiry into the physiological actions of theine, guaranine, cocaine and theobromine', *Edinburgh Medical Journal*, *19* (1873), pp. 323–41.

Besant, W., *East London* (London, Chatto and Windus, 1901).

Bourneville and Bricon, Drs, *Manual of Hypodermic Medication* (London, Lewis, 1887).

Brereton, W. H., *The Truth about Opium* (London, W. H. Allen, 1882).

British Medical Association, *Secret Remedies, What They Cost and What They Contain* (London, B.M.A., 1909).

More Secret Remedies, What They Cost and What They Contain (London, B.M.A., 1912).

British Pharmacopoeia (London, Spottiswoode, 1858).

Broomhall, B., *The Truth about Opium Smoking* (London, Hodder and Stoughton, 1882).

Browne, J. Collis, *Practical Instructions for the Treatment and Cure of Cholera and Diarrhoea by Chlorodyne* (London, n.d.).

Browne, W. A. F., 'Opiophagism', *Journal of Psychological Medicine*, n.s. *1* (1875), pp. 38–55.

Brunton, T. L., 'The influence of stimulants and narcotics on health', pp. 183–267 in M. Morris, ed., *The Book of Health* (London, Cassell, 1883).

Buchan, W., *The Maternal Management of Children, in Health and Disease* (London, Longmans, Orme, Brown, Green and Longmans, 1840).

Calkins, A., *Opium and the Opium Appetite* (Philadelphia, J. Lippincott, 1871).

'Opium and its victims', *Galaxy*, *4* (1867), pp. 25–36.

Campbell, J. D., *Samuel Taylor Coleridge. A Narrative of the Events of His Life* (London, Macmillan, 1894).

Cheadle, W. B., 'A lecture on the clinical uses of opium', *Clinical Journal*, *4* (1894), pp. 345–51.

Cheever, D. W., 'Narcotics', *North American Review*, *95* (1862), pp. 374–415.

Chemist and Druggist, *The Pharmacy and Poison Laws of the United Kingdom* (London, Chemist and Druggist, 1892).

'Messrs Morson give up the retail', *Chemist and Druggist*, *57* (1900), p. 650.

Chesson, F. W., 'The opium trade', *Fortnightly Review*, n.s. *10* (1871), pp. 351–7.

Child, S., *Every Man His Own Brewer* (London, J. Ridgeway, 10th edn 1802).

Christian Union for the Severance of the Connection of the British Empire with the Opium Traffic, Miscellaneous pamphlets, 1906–7.

Christison, R., *A Treatise on Poisons* (Edinburgh, Adam Black, 2nd edn, 1832).

Observations on the Adulteration of Drugs (Edinburgh, Adam Black, 1838).

'On the effects of opium eating on health and longevity', *Edinburgh Medical and Surgical Journal*, *37* (1832), pp. 123–35.

'Supplement to the preceding paper (by Little) on the habitual use of opium, more especially the mode of cure', *Monthly Journal of Medical Science*, *10* (1850), pp. 531–8.

'Observations on the effects of the leaves of erythroxylon coca', *British Medical Journal*, *1* (1876), pp. 527–31.

Clarke, J. St T., 'Treatment of the habit of injecting morphia by suddenly discontinuing the drug', *Lancet, 2* (1884), p. 491.

Clouston, T. S., 'Diseased cravings and paralysed control', *Edinburgh Medical Journal, 35* (1890), pp. 508-21, 689-705, 793-809 and 985-96. 'Observations and experiments on the use of opium, bromide of potassium and cannabis indica in insanity . . .', *British and Foreign Medico-Chirurgical Review, 46* (1870), pp. 493-511, and *47* (1871), pp. 203-20.

'The Cairo Asylum; Dr Warnock on hashish insanity', *Journal of Mental Science, 42* (1896), pp. 790-95.

'Confessions of an English opium eater', review in *The British Review and London Critical Journal, 20* (1822), pp. 474-88.

Cottle, J., *Reminiscences of Samuel Taylor Coleridge and Robert Southey* (London, Houlston and Stoneman, 1847).

Cowley and Staines, 'English opium', *Transactions of the Society . . . of Arts, 41* (1823), pp. 15-16.

'On the cultivation of the white poppy and on the preparation of English opium', *Technical Repository, 7* (1825), p. 145.

Crothers, T. D., *Morphinism and Narcomanias from Other Drugs. Their Etiology, Treatment and Medico-Legal Relations* (Philadelphia and London, W. B. Saunders, 1902).

Crumpe, S., *An Inquiry into the Nature and Properties of Opium* (London, G. G. and J. Robinson, 1793).

Curgenven, J. B., *The Waste of Infant Life* (London, Faithfull and Head, 1867).

Dickens, C., *The Mystery of Edwin Drood* (London, Chapman and Hall, 1870, Penguin edn 1974).

Disraeli, B., *Sybil, or The Two Nations* (London, Henry Colburn, 1845).

Dixon, W. E., 'The pharmacology of cannabis indica', *British Medical Journal, 2* (1899), pp. 1354-7.

Doré, G. and Jerrold, W. B., *London, A Pilgrimage* (London, Grant, 1872).

Dowdeswell, G., 'The coca leaf', *Lancet, 1* (1876), pp. 631-3 and 664-7.

Drury, H. C., 'Morphinomania', *Dublin Journal of Medical Science, 107* (1899), pp. 321-44.

Dudgeon, J., 'Opium in relation to population', *Edinburgh Medical Journal, 23* (1877), pp. 239-50.

Eaton, H. A., *Thomas De Quincey. A Biography* (O.U.P., 1936).

Eaton, V. G., 'How the opium habit is acquired', *Popular Science Monthly, 33* (1888), pp. 663-7.

Ellis, H. H., 'Mescal: a new artificial paradise', *Contemporary Review, 73* (1898), pp. 130-41.

My Life (London, Heinemann, 1940).

Enquire Within upon Everything (London, Houlston & Sons, 84th edn 1891).

Erlenmeyer, A., 'Cocaine in the treatment of morphinomania', *Journal of Mental Science, 31* (1885–6), p. 427.

'The morphia habit and its treatment', *Journal of Mental Science, 34* (1888–9), p. 116.

Everybody's Pocket Cyclopaedia (London, Saxon, 1893).

Ferriar, J., *Medical Histories and Reflections* (London, Cadell and Davies, 2nd edn 1810).

Fluckiger, F. A., and Hanbury, D., *Pharmacographia. A History of the Principal Drugs of Vegetable Origin, Met With in Great Britain and British India* (London, Macmillan, 1879).

Foot, A. W., 'On morphinism', *Dublin Journal of Medical Science, 88* (1889), pp. 457–72 and 531–3.

Forster, J., *The Life of Charles Dickens* (London, Chapman and Hall, 1874), vol. 3.

Francis, C. R., 'On the value and use of opium', *Medical Times and Gazette, 1* (1882), pp. 87–9 and 116–17.

Fry, E., 'China, England and opium', *Contemporary Review, 27* (1875–6), pp. 447–59.

'China, England and opium', *Contemporary Review, 30* (1877), pp. 1–10.

'China, England and opium: the Chefoo Convention', *Contemporary Review, 31* (1877–8), pp. 313–21.

Garrod, A. B., and Baxter, E. B., *The Essentials of Materia Medica and Therapeutics* (London, Longmans, 9th edn 1882).

Gaskell, E., *Mary Barton. A Tale of Manchester Life* (London, Chapman and Hall, 1848, Penguin edn 1970).

General Board of Health, 'Reports by W. Lee on the sanitary condition of various towns in the Fenland area' (London, W. Clowes, 1849–53).

Gillman, J., *The Life of Samuel Taylor Coleridge* (London, William Pickering, 1838).

Greenwood, J., 'An opium smoker in Tiger Bay', pp. 229–38 of *In Strange Company* (London, Henry S. King, 1873).

Gregory, W., 'On a process for preparing economically the muriate of morphia', *Edinburgh Medical and Surgical Journal, 35* (1831), pp. 331–8.

Hall, M., 'The effects of the habit of giving opiates on the infantine constitution', *Edinburgh Medical and Surgical Journal, 12* (1816), pp. 423–4.

Hardy, T., *The Trumpet-Major* (London, Smith, Elder, 1880).

Hardy, T., *The Trumpet-Major* (Smith, Elder, 1880).

Hassall, A. H., *Adulterations Detected: or Plain Instructions for the Discovery of Frauds in Food and Medicine* (London, Longman, Brown, Green, Longmans and Roberts, 1857).

Health News, *Exposures of Quackery. Being a Series of Articles upon, and Analyses of, Various Patent Medicines* (London, The Savoy Press, 1895–6).

Hehir, P., *Opium: Its Physical, Moral and Social Effects* (London, Bailliere, Tindall and Cox, 1894).

Hogg, J., *De Quincey and His Friends* (London, Sampson Low, Marston, 1895).

Homes for Inebriates Association, *Annual Report*, 1884 onward.

Howison, J., 'Essay on the preparation of opium in Britain', *Memoirs of the Caledonian Horticultural Society, 1* (1814), p. 365.

Hunter, C., *On the Speedy Relief of Pain and Other Nervous Affections by Means of the Hypodermic Method* (London, John Churchill, 1865).

'On the ipodermic/hypodermic treatment of diseases', *Medical Times and Gazette, 18* (1859), pp. 234–5, 310–11, 387–8 and·432.

Infant Mortality Committee, Report in *Transactions of the Obstetrical Society of London, 12* (1870).

Japp, A. H., *Thomas De Quincey: His Life and Writings* (London, John Hogg, 1890), including Appendix 1: W. C. B. Eatwell, 'A medical view of Mr De Quincey's case'.

Jeffreys, J., 'Observations on the improper use of opium in England', *Lancet, 1* (1840–41), pp. 382–3.

The Traffic in Opium in the East (London, Longman, Brown, Green, Longmans and Roberts, 1858), Appendix to *The British Army in India; Its Preservation.*

Jennings, O., *On the Cure of the Morphia Habit* (London, Bailliere, Tindall and Cox, 1890).

The Morphia Habit and its Voluntary Renunciation (London, Bailliere, Tindall and Cox, 1909).

The Re-education of Self-Control in the Treatment of the Morphia Habit (London, Bailliere, Tindall and Cox, 1909).

Jeston, J. W., 'English opium', *Transactions of the Society ... of Arts, 41* (1823), pp. 17–31.

Jones, T., 'British opium', *Transactions of the Society ... of Arts, 18* (1800), pp. 161–94.

Kane, H. H., *The Hypodermic Injection of Morphia. Its History, Advantages and Dangers*, New York, Chas. L. Bermingham, 1880).

Kerr, N., *Inebriety, its Etiology, Pathology, Treatment and Jurisprudence* (London, H. K. Lewis, 1888).

Kingsley, C., *Alton Locke* (London, 1850).

Ladies Sanitary Association, *Annual Reports*, 1881, 1882.

Levinstein, E., *Morbid Craving for Morphia (Die Morphiumsucht)* (London, Smith, Elder, 1878).

Little, R., 'On the habitual use of opium', *Monthly Journal of Medical Science, 10* (1850), pp. 524–31.

Lock, B. Fossett, 'The opium trade and Sir Rutherford Alcock', *Contemporary Review, 41* (1882), pp. 676–93.

McBride, C. A., *The Modern Treatment of Alcoholism and Drug Narcotism* (London, W. Rebman, 1910).

Macclesfield Infant Mortality Committee, *Infant Mortality in Macclesfield. Report of a Special Committee of the Town Council* (Macclesfield, Swinnerton and Brown, 1877).

Maltass, S. H., 'On the production of opium in Asia Minor', *Pharmaceutical Journal*, *14* (1854–5), pp. 395–400.

Manchester and Salford Sanitary Association, *Annual Reports*, 1856–7, 1861–4.

Mart, G. R., 'Effects of the practice of opium eating', *Lancet*, *1* (1831–2), pp. 712–13.

Moore, W. J., *The Other Side of the Opium Question* (London, J. and A. Churchill, 1882).

Morewood, S., *A philosophical and statistical history of the inventions and customs of ancient and modern nations in the manufacture and use of inebriating liquors; with the present practice of distillation in all its varieties; together with an extensive illustration of the consumption and effects of opium, and other stimulants used in the East, as substitutes for wine and spirits* (Dublin, W. Curry and W. Carson, 1838).

Murray, J., *A System of Materia Medica and Pharmacy* (Edinburgh, Adam Black, 6th edn 1832).

'Narcotics', *Chambers' Journal* (1875), pp. 396–9.

'The narcotics we indulge in', *Blackwood's Magazine*, *74* (1853), pp. 605–28.

'Noctes Ambrosianae', *Blackwood's Magazine*, *14* (1823), p. 485, and *28* (1830), p. 391.

Normandy, A., *Commercial Hand-book of Chemical Analysis* (London, George Knight, 1850).

Obersteiner, H., 'Chronic morphinism', *Brain*, *2* (1878–80), pp. 449–65; *5* (1884–5), pp. 324–31.

'Use of opiates among the operative population', *Chambers' Journal*, *3*, (1845), pp. 346.

'Opium dens in London', *Chambers' Journal*, *81* (1904), pp. 193–5.

'London opium dens', *Good Words*, *26* (1885), pp. 188–92.

'East London opium smokers', *London Society*, *14* (1868), pp. 68–72.

'Opium', *Penny Magazine*, *3* (1834), p. 397.

O'Shaughnessy, W. B., 'On the preparations of the Indian hemp ...', *Transactions of the Medical and Physical Society of Calcutta*, *8* part 2 (1842), pp. 421–61.

Osler, W., *The Principles and Practice of Medicine* (London, Y. J. Pentland, 1892).

Page, H. A., *Thomas De Quincey: His Life and Writings, with Unpublished Correspondence* (London, John Hogg, 1877).

Pannell's Reference Book for Home and Office (London, Granville Press, 1906).

Parkinson, J., *Medical Admonitions to Families, Respecting the Preservation of Health, and the Treatment of the Sick* (London, H. D. Symonds, 4th edn 1801).

Pavy, F. W., 'Report of a case of diabetes mellitus successfully treated by opium', *Transactions of the Clinical Society of London*, 2 (1869), pp. 44–56.

'Cases illustrating the influence of opium and some of its constituent principles in the treatment of diabetes', *British Medical Journal*, *1* (1870), p. 289.

Pereira, J., *Elements of Materia Medica* (London, Longman, Orme, Browne, Green and Longmans, 1839–40).

Pharmacopoeia of the Royal College of Physicians (London, G. Woodfall, 3rd edn 1815).

Platt, J., 'Chinese London and its opium dens,' *Gentleman's Magazine*, *279* (1895), pp. 272–82.

Quain, R., ed., *A Dictionary of Medicine* (London, Longmans, 1894).

Quincey, T. De, *Confessions of an English Opium Eater* (London, Taylor and Hessey, 1822; Penguin edn 1971).

Registrar General, *Annual Reports*, 1840–1910 (London, H.M.S.O.).

Reynolds, J. Russell, ed., *A System of Medicine* (London, Macmillan, 1866–79).

Richardson, B. W., 'On the morphia habit and its treatment', *British Medical Journal*, 2 (1883), p. 1194.

'Morphia habitués and their treatment', *Asclepiad*, *1* (1884), pp. 1–31.

Rowntree, J., *The Imperial Drug Trade* (London, Methuen, 1905).

Sainsbury, H., *Drugs and the Drug Habit* (London, Methuen, 1909).

Sharkey, S. J., 'The treatment of morphia habitués by suddenly discontinuing the drug', *Lancet*, 2 (1883), p. 1120.

'Morphinomania', *Nineteenth Century*, *22* (1887), pp. 335–42.

Squire, P., *A Companion to the Latest Edition of the British Pharmacopoeia* (London, J. and A. Churchill, 1886 and 1899).

Swayne, G., 'On the manufacture of British opium', *Quarterly Journal of Science, Literature and the Arts*, *8* (1820), pp. 234–40, and *9* (1820), pp. 69–80.

Symons, A., 'The opium smoker', in *Poems*, vol. 1 (London, Heinemann, 1902).

Taylor, A. S., *On Poisons in Relation to Medical Jurisprudence and Medicine* (London, John Churchill, 1848, 6th edn 1859).

Tott, Baron de, *Mémoires du Baron de Tott, sur les Turcs et les Tartares* (Amsterdam, no publisher, 1784).

Turner, F. S., *British Opium Policy and its Results to India and China* (London, Sampson Low, Marston, Searle and Rivington, 1876).

'Opium and England's duty', *Nineteenth Century*, *11* (1882), pp. 242–53.

Tweedie, A., ed., *George Harley, F.R.S.* (London, Scientific Press, 1899).

Vicars, G. Rayleigh, 'Laudanum drinking in Lincolnshire', *St George's Hospital Gazette*, *1* (1893), pp. 24–6.

Ward, M., *Facts Establishing the Efficacy of the Opiate Friction* (London, C. Wheeler, 1809).

'W. B. E.', *A Short History of Druggs and Other Commodities, the Produce and Manufactory of the East Indies* (London, eighteenth century, exact date uncertain).

Wilde, O., *The Picture of Dorian Gray* (London, Ward, Lock, 1891, Penguin edn 1966).

Wood, C. W., 'In the night watches', *Argosy*, *65* (1897–8), pp. 191–223.

Wood, G. B., *A Treatise on Therapeutics* (Philadelphia and London, J. B. Lippincott and H. Bailliere, 1856).

Woodville, W., *Medical Botany*, vol. 3 (London, James Phillips, 1793).

Young, J., 'English opium', *Transactions of the Society . . . of Arts*, *37* (1820), pp. 23–39.

Secondary Sources

Adams II, L. P., 'China: the historical setting of Asia's profitable plague', in A. W. McCoy, *The Politics of Heroin in South East Asia* (New York, Harper and Row, 1972), pp. 365–83.

Adlard, J., *Stenbock, Yeats and the Nineties* (London, Cecil and Amelia Woolf, 1969).

Alexander, H. G., *Joseph Grundy Alexander* (London, Swarthmore Press, 1920).

Anderson, M., *Family Structure in Nineteenth Century Lancashire* (Cambridge University Press, 1971).

Aries, P., *Centuries of Childhood: A Social History of Family Life* (London, Jonathan Cape, 1962).

Ashley, R., *Cocaine: Its History, Uses and Effects* (New York, St Martin's Press, 1975).

Austen, Jane, *Letters to her Sister Cassandra and Others*, ed. R. W. Chapman (O.U.P., 2nd edn 1952).

Beaton, C., and Buckland, J., *The Magic Image* (London, Weidenfeld and Nicolson, 1975).

Becker, H. K., 'Carl Koller and cocaine', *Psychoanalytic Quarterly*, *32* (1963), pp. 309–73.

Bell, W. J., *The Sale of Food and Drugs Acts, 1875 to 1907*, 5th edn by Charles F. Lloyd (London, Butterworth, 1910).

Bellot, H. H., *The Pharmacy Acts, 1851–1908* (London, Jesse Boot, 1908).

Benson, B. W., 'The nineteenth century British mortality statistics: towards an assessment of their accuracy', *Bulletin of the Society for the Social History of Medicine*, *21* (1977), pp. 5–13.

Berridge, V., 'Our own opium: cultivation of the opium poppy in Britain, 1740–1823', *British Journal of Addiction*, *72* (1977), pp. 90–94.

'Opium and the historical perspective', *Lancet*, *2* (1977), pp. 78–80.

'Fenland opium eating in the nineteenth century', *British Journal of Addiction*, *72* (1977), pp. 275–84.

'Opium eating and life insurance', *British Journal of Addiction*, *72* (1977), pp. 371–7.

'Opium eating and the working class in the nineteenth century: the public and official reaction', *British Journal of Addiction*, *73* (1978), pp. 107–12.

'Medical and pharmaceutical professionalisation and narcotic use in Britain', *Social History Society Newsletter*, *3*, Spring 1978.

'East End opium dens and narcotic use in Britain', *London Journal*, *4*, No. 1 (1978), pp. 3–28.

'War conditions and narcotics control: the passing of Defence of the Realm Act Regulation 40B', *Journal of Social Policy*, *7*, No. 3 (1978), pp. 285–304.

'Victorian opium eating: responses to opiate use in nineteenth century society', precis in *Bulletin of the Society for the Social History of Medicine*, *22* (1978), pp. 11–16.

'Working class opium eating in the nineteenth century: establishing the facts', *British Journal of Addiction*, *73* (1978), pp. 363–74.

'Victorian opium eating: responses to opiate use in nineteenth century England', *Victorian Studies*, *21*, No. 4 (1978), pp. 437–61.

'Opium over the counter in nineteenth century England', *Pharmacy in History*, *20*, No. 3 (1978), pp. 91–100.

'Professionalisation and narcotics: the medical and pharmaceutical professions and British narcotic use', *Psychological Medicine*, *8* (1978), pp. 361–72.

'Morality and medical science: concepts of narcotic addiction in Britain', *Annals of Science*, 36 (1979), pp. 67–85.

'The origins of the English drug "scene"', in J. Kramer, ed., *Drugs and the Arts* (California, forthcoming).

and N. Rawson, 'Opiate use and legislative control: a nineteenth century case study', *Social Science and Medicine*, *13A* (1979), pp. 351–63.

'Opium in the Fens in nineteenth century England', *Journal of the History of Medicine and Allied Sciences*, *34* (1979), pp. 293–313.

Bett, W. R., 'The discovery of morphine', *Chemist and Druggist*, *162* (1954), pp. 63–4 and 83.

'Cocaine, divine plant of the Incas. Some pioneers – and some addicts', *Alchemist*, *21* (1957), pp. 658–89.

'William Stewart Halsted (1852-1922), cocaine pioneer and addict', *British Journal of Addiction*, *49*, pp. 53–9.

Block, B. P., 'Cocaine and Koller', *Pharmaceutical Journal*, *180* (1958), p. 69.

Bragman, L. J., 'The case of Dante Gabriel Rossetti', *American Journal of Psychiatry*, *92* (1935-6), pp. 1111-22.

Breathnach, C. S., 'Francis Thompson, student, addict, poet', *Journal of the Irish Medical Association*, *45* (1959), pp. 98–103.

Brendon, P., *Hawker of Morwenstow. Portrait of a Victorian Eccentric* (London, Jonathan Cape, 1975).

Bryson, J., and Troxell, J. C., eds., *Dante Gabriel Rossetti and Jane Morris: Their Correspondence* (Oxford, Clarendon Press, 1976).

Burnby, J., 'Medals for British rhubarb', *Pharmaceutical Historian*, *2* (1971), pp. 6–7.

'John Sherwin and drug cultivation in Enfield: a re-examination' (Edmonton Hundred Historical Society occasional paper, n.s. 23, 1973).

Burnett, J., *Plenty and Want. A Social History of Diet in England from 1815 to the Present Day* (Harmondsworth, Penguin Books, 1968).

Bynum, W. F., 'Chronic alcoholism in the first half of the nineteenth century', *Bulletin of the History of Medicine*, *42* (1968), pp. 160–85.

Carlson, E. T., and Simpson, M. M., 'Opium as a tranquilliser', *American Journal of Psychiatry*, *120* (1963), pp. 112–17.

Carlson, E. T., 'Cannabis indica in nineteenth century psychiatry', *American Journal of Psychiatry*, *131* (1974), pp. 1004–7.

Checkland, S. G., *The Gladstones. A Family Biography 1764–1851* (Cambridge University Press, 1971).

Chemist and Druggist, 'The beginnings of pharmacy', *Chemist and Druggist*, *106* (1927).

'Evolution of hypodermics', *Chemist and Druggist*, *159* (1953), p. 607.

'Memories of the jug and bottle trade', *Chemist and Druggist*, *167* (1957), pp. 164–5, 274, 298, 322.

Collis, J. S., *An Artist of Life. A Study of the Life and Work of Havelock Ellis* (London, Cassell, 1959).

Cotterell, G., ed., 'A night in an opium den: by the author of A Dead Man's Diary', in *London Scene from the Strand* (London, Strand Magazine, 1975).

Coulthard, A. J., 'Arthur Devereux: chemist and poisoner', *Journal of Forensic Medicine*, *6* (1959), pp. 178–88.

Crellin, J. K., 'The growth of professionalism in nineteenth century British pharmacy', *Medical History*, *11* (1967), pp. 215–27.

Croft-Cooke, R., *Feasting with Panthers. A New Consideration of Some Late Victorian Writers* (London, W. H. Allen, 1967).

Darby, H. C., *The Draining of the Fens* (Cambridge, 2nd edn 1956).

Davies, M. Llewelyn, ed., *Life As We Have Known It* (London, Hogarth Press, 1931, Virago reprint 1977).

Davin, A., 'Imperialism and motherhood', *History Workshop*, 5 (1978), pp. 9–66.

Delamont, S., and Duffin, L., eds., *The Nineteenth Century Woman: Her Cultural and Physical World* (London, Croom Helm, 1978).

Duckworth, A., 'The rise of the pharmaceutical industry', *Chemist and Druggist*, centenary issue, *172* (1959), pp. 127–8.

Duster, T., *The Legislation of Morality* (New York, Free Press, 1970).

Edwards, G., 'Drug problems U.K./U.S.A.', in R. A. Bowen, ed., *Anglo-American Conference on Drug Abuse* (London, Royal Society of Medicine, 1973), pp. 2–6.

'Some years on: evolutions in the "British System"', in D. J. West, ed., *Problems of Drug Abuse in Britain* (Cambridge, Institute of Criminology, 1978), pp. 1–45.

'The British approach to the treatment of heroin addiction', *Lancet*, *1* (1969), pp. 768–62.

Unreason in an Age of Reason (London, Royal Society of Medicine, 1971).

Entract, J. P., 'Chlorodyne Browne: Dr John Collis Browne, 1819–84', *London Hospital Gazette*, *5* 73, no. 4 (1970), pp. 7-11.

Etang, H. L', 'Anstie and alcohol', *Journal of Alcoholism*, *10* (1975), pp. 27–30.

Figlio, K., 'Chlorosis and chronic disease in nineteenth-century Britain: the social constitution of somatic illness in a capitalist society', *Social History*, *3* (1978), pp. 167–97.

Flinn, M. W., ed., *Introduction to Chadwick's Report on the Sanitary Condition of the Labouring Population of Great Britain* (Edinburgh University Press, 1965).

Foot. M. R. D., and Matthew, H. C. G., eds., *The Gladstone Diaries, Vol. 3, 1840–47* (Oxford, Clarendon Press, 1974).

Foucault, M., *Madness and Civilisation. A History of Insanity in the Age of Reason* (London, Tavistock Publications, 1967).

The Birth of the Clinic. An Archaeology of Medical Perception (London), Pantheon Books and Tavistock Publications, 1973).

France, R. S., 'An Elizabethan apothecary's inventory', *Chemist and Druggist*, *172* (1959), p. 168.

Gerin, W., *Branwell Brontë* (London, Thomas Nelson, 1961).

Godwin, H., 'The ancient cultivation of hemp', *Antiquity*, *41* (1967), pp. 42 ff. and 137–8.

Goldsmith, M., *The Trail of Opium* (London, Hale, 1939).

Greenberg, M., *British Trade and the Opening of China, 1800–42* (Cambridge University Press, 1951).

Greene, H., ed., *The Rivals of Sherlock Holmes, Early Detective Stories* (London, Bodley Head, 1976).

343

Griggs, E. L., 'Samuel Taylor Coleridge and opium', *Huntington Library Quarterly*, *17* (1954), pp. 357–8.

Grinspoon, L., and Bakalar, J. B., *Cocaine. A Drug and Its Social Evolution* (New York, Basic Books, 1976).

Hayter, A., *Mrs Browning. A Poet's Work and Its Setting* (London, Faber and Faber, 1962).

A Sultry Month. Scenes of London Literary Life in 1846 (London, Faber and Faber, 1965).

Opium and the Romantic Imagination (London, Faber and Faber, 1968, paperback edn 1971).

Helmer, J., and Vietorisz, T., *Drug Use, the Labor Market and Class Conflict* (Washington, D.C., Drug Abuse Council, 1974).

Helmer, J., *Drugs and Minority Oppression* (New York, Seabury Press, 1975).

Hewitt, M., *Wives and Mothers in Victorian Industry* (London, Rockliff, 1958).

Himmelstein, J., 'Drug politics theory: analysis and critique', *Journal of Drug Issues*, *8* (1978), pp. 37–52.

Hindmarch, I., 'A social history of the use of cannabis sativa', *Contemporary Review* (1972), pp. 252–7.

Holloway, S. W. E., 'The Apothecaries' Act 1815; a reinterpretation', *Medical History*, *10* (1966), pp. 107–29 and 221–36.

'Medical education in England, 1830–58: a sociological analysis', *History*, *49* (1964), pp. 299–324.

Holmes, R., *Shelley, The Pursuit* (London, Weidenfeld and Nicolson, 1974).

Howard-Jones, N., 'A critical study of the origins and early development of hypodermic medication', *Journal of the History of Medicine and Allied Sciences*, *2* (1947), pp. 201–49.

Hunter, R., and MacAlpine, I., *Three Hundred Years of Psychiatry, 1535–1860* (London, O.U.P., 1963).

Inglis, B., *The Forbidden Game. A Social History of Drugs* (London, Hodder and Stoughton, 1975).

Jackson, H., *The Eighteen-Nineties* (London, Grant Richards, 1913).

Jellinek, E. M., *The Disease Concept of Alcoholism* (New Haven, Connecticut, Hill House Press, 1960).

Johnson, B., 'Righteousness before revenue: the forgotten crusade against the Indo-Chinese opium trade', *Journal of Drug Issues*, *5* (1975), pp. 304–26.

Jones, G. Steadman, 'Class expression *versus* social control?', *History Workshop*, *4* (1977), pp. 162–70.

Kalant, O. J., 'Report of the Indian Hemp Drugs Commission, 1893–94: a critical review', *International Journal of the Addictions*, *7* (1) (1972), pp. 77–96.

Koller, C., 'Historical notes on the beginning of local anaesthesia', *Journal of the American Medical Association*, *90* (1928), pp. 1742–3.

Kramer, J., 'Heroin in the treatment of morphine addiction', *Journal of Psychedelic Drugs*, *9* (1977), pp. 193–7.

Laurie, P., *Drugs. Medical, Psychological and Social Facts* (Harmondsworth, Penguin Books, 1974 reprint).

Lefebure, M., *Samuel Taylor Coleridge. A Bondage of Opium* (London, Victor Gollancz, 1974).

Levine, H. G., 'The discovery of addiction: changing conceptions of habitual drunkenness in America', *Journal of Studies on Alcohol*, *39* (1978), pp. 143–74.

Lewin, L., *Phantastica. Narcotic and Stimulating Drugs, Their Use and Abuse* (London, Kegan Paul, 1931).

Lindesmith, A. R., *Opiate Addiction* (Bloomington, Indiana, Principia Press, 1974).

Litchfield, R. B., *Tom Wedgwood, The First Photographer* (London, Duckworth, 1903).

Lomax, E., 'The uses and abuses of opiates in nineteenth century England', *Bulletin of the History of Medicine*, *47* (1973), pp. 167–76.

Lucas, C., *The Fenman's World* (Norwich, Jarrold and Sons, 1930).

Macht, D. I., 'The history of opium and some of its preparations and alkaloids', *Journal of the American Medical Association*, *64* (1915), pp. 477–81.

'The history of intravenous and subcutaneous administration of drugs', *Journal of the American Medical Association* (1916), pp. 856–9.

and Gessford, N. L., 'The unfortunate drug experiences of Dante Gabriel Rossetti', *Bulletin of the Institute for the History of Medicine*, *6* (1938), pp. 34–61.

Macleod, R. M., 'The edge of hope: social policy and chronic alcoholism, 1870–1900', *Journal of the History of Medicine and Allied Sciences*, *22* (1967), pp. 215–45.

Marchand, L. A., *Byron, a Biography* (London, John Murray, 1957).

Matthews, L. G., *History of Pharmacy in Britain* (Edinburgh and London, E. and S. Livingstone, 1962).

May, J. P., 'The Chinese in Britain, 1860–1914', pp. 111–24 in C. Holmes, ed., *Immigrants and Minorities in British Society* (London, George Allen and Unwin, 1978).

Michie, A., *The Englishman in China during the Victorian Era. The Career of Sir Rutherford Alcock* (London, William Blackwood and Sons, 1900).

Moon, J. B., 'Sir William Brooke O'Shaughnessy – the foundations of fluid therapy and the Indian telegraph service', *New England Journal of Medicine*, *276* (1967), pp. 283–4.

Moore, V., *The Unicorn, William Butler Yeats' Search for Reality* (New York, Macmillan, 1954).

Morse, H. B., *The International Relations of the Chinese Empire, 1910–18* (London, Longmans, Green, 1910-18).

Mortimer, W. Golden, *History of Coca, 'The Divine Plant' of the Incas* (San Francisco, Fitz Hugh Ludlow Library reprint, 1974. Published 1901).

Musto, D. F., *The American Disease. Origins of Narcotic Control* (New Haven and London, Yale University Press, 1973).

Newman, C., *The Evolution of Medical Education in the Nineteenth Century* (O.U.P., 1957).

Ng, K. C., *The Chinese in London* (London, Institute of Race Relations, 1968).

Nuttall, G. H. F., Cobbett, L., and Strangeways-Pigg, T., 'Studies in relation to malaria. I. The geographical distribution of anopheles in relation to the former distribution of ague in England', *Journal of Hygiene*, *1* (1901), pp. 4–44.

'Opium as a daily transaction', *Pharmaceutical Journal, 207* (1971), pp. 164, 214-15, 236.

Owen, D. E., *British Opium Policy in China and India* (New Haven, Yale University Press, 1934).

Parry, N. and J., *The Rise of the Medical Profession. A Study of Collective Social Mobility* (London, Croom Helm, 1976).

Peterson, M. J., *The Medical Profession in Mid-Victorian London* (Berkeley, University of California Press, 1978).

Phear, D. N., 'Thomas Dover, 1662–1742. Physician, privateering captain, and inventor of Dover's Powder', *Journal of the History of Medicine and Allied Sciences, 9* (1954), pp. 139–56.

Pickering, G., *Creative Malady* (London, Allen and Unwin, 1974).

Pinchbeck, I., *Women Workers and the Industrial Revolution, 1750–1850* (London, Frank Cass, 1969, 1st edn 1930).

and Hewitt, M., *Childhood in English Society*, vols. 1 and 2 (London, Routledge and Kegan Paul, 1969 and 1973).

Pollock, J., *Wilberforce* (London, Constable, 1977).

Porter, E., *Cambridge Customs and Folklore* (London, Routledge and Kegan Paul, 1969).

Poynter, F. N. L., ed., *The Evolution of Medical Practice in Britain* (London, Pitman, 1961).

The Evolution of Pharmacy in Britain (London, Pitman, 1965).

Quennell, P., ed., *Byron, A Self-Portrait. Letters and Diaries, 1798–1824* (London, John Murray, 1950).

Raine, K., *Yeats, the Tarot and the Golden Dawn* (Dublin, Dolmen Press, 1972).

Reader, W. J., *Professional Men. The Rise of the Professional Class in Nineteenth Century England* (London, Weidenfeld and Nicolson, 1966).

Reinert, R. E., 'The confessions of a nineteenth century opium eater: Thomas De Quincey', *Bulletin of Menninger Clinic*, *16* (1972), pp. 455–9.

Rhys, E., *Everyman Remembers* (London, J. M. Dent, 1931).

Roberts, R. S., 'The early history of the import of drugs into Britain', in F. N. L. Poynter, ed. (1965), op. cit.

Schneider, E., *Coleridge, Opium and Kubla Khan* (University of Chicago Press, 1953).

Scull, A., 'Museums of madness: the social organization of insanity in nineteenth century England' (Princeton Ph.D., 1974).

Searle, G. R., *Eugenics and Politics in Britain, 1900–1914* (Leyden, Noordhoff Publishing Co., 1976).

Shyrock, R. H., 'Nineteenth century medicine: scientific aspects', *Journal of World History*, *3* (1957), pp. 880–980; and 'Medicine and society in the nineteenth century', ibid., *5* (1959), pp. 116–46.

Sonnedecker, G., 'Emergence of the concept of opiate addiction', *Journal Mondiale Pharmacie*, No. *3* (1962), pp. 275–90, and No. *1* (1963), pp. 27–34.

Springall, L. M., *Labouring Life in Norfolk Villages* (London, G. Allen and Unwin, 1936).

Symonds, J., and Grant, K., eds., *The Confessions of Aleister Crowley* (London, Jonathan Cape, 1969).

Symonds, J., *The Great Beast. The Life and Magick of Aleister Crowley* (London, Macdonald, 1971).

Szasz, T., *Ceremonial Chemistry. The Ritual Persecution of Drugs, Addicts and Pushers* (London, Routledge and Kegan Paul, 1975).

Terry, C. E., and Pellens, M., *The Opium Problem* (Montclair, New Jersey, Patterson Smith 1970 reprint, first published 1928).

Victoria County History of Cambridge and the Isle of Ely (University of London, Institute of Historical Research, 1948).

Waddington, I., 'General practitioners and consultants in early nineteenth century England: the sociology of an intra-professional conflict', *Bulletin of the Society for the Social History of Medicine*, *17* (1976), pp. 11–12.

Walkowitz, J. and D., 'We are not beasts of the field: prostitution and the poor in Plymouth and Southampton under the Contagious Disease Acts', in M. Hartman and L. W. Banner, eds., *Clio's Consciousness Raised* (New York, Harper and Row, 1974).

Weeks, J., 'Sins and diseases: some notes on homosexuality in the nineteenth century', *History Workshop*, *1* (1976), pp. 211–19.

Coming Out. Homosexual Politics in Britain, from the Nineteenth Century to the Present (London, Quartet Books, 1977).

'Winslow opium, British production in the early 1800s', *Pharmaceutical Journal*, *160* (1948), p. 151.

Wohl, A., 'Working wives or healthy homes?', *Bulletin of the Society for the Social History of Medicine, 21* (1977), pp. 20–24.

Wood, A. C., *A History of the Levant Company* (O.U.P., 1935).

Woodward, J., and Richards, D., eds., *Health Care and Popular Medicine in Nineteenth Century England. Essays in the Social History of Medicine* (London, Croom Helm, 1977).

Wootton, A. C., *Chronicles of Pharmacy* (London, Macmillan, 1910).

Wu, W. T., *The Chinese Opium Question in British Opinion and Action* (New York, Academy Press, 1928).

Index

349